Let's eat at home

Let's eat at home

JULIE BENELL

Thomas Y. Crowell Company, New York

ESTABLISHED 1834

Manufactured in the United States of America by the Cornwall Press, Cornwall, New York

Library of Congress Catalog Card No. 61-17468

This book is dedicated
To *my Al* for his patience and
help in testing and tasting

AND

To *Chef Edmond Kaspar,* who helped
to make the low-cholesterol basic menus
delightful food with his creative
touch

AND

To *Helen Haycraft,* who for ten years
has been my right hand.

Contents

Introduction

ONCE UPON A TIME a charming woman told me that she hated food, that she couldn't stand to cook, and that she would be glad when we had different colored pills to take for the three meals a day. About a year later I was invited to her home for dinner and I have never seen such a beautiful meal. I think I knew, down deep in my heart, that this woman really didn't hate to cook, but that she had fallen into a dull routine in meal preparation that of course is fatal to any creative ability one might have in the preparation of fine and handsome foods.

Routine is the villain we all want to avoid in meal planning and that is why good cookbooks are always a source of inspiration to a woman who will take the time to read them.

My collection of recipes is made up of some old, some new, some borrowed—but no blue. My grandmother first taught me to cook when I was five years old. My dad made a little box for me to stand on so I could watch her at the kitchen table. She was an inspirational cook—a pinch of this, a dab of that, then turn your back and put in as much butter as your conscience will allow. From this early training I developed a healthy respect for food, and I sincerely think that the preparation of food can be as creative as painting a beautiful picture or designing a lovely gown.

In my job as Food Editor for the *Dallas Morning News*, and for WFAA-TV, I receive much help from the test kitchens of the food companies throughout the country. For this I am most grateful. I also have recipes sent to me by readers and viewers, and this is one of my great joys. Because, on a large scale, I am a next-door neighbor, and these women are sharing their favorites with me. Of course I pass them along.

A good recipe never dies, it justs passes from one homemaker to another. For instance, the German's Sweet Chocolate Cake recipe has traveled around the world and has been made in kitchens in every country. This was first sent to me by a Texas woman named Mrs. Henry Clay; and from this point, because it is a fabulous cake, it has traveled on its own merits.

This is a cookbook for everyone: the new bride who really hasn't found her way around her new kitchen; the homemaker who has been planning meals for one hundred and forty-five years as I have; and the man of the house who wants to pick up a cookbook, whip something together, and surprise his wife who is working late at the Red Cross.

I hope you enjoy these recipes. It has been my pleasure to gather them together for you. Happy eating!

Julie Benell

Let's eat at home

I

Dips, dunks, and hors d'oeuvres

THIS IS A VERY IMPORTANT TYPE of food, because it is a way of entertaining in a quick and modern manner, or it can be a pleasant hour before a family dinner, or it might be a quick "pick-up" type of snack for unexpected company. With so much emphasis now on keeping our waistlines down and our figures slim (and I find that men are really more conscientious calorie counters than women), it is a wise hostess who will plan just a few hors d'oeuvres, or one hot dip and one cold dip, and not only crackers or corn chips for dunking, but cauliflowerets, and two-inch stalks of crisp celery, slivers of peeled and crisped cucumber, celery sticks, and other green vegetables.

If you are planning on having a low-calorie dip for your calorie-conscious friends, use yogurt or the low-calorie cottage cheese. Whiz it in the blender, add Worcestershire sauce and whatever seasonings you want, and serve with a platter of small bits of fresh vegetables. Even crisp scraped turnips are delicious with a dip.

If you are planning a cocktail party, where the food is all going to be snack food, then plan on at least one hot dip and one hot hors d'oeuvre.

You'll find some old favorites in this chapter and also some brand-new ideas. If you have nondrinking friends, have chilled tomato juice or Soup on the Rocks—beef bouillon poured over ice cubes and served in old-fashioned glasses. A twist of lemon is a nice addition.

Exotic Cheese Dip

1 cup cream cheese
½ cup commercial sour cream
1 package Exotic Herb or Blue Cheese salad mix

Mix thoroughly and chill. Use as a dip. Substitute cottage cheese for the cream cheese if fewer calories are desired.

Cheese and Red Caviar

1 cup cream cheese
2 tablespoons cream
1 teaspoon onion juice
1 teaspoon lemon juice
2 tablespoons red caviar

Soften cream cheese with cream and onion juice. Add lemon juice and mix in the caviar very carefully to avoid breaking the eggs. Serve with dark rye bread.

Olive Cheese Balls

1 cup cream cheese
½ cup chopped ripe olives
1 tablespoon butter
Coarsely chopped walnuts

Cream together thoroughly the cream cheese, olives, and butter. Form into little balls and roll in coarsely chopped walnuts. Serve on toothpicks.

Egg and Swiss Cheese Spread

6 hard-cooked egg yolks, sieved
1 cup grated Swiss cheese
1 teaspoon prepared mustard
Mayonnaise to bind ingredients to a smooth paste
Salt and pepper to taste

Blend, using enough mayonnaise to bind the ingredients to a smooth paste of spreading consistency.

Clam Dip

1 7½-ounce can minced clams, drained
1 teaspoon Worcestershire sauce
1 teaspoon lemon juice
2 3-ounce packages cream cheese

Add Worcestershire sauce and lemon juice to the drained clams and mix with cream cheese. Chill and serve.

Lobster and Cucumber Spread

1 cup lobster meat, chopped fine
Melted butter to sauté
1 cucumber, chopped fine
Salt
Paprika
Mayonnaise

Sauté lobster in melted butter. Cool and add cucumber. Season with salt and paprika, and use enough mayonnaise to make of spreading consistency.

Blue Cheese Dip

¼ pound Blue cheese, crumbled
½ cup chili sauce
3 tablespoons salad dressing *or* mayonnaise
¼ teaspoon garlic salt
¼ cup chopped parsley
2 tablespoons minced onion

Combine all ingredients, blend well, and chill until serving time. MAKES 1 CUP.

Curried Olive Spread

1 3-ounce package cream cheese
2 tablespoons milk
⅛ teaspoon curry powder
¼ teaspoon onion powder
½ cup chopped ripe olives
Dash each of pepper and paprika

Mix cream cheese and milk until smooth and of spreading consistency. Add remaining ingredients and blend. Serve in a bowl, to be spread on crisp crackers, but let your guests spread their own. In this way the crackers don't get soggy. MAKES ¾ CUP.

Black Bean Soup Dip

1 can condensed black bean soup
2 3-ounce packages cream cheese
¼ teaspoon powdered thyme
1 teaspoon Worcestershire sauce
½ teaspoon salt
¼ teaspoon powdered garlic

Beat together well to blend and serve with potato or corn chips.

Hawaiian Teriyaki

- 1 pound beef steak, preferably sirloin
- 1/8 cup soy sauce
- 1/8 cup water
- 1 tablespoon sugar
- 1 clove garlic, minced
- 1 tablespoon minced fresh ginger *or* 1/8 teaspoon powdered ginger

Cut steak into 1-inch cubes. Combine remaining ingredients and marinate steak in sauce for at least 1 hour. Place 1 or 2 cubes on bamboo skewers and broil about 5 minutes on each side. If you have a little hibachi, it's great fun to broil these over charcoal right at the table. MAKES APPROXIMATELY 40 CUBES.

Crusty Cheese Balls

- 3/4 cup flour
- 1 pound grated sharp cheese
- 2 egg whites, beaten stiff
- 8 drops Tabasco sauce
- 1 teaspoon Worcestershire sauce
- 1 tablespoon parsley flakes, onion flakes or caraway seed
- 1 teaspoon salt
- 1 teaspoon paprika

Combine cheese and flour. Add Tabasco, Worcestershire, flakes, and seasonings. Mix in beaten egg whites. Roll mixture into balls about the size of a walnut and either deep fry them at 375° F. in hot oil or skillet fry them in 1/2 inch of oil. Cook only until they are a light brown, drain on brown paper, and serve warm.

Seviche

This recipe for Seviche which is an uncooked-by-heat fish appetizer has some painful memories for me. I tried in all of the hotels in Acapulco to find a good Seviche recipe. Everyone looked at me with a blank stare when I suggested that I would like to know how the dish was prepared. So I went out on the beach with a friend of mine who is a Seviche admirer, and we found a little old Mexican man who was just at that moment marinating the raw fish in lemon and lime juice. He spoke no English and I speak no Spanish, but the language of food is international. I watched him through the whole process and made little notes. Then I returned to the hotel and ordered up raw fresh fish and the ingredients and made it immediately so I wouldn't forget how to put it together.

Seviche is a delightful appetizer, and if you don't tell your guests that it is raw fish, they will love it. Of course the combination of lime and lemon juice marinade does cook the fish, but it's hard to convince people that they are not being cannibalistic.

- 1 pound fish fillets
- 6 ounces lemon or lime juice or combination of both
- 2 large tomatoes, peeled and chopped
- 1 large onion, chopped fine
- 1 4-ounce can green chilies, chopped
- Salt and pepper
- 3/4 teaspoon orégano
- 2 tablespoons good oil
- Bottle small Italian-type olives

If you are using frozen fish fillets, defrost them before starting to prepare the Seviche. Chop fish fine and marinate for at least 2 hours in juice. Combine tomatoes, onion, chilies; add to fish at the end of marinating period. Add remaining ingredients. Chill and serve very cold with tostados or crisp crackers. Use in place of a shrimp or crab cocktail.

Tiny Spiced Meat Balls

- 1/2 pound ground lean beef
- 4 tablespoons fine bread crumbs
- 1/2 teaspoon salt
- 1/4 teaspoon pepper
- 1/2 teaspoon caraway seeds
- 1/8 teaspoon nutmeg
- 1 1/2 teaspoons minced onion
- 1/4 teaspoon horseradish
- 1 tablespoon mayonnaise
- Dash of Tabasco sauce
- 2 tablespoons bacon drippings
- Parmesan cheese

In a mixing bowl, combine all ingredients except the bacon drippings and the grated Parmesan cheese. Mix and blend well and then shape into 24 tiny meat balls. Sauté the balls in the bacon drippings until all sides are thoroughly browned, about 4 minutes. Drain briefly on paper toweling, then roll each ball in the grated Parmesan cheese. Insert a toothpick in each ball and serve in a chafing dish over hot water to keep them hot.

Tommy Lumby's Tamale Balls

Tommy Lumby used to be food editor for one of the Texas papers, but is now a most successful real estate woman. She loves to cook, and has enough blue ribbons in cooking contests to paper the walls of her den. This Tamale Ball recipe is one of her greatest. At Christmas time she makes gallons of this recipe, freezes it, and gives it as gifts to the grocery store manager, the meat man, to me, and to all of her friends. It freezes very well.

- 1 pound ground beef
- 1 pound ground pork
- 1½ cups corn meal
- ¾ cup tomato juice
- ½ cup flour
- 4 garlic pods, minced, *or* 1 teaspoon garlic purée
- 1 tablespoon chili powder
- 2 teaspoons salt

Combine beef and pork, add all other ingredients, and mix well with hands. Form into small balls, about the size of large marbles. Place in sauce and simmer for 2 hours. Keep hot in chafing dish. Serve on toothpicks.

Sauce

- 2 large cans (5 cups) tomatoes
- 1 tablespoon chili powder
- 2 teaspoons salt

Mash tomatoes with a fork, add chili powder and salt, and bring to a simmer. Add tamale balls and simmer about 2 hours.

Deviled Eggs Angostura

- 6 hard-cooked eggs
- 1 teaspoon Angostura bitters
- Mayonnaise

Slice hard-cooked eggs in half lengthwise and remove yolks. Put yolks through a sieve, add mayonnaise to make the desired consistency, and add Angostura bitters to mixture. Restuff whites with filling. Chill.

Vegetable Dunking Bowl

- 1 pound cottage cheese
- ½ cup finely cut green onions
- ¼ cup grated raw carrot
- ¼ cup heavy cream
- 4 radishes, sliced
- ¼ cup chopped green pepper
- Salt to taste

Blend all ingredients together in food blender. Serve in a bowl with crisp carrot strips and cauliflowerets for dunking.

Salted Parmesan Bits

1 cup sifted flour
½ teaspoon salt
Dash of pepper
1 3-ounce can grated Parmesan cheese
½ cup soft butter
Slightly beaten egg or milk for brushing bits

Combine flour, salt, pepper, and cheese. Cut in soft butter until particles are the size of small peas. Knead and work with hands or spoon until a smooth ball is formed. Roll out on floured pastry cloth or board to ½-inch thickness. Brush with slightly beaten egg or milk. Cut into ½-inch cubes. Place on a greased baking sheet and bake in a moderate oven, 375° F., 20 to 25 minutes. Cool. Store in a tightly covered container.

Melba Toast Parmesan

Cut thin slices of white or protein bread and brush the slices with soft butter. Sprinkle with grated Parmesan cheese and a little paprika. Toast slowly in a 250° F. oven until crisp and nicely browned.

Chili Walnuts

½ pound shelled walnuts
Butter *or* margarine
Chili powder
Salt

In a skillet, lightly sauté walnuts in hot butter, stirring constantly. When the nuts are crisp and lightly browned, dust them liberally with chili powder and salt. Place on paper towels to drain before serving.

Pimiento Cream Cheese Dip

2 3-ounce packages cream cheese
1 pimiento, minced
½ cup ripe olives, chopped
¼ cup English walnuts, chopped
Tabasco sauce to taste
Cream to make dipping consistency

Combine all ingredients and blend, using just enough cream to make the mixture a good dipping consistency. Serve with corn or potato chips and tostados.

Cream Cheese Puffs

- 2 3-ounce packages cream cheese
- 1 egg
- ½ teaspoon onion, grated
- Rounds of bread, toasted on one side

Beat cream cheese with egg until thoroughly blended, light, and smooth. Add grated onion and heap on rounds of bread that have been toasted on one side. Broil about 1 minute or until brown and puffy. Serve hot.

Anchovy Teasers

Mix equal parts of chopped anchovies, mashed Roquefort cheese, and soft butter. Blend together until smooth and serve on Melba toast.

Chicken Liver Pâté

- 3 chicken livers
- 1 onion, minced
- Butter
- 3 hard-cooked eggs
- Salt and pepper

Cook chicken livers until tender. Sauté onion in butter until golden brown. Combine all ingredients in wooden bowl, seasoning with salt and pepper to taste. Chop very fine, blend to make a paste, and serve on crackers or Melba toast.

Parmesan Garlic Dip

- 2 3-ounce packages cream cheese, softened
- ½ cup evaporated milk
- 2 teaspoons grated onion *or* ½ teaspoon onion powder
- ¼ teaspoon garlic powder
- 1 teaspoon Worcestershire sauce
- ¼ cup grated Parmesan cheese

Gradually add evaporated milk to softened cream cheese, blending well. Add remaining ingredients and mix thoroughly. If the dip is too thick, add more milk until the mixture is the desired consistency.

Onion Soup Dip

This Onion Soup Dip, which came originally from the test kitchens of Lipton's, is one of the greatest spur-of-the-moment dips. It has traveled all around the world; in fact, a copy of it was sent to me recently from Japan.

- 1 package dehydrated onion soup mix
- 1 pint commercial sour cream
- Tabasco sauce

Mix together the onion soup mix and sour cream until well blended. Add a touch of Tabasco and serve as a dip. If the dip becomes too thick while standing, thin it with more sour cream.

Caesar Dip

- 1 3-ounce package cream cheese
- ½ cup commercial sour cream
- 2 packets garlic-olive dip mix
- 2 tablespoons milk
- 1 teaspoon lemon juice
- 1 teaspoon finely chopped anchovies

Blend cream cheese and sour cream together until smooth. Add dip mix and blend. Add milk, lemon juice, and anchovies; beat until smooth. Refrigerate several hours before serving. MAKES 1 CUP.

New Roquefort Dip

- 2 3-ounce packages cream cheese
- 2 ounces Roquefort cheese or to taste
- 1 tablespoon heavy cream
- ¼ teaspoon onion juice
- 1 tablespoon sherry wine

Blend all ingredients, using more Roquefort if needed to make a creamy consistency. Let stand a few hours before serving.

Mushrooms with Crabmeat Stuffing

- Large mushroom caps
- 1 pound fresh crabmeat
- 1 small onion, finely chopped
- Butter *or* margarine
- ¼ cup brandy

Break off the stems of the mushrooms and save them for soup or a casserole dish. Pick over the crabmeat very carefully and remove any tendon that might be lurking in it. Sauté the finely chopped onion in butter or margarine. When a light yellow, add the crabmeat. Handle it gently, but toss lightly with the onions, turning the mixture over and over until the crabmeat is heated and well combined with the onion and butter. Make a well in the middle of the skillet and add brandy. Let the brandy heat in the middle of the skillet and, when hot, blend it into the crabmeat mixture. Stuff the mushroom caps and set them in an open baking pan. Pour about ¼ inch water in the pan. Bake in a moderate (350° F.) oven for 25 to 30 minutes. Serve hot.

Onion Cheese Puffs

12 2-inch bread rounds
¼ cup mayonnaise
2 packets onion dip mix
2 tablespoons grated Parmesan cheese
1 egg white

Cut rounds from thin bread slices with a 2-inch biscuit cutter. Mix together mayonnaise, dip mix, and Parmesan cheese. Beat egg white until stiff and fold into mayonnaise mixture. Spread on bread. Bake in a hot oven, 450° F., for 10 minutes. Serve hot. MAKES 12 PUFFS.

Mystery Dip

1 can frozen condensed cream of shrimp soup, thawed
½ cup commercial sour cream
1 tablespoon horseradish
¼ teaspoon Worcestershire sauce

Combine all ingredients thoroughly. Let stand in the refrigerator for at least 1 hour to allow flavors to blend.

Liptauer Spread

Mrs. Frank Krusen, the wife of Dr. Frank Krusen of the Mayo Clinic in Rochester, Minnesota, gave me this Liptauer Spread recipe. It's a good standby spread to have in the refrigerator for a bite or two before dinner, and it is also a wonderful addition to a buffet table. Mrs. Krusen packs the spread in little stone crocks.

2 3-ounce packages cream cheese
1 can anchovies
1 tablespoon butter *or* margarine
1 teaspoon capers
1 teaspoon caraway seeds
1 teaspoon paprika
1 teaspoon chopped onion

All ingredients must be at room temperature. Combine all ingredients and mix very thoroughly. Chill and serve with crackers or chips.

Marinated Garbanzo Beans

Mexican garbanzo beans are also called chick peas. I felt there might be some areas in the United States where the garbanzo bean influence had not been felt. Any canned product that bears the name "chick peas" is the right ingredient for this recipe.

These taste even better if they are prepared several days before serving.

5 cups (2 No. 2 cans) garbanzo beans
¼ cup lemon juice
¼ cup red wine vinegar
1⅓ cups olive oil *or* salad oil
1 clove garlic, split
4 tablespoons finely chopped green onions
2 tablespoons chopped fresh parsley

Drain the beans thoroughly. Mix all other ingredients together and then combine with the beans. Chill and marinate at least several hours. Before serving, drain off some of the marinade. Place the beans in a bowl and sprinkle with additional parsley. Serve cold.

Little Mexican Turnovers

Elena Zelayeta, who is probably the most outstanding authority on Mexican cookery in this country and the author of many cookbooks, has a wonderful recipe for Little Mexican Turnovers. This simplified version that we use in Texas is always one of the stars of a hot hors d'oeuvres collection.

These bite-sized hot canapés are called *empanaditas* and they are bits of rich pie dough baked with any kind of filling you want in them. Use anchovy paste, deviled ham, grated cheese mixed with butter, or creamed chicken or tuna.

2 cups flour
1 teaspoon salt
⅔ cup lard *or* other shortening
Ice water (just enough to blend the pastry)

Combine flour and salt, cut in shortening, and add just enough ice water to blend. Roll out and cut into rounds with a biscuit cutter. Place a spoonful of any desired filling on half of each circle. Dampen the edges, fold over, and press edges together. Bake in a hot (400° F.) oven until golden, 15 to 20 minutes.

The turnovers may also be fried in deep fat until golden, but if you plan to fry them, use ½ cup shortening instead of ⅔ cup.

Shad Roe en Brochette

Buy canned shad roe and cut it into small squares (about ¾ inch square). Wrap each square in small strips of bacon, secure with a toothpick, and place under the broiler until the bacon is crisp. Serve hot.

Chinese Chicken Livers

1 pound chicken livers
¼ cup soy sauce
¼ cup sugar
1 teaspoon salt
1 teaspoon brandy *or* sherry
¼ cup cornstarch

Cut livers into 1-inch pieces. Mix soy sauce, sugar, salt, and brandy or sherry. Add the livers and marinate in a covered dish for about 30 minutes. Dip each piece of liver in cornstarch and fry in deep hot fat (370° F., as for fritters) for 2 minutes. Serve hot. Be sure you cover the deep fryer when cooking the livers—they pop.

Hot Tomato Cheese Whiz Dip

1-pound jar Kraft's Cheese Whiz
⅓ cup chili sauce
½ teaspoon celery seed
1 teaspoon minced onion

Place all ingredients in a saucepan, mix well, and heat over very low heat. Serve hot as a dip with corn chips.

Curried Celery Sticks

1 3-ounce package cream cheese
1 tablespoon chopped parsley
2 teaspoons mayonnaise *or* salad dressing
1 teaspoon grated onion
¼ teaspoon curry powder
¼ teaspoon salt
Celery stalks

Blend all together and stuff celery stalks. Cut into bite-size pieces. Filling keeps well for days in refrigerator.

Idiot's Delight

1 can Chinese fried noodles
½ pound Spanish peanuts (the red ones)
1 teaspoon butter
½ teaspoon Ac'cent
½ teaspoon salt

Toss noodles and peanuts together in a frying pan, adding butter, Ac'cent, and salt. Heat gently until butter is melted, stirring constantly so that ingredients won't burn. Drain on paper and serve either warm or cold.

Bologna Bites

- 2 3-ounce packages cream cheese, softened
- 2 teaspoons grated onion
- 2 teaspoons horseradish
- Dash of Worcestershire sauce
- 2 tablespoons Rhine wine
- 6 thin slices round bologna sausage

Combine softened cream cheese, grated onion, horseradish, Worcestershire, and Rhine wine; blend well. Spread each bologna slice with some of this mixture, stack the slices, and chill thoroughly. Cut in wedges and spear with wooden picks.

Hot Chili Roquefort Canapés

- 4 ounces cream cheese
- 1½ ounces (2 tablespoons) crumbled Roquefort cheese
- 1 tablespoon catsup
- 1¾ teaspoons chili powder
- ¼ teaspoon paprika
- 1/16 teaspoon garlic powder
- 10 slices of bread

Soften the cream cheese and blend with the Roquefort cheese. Add catsup and spices and mix well. Trim crusts from bread and toast slices on both sides. Spread the cheese mixture on the toast and cut each piece in 3 finger-length strips. Broil until browned and bubbly. Sprinkle with additional paprika. MAKES 30 CANAPÉS.

Hot Peppered Shrimp

- 3 to 4 pounds shrimp
- 2 teaspoons salt
- 1 onion, sliced
- 1 carrot, sliced
- 4 stalks celery
- 2 cloves garlic
- 3 teaspoons mixed pickling spices
- ¼ pound butter
- 1 to 2 teaspoons coarsely ground black pepper
- Thin slices of rye bread
- Minced parsley creamed with soft butter

Make a court bouillon of enough water to cover the shrimp, salt, onion, carrot, celery, garlic. Tie the pickling spices in a little cloth bag, drop it into the liquid, and boil all together. Clean and devein the shrimp. When the court bouillon reaches a slow boil, drop the shrimp into the bouillon and let it come to a boil again. Cook a few minutes until the shrimp are tender, then turn off the heat and let the shrimp cool in the broth. Remove the shrimp, drop them into a shallow casserole, add about ¼ pound butter and much more freshly ground black pepper than you think you need, about 1 to 2 teaspoons. Cover the casserole, and heat in a moderate oven just before serving time. To serve, surround the casserole with paper-thin slices of small rye bread spread with parsley butter and let the guests use the bread, tortilla fashion, folding each slice around a buttery, peppery shrimp.

Parmesan Canapés

Cut rounds of sliced bread with a biscuit cutter. Top each with a slice of thin white onion. Combine ½ cup mayonnaise and 3 tablespoons grated Parmesan cheese. Place the rounds on an ungreased baking sheet. Top each slice with 1 teaspoon of cheese mixture and sprinkle with additional Parmesan cheese. Just before serving, place under broiler until golden brown. Serve piping hot.

Guacamole

- 3 tablespoons finely chopped onion
- 1 tomato, peeled and chopped
- 2 avocados, peeled and mashed
- 1 teaspoon salt
- 2 teaspoons chili powder
- 1 tablespoon lemon juice

Combine the onion, tomato and avocado; mash until smooth. Add the salt, chili powder, and lemon juice. Mix well. Serve as a dip with tortillas, or with potato or corn chips.

Crisp Rye Curls

- 1 loaf icebox rye bread
- ½ cup butter *or* margarine, melted
- Grated Parmesan cheese

With a very sharp knife or slicer, cut rye bread into paper-thin slices. Place slices in single layer on trays and allow to dry in the air until they are crisp and the edges curl. Spread half the melted butter over the bottom of a large baking pan at least 2 inches deep. Scatter the rye bread slices over the butter. Dribble the remaining butter over the top. Broil about 4 inches from heat until delicately browned. Don't let chips get too dark. Stir occasionally so that the bottom pieces can brown. Sprinkle with grated Parmesan cheese while still hot.

Fried Camembert Cheese

Cut Camembert cheese in desired portions after removing rind. Dip in beaten eggs and fresh bread crumbs. Harden in refrigerator. Before serving, fry very quickly in hot deep fat. Currant jelly or bar-le-duc and Melba toast may be served with it.

NOTE: I have found that if you refrigerate the cheese before you remove the rind it is easier to handle.

Italian Scampi

2 pounds unshelled shrimp
¼ pound butter *or* margarine
1 clove garlic, minced fine
Salt and pepper to taste

Remove shells from all but the tail portion of raw shrimp. Cut the shrimp down the center of the back and remove the sand vein. Melt butter and add garlic. Simmer 3 minutes. Place shrimp on individual, flameproof platters or large broiling pan and pour garlic butter over them. Sprinkle with salt and pepper. Place in a preheated broiler, 3 inches from the heat, and broil 5 to 7 minutes or until browned and tender. SERVES 4 TO 5.

Blue Cheese Mousse

¼ pound Blue cheese
¼ cup light cream
½ cup heavy cream

Press the cheese through a fine sieve. Add the light cream and mix thoroughly. Place in the top of a double boiler over boiling water and stir until smooth. Remove from heat and chill. Beat in heavy cream. Turn the mixture into a shallow mold and freeze 4 hours or until the mousse is firm. Unmold onto a chilled serving dish and surround with rounds of dark bread. This mixture will keep for a week. MAKES 1 CUP.

Fondue Neuchateloise

½ pound Swiss cheese, grated
1 tablespoon flour
1 cut clove garlic
1 cup dry white wine
Salt, pepper, and nutmeg
3 tablespoons Kirsch
French bread, cubed

Dredge the grated Swiss cheese with the flour. Rub a chafing dish or an electric skillet with the cut clove garlic. Add the wine and bring the mixture almost to the boiling point. Add grated cheese and stir constantly with a fork until cheese is all melted. Add salt, pepper, and nutmeg to taste. When the fondue starts to boil, add Kirsch. Bring to the table in a chafing dish or casserole over an electric plate. The fondue must be kept very hot or it will become stringy. Each guest dips his own cubes of bread into the hot fondue.

Hot Deviled Ham Dip

- 1/4 pound Velveeta cheese
- 1 2 1/4-ounce can deviled ham
- 1/2 cup mayonnaise
- 1 teaspoon grated onion
- Potato chips *or* potato crackers

Melt cheese in a chafing dish or in the top of a double boiler, add deviled ham, and mix until well blended. Add mayonnaise and onion and mix again. Serve hot or cold with potato chips or crackers. This may also be served hot over fluffy rice.

Chive Balls

- 1 cup cream cheese
- 1/2 cup chopped chives *or* chopped green onions
- 1 teaspoon French mustard
- 1/2 teaspoon salt
- 1/2 teaspoon pepper

Cream well and shape into balls. Serve on toothpicks.

Cheese-Crab Dip

- 1/2 cup Roquefort *or* Blue cheese
- 1/3 cup cream cheese
- 2 tablespoons Worcestershire sauce
- 1 small clove garlic, finely chopped
- 1 teaspoon lemon juice
- 1/2 cup crabmeat

Cream the cheeses together until soft, then add the rest of the ingredients and mix well. Place in a bowl on a large tray and surround with potato chips that have been sprinkled with garlic salt and heated.

Fontina

- 1 tablespoon butter
- 3 tablespoons flour
- 2 cups milk
- 1 pound Swiss cheese, grated
- Salt, pepper, nutmeg
- French bread, cubed

Melt butter in chafing dish or electric skillet; add flour and blend well. Stir in milk, a little at a time. When all milk is added, bring to a boil and add Swiss cheese, stirring constantly with a fork until melted. Add salt, pepper and nutmeg to taste. Serve very hot, with cubes of French bread for dunking.

Mexican Cheese Balls

1½ cups cream cheese
1 tablespoon chopped green pepper
1 tablespoon chopped pimiento
1 tablespoon chopped or minced onion
½ teaspoon salt
Pignolia (pine) nuts

Mix well, form into balls, and roll in coarsely chopped pignolia nuts. Serve on toothpicks.

Cheese Shortbread

¼ pound butter *or* margarine
¼ pound sharp cheese, coarsely grated
1 cup sifted flour
Worcestershire sauce
Paprika
Cayenne (or any other seasoning desired)
Pecan or walnut halves

Combine all ingredients, working with the hands for a good blend, then form into balls. Place the balls on an ungreased cooky sheet and flatten each one with a fork. Put a half pecan or walnut on top of each and bake in a moderate (325° F.) oven for 25 minutes.

Cream Cheese Puffs

2 3-ounce packages cream cheese
2 egg yolks
1 small onion, grated
2 teaspoons baking powder
Crisp crackers

Let the cream cheese stand at room temperature so that it will soften. Blend with egg yolks and grated onion. A few minutes before serving, add the baking powder to the cream cheese mixture, blend well, and heap onto crisp crackers or Triscuits. Broil for a minute or two until bubbly and brown. Serve hot.

Anchovy Spread I

Mix equal parts of chopped anchovies, mashed Roquefort, and butter. Blend together until smooth and serve on Melba toast.

Anchovy Spread II

12 anchovy fillets, chopped
1 tablespoon chopped fresh dill
2 tablespoons chopped chives
1 cup soft cream cheese

Combine all ingredients and blend until smooth.

Anchovy Spread III

6 hard-cooked eggs, finely chopped
3 tablespoons anchovy paste
½ cup mayonnaise
Salt and pepper

Blend chopped eggs with anchovy paste and mayonnaise; season to taste with salt and pepper. Spread on toast rounds.

Ham-Stuffed Eggs

8 hard-cooked eggs
1 3-ounce can deviled ham
Mayonnaise
½ teaspoon onion juice
½ teaspoon prepared mustard
Salt and pepper
Water cress

Cut eggs in half lengthwise and remove yolks. Mash the yolks with the deviled ham spread, moisten with mayonnaise, and add the onion juice, mustard, salt, and pepper. Stuff the egg whites with this mixture and chill. Garnish with water cress just before serving.

Curried Tuna Spread

1 7-ounce can tuna
¼ teaspoon salt
½ teaspoon curry powder
2½ tablespoons mayonnaise
2 teaspoons lemon juice
2 teaspoons onion powder
Pimiento strips
Parsley sprigs

Drain the tuna and break it into small pieces. Add the remaining ingredients and toss lightly together with a fork until well mixed. Garnish with strips of pimiento and parsley and serve with crackers. MAKES 1 CUP.

Chile Con Queso

Chile Con Queso demands that you use red chili purée as the main ingredient. Sometimes it is difficult to find in markets where Mexican-type products are not too popular. However, Ashley's of

El Paso, Texas, have a very good one, either mild or hot-flavored. They would be very glad to send you a catalog of their complete line if you care to go the Mexican food route.

1 onion, finely chopped
2 green chilies, peeled
2 tablespoons bacon fat
½ cup red chili purée
1 cup processed cheese, cut into small chunks
Salt, pepper, and garlic salt

Fry finely chopped onion and chili pepper in hot bacon fat until light brown. Add chili purée and cheese chunks. Reduce heat and simmer, stirring constantly, until all cheese is thoroughly melted. (The secret is never to let this boil.) Season to taste. Serve piping hot with tostados.

Water Cress Cornucopias

Thin-sliced bread, crusts removed
Softened butter
Crisp water cress, well washed

Remove crusts from thinly sliced white bread, spread generously with softened butter and roll into cornucopias, fastening each with a toothpick. Place a sprig of water cress in each cornucopia so that the leafy part shows.

Cheese Wafers

1 package Snappy cheese
¼ cup butter
½ cup flour
Salt

Mix all ingredients well and set in refrigerator till hard. (The dough may be prepared the night before.) Roll out to the thickness of pie crust and cut into small circles with a biscuit cutter. Sprinkle with paprika and bake in a moderate (350° F.) oven for 15 minutes. Serve hot.

Caviar Spread

1 small jar black caviar
½ pint commercial sour cream
Lemon juice
Pumpernickel bread

Mix into the caviar a few drops lemon juice. Serve sour cream and caviar in separate containers, allowing your guests to help themselves to bread, sour cream, and caviar in the proportions they like best.

Avocado-Roquefort Dip I

1 clove garlic, grated or chopped
2 ounces Roquefort cheese
2 tablespoons lemon juice
2 very ripe avocados, peeled
½ teaspoon salt
½ teaspoon chili seasoning
1 teaspoon Worcestershire sauce

Combine all ingredients and beat well with a fork. As the mixture tends to darken on standing, beat or stir it occasionally to keep it light.

Avocado-Roquefort Dip II

1 or 2 avocados, peeled
¼ cup mashed Roquefort cheese
1 tablespoon lemon juice
Olive oil
Seasonings to taste

Press peeled avocados through a sieve to make 1 cup purée. Add Roquefort, lemon juice, and enough olive oil to make the dip a smooth consistency. Add seasonings to taste, and chill.

Anchovy-Deviled Eggs

6 hard-cooked eggs, cut in half lengthwise
2 teaspoons anchovy paste
1 teaspoon sugar
½ cup mayonnaise
Finely chopped parsley
Water cress

Mix egg yolks with anchovy paste, sugar, and mayonnaise. Fill the egg whites with this mixture. Sprinkle with finely chopped parsley and serve on water cress. This is a nice addition to a canapé tray.

Pâté de Foie Gras

1 2-ounce can chopped mushrooms
1 small can liver pâté
4 ounces melted butter
2 tablespoons brandy

Sauté the mushrooms in a little butter until they are lightly browned; do not allow them to dry out. Blend mushrooms, liver, and butter; then add brandy. Chill in the refrigerator overnight. The butter will rise to the top of the crock and form a thin covering for the pâté. Serve as a spread for canapés.

Cheese-Nut Dip

- ½ cup cottage cheese
- 1 3-ounce package cream cheese
- ½ cup sour cream
- Dash of Tabasco sauce
- Dash of garlic powder
- Pinch of black pepper
- ¼ teaspoon salt
- ½ cup chopped nuts

Blend all the ingredients together and chill thoroughly. Serve with potato chips or corn chips.

Crab au Gratin

- White bread, sliced
- Butter
- 1 can crabmeat
- ½ cup sharp Cheddar cheese, grated
- Sherry wine

Toast one side of a slice of white bread, butter the untoasted side, and spread with the crabmeat. Sprinkle the crabmeat thickly with grated cheese and broil until the cheese is melted. A moment before removing from the broiler, pour on a tablespoon of sherry, heat and serve. To make a hot canapé, cut each slice of toast into four sections. For a first course, each slice is one serving.

Chicken Livers Madeira

- ½ pound chicken livers
- Butter for frying
- Salt and pepper
- 3 tablespoons Madeira wine
- 1 tablespoon butter
- 1 tablespoon lemon juice

Fry chicken livers rapidly in butter for 5 minutes; season with salt and pepper. Add Madeira wine and bring to a boil, then add a tablespoon of butter and the lemon juice. Toss and remove from heat without further cooking. Serve on toast points. SERVES 2.

Roquefort Dip

- 2 3-ounce packages cream cheese
- Roquefort cheese to taste
- 1 tablespoon heavy cream
- ¼ teaspoon onion juice
- 1 tablespoon sherry wine

Blend all ingredients, using enough Roquefort to make a creamy consistency. Let stand a few hours before serving with potato chips, corn chips, or crackers. If you'd rather serve this mixture as a spread, omit the heavy cream.

Blue Cheese Crisps

¼ cup softened butter *or* margarine
½ cup grated processed Cheddar cheese
1 teaspoon grated onion
¾ cup sifted flour
¾ cup crumbled Blue cheese

Combine all ingredients and mix until well blended. Shape into balls about ¾ inch in diameter and place on an ungreased baking sheet. Press down with the tines of a fork. Chill several hours. Bake in a very hot oven, 450° F., for 8 to 10 minutes or until golden brown. MAKES 30 TO 36 CANAPÉS.

Hot Maine Sardine Dip

2 cans Maine sardines
3 hard-cooked eggs
1 tablespoon minced parsley
1 teaspoon minced onion
1 teaspoon prepared mustard
½ cup mayonnaise
½ cup creamy processed American cheese
1 teaspoon Worcestershire sauce
Salt and pepper to taste

Drain and mash the sardines. Put the eggs through a sieve. Combine all ingredients in the top of a double boiler, heat, and season as desired. For a thinner mixture, stir in a little heavy cream or more mayonnaise. Keep the dip hot in a chafing dish and serve with crisp crackers or corn chips.

Sour Cream and Olive Dunk

2 cups thick commercial sour cream
¾ cup finely chopped ripe olives
1 tablespoon grated onion
Salt and pepper to taste

Combine all ingredients and use as a dunk for raw vegetables.

Bacon Olives

Wrap half slices of bacon around large stuffed olives and fasten with a pick. Place on a rack in a shallow pan. Bake in a hot oven, 400° F., until bacon is crisp, about 12 to 15 minutes. Serve hot.

Bacon Roll-Ups

Mash liverwurst and blend it with enough finely mashed hard-cooked egg yolk to hold together. Season well with Tabasco and

Worcestershire sauces. Spread the mixture on strips of bacon, roll them up, and fasten with toothpicks. Skillet fry or broil until rolls are crisp. Serve hot.

Holiday Cheese Ball

This Holiday Cheese Ball recipe has become a tradition on holiday buffet tables, but it is equally good to give to a friend who might be having a few guests for cocktails. I'm sure it isn't an exaggeration to say that we have made millions of these cheese balls. This year, to change the appearance of them, we divided the cheese mixture in three parts, lined small bowls with foil, and packed the cheese into small balls. Before we put them on the table, we rolled one in chopped ripe olives and another in finely chopped parsley. We molded chopped red pimientos over the third one. They looked beautiful on a serving tray surrounded by an assortment of crackers.

- 6 ounces Blue cheese
- 2 5-ounce jars processed Cheddar cheese spread
- 4 3-ounce packages cream cheese
- 2 tablespoons grated onion
- 1 teaspoon Worcestershire sauce
- ½ teaspoon Ac'cent
- 1 cup ground pecans
- ½ cup finely chopped parsley

Have cheeses at room temperature. Mix cheeses, onion, Worcestershire sauce, and Ac'cent together until thoroughly blended. Add ½ cup pecans and ¼ cup parsley. Shape the mixture into a ball. Place in bowl lined with waxed paper or foil and chill overnight. About 1 hour before serving, roll the ball in a mixture of the remaining pecans and parsley. Place on platter and surround with crisp crackers.

Cheese Spread

- 1 pound Roquefort *or* Blue cheese
- 5 tablespoons lemon juice
- 5 tablespoons Worcestershire sauce
- 2 tablespoons A-1 sauce
- 1 teaspoon dry mustard
- ¼ teaspoon pepper
- 4 3-ounce packages cream cheese *or* 1 pound cottage cheese

Cut Roquefort cheese in small pieces. Place in electric mixer bowl. Add lemon juice, Worcestershire and A-1 sauces, mustard, and pepper. Beat at low speed until light and smooth. Add cream cheese or cottage cheese and beat again until the mixture is the consistency of heavy whipped cream.

This spread can be kept for weeks in the refrigerator in a tightly covered jar.

Curried Cream Cheese

1 cup soft cream cheese
½ teaspoon curry powder
2 tablespoons chopped preserved ginger
3 tablespoons chopped chutney
2 tablespoons grated fresh coconut

Combine all ingredients and mix well. Use as a spread.

Garlic Cheese

1 cup cottage cheese
¼ cup milk
2 cloves garlic, crushed
Salt

Combine cottage cheese, milk, and crushed garlic; force through a fine sieve or whip in an electric blender. Add a generous amount of salt and, if necessary, a little more milk to make a spread or a dip soft enough to pick up on potato chips.

Angostura Appetizer Sauce

1 cup mayonnaise
1 teaspoon curry powder
1 teaspoon prepared mustard
½ teaspoon onion salt
1 teaspoon Angostura bitters
½ teaspoon paprika

Blend all ingredients together and chill. Use this as a dip for cold rock lobster tails. Cut the cooked lobster meat into chunks and arrange them around your dip bowl.

Hollywood Dunk

1 cup heavy cream, whipped
1 2¼-ounce can deviled ham
2 tablespoons minced chives
1 tablespoon grated onion *or* onion juice
4 tablespoons horseradish
Dash of garlic salt
Dash of celery salt

Combine all ingredients and blend well. Serve with potato or corn chips.

Garlic Almonds

1 pound almonds
1 tablespoon butter
2 cloves garlic, minced
Salt

Shell and blanch the almonds. Place in a shallow pan with butter, garlic, and plenty of salt. Toast in a slow oven, 300° F., stirring often, until the almonds are brown. Remove the garlic and drain the almonds on paper towels before serving.

Franks under Wraps

Slit 6 frankfurters lengthwise. Brush each opening with mild mustard, insert a sliver of American cheese, wrap up with thin strips of boiled ham and fasten with 3 or 4 cocktail picks. Heat in a hot oven, 400° F., until the cheese starts to melt. Cut into bite-size sections, leaving in the cocktail picks. Serve on a platter as hot canapés.

Shrimp Portuguese

2 pounds large raw shrimp
½ cup butter *or* margarine
1 large garlic clove, minced, *or* ¼ teaspoon garlic purée
½ teaspoon salt
⅛ teaspoon pepper
½ cup minced parsley

Peel and devein the shrimp. Melt the butter in a large frying pan, add the garlic and salt, and cook until the butter is light brown. Add shrimp and cook, turning them over and over, for about 10 minutes or until the shrimp are pink, tender, and well done. Add pepper and additional salt if needed. Add parsley and mix through the cooked shrimp and cook 1 minute longer. Transfer to the double boiler part of a chafing dish. Put hot water in the lower part and keep the shrimp warm, to be speared out one at a time or served, three to a serving, on hors d'oeuvre plates.

Roquefort Cheese Spread

½ pound Roquefort cheese
4 3-ounce packages cream cheese
Port wine

Blend cheeses and enough port wine to form a paste and chill thoroughly. Serve with toasted crackers.

French-Fried Mustard Shrimp

Dip cooked shrimp in prepared mustard. Roll the shrimp in fine dry bread crumbs; be sure they are well coated. Drop into hot deep fat, 365° F., and fry until golden brown. Serve on toothpicks.

Cream Cheese Puff Canapés

Beat 3 ounces cream cheese and add just a bit of tarragon, salt, pepper, and 1 teaspoon of minced onion. Add 1 egg yolk and beat. Spread ½ inch thick on small bread rounds that have been fried in butter and place under the broiler so they will puff up. SERVE HOT!

Roquefort-Stuffed Olives

Use the pitted olives that have no stuffing (or pry the pimiento out of stuffed ones). Fill with softened Roquefort or Blue cheese. Chill and serve.

2

Main dishes

MAIN DISHES FALL NATURALLY into four different categories. Fish and seafood, of course, red meat, poultry, and those wonderful casserole dishes that help to balance the budget.

Once while I was autographing a cookbook for a man's wife, he asked me, "Does every casserole dish *have* to start with macaroni or spaghetti?" Of course it doesn't! There are hundreds of delicious combinations of meat and vegetables that can be put together without any of the pastas. If you have a freezer, put away small portions of leftover vegetables and meat, labeling them so you don't have to look into your crystal ball to know what's in each specific package. Then some night when the food budget is low, whip out a cup of cooked peas, a half cup of lima beans, and the tag end of a baked ham or beef roast; put it all together with a tomato or mushroom sauce, and you have done a creative job of building a new casserole dish. Oven temperature for these creations should be 350 degrees, and baking time, with the food already cooked, is usually about 25 to 30 minutes.

In this chapter of main dishes many old favorites have been left out, because I wanted to give you some new ideas that I have worked out for serving the same fine foods in different ways. Enjoy them in good health!

Seafarers' Tuna Chowder

Almost no one considers a chowder a main dish, but after you have eaten a large bowl of this hearty fare, with a tossed green salad and hot French bread, you couldn't possibly want anything other than a sweet dessert of some kind.

- 2 7-ounce cans solid pack tuna
- ½ pound fresh mushrooms, sliced
- 2 cups sliced carrots
- 1 cup sliced onions
- 1 cup sliced celery
- 1 quart milk
- 1 tablespoon Worcestershire sauce
- 1½ teaspoons garlic salt
- ½ teaspoon salt
- ¼ teaspoon pepper

Drain the tuna, reserving ¼ cup of the oil. Heat the oil in a large saucepan, add the vegetables, and cook until the onions are tender, stirring occasionally. Break the tuna into pieces. Add the tuna and remaining ingredients to the vegetable mixture, cover, and cook over low heat for 30 minutes, stirring occasionally. SERVES 5 OR 6.

Galley Tuna Chowder

- 2 7-ounce cans solid pack tuna
- ½ cup sliced onions
- 3 cups diced potatoes
- 1 10-ounce package frozen chopped spinach
- 1 quart milk
- 1 tablespoon celery seed
- 1 teaspoon salt
- ¼ teaspoon pepper
- 2 tablespoons sherry wine

Drain the tuna, reserving ¼ cup oil. Heat the oil in a large saucepan, add the onions and potatoes, and cook until the onions are tender. Meanwhile, cook the spinach, covered, in a small amount of boiling salted water for 5 minutes. Drain the spinach and force it through a sieve or food mill. Break the tuna into pieces. Add the tuna, spinach, purée, milk, celery seed, salt, and pepper to the onion mixture. Cover and cook over low heat, stirring occasionally, for 45 minutes or until the potatoes are tender. Add sherry just before serving, and mix well. SERVES 5 OR 6.

Oyster Stew

- 1 pint oysters
- ¼ cup butter *or* margarine
- ½ teaspoon salt
- Dash of Cayenne pepper
- ⅛ teaspoon pepper
- 1 teaspoon Worcestershire sauce
- 1½ quarts milk, scalded
- 2 tablespoons butter
- ¼ teaspoon paprika

Heat the oysters in their own liquor and add ¼ cup butter, seasonings, and Worcestershire. When the edges of the oysters curl, add the scalded milk and bring just to boiling, stirring occasionally. Remove from heat at once. Cut remaining 2 tablespoons butter into 6 pieces and place one piece in each of six heated soup plates. Pour in soup and sprinkle with paprika. SERVES 6.

Crab Gumbo

- ½ cup sliced onion
- 4 tablespoons butter
- 2 tablespoons flour
- 1 pound fresh or frozen crabmeat
- 4 cups (2 No. 303 cans) tomatoes
- 1 pound okra, cut in ¼-inch pieces
- 1 cup diced green pepper
- 2 cloves garlic, crushed
- 1 teaspoon nutmeg
- 2 teaspoons salt
- ¼ teaspoon freshly ground black pepper
- 2 cups water
- 1 teaspoon gumbo filé powder

Sauté the onion in the butter; stir in flour and cook until brown. Add crabmeat, vegetables, and all seasonings and spices *except* gumbo filé. Add 2 cups water. Bring to boiling, then reduce heat and simmer for 1 hour. Remove from heat and add gumbo filé powder; stir. Serve over fluffy rice immediately. SERVES 6.

Seafood Gumbo

- 1 cup sliced onions
- 8 tablespoons butter *or* margarine
- 4 tablespoons flour
- 1 pound crabmeat, fresh or frozen
- 1 pound cooked, diced lobster *or* flaked fish fillets
- 1 pint standard size oysters
- 1 pound cooked, deveined shrimp
- 8 cups (4 No. 303 cans) tomatoes
- 2 pounds okra cut in ¼-inch pieces *or* 4 packages frozen okra
- 2 cups diced green pepper
- 4 teaspoons salt
- 4 cloves garlic, crushed
- 2 teaspoons nutmeg
- 4 cups water
- 2 teaspoons gumbo filé powder
- ½ teaspoon fresh ground black pepper

Sauté the onions in butter or margarine. Stir in the flour and brown. Add the seafood, vegetables, salt, and all spices except gumbo filé,

Add 4 cups water. Bring to a boil, stirring constantly to prevent sticking; then reduce heat and simmer for 2 hours (cover the saucepan for the first hour and uncover it for the second hour). Remove from heat and add gumbo filé powder. Serve with fluffy rice. This freezes well. SERVES 16 TO 20.

German Vegetable Soup

A good vegetable soup is a thing of beauty and a joy forever. Judy Strain, one of our executive secretaries at the television station, came up with this favorite that was her grandmother's recipe. With hot French bread, it's a meal in itself.

The meat should be cut in large enough chunks so that the soup can be served with a big chunk of meat in each bowl.

- 4 pounds boneless boiling beef, cut in large chunks
- 1 soup bone, cracked
- 3⅓ cups (No. 2½ can) tomatoes
- 3 onions, sliced
- 4 stalks celery, diced
- 1 bay leaf
- 1 tablespoon dehydrated parsley flakes
- Salt and pepper to taste
- 1 rutabaga, diced
- 3 turnips, diced
- 3 potatoes, diced
- 1 small head cabbage, shredded (4 cups)
- 2 packages frozen mixed vegetables

Put the beef, soup bone, tomatoes, onions, celery, bay leaf, and parsley flakes in a large kettle. Cover with water and season with salt and pepper (you'll be adjusting the seasoning later). Bring to a boil and let simmer for 2 hours. If the water should boil away, add water during the simmering time. Add the diced rutabaga, turnips, potatoes, and shredded cabbage; let simmer for another hour. Add the frozen mixed vegetables and continue cooking until they are done. Taste, and adjust the seasonings. Serve in big bowls with hot French bread.

You should end up with a whole big kettle of soup and vegetables. It can be frozen in quart containers and used later. Good, old-fashioned soup is always made in large quantities.

Crabmeat Sauté

- 1 clove garlic
- ¼ pound butter
- 1 small onion, minced or grated
- 1 pound lump crabmeat

Rub the inside of the skillet with the cut clove of garlic, holding it with a fork, then remove the garlic. Melt the butter and lightly sauté the onion (don't let it turn brown). Add the crabmeat and turn it gently in the butter and onion until it begins to take on a golden color. Pile the sautéed crabmeat in crab shells (be sure they are *hot,* so they keep the mixture hot). Serve with a tomato and cucumber salad with French dressing. SERVES 2 OR 3.

Baked Imperial Crabmeat

- 1 pound fresh crabmeat
- 4 shallots *or* 1/4 of an onion
- 1/4 cup butter
- 2 tablespoons A-1 Sauce
- 1 teaspoon Worcestershire sauce
- 1 cup soft white bread crumbs
- 1 teaspoon salt
- 6 drops Tabasco sauce
- Juice of 1/2 lemon
- 2 teaspoons white wine
- 1 egg, slightly beaten
- 1 teaspoon dry mustard

Break the crabmeat into large pieces and pick over carefully to be sure that there are no pieces of shell or tendon. Chop the shallots or onion fine and sauté them in about 1 tablespoon butter until transparent. Combine the A-1 Sauce, Worcestershire, 1/2 cup bread crumbs, salt, Tabasco, lemon juice, wine, egg, and mustard; mix well. Add the crabmeat. Melt the remaining 3 tablespoons butter in a skillet, add the crabmeat mixture, and cook until the bread crumbs are slightly browned. Spoon into scallop shells or shallow baking dishes and top with remaining bread crumbs which have been tossed in a little melted butter. Bake in a moderate oven, 350° F., for about 30 minutes. SERVES 4.

Crab Isabella

- 2 cups cooked crabmeat
- 4 tablespoons butter *or* margarine
- 1 tablespoon flour
- 3/4 cup milk
- Salt
- Dash of Cayenne pepper
- Dash of mace
- 2 egg yolks, well beaten
- Lemon juice
- 2 tablespoons sherry wine
- 2 avocados
- 6 slices toast

Simmer the crabmeat in butter for about 3 minutes. Remove the crabmeat from the pan. Blend the flour into the butter and add milk, 1/4 teaspoon salt, Cayenne pepper, and mace. Cook and stir until thickened. Add the egg yolks while stirring. Add crab. Stir in 2 tablespoons lemon juice and wine just before serving. To prepare the avocados, cut each one into halves lengthwise, remove seed and skin, and cut into thin lengthwise slices. Sprinkle with salt and lemon juice. Arrange avocado slices on hot toast, reserving some for garnish. Top with the crab mixture and garnish with remaining avocado slices. Serve at once. SERVES 6.

Crab Pilau

- 1 cup shredded coconut
- 1 1/4 cups milk
- 2 cups crabmeat, fresh, frozen or canned
- 1 tablespoon butter
- 2 tablespoons oil
- 1 medium onion, minced
- 1 or 2 tomatoes, peeled and chopped
- 1 1/2 teaspoons salt
- Pinch of curry powder
- 1 cup rice
- 1 cup water
- 2 tablespoons Jamaica rum

Soak the shredded coconut in the milk while preparing the vegetables, then strain, squeezing coconut dry. Discard the coconut, saving the milk. You should have 1 cup coconut milk. Heat the butter and oil together, add the chopped onion and tomato, and cook until soft. Add the crabmeat, salt, and curry powder; simmer 1 minute. Add rice, 1 cup water, and coconut milk. Cover and cook over very low heat for 25 to 30 minutes or until all the liquid is absorbed. During the last 5 minutes, add the rum. SERVES 6.

Crab St. Jacques

- 1 cup ripe olives
- 2 cups fresh or canned crabmeat
- 2 tablespoons butter *or* margarine
- 1/2 cup cracker crumbs
- 1 1/4 cups milk
- 2 eggs, beaten
- 1/4 teaspoon curry powder
- 1/8 teaspoon dry mustard
- Pinch of Cayenne pepper
- Dash of Tabasco sauce
- 1/4 cup sauterne *or* Chablis wine
- 1 tablespoon lemon juice

Slice the ripe olives. Flake the crab, removing any pieces of shell or tendon. Melt the butter, add the cracker crumbs and milk, and cook until thick. Stir a little of the hot mixture into the beaten eggs.

Combine with remaining hot mixture, stirring constantly. Add curry, mustard, cayenne and Tabasco. Cook slowly, stirring constantly, until thickened. Remove from heat and stir in wine, lemon juice, olives, and crab. Turn into individual shells, ramekins, or custard cups and bake in a moderate (350° F.) oven for 15 minutes. SERVES 8 TO 12.

Fish Divan

- 1 pound sole *or* halibut fillets
- ½ lemon
- 2 green onions
- ½ cup white wine
- 1 pound fresh *or* 2 packages frozen broccoli, chopped
- Salt and white pepper
- 2 tablespoons butter *or* margarine
- 2 tablespoons flour
- ½ cup half and half *or* light cream
- ½ teaspoon salt
- ½ cup grated Parmesan cheese
- 1 teaspoon lemon juice
- ¼ cup slivered almonds

Rub the fish with cut side of lemon. Slice the onions into a shallow pan, add wine, and heat to simmering. Lay the fish in the wine. Poach, basting gently, till it is white and flaky, which should take about 5 minutes. Cook the broccoli in boiling salted water, drain, and place in a shallow baking dish. Cover with the fish fillets and sprinkle with salt and pepper. Melt the butter and smooth in the flour. Blend in the cream, ½ cup wine from the fish, and salt. Cook and stir until the sauce boils and thickens. Smooth in the cheese, saving a little for the top. Add lemon juice and pour hot over fish and sprinkle with cheese and almonds. Bake in a moderate oven, 350° F., for about 20 minutes or until bubbly. SERVES 4.

Halibut Florentine

- 1½ pounds halibut fillets *or* 2 packages frozen halibut, semi-thawed
- 1 cup water
- ¼ cup white wine
- 4 tablespoons lemon juice
- 1 cup medium thick white sauce
- 1 package frozen chopped spinach *or* 1¼ cups cooked and drained fresh spinach
- 3 green onions, finely chopped
- ¾ cup grated sharp cheese
- Salt and pepper
- 3 egg yolks *or* 2 whole eggs
- 1 tablespoon soft butter

Place the halibut in a shallow saucepan or casserole. Add 1 cup water, wine, and lemon juice. Cover and boil 5 minutes. Drain the broth from the halibut into another saucepan. Boil the broth, uncovered, until it is reduced in quantity to two thirds the original amount. Add the white sauce, spinach, onions, and 1/4 cup cheese. Season the sauce with salt and pepper to taste. Stir and bring to a boil. Remove from heat and quickly stir in the egg yolks or slightly beaten whole eggs. Sprinkle the fillets with salt and pepper. Pour the sauce over the halibut and sprinkle with the remaining cheese. Dot the top with butter. Bake in a hot oven, 400° F., until golden brown, 8 to 10 minutes. Serve immediately. SERVES 4 TO 6.

Baked potatoes and crusty French garlic bread were served at Tarantino's with this delicious fish.

Escalloped Oysters

- 1 pint oysters
- 1 1/2 cups medium-coarse cracker crumbs
- 1/3 cup melted butter *or* margarine
- 1/2 teaspoon salt
- Dash of pepper
- 1/4 teaspoon Ac'cent
- 1/2 cup heavy cream
- 1/4 cup oyster liquor
- 1/2 teaspoon Worcestershire sauce

Drain the oysters, saving the liquor. Combine the cracker crumbs, butter, salt, pepper and Ac'cent. Spread one third of the buttered crumbs in a greased baking dish, cover with oysters, use another third of the crumbs for the second layer, then oysters. Combine cream, oyster liquor and Worcestershire, pour over oysters and top with the last of the crumbs. Bake in a preheated, moderate (350° F.) oven for 25 minutes. SERVES 4.

Salmon Croquettes

- 1 1-pound can salmon
- Milk
- 1/4 cup butter
- 2 tablespoons minced onion
- 1/3 cup flour
- 1/4 teaspoon salt
- 3/4 teaspoon Tabasco sauce
- 1 tablespoon lemon juice
- About 1 cup corn flake crumbs

Drain the liquid from the salmon into a measuring cup and add milk to make 1 cup of liquid. Melt the butter in a saucepan, add the onions, and cook until they are tender but not brown. Blend in flour, salt, and Tabasco. Add milk mixture and cook over medium heat, stirring constantly, until thickened. Flake the salmon and add it to the sauce with the lemon juice. Stir in ½ cup corn flake crumbs. Refrigerate the mixture until it is chilled and firm enough to handle. Divide into 8 or 10 portions and shape into cones. Roll the cones in the remaining corn flake crumbs; they should be well coated. Place them on a greased baking sheet and bake in a hot oven, 400° F., for 20 to 25 minutes or until golden brown. Serve with Tabasco tartare sauce. SERVES 4.

Tuna or crabmeat may be substituted for the salmon in this recipe.

Butterfly Shrimp

4	to 5 pounds shrimp		Ground black pepper
1	large onion	1½	teaspoons salt
1	to 1½ pints evaporated milk		Flour
4	large cloves garlic, cubed	¾	teaspoon baking powder
	Dash of Tabasco sauce		Fat for deep frying
1	teaspoon sugar		

Clean the shrimp and remove all of the shell except the last segment and the tail. Slit each shrimp lengthwise through the body down to the last segment of shell, leaving two long strips of flesh hanging loose (these curl back when shrimp is placed in the hot deep fat). Make a marinade by scraping the onion into the evaporated milk then adding garlic cubes, Tabasco, sugar, pepper, and salt. Marinate the shrimp for *at least* an hour, preferably a good deal longer. When you are ready to cook the shrimp, drop a few at a time into a paper bag into which you have placed some flour and a few pinches of baking powder. Change the flour and baking powder mixture for a fresh mixture when it becomes damp, otherwise the coating on the shrimp will be heavy instead of light and crisp. Fry the shrimp in deep, hot fat, 375° F. Serve hot with tartare sauce. SERVES 8 TO 10.

Charcoal-Broiled Shrimp

Figure on about 6 to 8 shrimp, if they are good-sized, per serving. Shell the shrimp and cut out the little sand vein. Marinate them for about half an hour in a mixture of melted butter or margarine, coarsely ground black pepper, Ac'cent, and salt. When you get ready to charcoal-broil them, put them in a closed grill where you can turn them all at one time. (This is a grill with two sides that clamp shut with a piece of ringed steel. It's a wonderful addition to your barbecue equipment because it can be used for fish, lobster tails, chops, or chicken.) Keep basting the shrimp while they are over the charcoal fire, using either the marinade that you used for the shrimp originally or highly seasoned, melted margarine. When the shrimp turn pink, after about 5 minutes on each side, slip out one shrimp and try it. It's the only safe way of telling when they are done because the heat of charcoal fire varies.

Serve the shrimp piping hot with baked potatoes, tomato slices with garlic dressing and hot French bread. If you have a warming oven above your charcoal grill, wrap the bread in foil and put it up there to warm. If you'd like to bake your potatoes on the grill, wrap them in foil and allow 1 hour, turning them several times.

Shrimp Bake

¾ to 1 pound fresh mushrooms	¼ cup chopped pimiento
¾ cup butter *or* margarine	2½ cups (No. 2 can) tomatoes, drained
2 cups cleaned cooked shrimp	¾ teaspoon salt
2 cups cooked rice	½ teaspoon chili powder
1 cup chopped green pepper	Parsley
1 cup chopped onion	Stuffed olive slices
½ cup chopped celery	

Cook the mushrooms in ¼ cup butter until just tender. Combine with shrimp, rice, green pepper, onion, celery, pimiento, tomatoes, salt, and chili powder. Place in a greased 2-quart casserole. Melt the remaining ½ cup butter, pour over all, and bake in a slow oven, 300°F., for 50 to 60 minutes. Trim with a wreath of parsley and stuffed olive slices. SERVES 6 TO 8.

Chinese Fried Shrimp and Mushrooms

1 tablespoon olive oil *or* butter	2 teaspoons powdered ginger
1 pound cooked shrimp, shelled and deveined	1 tablespoon minced preserved ginger
1 pound fresh *or* 1½ cups canned button mushrooms, sliced	1 tablespoon cornstarch
1 cup Chinese bamboo shoots, *or* water chestnuts, *or* bean sprouts	½ cup chicken stock *or* bouillon
	½ teaspoon salt
	¼ teaspoon pepper
	1 tablespoon soy sauce

Heat the fat in a large chafing dish over direct heat; add shrimp and sauté until well coated and heated through. Add the mushrooms and mix with shrimp, cooking slowly until mushrooms are tender, about 5 minutes. Stir in bamboo shoots, water chestnuts, or bean sprouts; mix and cook for 2 minutes. Stir in powdered and minced ginger and continue to cook and stir until the bamboo shoots are tender, about 8 minutes. Push the cooked mixture to one side of the pan, pour in combined cornstarch and stock, and cook, stirring, until thickened, 3 or 4 minutes. Mix with shrimp and vegetables, add salt, pepper, and soy sauce. Mix and heat 1 or 2 minutes. Serve on hot, fluffy rice. SERVES 4.

Curried Shrimp, Bombay Style

- 2 pounds shrimp
- 2 teaspoons salt
- ¼ teaspoon pickling spice
- 4 tablespoons butter
- 1 tablespoon minced onion
- 1 tablespoon minced apple
- ⅓ cup flour
- 1 tablespoon curry powder
- 2 cups light cream
- 1 teaspoon lemon juice

Combine the shrimp, 3 cups water, salt, and pickling spice; bring to a boil and cook 5 minutes. Drain, reserving 1 cup stock. Shell and devein the shrimp. Melt the butter in a saucepan and sauté the onion and apple in it for 3 minutes. Stir in the flour and curry powder. Gradually add the cream and reserved stock, stirring steadily until the mixture boils. Reduce heat and cook over low heat for 5 minutes. Add the shrimp and cook 3 minutes longer. Stir in the lemon juice and taste for seasoning. Serve with rice and French fried onions. SERVES 6.

Curried Shrimp

- 3 pounds shrimp
- Slice of lemon
- Slice of onion
- Bay leaf
- Few black peppercorns
- ½ cup celery leaves, packed down
- ½ teaspoon salt
- 4 tablespoons butter *or* margarine
- 1 onion, chopped
- ¼ cup chopped apple
- ¼ cup finely chopped celery
- 2 tablespoons curry powder
- 2 cups light cream
- Salt and pepper

Cook the shrimp in boiling water with slices of lemon and onion, bay leaf, peppercorns, celery leaves, and salt. Simmer about 15 minutes, then drain, saving the liquid they have been cooked in. Run cold water over the shrimp, shell them, and remove the sand vein. Put the butter in a skillet and add the chopped onion, apple and celery. When all are limp, add 1½ cups liquid from the shrimp (with water added if necessary to make 1½ cups). Let simmer gently until the celery and apple are tender and most of the liquid has cooked away. Add the curry powder and stir it into mixture. Add the cream and the shrimp. Cook slowly until the cream is reduced to the desired consistency for a sauce. Season to taste with salt and pepper. SERVES 6.

Curried Shrimp à la Ceylon

- 2 tablespoons butter *or* margarine
- 1 cup chopped onion
- ½ cup chopped green pepper
- ½ cup chopped celery
- 2 tablespoons flour
- 2 teaspoons curry powder
- 3 teaspoons soy sauce
- 2 cups (No. 303 can) solid pack tomatoes
- 1 cup uncooked white rice
- 1 teaspoon salt
- 3 cups water
- 1 pound frozen, thawed shrimp *or* 2 5-ounce cans shrimp

Melt the butter or margarine in a skillet or saucepan. Add the onion, green pepper and celery; cook, stirring occasionally, until the onion is yellow. Blend in the flour. Stir in the curry powder and soy sauce. Stir in 1 cup water and the tomatoes and cover and simmer for 20 minutes. While the sauce cooks, put the rice, salt and 2 cups water in a 2-quart saucepan and cook according to directions, until tender. Peel the frozen, thawed shrimp. Remove the sand vein and wash the shrimp in clear water; drain. Place the shrimp in boiling salted water, cover and return to the boiling point, then lower the heat and simmer for 5 minutes. Drain. When the sauce is done, stir in the cooked shrimp and heat for 5 minutes over low heat. Arrange the cooked rice on a hot platter and pour shrimp and sauce over the rice. SERVES 6.

Singing Shrimps à la Schweizerhof

This shrimp recipe sang its way over from Switzerland. The Schweizerhof is a fabulous hotel noted for its fine food.

The dry hot fluffy rice is an essential part of the recipe. If you have any trouble cooking rice, try Minute Pre-Cooked Rice. You just can't end up with anything but fluffy rice, because all you do is to combine equal amounts of Minute Rice and boiling water, add a little salt, and cover your saucepan. When the rice comes to the boiling point again, set the pan off the heat unit. Don't peek, and in 5 minutes you'll have beautiful rice. We're very proud of this rice because it got its start in the rice fields of Texas. It's a wonderful long-grain rice.

- 6 mushrooms, cut in strips
- 4 tablespoons butter
- 12 jumbo shrimp, cleaned and deveined
- Salt and pepper to taste
- 2 ripe tomatoes, peeled and julienned
- 3 teaspoons catsup
- ¾ cup white wine
- ¾ cup water
- 2 tablespoons olive oil
- Chopped parsley
- 1 tablespoon whiskey

Sauté the mushrooms in the butter until golden brown. Add the shrimp, salt, and pepper; cook over medium heat, stirring to blend with the mushrooms, for 1 to 2 minutes. Add the tomatoes, catsup, wine, and ¾ cup water. Let boil, uncovered, to reduce the liquid, for about 7 minutes. Have a second pan handy with the olive oil smoking hot. Remove it from the heat, add the shrimp mixture, and at the very last moment before serving, add the parsley and whiskey. Serve immediately over dry, hot, fluffy rice. SERVES 3 OR 4.

Shrimp Creole on Rice

- 1½ tablespoons butter *or* margarine
- ½ cup chopped onion
- 1 garlic clove, cut fine, *or* ¼ teaspoon garlic purée
- ½ cup chopped green pepper
- 6 medium ripe tomatoes
- 2 bay leaves
- 2 teaspoons salt
- ⅛ teaspoon pepper
- Dash of Tabasco sauce
- Dash of Cayenne pepper
- 1 pound fresh shrimp, cleaned and deveined
- 3 cups hot cooked rice

Heat butter and add onion, garlic, and green pepper. Cook uncovered over low heat about 10 minutes, stirring occasionally. Peel the tomatoes and cut them into eighths; add with bay leaves, salt, pepper, Tabasco and Cayenne. Cook 10 minutes longer, stirring occasionally. Add the shrimp and cover the saucepan; cook 8 to 10 minutes longer, depending upon the size of the shrimp. Remove the bay leaves and serve hot over fluffy rice. SERVES 4.

Shrimps Delicious

- 8 tablespoons butter
- 8 tablespoons flour
- 4 cups milk
- 2 generous tablespoons curry powder
- 1/4 pound sharp cheese
- Worcestershire sauce
- Salt and pepper
- 4 hard-cooked eggs, cut in chunks
- 1/4 pound blanched almonds, diced
- 3 pounds shrimp, cooked and deveined
- 1/2 cup dry sherry

Make a cream sauce with the butter, flour, and milk. Add the curry powder, stirring constantly until blended, then add the cheese and keep stirring until it is completely blended into the sauce. Add Worcestershire and salt and pepper to taste. Just before serving, add the hard-cooked eggs, almonds, and shrimp. Have the mixture piping hot over very low heat, then add dry sherry and serve over crisp Chinese noodles. SERVES 10.

Shrimp Jambalaya

- 3 tablespoons drippings *or* shortening
- 2 onions, chopped fine
- 2 cloves garlic, chopped fine
- 1/2 pound cured ham, diced
- 2 1/2 cups (No. 2 can) tomatoes
- 2 1/2 cups uncooked rice
- 1 pound fresh or frozen, cleaned, uncooked shrimp
- 2 bay leaves
- Pinch of thyme
- 1 tablespoon chopped fresh parsley
- 1/2 tablespoon chopped celery
- Salt and pepper to taste
- Dash of Cayenne pepper
- 1 teaspoon sugar

Melt the drippings in a heavy skillet or Dutch oven, brown the onions and garlic, then add the diced ham. Sauté the ham with the onions and garlic for 5 minutes, then add the tomatoes and cook for 3 minutes. Wash the rice thoroughly and place it in the pot. Add shrimp, bay leaves, thyme, parsley, celery, and seasonings; let cook slowly for about 45 minutes. SERVES 6.

As a variation, one pint of oysters may be used instead of the shrimp.

South-of-the-Border Shrimp

- 1 pound uncooked shrimp, cleaned and deveined
- 2 tablespoons vegetable oil
- 2 medium onions, sliced
- 1 clove garlic, minced
- 3 stalks celery, chopped
- 1 tablespoon flour
- 1 No. 2 can (2½ cups) tomatoes
- 1 bay leaf
- ¼ teaspoon thyme
- 1 teaspoon chili powder
- 1 4-ounce can pieces and stems mushrooms, drained
- 2 pimientos, chopped
- Salt and pepper
- Hot cooked rice

Heat oil in a large frying pan. Add onions, garlic and about two-thirds of the celery. Cook until onions and celery are tender. Sprinkle in flour and continue cooking, stirring constantly, until mixture is slightly browned. Add tomatoes, bay leaf, thyme, chili powder, mushrooms and pimientos. Season to taste with salt and pepper. Cook 10 minutes. About 10 minutes before serving time, add the shrimp and the remainder of the celery. Serve on rice. SERVES 4.

Sole l'Enfante

- 2 tablespoons butter *or* margarine
- 1 slice onion, finely chopped
- 2 tablespoons flour
- 1 cup milk
- ½ teaspoon salt
- ½ pound mushrooms, cleaned and finely chopped
- Few drops lemon juice
- 1 pound sole fillets *or* other white fish fillets
- ½ cup dry white wine
- 2 tablespoons grated Parmesan cheese

Melt the butter, add the onion, and cook until the onion is soft but not brown. Add the flour and blend it well with the butter. Add milk and continue to cook, stirring constantly, until the mixture thickens. Add salt. Add the mushrooms which have been sprinkled with the lemon juice and continue cooking, stirring occasionally, until mixture is quite thick. Rub through a fine sieve or put through a Foley mill. Season the fish and put it in a shallow, heatproof, buttered baking dish. Pour the wine over the fish, cover, and cook in a hot oven, 400° F., about 20 minutes or until the fish flakes easily when tested with a fork. Remove from the oven, drain the liquid into the mushroom mixture, and add cheese. Pour over the fillets and place under the broiler to brown the top. SERVES 4.

Sole in Wine Sauce

1½ pounds broccoli
1½ pounds fillet of sole
Juice of 1 lemon
1 cup sauterne, Rhine, or any white table wine
1 cup fresh mushrooms
2 tablespoons butter
2 tablespoons flour
½ cup light cream
½ teaspoon salt
1 cup grated sharp Cheddar cheese

Cook the broccoli until just tender. (If you use frozen broccoli, be sure you get the stalks and not the cuts.) Sprinkle the sole with lemon juice and let stand a few minutes. Drain and poach in heated wine (exactly as you poach eggs). Place the fish and broccoli in a shallow baking dish. Slice the mushrooms and sauté them lightly in the butter. Blend in the flour, stir in the cream and ½ cup of the wine in which the fish was poached. Cook and stir until mixture boils and is thickened. Blend in salt and cheese and stir over very low heat until cheese is melted. Pour over fish. Bake in a moderate oven, 350° F., for 20 to 30 minutes and serve at once. SERVES 6.

Sole Supreme

1 pound sole fillets
Salt and pepper
2 green onions, chopped
½ cup sauterne wine
1 tablespoon flour
1 tablespoon melted butter *or* margarine
Cayenne pepper
1 tablespoon chopped parsley
2 teaspoons lemon juice
½ cup ripe olives, cut from pits

Place the fillets in a greased shallow pan; sprinkle with salt, green onions, and wine. Bake in a hot oven, 400° F., for 15 minutes. Blend the flour into the melted butter. Drain the wine from fish, add it to the flour and butter, and cook and stir until thickened. Season with salt, pepper and Cayenne. Add parsley, lemon juice, and ripe olives. Pour the sauce over the hot fish and serve. SERVES 3 GENEROUSLY.

Any sweet fish fillet may be used for this recipe.

Red Snapper Fillets

Have your fishman fillet red snapper and plan on serving one fillet for each serving.

Red snapper fillets
Lemon slices
Lemon juice
Melted butter *or* margarine
Salt, pepper, and Ac'cent

Cut aluminum foil to cover the broiler pan. Place 3 lemon slices under each fish fillet—at the top, middle, and tail. Mix lemon juice with melted butter or margarine; brush the fillets with this mixture. Season with salt, pepper, and Ac'cent; let stand for about 30 minutes before broiling. Broil, close to the broiler heat, until the fillets are a lovely golden brown. Then bake in a moderate (350° F.) oven, basting several times with butter and lemon juice marinade, until the fish flakes easily when you test it with a silver fork. Don't overcook the fish, because it will dry out. Serve with lemon slices and tartare sauce.

Baked potatoes, pineapple and cream cheese salad, and a simple sherbet dessert complete a delicious meal.

Red Snapper à la Creole

- 1 3-pound red snapper
- 2 tablespoons butter, softened
- Juice of ½ lemon
- Salt and pepper
- 4 slices bacon
- 3 onions, chopped
- 1 clove garlic, mashed, *or* ¼ teaspoon garlic purée
- 4 cups cooked tomatoes
- 2 tablespoons chopped parsley
- ⅛ teaspoon savory
- 2 bay leaves
- White wine or water

Wipe the dressed fish. Rub with butter and place in a large, shallow, greased baking dish. Sprinkle with lemon juice, salt, and pepper. Bake in a moderate oven, 350° F., for 15 minutes. While the fish is baking, cook the bacon until crisp. Remove the bacon from the pan and add to the pan all remaining ingredients except wine or water. Cover and simmer, stirring occasionally, until thickened. Pour the sauce over the fish, sprinkle with crumbled bacon, and bake 30 minutes longer, basting frequently with the sauce. It may be necessary to add white wine or water to make the sauce a little more liquid. When the fish is tender, remove bay leaves and serve with lemon wedges. SERVES 6.

Tuna Scallop Royal

2 avocados
Salt
1 can condensed cream of chicken *or* mushroom soup
1 7-ounce can tuna
Potato chips
Lime or lemon wedges

Cut each avocado in half lengthwise, remove seed, and sprinkle with salt. Combine undiluted soup and tuna; heat thoroughly. Place the avocado halves in a baking pan containing ¼ inch of warm water. Fill the halves generously with the tuna mixture and cover the tops with crushed potato chips. Bake 10 to 15 minutes in a 325° F. oven. Garnish with lime or lemon wedges. Serve immediately with Melba toast or hot biscuits. SERVES 4.

Sherry Tuna with Olives

4 cans solid pack tuna, well drained
1 teaspoon coarsely grated lemon rind
2 tablespoons lemon juice
⅔ cup sherry wine *or* dry sauterne
¼ teaspoon pepper
1½ tablespoons butter *or* margarine
1½ tablespoons flour
2 tablespoons chopped parsley
1 cup ripe olives, drained

In a saucepan gently heat together the tuna, lemon rind, lemon juice, wine, and pepper. In a separate saucepan, melt the butter or margarine, stir in the flour, and cook until bubbling hot and lightly browned. Drain hot liquid from tuna into measuring cup and add more sherry if necessary to make 1 cup. Add this liquid to the flour mixture and cook, stirring constantly, until smooth and thickened. Turn the hot tuna into a serving dish or chafing dish, pour on the sauce, sprinkle with chopped parsley, and garnish with olives. If you wish, you may heat the olives in a small amount of salad oil. SERVES 8.

Asparagus with Eggs Parmesan

1 package frozen asparagus pieces
4 eggs
Salt and pepper
½ cup grated Parmesan cheese

Cook asparagus in boiling, salted water until tender. Drain and place in baking dish. Top with unbeaten eggs. In other words, just break the 4 eggs on top of the asparagus. Sprinkle with salt, pepper, and cheese and bake in a slow oven, 325° F., until the eggs are done. SERVES 4.

Toasted English muffins, orange marmalade, and fragrant coffee round out a supper or brunch menu.

Cabbage Mexicana

- 1 large head cabbage
- 1 pound ground sausage
- ½ pound ground beef
- ½ cup uncooked rolled oats
- 1 8-ounce can tomato sauce
- 2 teaspoons salt
- ½ teaspoon pepper
- 1 green pepper, seeded and chopped
- 1 large onion, chopped
- 2 tablespoons shortening
- 1 cup hot water
- 1 tablespoon chili powder

Remove 12 cabbage leaves from head and immerse in boiling, salted water. Cook until pliable and almost translucent, then drain. Combine sausage and beef with rolled oats, tomato sauce, salt, and pepper; mix thoroughly. Cut out the heavy end of the spine of each cabbage leaf so it will roll more easily. Spoon some of the meat mixture onto each leaf, roll, and tie securely or fasten with toothpicks. Sauté the green pepper and onion in hot shortening; add 1 cup hot water and the chili powder. Add the cabbage rolls, cover, and cook over low heat for 1¼ hours or until tender. SERVES 6.

Meat-Filled Cabbage

Meat-Filled Cabbage is a dish that is typical of Greek and Lebanese cooking. This recipe was given to me by a most charming young Greek homemaker, who said, "I think that you'll love this once in a while at your house." And we do, we certainly do!

- 1 pound ground beef
- ¼ cup uncooked rice
- 1 egg
- 1 onion, grated
- 1 carrot, grated
- ¼ teaspoon salt
- 1 dozen cabbage leaves
- ¼ cup lemon juice
- ½ cup brown sugar
- ¾ cup tomato catsup
- ½ cup raisins

Combine the ground meat, rice, and egg; add onion, carrot, and salt. Blanch the cabbage leaves by placing them in boiling water. Cover the pan and remove it from the heat. Let the leaves stand in the water for 20 minutes. Drain. Place a ball of the meat mixture in the center of each leaf and roll up, tucking in the ends securely so the filling doesn't escape. Place the rolls close together in a heavy frying pan. Combine lemon juice, brown sugar, catsup, and raisins. Pour this mixture over cabbage rolls, add enough water to cover. Cover the pan tightly and cook over medium heat for 30 minutes. Reduce heat and simmer for an additional 20 minutes, then bake, uncovered, for about 20 minutes in a moderate (350° F.) oven to brown the tops of the rolls. Water should be added if necessary during the baking period. SERVES 4.

Olive Chow Yuk

This recipe came to me from the California Foods Research test kitchens, and you'll probably say the same thing I said when I first read it: "She's out of her mind." But believe me, it's a very tasty combination of vegetables.

- ⅔ cup ripe olives, cut in large wedges
- 2 medium onions
- 2 cups coarsely sliced celery
- 1 cup green pepper strips
- 2 tablespoons cooking oil
- 1 cup hot water
- ¼ teaspoon sugar
- ¼ teaspoon salt
- 1 chicken bouillon cube
- 1 tablespoon cornstarch
- 1 tablespoon soy sauce
- Steamed fluffy rice

Cut the olives into large wedges. Quarter the onions and pull the layers apart. Cook the onion, celery, and green peppers slowly in the oil for about 10 minutes. Add 1 cup hot water in which the sugar, salt, and bouillon cube have been dissolved; cover and cook 10 minutes longer. Moisten the cornstarch in soy sauce and stir into the liquid in the pan. Blend in the olives and serve on hot steamed rice. SERVES 4.

Barbecued Frankfurters

- 8 frankfurters
- 1 to 2 tablespoons butter
- 2 cups tomato sauce
- 1 tablespoon chopped pickle
- 1 tablespoon chopped onion
- 1 teaspoon minced parsley
- 4 cloves
- 1 teaspoon minced chives *or* green onion tops
- 1 teaspoon mixed fresh herbs (optional)
- ½ teaspoon sugar
- ½ teaspoon Worcestershire sauce

Cut a slit in each frankfurter. Melt the butter in a chafing dish pan over direct heat or in a skillet on the range. Add the frankfurters and cook them, turning them often, till they are slightly browned. Mix all the remaining ingredients together and pour over the franks. Stir and mix for 5 minutes or until the sauce is hot and steaming but not boiling. Serve with baked potatoes, a green salad, and a lush dessert. SERVES 4.

Corny Dogs

This recipe for Corny Dogs is one that doesn't even get cold in my file until someone asks for it again. It's fun for a teen-age party, and I know several homemakers who use it for Saturday night supper.

- 2/3 cup corn meal
- 1 cup flour
- 2 teaspoons sugar (optional)
- 1 1/2 teaspoons baking powder
- 1 teaspoon salt
- 2 tablespoons shortening
- 3/4 cup milk
- 8 frankfurters
- 1 egg, slightly beaten

Mix the dry ingredients and cut in the shortening. Combine milk and beaten egg; mix with dry ingredients. Dip frankfurters in the batter and deep fry at 365° F. until they are browned. If you want them on a stick, insert a wooden skewer in the end before dipping. Be sure you have mustard in the house when you make these—they call for a liberal use of it. SERVES 4.

Frankfurters Italian Style

- 1 pound frankfurters
- 1/4 cup minced onion
- 2 tablespoons bacon drippings or fat
- 3 medium potatoes, pared and diced small
- 1 6-ounce can tomato paste
- 1/2 tomato paste can of water
- 1 teaspoon salt
- 1/8 teaspoon pepper

Cut the frankfurters lengthwise into quarters. Cook onion in hot fat for about 5 minutes then add potatoes, tomato paste, water, salt, and pepper. Cover and cook over low heat for 20 minutes or until potatoes are tender. Add franks and cook until heated through. Serve immediately. SERVES 4.

A green salad and crusty French bread is all you need for this supper menu.

Beef in Burgundy Wine

- 2 tablespoons oil *or* shortening
- ¼ pound salt pork *or* bacon, diced
- 3 pounds round steak, cut into 2-inch cubes
- 18 small onions, peeled
- 6 scraped carrots, cut in 2-inch lengths
- 1½ cloves garlic, minced
- 3 tablespoons flour
- 2 cups Burgundy wine
- 1 bay leaf
- 6 sprigs parsley
- 2 sprigs green celery tops
- 6 whole black peppers
- 2 teaspoons salt
- 1 4-ounce can sliced mushrooms

In a heavy skillet, heat the oil and add the salt pork or bacon. Cook gently, stirring frequently, until the cracklings become golden or the bacon is crisp. Remove from skillet and reserve. In the drippings, brown the meat, then add the onions and carrots and let them brown slightly. Add the garlic, sprinkle the meat mixture with the flour, and stir until the flour disappears. Add wine, bay leaf, parsley, celery tops, whole black peppers and salt. Cover and simmer over low heat until the meat is tender, 1½ to 2 hours. Remove the bay leaf, parsley, and celery tops. Add the salt pork or bacon and mushrooms and reheat. SERVES 6.

Chinese Pepper Steak

- 2 pounds boneless beef chuck
- 2 tablespoons fat
- 1 bunch green onions, cut in inch pieces
- 1½ cups sliced celery
- 2 cloves garlic, minced *or* ½ teaspoon garlic purée
- 1½ teaspoons salt
- ⅛ teaspoon pepper
- 2 beef bouillon cubes
- 2 large green peppers, cut in eighths
- 2 tablespoons cornstarch
- 1 tablespoon soy sauce

Trim the fat from the beef and cut the meat in thin strips, about 1 by 2 inches. Melt the fat in a Dutch oven and brown the meat, then cover and cook until tender. Stir frequently to keep the meat from burning. Add onions, celery, garlic, salt, pepper, and bouillon cubes dissolved in 1 cup hot water. Cook until the vegetables are still crisp but partially cooked. Add the green pepper pieces and cook about 5 minutes over very low heat. Blend the cornstarch with ¼ cup cold water, add to the meat, and cook until the gravy is thickened. Add the soy sauce (use more soy sauce if you like a heavier flavor). Serve on hot fluffy rice or canned Chinese noodles. SERVES 6.

Cube Steaks Parmesan

- 3 eggs
- 1½ teaspoons salt
- ½ teaspoon pepper
- 1½ cups fine dry bread crumbs
- 9 tablespoons Parmesan cheese
- 6 cube steaks
- ½ cup olive oil
- 2 8-ounce cans tomato sauce

Combine eggs, salt, and pepper; beat well. Mix dry bread crumbs with 5 tablespoons of the Parmesan cheese. Dip the steaks into the egg mixture and then into the crumbs. Brown in hot olive oil in a heavy skillet. When the steaks are brown on both sides, add the tomato sauce and top with the remaining 4 tablespoons Parmesan cheese. Bake uncovered in a slow (325° F.) oven for 20 minutes. SERVES 6.

Braised Short Ribs with Sesame Seeds

- 6 pounds short ribs, cut in serving portions
- Flour, salt, and pepper for dredging
- Beaten egg for dipping
- Sesame seeds
- Butter
- 1 cup tomato purée
- 2 tablespoons chili powder
- 4 cloves garlic, crushed
- 2 tablespoons chopped parsley
- 1 teaspoon cumin seed
- ½ teaspoon coriander
- 2 hot chili peppers
- ½ cup beef broth or bouillon
- ½ cup pitted ripe olives, sliced
- ½ cup blanched almonds

Dredge the ribs in seasoned flour, dip them in beaten egg, and roll them in sesame seeds. Brown the ribs in butter in a skillet, then place them in a casserole and add the tomato purée, chili powder, garlic, parsley, cumin seed, coriander, chili peppers, and beef broth. Cover and bake in a slow oven, 300° F., for about 2 hours. Baste the ribs frequently and add a little more broth if necessary. After 2 hours' cooking, add sliced ripe olives and almonds. Cook 15 minutes longer or until the meat is tender. Serve with baked potatoes and tossed green salad or broccoli stalks with browned butter. SERVES 4 TO 6.

Round Steak Royale

- 1 round steak, at least ½ inch thick
- 1 clove garlic
- ¼ cup flour
- 2 tablespoons paprika
- 1 teaspoon salt
- ¼ teaspoon pepper
- ¼ cup butter *or* margarine
- ¼ cup sliced onions
- 1 4-ounce can mushrooms, drained
- ½ cup water *or* bouillon
- ½ cup commercial sour cream

Cut the steak in 4 pieces and rub each piece on both sides with the cut clove of garlic. Combine the flour, paprika, salt and pepper; pound this mixture into the steak. Heat the butter or margarine, and add the steak and brown it on both sides. Top with onions and mushrooms. Add water or bouillon, cover, and cook over low heat until the meat is tender, which should take about 1 hour. Add more liquid as needed. Remove the steak to a warm platter. Spoon off the excess fat and add sour cream to liquid in pan. Dilute to right consistency with water if necessary. Reheat the sauce and serve it over the meat. SERVES 4.

Spicy Swiss Steak

- 2 pounds round steak, 1½ inches thick
- ¼ cup flour
- 2 tablespoons drippings *or* fat
- 2 teaspoons salt
- ¼ teaspoon pepper
- 2 cups (No. 303 can) tomatoes
- 2 medium onions, sliced
- 1 stalk celery, diced
- 1 bay leaf
- 2 teaspoons Worcestershire sauce

Place the steak on a board, sprinkle with the flour, and pound the flour into the steak with a meat pounder or edge of a heavy saucer. Brown slowly in hot fat in a heavy skillet. Sprinkle with salt and pepper and add remaining ingredients. Cover and cook over low heat or in a 325° F. oven for 2 hours or until meat is tender. Add a small amount of water during cooking if necessary. Serve the steak with the tomato gravy spooned over it. For a thicker gravy, mix 2 tablespoons flour and ¼ cup of water and stir into the sauce after the meat has been removed. Cook over low heat, stirring until gravy becomes smooth and thickened. Season to taste with salt and pepper. SERVES 4 TO 6.

If you want to experiment with other spices, the ones that usually go with a dish of this kind are marjoram, thyme, basil, garlic, chili powder, or mustard.

Spanish Pot Roast

- 5 pounds pot roast, chuck or rump
- Flour for dredging
- 3 tablespoons olive oil
- 1 small onion, sliced
- 1 cup plus 1 tablespoon sherry wine
- ½ cup sliced carrots
- ½ cup sliced celery
- Whole small onions
- Whole small potatoes *or* large cubes of potatoes
- 12 stuffed green olives

Dredge the pot roast in flour then brown it in olive oil, adding sliced onion and 1 tablespoon sherry. Cover tightly and simmer for 2 to 3 hours. Add 1 cup sherry and the carrots, celery, whole onions, and potatoes. Cook until the vegetables are tender, then add the green olives. SERVES 6.

Steak Hawaiian

Chop a clove of garlic very fine and put it in a large shallow glass baking dish or platter. Add ½ to 1 cup soya sauce and mix. Marinate your steak in this for 15 minutes, turning it several times to flavor the meat with the seasoning and soak up the sauce. Then barbecue, fry, or broil the steak as you prefer. At Trader Vic's, this steak dish is cooked in a huge Chinese oven.

Steak Smothered with Onions

- 1 pound round steak cut ¾ inch thick
- Flour
- Salt and pepper
- 3 tablespoons fat
- 4 onions, sliced thin

Cut the steak into four pieces, dip each piece in flour, and sprinkle with salt and pepper. In a heavy skillet, melt the fat, add the steak, and cook until the meat is browned. Add ½ cup water, cover, and cook over low heat about 30 minutes. Add onions and season to taste. Cover the skillet and continue cooking for another 30 minutes or until meat is fork tender and onions are done. SERVES 4.

Baked potatoes and a green salad go well with this meat dish.

Apple Puffs with Baked Ham

- 6 ½-inch apple rings, unpeeled
- 1 egg, beaten
- 1 cup sweetened fresh applesauce
- 3 cups mashed sweet potatoes
- 4 tablespoons melted butter
- 1 teaspoon cinnamon
- ½ teaspoon salt
- 6 to 8 tablespoons fine corn flake crumbs

Brown the apple rings in a little butter until almost tender. Mix together all the remaining ingredients. Place the apple rings on a heatproof platter. Force the applesauce-potato mixture through a pastry tube, making mounds on the apple rings. Place in a hot oven, 400° F., for about 15 minutes just before serving. Serve with baked ham. SERVES 6.

Baked Ham Steak

- 1 ham steak, 1½ inches thick
- 1½ cups crushed pineapple
- 2 ounces rum

Slash the fatty edge of the ham steak to prevent it from curling. Place the ham in a casserole and pour the crushed pineapple over it. Cover and bake in a moderate (325° F.) oven for 1 hour and 20 minutes. Uncover and add rum, then bake 15 minutes longer. SERVES 4.

Sweet potato puffs or baked sweet potatoes, a green salad, and French rolls are delicious accompaniments.

Ham with Corn Stuffing

Place a 1-inch thick slice of ready-to-eat baked ham in the bottom of a greased baking dish. Top with corn stuffing and bake, uncovered, for 30 minutes in a moderate (350° F.) oven. SERVES 4 TO 6.

Corn Stuffing

- 3 tablespoons melted butter *or* margarine
- ¼ cup minced onion
- 3 tablespoons chopped celery
- 2 cups stale, coarse bread crumbs
- 1 tablespoon chopped green pepper
- ⅛ teaspoon salt
- Dash of pepper
- ⅛ teaspoon poultry seasoning
- ½ cup cooked or canned whole-kernel corn

In a large skillet, melt the butter, add the onion, and sauté until tender but not brown. Add the celery, bread crumbs, green pepper, salt, pepper, and poultry seasoning. Blend well and add corn. Heat thoroughly, stirring, and place on top of the ham in the casserole.

Island-Style Ham and Sweet Potatoes

- 6 medium sweet potatoes
- 3 tablespoons butter *or* margarine
- ½ teaspoon salt
- ⅛ teaspoon pepper
- Pinch of nutmeg
- Milk
- 2 cups coarsely cut up, cooked ham
- ½ cup green pepper *or* pimiento strips
- 1½ cups pineapple chunks, drained
- 2 tablespoons brown sugar
- 1 tablespoon cornstarch
- ¾ cup drained juice from pineapple
- 2 tablespoons vinegar

Cook and then mash the potatoes. Add 1 tablespoon butter or margarine, salt, pepper, nutmeg, and enough milk to whip. Heat the oven to 400° F. In a skillet, sauté the ham in the remaining 2 tablespoons butter or margarine, stirring until golden. Add the green peppers or pimientos and pineapple chunks; cook 2 to 3 minutes. Stir in the combined brown sugar and cornstarch, then add the pineapple juice and vinegar. Cook, stirring constantly, until the sauce is thickened and clear. Pour the mixture into a 9-inch pie plate, drop spoonfuls of potato on top, and bake 20 to 25 minutes until bubbling hot. SERVES 4.

Braised Pork Shoulder Steaks with Lima Beans

- 1 cup dried lima beans
- 2 teaspoons salt
- 4 pork shoulder steaks
- 3 tablespoons fat
- 1 small onion, chopped
- ⅛ teaspoon pepper
- 1 bay leaf
- 2 tablespoons brown sugar
- 2 tablespoons vinegar
- 1 cup hot water

Rinse the beans, add 2½ cups hot water, and boil for 2 minutes. Remove from heat, cover, and let stand for 1 hour. Add 1 teaspoon salt and simmer for 1 hour or until the beans are tender. Add more water during the cooking time if necessary. (You may also use canned, dry limas with their liquid.) Brown the steaks in hot fat in a skillet, add onion and cook until lightly browned. Remove steaks from skillet. To the drippings, add the beans and their liquid, 1 teaspoon salt, pepper, bay leaf, brown sugar, vinegar, and 1 cup hot water. Arrange the steaks on top of the beans in the skillet. Cover and cook over low heat for 1 to 1¼ hours or until meat is tender or bake, covered, in a moderate (350° F.) oven until tender. SERVES 4.

Glazed Pork Shoulder Steaks

If your butcher doesn't have shoulder steaks of pork he can make a suggestion for a substitute, possibly pork fillets.

6 pork shoulder steaks
¼ cup flour
3 tablespoons fat
1 teaspoon salt
¼ teaspoon pepper
½ cup water
⅓ cup currant jelly
⅛ teaspoon allspice

Roll the steaks in flour and brown them on both sides in hot fat in a large skillet. Sprinkle with salt and pepper, add ½ cup water, and cover skillet. Cook over low heat 1 hour or until meat is tender, adding more water if necessary. Using a fork, mash the jelly and mix in the allspice. Spread half the mixture over the steaks and broil 5 minutes; turn the steaks, brush on the remaining jelly, and broil 3 minutes longer or until the jelly melts. SERVES 6.

Herbed Pork Roast

1 4- to 5-pound pork loin roast
Olive oil
Salt
Dried thyme
Dried orégano
Freshly ground pepper
Fennel *or* anise seeds
Flour
1 medium onion, sliced very thin

Rub the roast lightly with the very best olive oil and sprinkle with a mixture of salt, thyme, orégano, freshly ground pepper, fennel or anise seeds, and flour. Lightly pat the roast so that the herbs will adhere to it. With toothpicks, fasten the onion slices, cut almost paper thin, over the meat. Wrap the prepared roast in Saran Wrap and let it stand in the refrigerator for about 12 hours, so that the flavors of the herbs will be absorbed. Just before putting the roast in the oven make the following basting liquor.

1 cup chicken broth	1 clove garlic
¾ cup dry white wine	⅛ teaspoon ground nutmeg

Cook together in a saucepan for about 5 minutes the chicken broth, dry white wine, garlic, and nutmeg. Keep this sauce warm over very low heat. To cook, remove the meat from the refrigerator, remove wrapping and place meat in a roasting pan, rib side down. Cook in a preheated 375° F. oven for 30 minutes then pour in the basting liquid, turn oven down to 325° F. and let roast cook about 35 minutes to the pound: If you use a meat thermometer it should register 185° F. for the inside of the roast. Baste frequently. When the roast is done, remove it to a hot platter and keep it warm. Leave the onion slices pinned to the roast. They will be black, but they taste wonderful. Prepare the gravy.

Chicken broth	2 tablespoons butter
Dry white wine	½ cup commercial sour cream
2 tablespoons flour	

Skim excess fat from the basting liquid in the roaster and add enough chicken broth and white wine in equal parts to make 2 cups of liquid. Blend the flour and butter together thoroughly to make a roux. Mix the roux with the liquid in the roaster or add a little of the hot liquid to the roux and stir until it is a thin paste. Then add the commercial sour cream and cook, stirring constantly, until the gravy is thickened and smooth. Serve the gravy separately.

Jeanne's Cranberry Pork Chops

Jeanne—Mrs. Ernest Foree—is a favorite cousin of mine. She has a delightful brood of three healthy children who are always hungry and always running through the kitchen for a handout. This recipe is a family favorite at the Foree house.

6 pork chops, cut 1 inch thick	1 cup sugar
Flour	1 cup water
2 cups fresh cranberries	

Dredge the pork chops in flour and brown them in a little fat in a skillet. Add cranberries, sugar, and water; cover the skillet. Bake in a moderate oven, 350° F., for 30 minutes. Uncover and continue baking for another 30 minutes. Cranberries, sugar, and water make a delightful fruity sauce for the chops. Serve with baked sweet potatoes.

Orange-Raisin Pork Chops

- 4 pork chops, 3/4 to 1-inch thick
- 2 medium oranges
- 1/4 cup sugar
- 1 tablespoon cornstarch
- 1/8 teaspoon allspice
- 1 1/4 cups hot water
- 2 tablespoons lemon juice
- 1/4 cup orange juice
- 1/4 cup raisins

Dredge the chops with flour, brown them in hot fat, and sprinkle them with salt. With a sharp knife, peel the oranges and free the orange sections from membrane. Place two sections on each chop.

Make sauce as follows: mix together the sugar, cornstarch, and allspice. Gradually stir in 1 1/4 cups hot water and cook until thick. Add the lemon juice, orange juice, and raisins. Pour the sauce over the chops and cook, covered, over low heat for 1 hour; or cover the skillet and bake in a moderate (350° F.) oven for 1 hour. SERVES 4.

Pork Chops with Rice Burgundy

- 4 pork chops, about 1 inch thick
- Salt and pepper
- 2 tablespoons fat
- 1/2 teaspoon poultry seasoning
- 4 thick slices onion
- 4 rings green pepper
- 1/2 cup uncooked rice
- 2 8-ounce cans tomato sauce
- 3/4 cup California Burgundy wine

Dust the pork chops with salt and pepper. Heat the fat in a large, heavy skillet with a tight-fitting lid and brown the chops slowly on both sides. Sprinkle the chops with poultry seasoning, place a slice of onion on top of each one, and then top each with a green pepper ring. Scatter the rice around the chops. Mix tomato sauce and wine, heat to boiling, and pour over chops and rice. Cover tightly and bake in a moderate oven, 350° F., for 1 1/2 to 2 hours. SERVES 4.

Scrapple

You can make pork scrapple with 3 pounds of bony pieces of pork. Simmer in 3 quarts of water until the meat drops from the bone. Strain off the broth and remove the bone, taking care to get out all the tiny pieces. Chop the meat fine. There should be about 2 quarts of broth; but, if necessary, add water to make this quantity. Bring the broth to the boiling point and slowly add 2 cups corn meal. Cook the mixture until it is a thick mush, stirring almost constantly. Add the chopped meat, salt, and any other seasonings desired, such as onion juice, sage, and thyme. Pour the hot scrapple into a large loaf pan that has been rinsed with cold water. Let stand until cold and firm. Slice and brown in a hot skillet. This can be refrigerated and used as you need it. Scrapple is delicious with maple syrup.

Sweet and Pungent Pork with Almonds

- 1 pound lean pork
- Cornstarch
- ¼ cup oil
- 1 green pepper, cut in 1-inch squares
- 2 slices pineapple, cut into wedges
- ½ cup pineapple juice
- ½ cup chicken stock
- 1 teaspoon soy sauce
- ½ cup blanched almonds
- ¼ cup vinegar
- ¼ cup sugar
- 2 tablespoons cornstarch
- ¼ cup cold water

Cut the pork in 1-inch cubes and roll the cubes in cornstarch to coat them thoroughly. Heat the oil in a skillet, add the pork, and cook until well done and nicely browned. Add the green pepper, pineapple, juice, chicken stock, soy sauce, almonds, vinegar, and sugar. Mix 2 tablespoons cornstarch with water and stir into the sauce. As soon as sauce is thickened and clear, serve with hot, fluffy rice. SERVES 4.

Barbecued Ribs

- 3 pounds ribs, cut in serving pieces
- 1 to 2 tablespoons liquid smoke
- 1 cup catsup
- ¼ cup Worcestershire sauce
- ¼ cup lemon juice
- 1 teaspoon salt
- 1 teaspoon chili powder
- 1 cup water
- 1 teaspoon celery seed

Place ribs in shallow pan, meaty side up, brush with liquid barbecue smoke. Roast in a very hot oven, 450° F., for 30 minutes. Combine remaining ingredients in a saucepan; heat to boiling, and pour over ribs. Continue baking in a moderate (350° F.) oven for 1 hour or until the ribs are tender. (The time will depend on the meatiness of the ribs.) Baste with the sauce every 15 to 20 minutes. SERVES 4.

Barbecued Sweet-Sour Spareribs

Whenever you buy spareribs, it's a good rule of thumb to buy 1 pound of spareribs per serving. Sometimes you'll find that the ribs are very meaty, but it's always best to have a little more than you need. This recipe is a great favorite in the Southwest.

- 3 pounds pork spareribs
- Salt and pepper
- ¼ cup coarsely chopped onion
- ¼ cup coarsely chopped celery
- ¼ cup coarsely chopped green pepper
- 2 tablespoons butter *or* margarine
- 1 tablespoon cornstarch
- 2½ cups (No. 2 can) crushed pineapple
- 4 tablespoons vinegar
- 1 tablespoon soy sauce

Spread the spareribs, meaty side up, in a shallow pan. Salt and pepper them lightly, then roast in a hot oven, 400° F., for 30 minutes. Meanwhile, cook chopped onion, celery, and green pepper in butter for about 5 minutes. Sprinkle with cornstarch, stir, and add the crushed pineapple, syrup and all. Continue to cook, stirring constantly, until it boils. Add vinegar and soy sauce. Drain off excess fat from the roasting pan, then pour the hot pineapple mixture over ribs, put them back into the oven, and reduce the heat to 350° F. Continue cooking, basting occasionally with the sauce in the pan, for about 45 minutes or until meat is well browned and done. SERVES 4.

Fruited Spareribs

- 2 pounds spareribs, cut in 2-rib pieces
- ¼ cup flour
- 1 cup orange juice
- ½ cup crushed pineapple
- ½ teaspoon salt
- ¼ teaspoon allspice
- 1 cup commercial sour cream

Dredge the spareribs with flour and brown them in a little hot fat. Combine orange juice, pineapple, salt, and allspice; pour over browned meat. Cover and cook over low heat or bake in a moderate oven, 350° F., for 45 minutes or until fork tender. Remove the ribs to a warm platter. Add the sour cream to the sauce in the skillet. Stir and cook until heated. Pour the sauce over the meat and serve. SERVES 4.

Cantonese Spareribs

2 sides pork spareribs
2 cups soy sauce
1 cup sugar
2 teaspoons salt
2 tablespoons catsup

Trim the ribs and marinate them for an hour in a mixture of the soy sauce, sugar, salt, and catsup. Roast in a moderate (350° F.) oven for approximately 1 hour and 10 minutes. Baste them at least three times during the roasting. The roasting time will vary with the thickness of the ribs. Serve with barbecue sauce.

This recipe is ideal for an outdoor barbecue.

Honey-Sherry Glazed Spareribs

1 8-ounce can tomato sauce
2 tablespoons wine vinegar
2 tablespoons minced onion
Salt and pepper to taste
½ cup honey
1 clove garlic, minced
1 teaspoon Worcestershire sauce
1 teaspoon celery seed
½ cup dry sherry
4 pounds meaty spareribs

Combine tomato sauce, vinegar, minced onion, salt, pepper, honey, garlic, Worcestershire sauce, celery seed, and sherry; simmer about 20 minutes. Cut the ribs in serving pieces. Cook the meat over charcoal about 30 minutes to cook out fat or cook in a hot oven, 400° F., for 30 minutes. Pour off the drippings and continue cooking the ribs, basting frequently with sauce, for 1 hour in a moderate oven, 350° F., or about 2 hours over charcoal. SERVES 4 TO 5.

Veal Chops Italia

3 green peppers, seeded and thinly sliced
1 medium onion, chopped
3 tablespoons olive oil
6 stuffed olives, chopped
1 tablespoon capers
1 No. 303 can (2 cups) tomatoes
1 teaspoon Ac'cent
½ garlic clove, chopped or put through press
4 loin veal chops
1 tablespoon flour
1 tablespoon butter *or* margarine
Salt and pepper
2 tablespoons white wine

Cook the peppers and onion in 1 tablespoon of the olive oil until the peppers are almost tender. Add olives, capers, tomatoes, and

Ac'cent; let simmer for 20 minutes. Meanwhile, chop the garlic or put it through a press, cook in 1 tablespoon oil until lightly browned, and add it to the tomato mixture. Remove from heat. Dust the chops with flour, brown them in butter or margarine with the remaining 1 tablespoon oil, and cook over low heat for 20 minutes or until chops are done. Sprinkle the chops with salt and pepper and remove them to a platter. Pour the wine into the pan in which the chops were cooked, stir well, heat, and pour over the chops. Top with the tomato mixture. SERVES 4.

Oven-Barbecued Spareribs

Have spareribs cut into serving pieces and figure on 1 pound to a person. Put them in an open roasting pan in a hot (450° F.) oven for 30 minutes. In the meantime, make up the barbecue sauce and cover the ribs with it. Reduce the oven temperature to moderate (350° F.) and bake for 1 hour. (I cover the ribs with foil for the first half hour of the baking time at 350° F., then remove the cover and let the sauce glaze and reduce in quantity.)

Barbecue Sauce

- ¼ cup salad oil
- 1 medium onion, minced
- ¼ cup vinegar
- 1 cup tomato sauce
- 1 cup water
- 1 teaspoon salt
- ⅛ teaspoon Cayenne pepper
- 2 teaspoons Angostura bitters

Heat the oil, add the onion, and cook until yellow. Add all other ingredients and mix well.

This sauce is also very good with barbecued chicken.

Chili Bean Meat Loaf

- 2 pounds ground chuck
- 3 tablespoons instant minced onion
- 2 tablespoons sweet pepper flakes
- 2 teaspoons salt
- 2 teaspoons chili powder
- ¼ teaspoon ground black pepper
- ¼ teaspoon garlic powder
- 2 eggs, slightly beaten
- ½ cup fine dry bread crumbs
- 1 cup canned tomatoes
- 1 1-pound can red kidney beans

Place all ingredients except the kidney beans in a large mixing bowl. Drain the beans, mash them, and add them to the meat mixture. Mix well. Pack into a greased 9 x 5 x 3-inch loaf pan. Bake in a preheated moderate (350° F.) oven for 1 hour or until done. SERVES 8 TO 10.

Chinese Meat Loaf

It's been said that "a meat loaf is a meat loaf is a meat loaf"—but not so. There are many different types of meat loaf and this one not only tastes wonderful, but also freezes like a dream.

- 1 8-ounce can tomato sauce
- ¼ cup brown sugar, packed
- ¼ cup vinegar
- 1 teaspoon prepared mustard
- 1 egg, slightly beaten
- 1 onion, minced
- ¼ cup crushed saltines
- 2 pounds ground beef
- 1½ teaspoons salt
- ¼ teaspoon pepper
- ¼ teaspoon Ac'cent

In a saucepan, mix the tomato sauce with the brown sugar, vinegar, and mustard; stir over medium heat until the sugar dissolves. Combine the egg, onion, saltines, meat, salt, pepper, Ac'cent, and ½ cup of the tomato sauce mixture; mix lightly but thoroughly and shape into a loaf in an uncovered baking pan. Pour the remainder of the tomato sauce mixture over the meat loaf. Bake in a preheated moderate (350° F.) oven for 1 hour, basting frequently with the sauce. Lift out onto a platter and serve the sauce separately or over the loaf. SERVES 6 TO 8.

Tiny frozen potatoes, parboiled and browned in butter in the same oven, are elegant with this meat loaf, or you can use buttered noodles and sprinkle some caraway seed on them.

Mable's Twin Meat Loaves

Mable is my housekeeper and she makes the best meat loaf I have ever eaten. Remember that when you work with ground meat you must treat it like a baby. If you don't handle it gently, you won't get the heavenly airy quality that Mable does. Incidentally, the idea of making twin meat loaves is to eat one and freeze the other.

- 4 pounds ground beef
- 1 pound ground veal
- 1 pound ground pork
- 2 slices bread
- ½ cup milk
- 2 eggs
- 1 large onion, chopped fine
- Salt, pepper, Ac'cent to taste
- 1 can condensed tomato soup

Have the meat ground together or mix it thoroughly by hand. Soak bread slices in the milk and add them and the milk to the meat mixture along with the eggs, onion, salt, pepper, and Ac'cent and about ¼ can of the tomato soup. Mix thoroughly and shape into two long meat loaves. Spread the tops with the remaining tomato soup. Bake the loaves in a shallow baking dish or pan for 30 minutes in a moderate (375° F.) oven. Reduce heat back to 350° F. and bake 30 minutes longer. Use one loaf and freeze the other, wrapping it securely in foil after it is cold. EACH LOAF SERVES 6.

Paprika Chicken with Sour Cream Gravy

1 2½-pound fryer
½ cup flour
1 tablespoon salt
¼ cup fat
½ cup diced onion
2 tablespoons flour
2 teaspoons paprika
½ cup water
1 tablespoon flour
1 cup commercial sour cream
1 teaspoon grated lemon peel

Cut the chicken in serving pieces and dredge in a mixture of ½ cup flour and 1 tablespoon salt. Fry in the hot fat until brown. Combine the onion, 2 tablespoons flour, paprika, and ½ cup water and add to the chicken. Cover and simmer until the chicken is tender, which should take about 30 minutes. Remove chicken, add 1 tablespoon flour and the sour cream to the mixture in skillet and stir until thickened. Add the lemon peel and serve chicken with sauce over fluffy rice. SERVES 4.

Broiled Chicken Sauterne

2 broilers, about 1½ pounds each
1 small onion, sliced
1 cup cold water
1 sprig parsley
1 cup sauterne wine
2 tablespoons lemon juice
Salt and pepper
2 tablespoons salad oil
1 tablespoon flour
1 tablespoon butter

Have the broilers split and the backbones removed. Cut off necks and put them with backbones in a saucepan with the giblets, onion, parsley, and 1 cup cold water. Cover and simmer until the giblets are tender. Add the wine and strain. (This sauce is to be used for basting during the broiling.) Chop the giblets fine and set them aside. Sprinkle the chickens with lemon juice, salt, and pepper; brush with oil. Place them skin side down in a shallow pan and place the pan low under the broiler. Turn the chicken occasionally and baste frequently with the wine sauce. When the chicken is tender and well browned (about 30 minutes) remove it from broiler. Thicken the sauce with flour and butter rubbed together. Add the giblets, season to taste, and pour a little of the sauce over each serving of chicken. SERVES 4.

Chicken Cacciatore

2 fryers, disjointed
Olive oil
2 large onions, chopped
1 pound mushrooms, sliced
3½ cups (No. 2½ can) tomatoes
1 clove garlic
1 tablespoon orégano
1 tablespoon salt
Black pepper to taste
1 cup Rhine wine
1 cup chicken stock
½ cup pitted, sliced, green olives
Noodles

Sauté the chicken in olive oil until brown. Add the onions, mushrooms, tomatoes, garlic, orégano, salt, and black pepper; brown slightly. Add wine and simmer for 20 minutes. Add chicken stock, reduce heat, and add olives. Cover and continue to cook until chicken is fork tender. Serve with noodles. SERVES 6.

Chicken Fancy

This excellent recipe for Chicken Fancy first came into my test kitchen from one of my television viewers, whose name has somehow strayed from the original recipe. I hope she will forgive me, and will understand that it is because I prize the recipe so highly that I am passing it along to the whole world.

1 frying chicken, cut in serving pieces
½ cup butter *or* margarine
1 clove garlic, cut in half
½ teaspoon salt
¼ teaspoon savory
⅛ teaspoon pepper
1½ cups finely crushed potato chips
1½ cups finely crushed corn flakes

Remove the skin from the chicken pieces. In a shallow baking dish, combine the butter, garlic, salt, savory, and pepper. Place in a moderate (350° F.) oven until the butter is melted. Mix potato chips and corn flakes in a pie plate. Dip the chicken pieces, one at a time, into the melted butter mixture and then into the crumbs, coating the pieces well. Arrange the chicken in a single layer in a large shallow baking pan. Remove the garlic from the butter mixture. Sprinkle the remaining potato chips and corn flakes over the chicken. Bake in a moderate oven, 350° F., for 1 hour or until the chicken is crispy brown, and tender when tested with a fork. Serve with hot fluffy rice. SERVES 4.

Chicken Shortcake

1 6-pound stewing chicken
1 package corn-bread mix
1 large can broiled-in-butter mushrooms
2 or 3 cans cream of chicken soup
Salt and pepper
Butter

Cook the chicken and giblets. Save the broth. Remove the chicken from the bones, set the dark meat aside for other uses, and cut the white meat in large dice for this shortcake. Prepare the corn-bread mix according to package directions and bake in a 9-inch square pan.

Skim the fat from 2½ cups of the chicken broth. Dice the mushrooms and giblets; add to the broth. Add the cream of chicken soup and season to taste with salt and pepper. Heat thoroughly over low heat or in the top of a double boiler.

Cut the hot corn bread into squares; split and butter each square. Place the bottom half of each square on a plate, top with some chicken, add the top half of the corn bread square, and finish off with more chicken. Serve with a spiced peach or crabapple. SERVES 6 TO 8.

Chicken and Rice au Gratin

1 5-pound stewing chicken
1 tablespoon instant minced onion *or* 1 small onion, finely chopped
½ teaspoon thyme
Salt and pepper
Sprig of parsley
Celery stalk and leaves
Bay leaf
4 cups chicken broth
1 teaspoon salt
2 cups uncooked long-grain rice
2 tablespoons butter *or* margarine
Mornay sauce (recipe below)
¼ cup grated Swiss *or* Parmesan cheese
Parsley for garnish

Cover the chicken with cold water and add the onion, thyme, salt, and pepper. Tie the parsley, celery, and bay leaf in a cheesecloth bag and place it in the water with the chicken. Cover and simmer until chicken is tender, about 3 hours. Remove the chicken. Skim the fat from broth for Mornay sauce. Discard the cheesecloth bag. If necessary add water to the broth to make 4 cups, bring to a boil, and add 1 teaspoon salt. Add the rice and cook, covered, for 25 minutes or until the rice is fluffy and tender. Remove the chicken from bone in large slices and keep warm. Make a ring of rice around an ovenproof platter and dot with butter. Put the chicken in center, cover with Mornay sauce and sprinkle with cheese. Place in a hot oven, 400° F., for 10 minutes to melt the cheese. Garnish with parsley. SERVES 6 TO 8.

Mornay Sauce

- 1 tablespoon instant minced onion *or* 1 small onion, finely chopped
- 1 cup milk
- 2 tablespoons flour
- 2 tablespoons chicken fat
- 1 cup light cream
- ¼ cup grated Swiss or Parmesan cheese
- 1 egg yolk, beaten
- Salt and pepper to taste

Combine onion with milk and let stand. In a saucepan, blend the flour and chicken fat, add the cream and the onion-milk mixture, and cook over low heat, stirring, until thick and smooth. Blend in the cheese. Add some of the hot mixture to the egg yolk, then combine the two mixtures and season to taste.

Chicken Italiano

- 1 frying chicken, cut as for fricassee
- 2 tablespoons olive oil
- 2 tablespoons butter *or* margarine
- Salt and pepper
- 1 clove garlic, minced
- 1 onion, finely sliced
- ½ cup canned *or* diced fresh peeled tomatoes
- ½ cup water
- Juice of 1 lemon
- 1 tablespoon chopped parsley

Wipe the chicken dry and sauté it until brown in olive oil and butter or margarine. Salt and pepper while browning. When the chicken pieces are well browned, add the garlic and onion and cook slowly until the onion is soft. Then add the tomatoes, ½ cup water, and lemon juice. Cover and cook slowly for 30 minutes longer or until the chicken is fork tender. Serve over fluffy rice on a warm platter; sprinkle with parsley. Any juice left in pan should be served over the chicken. SERVES 4.

Chicken with Orange-Honey Glaze

- 2 fryers, split
- Salt and pepper
- Butter *or* margarine
- 4 onion slices
- 4 orange slices
- ½ cup honey
- ¼ cup melted butter *or* margarine
- 2 tablespoons grated orange rind
- ½ teaspoon beef concentrate

Season the insides of split fryers with salt and pepper; rub inside and out with soft butter or margarine. In each cavity, place a slice of onion and a slice of orange. Fold the halves together and place them in a paper bag which has been greased inside with margarine or shortening. Close the bag and place it on rack in a shallow pan. Bake in a moderate (375° F.) oven for about 1¼ hours. When the chicken is tender, tear off the paper, letting juices run into bottom of pan. Have ready the mixture for the glaze. Prepare glaze by combining honey, melted butter or margarine, grated orange rind and beef concentrate. Pour half of this glaze over the chicken and slip under broiler to brown. Turn, adding remaining glaze, and brown the other side. SERVES 4.

Chicken Stroganoff

- 3 frying chickens, disjointed
- Butter
- Vegetable shortening
- 1 large onion, diced
- ½ cup chicken stock
- 2 fresh tomatoes *or* 2 cups (No. 303 can) solid pack tomatoes
- 1 teaspoon prepared mustard
- Salt and pepper
- 1 cup sliced fresh mushrooms
- 1 cup commercial sour cream

Sauté the chicken pieces in half butter and half vegetable shortening. Add the onion, stock, tomatoes, mustard, salt, and pepper.

Sauté the mushrooms separately and add them to the chicken. Cover and let cook over medium heat for about 40 minutes or until the chicken is tender. Remove the chicken pieces from the pan. Add sour cream to the sauce in the pan, stirring slowly but constantly until well blended. Serve at once over fluffy rice. SERVES 10 TO 12.

Swiss Enchiladas

Believe it or not, this recipe for Swiss Enchiladas came from Mexico City. It's a wonderful way to use up cooked chicken or cooked turkey. The tortillas are no problem, no matter where you live, because you can buy them frozen in stacks of twelve or in vacuum-packed cans. Jack cheese is a mild, bland white cheese and, if you can get it, use it instead of the American cheese.

- 1 dozen tortillas
- 6 chicken bouillon cubes
- 3 cups hot light cream
- 1 chopped onion
- 2 tablespoons oil
- 1 clove garlic, crushed
- 2 cups tomato purée
- 2 green chilies, chopped
- 2 cups chopped, cooked chicken
- Salt and pepper to taste
- ½ pound American *or* Jack cheese
- Slices of avocado, hard cooked eggs, and olives for garnish

Fry tortillas in about 1 inch of hot oil. Do not let them crisp as they are to be rolled. Heat the cream and dissolve the bouillon cubes in it. Dip each tortilla into this cream mixture, cover it generously with the chicken filling, and roll. For the filling, sauté the onion in oil until soft and add the garlic, tomato purée, chilies, chicken, and salt and pepper. Simmer about 10 minutes.

After filling and rolling the tortillas, arrange them in a baking pan and pour the remaining cream mixture over them. Top with grated cheese and bake in a moderate oven, 350° F., about 30 minutes. Garnish with slices of avocado, hard cooked eggs, and ripe and green olives. SERVES 6 TO 8.

Golden Glazed Chicken with Orange-Rice Stuffing

- 1 4- to 5-pound roasting chicken
- ½ cup prepared mustard
- ½ cup orange marmalade

Prepare the chicken for roasting, stuff with orange-rice stuffing, and truss. Place on the rack in a baking pan. Combine mustard and marmalade and brush generously over chicken. Roast, uncovered, in a slow oven, 325° F., 3 to 3½ hours or until tender. Baste the chicken every 45 to 60 minutes with the mustard-marmalade mixture. Add any remaining mustard mixture to pan drippings when making gravy. SERVES 6 TO 8.

Orange-Rice Stuffing

- 2 tablespoons butter *or* margarine
- 1 cup diced celery
- 2 cups cooked rice
- ½ cup coarsely chopped orange sections
- 1 teaspoon seasoning salt
- 1 teaspoon herb seasoning
- ¼ teaspoon coarsely ground black pepper

Melt the butter, add the celery, and cook slowly until tender. Combine with remaining ingredients and toss lightly to mix thoroughly. Stuff chicken loosely.

Sautéed Breast of Chicken Supreme

- 1 pound fresh or frozen chicken breasts
- 2 tablespoons lemon juice
- 1 teaspoon salt
- ¼ teaspoon pepper
- ⅓ cup flour
- 3 tablespoons shortening for frying
- Melted butter

Dip the chicken breasts in lemon juice, season with salt and pepper, and roll in flour. Heat an electric skillet or fry pan to 350° F., add shortening and, when it melts, sauté the chicken until delicately golden on both sides. Reduce heat to 200° F., cover, and continue cooking until the chicken is tender. Sprinkle melted butter over the chicken pieces and serve immediately with hot, fluffy rice. SERVES 2 OR 3.

Spicy Chicken

- 1 2½- to 3-pound chicken
- ½ cup flour
- Salt and pepper
- Drippings
- 3 medium onions, sliced
- 2 cups tomato juice
- ⅓ cup chopped sweet pickles
- 2 teaspoons Worcestershire sauce
- 1 teaspoon sugar
- 1½ teaspoons salt
- ¼ teaspoon dry mustard
- ¼ teaspoon orégano
- 1 small bay leaf

Cut the chicken into serving pieces and roll the pieces in flour seasoned with salt and pepper. Melt the drippings in a large, heavy, covered frying pan and brown chicken on all sides. Remove from heat and drain off fat. While the chicken is browning, combine the remaining ingredients. Pour mixture over the browned chicken in the frying pan, cover, and bring to a boil. Then reduce heat and simmer until the chicken is fork tender, which should take 45 minutes to 1 hour. SERVES 4 TO 6.

Skillet-Barbecued Chicken

- 1 large fryer, cut in serving pieces
- ½ cup flour
- Salt and pepper
- ¼ cup butter *or* margarine
- ¼ cup chili sauce
- 3 tablespoons catsup
- 3 tablespoons horseradish
- ¾ teaspoon Worcestershire sauce
- 1 tablespoon lemon juice
- Few drops Tabasco sauce

Dredge the chicken in flour seasoned with salt and pepper. Heat the butter in a large skillet and brown the chicken pieces in it. Combine the chili sauce, catsup, horseradish, Worcestershire, lemon juice, and Tabasco. Pour this mixture over the well-browned chicken. Cover the skillet and simmer gently, stirring occasionally. As the sauce cooks down, add water as needed (about ½ cup) to prevent chicken from sticking. Cook about 45 minutes or until the chicken is fork tender. Serve with hot rice. SERVES 4.

Mexican Chicken I

In our recipe files at the test kitchen we have six Mexican chicken recipes. I thought it might be confusing if we included all of them, so here are two that might be new to you. This one includes little green olives, which are a standard ingredient for chicken dishes in Mexico; the second includes chocolate to give a molé flavor.

- 2 fryers, cut in fricassee pieces
- Seasoned flour for dredging
- 3 medium onions, finely chopped
- 3 garlic cloves, finely chopped
- 1 cup claret *or* Burgundy wine, heated
- 1 teaspoon sesame seeds
- ½ teaspoon caraway seeds
- ⅛ teaspoon mace
- ⅛ teaspoon marjoram
- 2 cups hot chicken broth
- Salt and pepper to taste
- 1 cup blanched almonds
- 1 cup pitted green olives
- 4 tablespoons chili powder

Dredge the chicken pieces in seasoned flour, brown them lightly in a skillet, and arrange them in an oven casserole. Add the finely chopped onions and garlic, wine, sesame seeds, caraway seeds, mace, marjoram, and boiling broth. Season to taste with salt and pepper, cover the casserole, and bake in a 325° F. oven for 30 minutes. Add almonds, green olives, and chili powder; cover again and bake for 40 minutes longer, basting the chicken occasionally. If you would like to thicken the gravy or sauce, remove the chicken to a heated platter and use a flour-water paste to thicken sauce. Serve with hot fluffy rice, buttered noodles, or baked potatoes. SERVES 6.

Mexican Chicken II

- 1 large chicken, disjointed
- ½ cup salad oil
- 1 green pepper, chopped
- 1 onion, chopped
- 1 clove garlic, minced *or* ¼ teaspoon garlic purée
- 2 8-ounce cans tomato sauce
- 1 to 2 teaspoons chili powder
- 1 teaspoon salt
- ¼ teaspoon Tabasco sauce
- 2 whole cloves
- ½ ounce (½ square) unsweetened chocolate

Coat the chicken with the oil. Brown the pieces and arrange them in a baking dish. Pour off all but 3 tablespoons oil and browned bits; add green pepper, onion, and garlic and cook until soft. Combine with remaining ingredients and heat until chocolate is melted. Pour over chicken. Cover and bake in a moderate (350° F.) oven for 45 minutes or until the chicken is done. SERVES 6.

Serve Spanish rice, a garlicky green salad, and French bread or Italian bread sticks with this chicken dish.

Mexican Chicken in Orange Juice

- 1 large fryer, disjointed, *or* comparable chicken pieces
- Salt and pepper
- 3 tablespoons butter *or* margarine
- ½ cup sliced almonds
- ½ cup seeded raisins
- 1 cup crushed pineapple
- ⅛ teaspoon ground cinnamon
- ⅛ teaspoon ground cloves
- 2 cups orange juice
- 1 tablespoon flour
- 2 tablespoons cold water
- Avocado slices

Sprinkle the chicken pieces with salt and pepper. Melt the butter in a large, heavy skillet; add the chicken and sauté until the pieces are brown on all sides. Add almonds, raisins, pineapple, cinnamon, cloves, and orange juice. Cover the skillet tightly and simmer for 45 minutes or until the chicken is fork tender. Mix the flour with 2 tablespoons cold water to make a smooth paste and stir into the pan juices after removing chicken to a warmed platter. Pour a little of the sauce over the chicken and serve the rest in a gravy boat. Garnish the chicken platter with slices of avocado and serve with fluffy rice. SERVES 4.

Orange Fried Chicken

- 1 large fryer, cut in pieces
- 4 teaspoons grated orange rind
- ⅔ cup orange juice
- ½ teaspoon salt
- ½ teaspoon dry mustard
- ⅛ teaspoon pepper
- ¼ teaspoon Tabasco sauce
- ¾ cup flour
- 2 teaspoons paprika
- 1½ teaspoons salt
- ⅛ teaspoon pepper

Place chicken pieces, one layer deep, in a shallow dish. Combine 2 teaspoons grated orange rind with the orange juice, salt, mustard, pepper, and Tabasco. Pour this marinade over chicken and let stand from 1 to 3 hours. Drain, reserving the marinade for the gravy. Combine the remaining 2 teaspoons orange rind, flour, paprika, salt, and pepper in a paper bag. Place the chicken pieces, a few at a time, in the bag and shake them until they are well coated with the flour mixture. Save any extra flour after coating for the gravy. Brown the chicken in ½ inch of hot fat in a skillet, turning the pieces occasionally so that they brown evenly. When the chicken is lightly browned, 15 to 20 minutes, add 1 tablespoon water and cover skillet tightly. Cook slowly until the thickest pieces are fork tender, which should take about 30 minutes longer. Turn several times for even browning. When the chicken is tender, uncover and continue cooking slowly for about 5 minutes to restore crispness to the coating. Remove the chicken to a warm platter and prepare the gravy.

Pour off all but 2 tablespoons of drippings from skillet. Add 2 tablespoons of the reserved flour mixture and a little salt and pepper; heat until the mixture bubbles. Add water to marinade mixture to make 1½ cups, then add all at once to flour mixture and cook, stirring constantly until thickened. Taste for seasonings and adjust if necessary. SERVES 4.

Ranch Style Chicken Pie with Peaches

- ½ cup sifted flour
- 2 teaspoons salt
- 1 teaspoon paprika
- ¼ teaspoon pepper
- ½ teaspoon onion powder
- 1 frying chicken, cut in serving pieces
- ¼ cup shortening
- 3½ cups (No. 2½ can) cling peach halves
- Cinnamon
- Cloves
- 1 cup evaporated milk
- 1 package ready-to-bake biscuits
- Sharp cheese spread

Sift flour with salt, paprika, pepper, and onion powder. Dip the chicken pieces in the flour mixture, then brown them slowly in shortening in a heavy skillet. Cover and cook over low heat about 30 minutes. Meanwhile, drain the peaches, place them in a shallow baking dish, and sprinkle them with cinnamon and cloves. Remove chicken pieces to a 2-quart baking dish and keep warm. Stir into drippings in skillet 2 tablespoons flour left from dipping the chicken, stir in 1 cup water, and cook and stir until mixture boils and is thick. Stir in evaporated milk; heat, but do not boil. Pour this over the chicken and top with biscuits. Spoon a little cheese spread over the tops of the biscuits. Bake in a hot oven, 425° F., along with the peaches, for about 15 minutes or until the biscuits are browned. Serve at once. SERVES 6.

Pickled Chicken Breasts

This is an excellent appetizer for a dinner or a wonderful luncheon main dish.

- 4 onions, sliced thin
- 6 chicken breasts *or* 6 Rock Cornish hens, whole or halved
- 2 cloves garlic, minced
- 2 pimientos, sliced thin
- 3 tablespoons chopped parsley
- 1 stalk celery, chopped
- 4 bay leaves
- ½ cup tarragon vinegar
- ½ cup white wine
- 1 cup olive oil
- ½ teaspoon black pepper
- ⅛ teaspoon dried ground chili peppers
- 2 teaspoons salt

Place half the onions in an earthenware casserole or enamel saucepan. Arrange the chicken breasts or hens on top and cover with the remaining onions and the garlic, pimientos, parsley, celery, and bay leaves. In a bowl, combine vinegar, wine, olive oil, pepper, chili peppers, and salt. Pour over contents of casserole. Cover and cook over low heat for 45 minutes or until the poultry is tender. Remove the poultry and continue boiling the sauce, uncovered, until it is reduced to about half the original quantity. Pour the sauce over the poultry and place in refrigerator until cold. Serve cold, together with the sauce. SERVES 6.

Polynesian Fried Chicken

- 3 fryers, quartered
- 3 eggs
- ½ cup milk
- 2 tablespoons salt
- 1 cup orange juice
- 2 cups shredded coconut
- 1½ cups butter
- 3 oranges, peeled and sectioned

Dip the chicken pieces into the combined eggs, milk and salt. Dip into the orange juice, then into the coconut, coating the pieces thoroughly. Melt the butter in a shallow baking pan in a hot (400° F.) oven. Remove pan from the oven and place the chicken pieces in it, turning them so that they are coated with butter. Arrange the pieces skin side down in a single layer and bake for 30 minutes; turn and bake 30 minutes longer or until tender. Serve hot, garnished with orange sections. SERVES 10 TO 12.

Spanish Chicken Livers

- 1 pound chicken livers, cut in half
- ¼ cup flour for dredging
- 4 tablespoons butter *or* margarine
- 2 tablespoons minced green onions
- ½ cup white wine
- ½ cup chicken stock
- ¼ cup slivered green olives
- Salt and pepper to taste
- Fluffy cooked rice

Roll the chicken livers in flour and sauté them in melted butter or margarine, then add the green onions. Stir and cook gently for 3 or 4 minutes or until the blood stops running, then add wine, chicken stock, olives, and salt and pepper to taste. Cook a few minutes more, until the livers are done. Serve over fluffy rice. Asparagus spears go well with the chicken livers. SERVES 3 OR 4.

Turkey à la King

- ½ pound fresh mushrooms, sliced
- 1 green pepper, coarsely chopped
- ½ cup butter
- 2 cups diced cooked turkey
- 2 sliced pimientos
- ½ cup sherry wine
- 1 pint light cream
- 2 egg yolks, beaten
- 1 tablespoon butter
- Nutmeg
- Salt and white pepper
- 1 cup toasted almonds, slivered
- Patty shells

Sauté the mushrooms and chopped green pepper in butter for 5 minutes or until they are soft. Stir in the turkey and the pimientos. Add sherry wine and cook until the wine has been absorbed. Add light cream and simmer for 5 minutes. Thicken the sauce with egg yolks and add 1 tablespoon butter. Season to taste with nutmeg, salt, and white pepper. Serve in patty shells and sprinkle with toasted almonds. SERVES 4 OR 5.

Rich Turkey à la King

- 2¾ cups biscuit mix
- 1 cup grated American cheese
- 1¼ cups milk
- 6 tablespoons butter *or* margarine
- 6 tablespoons flour
- 1 teaspoon salt
- 2½ cups milk
- ¾ cup ripe olives, cut in large pieces
- 2½ cups diced cooked turkey
- 3 tablespoons diced pimiento

This is turkey à la king in a biscuit ring. To make the ring, combine biscuit mix, grated cheese, and milk. Blend well and turn into a greased, 8-inch ring mold, smoothing the top of the dough with a spoon. Bake in a hot oven, 400° F., about 20 minutes or until well browned.

While the biscuit ring is baking, make the sauce: Melt the butter and blend in the flour and salt to make a smooth paste. Add milk gradually and cook over medium heat, stirring constantly, until the mixture is thickened. Add the olives, turkey, and pimiento; heat thoroughly.

Turn the biscuit ring out onto a serving plate and fill the center with the olive-turkey sauce. Serve at once. SERVES 6 TO 8.

Roast Turkey to Perfection

The art of roasting turkey to perfection is a simple one. There are two important points to remember: Roast at a low oven temperature of 325° F. and keep the bird uncovered. Before stuffing turkey, be sure to remove the giblets from the neck and body cavity. Simmer the giblets in salted water about 1½ hours or until gizzard is tender, then chop them for use in stuffing or gravy.

Rub inside the body cavity with salt, then stuff the bird with your favorite dressing, being careful to make a loose pack. Fold the wings to the back and pull the neck skin over the wing tips. Fasten in place with a long skewer. Brush the bird with melted butter and place on the rack of the roasting pan. Use a shallow, uncovered pan for roasting. Baste with melted butter or drippings from time to time during baking. (I cover turkey with cheesecloth dipped in salad oil and baste from time to time during baking period.)

TIMETABLE FOR ROASTING

6 to 10 pounds	3 to 3½ hours
10 to 16 pounds	3½ to 4½ hours
18 to 25 pounds	4½ to 6 hours

If you use a roasting thermometer, roast at the same temperature until thermometer reaches poultry temperature. You'll find turkey much easier to carve if you allow the bird to stand for 30 minutes after it is taken from the oven. The meat will slice in firm, even slices.

Baked Turkey Croquettes

⅔ cup salad dressing *or* mayonnaise
1½ teaspoons Worcestershire sauce
1 tablespoon grated onion
1 tablespoon chopped parsley
1 tablespoon lemon juice
½ teaspoon salt
Dash of pepper
2 cups cooked rice
3 cups diced cooked turkey
Fine dry bread crumbs

Combine the salad dressing, Worcestershire, onion, and chopped parsley. Add lemon juice, seasonings, rice, and turkey; mix well. Chill the mixture. When it is cold, shape it into croquettes and roll them in the crumbs. Place the croquettes in an ungreased baking dish and bake in a hot oven, 450° F., for 15 to 20 minutes or until brown. Garnish each serving with a sprig of parsley. SERVES 6.

If you have any giblet gravy left from your turkey, heat it and serve with the croquettes.

Gourmet Turkey Casserole

- 1½ cups sliced celery
- 1 medium onion, minced
- 8 tablespoons butter *or* margarine
- 8 tablespoons flour
- Salt and pepper
- 3½ cups milk
- 1 can condensed cream of mushroom soup, undiluted
- 2 cups cubed cooked ham
- 2½ cups cubed cooked turkey
- 2 tablespoons minced pimiento
- ¼ teaspoon dried basil
- 3 tablespoons sherry
- ½ cup grated sharp American cheese
- Parsley sprigs

Sauté the celery and onion in butter until just tender. Stir in flour, salt, pepper, and milk. Cook over medium heat, stirring constantly, till the sauce is thickened. Add the condensed soup, ham, turkey, pimiento, basil, and sherry. Taste and add more seasonings if needed. Turn into a large casserole and top with cheese. Bake, uncovered, in a moderate (350° F.) oven for 1 hour. Garnish with parsley. SERVES 8.

Hawaiian Turkey Curry

- 3½ cups (No. 2½ can) pineapple chunks
- 1 cup sliced onion
- ¼ cup chopped green pepper
- ⅓ cup butter *or* margarine
- ⅓ cup flour
- 2 cups turkey or chicken bouillon
- 2 tablespoons lemon juice
- 1 teaspoon thinly sliced lemon peel
- 2 cups cooked turkey, cut in ½-inch cubes
- 1 teaspoon curry powder
- ½ teaspoon salt

Drain juice from pineapple and reserve. Pan fry onion and green pepper in butter in a 3-quart saucepan until onion is transparent but not brown. Stir in flour, add bouillon, pineapple juice, and lemon juice. Stir constantly until thickened. Add pineapple chunks, lemon peel, turkey, and seasonings. Simmer for 20 minutes. Serve on hot rice or crisp noodles. SERVES 6.

Turkey Almond Curry

- 1/3 cup chopped onion
- 2/3 cup thinly sliced celery
- 5 tablespoons butter *or* margarine
- 5 tablespoons flour
- 1 to 2 teaspoons curry powder (depending on taste)
- 1 cup milk
- 1 cup stock *or* bouillon
- 2 cups diced cooked turkey
- 1/3 cup chopped, blanched almonds

Cook the onion and celery slowly in butter or margarine until the vegetables are light yellow and wilted, but not browned. Blend in the flour and curry powder (the amount of curry powder may be varied to suit your taste). Add the milk and stock and cook until thickened. Blend in the turkey. Cover and cook over very low heat for 5 minutes. Just before serving, stir in the almonds. Serve on hot fluffy rice. SERVES 4.

Swiss Turkey and Squash

- 4 acorn squash
- 1/4 cup butter *or* margarine
- 1/4 cup chopped onion
- 1/2 cup canned sliced mushrooms
- 1/4 cup flour
- 2 teaspoons prepared mustard
- 1/2 teaspoon salt
- 1/4 teaspoon pepper
- 1 cup turkey broth *or* 1 cup chicken bouillon
- 1 cup light cream
- 2 cups cooked diced turkey
- 1 cup grated Swiss cheese

Cut the squash in half crosswise, remove seeds, and sprinkle the halves with salt. Place them cut side down, in a shallow pan. Add water to a depth of 1/4 inch and bake in a moderate oven, 375° F., for 45 minutes or until tender.

Melt the butter, add the onion and mushrooms, and sauté until onions are yellow. Sprinkle the flour over the mixture and blend well. Add mustard, salt, and pepper; blend well. Gradually add turkey broth and cream and continue cooking over medium heat until thick, stirring constantly. Add diced turkey and 1/2 cup cheese; cook until cheese melts. Fill the squash halves with the turkey mixture, top with remaining cheese, and bake in a moderate oven, 350° F., about 25 minutes or until piping hot. SERVES 8.

Turkey Pilaf

- ½ cup butter *or* margarine
- 2 cups cooked turkey, cut into strips
- ¼ cup diced onion
- 2 teaspoons salt
- ⅛ teaspoon pepper
- ½ teaspoon orégano
- 1 cup turkey broth *or* 1 cup chicken bouillon
- ½ cup chopped canned tomatoes, drained
- ½ cup chopped walnuts

Melt the butter or margarine in a skillet; add the turkey and onion and brown. Add salt, pepper, and orégano. Slowly add the turkey broth, tomatoes, and walnuts. Cover and bring to a boil, then reduce heat and simmer for 20 minutes. Serve over fluffy rice. SERVES 6.

Wild Rice and Turkey Casserole

I can just hear you when you read the first ingredient for this wild rice and turkey casserole: "One and a half cups of wild rice? It will shoot my food budget, it's so expensive!" Yes, it is expensive, but this is a company-casserole type of recipe, and I think with a tossed green salad or a fruit salad with poppy seed dressing you could even stretch this recipe to serve twelve people. In a gaily colored baking dish, it's a lovely looking finished dish for a buffet supper.

- 1½ cups uncooked wild rice
- 1 teaspoon salt
- 1 pound bulk pork sausage
- 1 4-ounce can whole mushrooms, undrained
- 2 cans condensed cream of mushroom soup, undiluted
- 1 teaspoon Worcestershire sauce
- 12 slices roast turkey *or* chicken
- 1½ cups day-old bread crumbs
- ¼ cup melted butter *or* margarine

Wash the wild rice in several waters. In a large saucepan, bring 4 cups water to a boil, add salt, then sprinkle the rice on the water very gradually so that the water does not stop boiling. Cover, reduce heat, and cook gently for 30 to 40 minutes or until the rice has absorbed the water and is tender. Drain. Meanwhile, in skillet, cook the sausage over medium heat until browned, stirring to break it up. Drain off the fat as it accumulates. Stir in mushrooms, soup, and Worcestershire sauce. Lightly stir this mixture into the cooked, drained rice. Spoon half the mixture into a greased 12 x 8-inch baking dish. Arrange the turkey or chicken slices on top and spoon rest of rice mixture over them. Mix the crumbs with butter or margarine and sprinkle over the rice in a 1-inch border around the edge of the casserole. Bake in a moderate (375° F.) oven about 30 minutes. SERVES 8.

Rock Cornish Hens

Many people like to stuff these little Rock Cornish hens. If you use stuffing, use a regular bread and poultry seasoned dressing. However, I don't stuff mine; in fact, I don't even stuff a turkey. Instead, I bake the dressing in a casserole along with the turkey.

During the season for the little white seedless grapes, if you'll pick a bunch of them off the stalk and put them inside the little hens, they will impart a delicious and unusual flavor.

Rub breast and tops of the drumsticks with butter. Put in an open roasting pan without adding any liquid and cook in a preheated hot (450° F.) oven for 20 minutes. Then cover the roaster and reduce oven temperature to moderate (350° F.) and bake for another 20 minutes. Uncover the roaster and cook for 20 minutes longer. This gives them a beautiful browned look. Baste with the juices several times. If you like, you can add a half cup of sherry to the basting juices or you may use just the juices alone. This is the timing for the 12- and 14-ounce birds. If yours are larger, increase the cooking time during the covered period.

Orange Duck

- 4 tablespoons butter
- 2 cups diced cooked duck
- Salt and pepper
- 1 cup orange juice
- ¾ cup sugar
- 2 tablespoons cornstarch
- ½ teaspoon butter

Melt the butter in a chafing dish. Add the duck, salt, and pepper; brown slightly. Remove from direct heat and cook over boiling water for about 20 minutes. Serve with orange sauce made by heating the orange juice, then adding the sugar which has been blended with the cornstarch. Cook until thickened, stirring constantly. Add ½ teaspoon butter after removing from the heat. Stir well and serve hot over the hot duck. SERVES 2 OR 3.

Doves with Cream Gravy

6 to 8 doves
Flour, salt, pepper
¼ cup pan drippings
3 tablespoons flour
2 cups milk

If the doves are frozen, thaw them slightly. Dredge the birds in seasoned flour and brown them in hot fat in a skillet. Remove the birds and make the gravy. Drain off all but ¼ cup pan drippings. Add the flour to the pan and blend in well. When smooth, add the milk and cook over medium heat, stirring all the while, until the gravy is thickened. Return the birds to the pan, cover, and bake in a moderate (350° F.) oven for 30 to 45 minutes. SERVES 3 OR 4.

Golden-Brown Fried Rabbit

1 1¾- to 2-pound dressed rabbit
1½ teaspoons salt
⅛ teaspoon pepper
1 egg, slightly beaten
1 cup fine dry bread crumbs
Fat for frying

Wash and wipe the rabbit with damp cloth and cut into 6 pieces for serving. Add salt, pepper, and 2 tablespoons water to the beaten egg. Dip the rabbit pieces into the egg mixture, roll them in crumbs, and brown in ¼ inch of hot fat. Reduce heat, cover, and cook slowly for 30 minutes longer or until tender. Serve on a bed of boiled rice, with brown gravy made as follows:

Drain off all fat remaining in pan except 3 tablespoons. Add to the fat in the pan 3 tablespoons flour, ¾ teaspoon salt, and ⅛ teaspoon pepper. Blend well and cook over medium heat, stirring constantly, until brown. Stir in 1½ cups water or rabbit stock and boil for 2 minutes, stirring constantly. SERVES 3 TO 4.

Quail in Red Wine

In our part of the country, we have lots of quail. When you freeze them after your husband has come in from a hunting trip, use either the water method, which means packing them in a freezer carton and covering them with water to within an inch of the top of the carton; or freeze them in bags in the number that you know that you can use for one meal. You'll find that the water method for both quail and dove keeps them fresh and tender with no freezer burn.

- 6 quail
- Brandy
- Flour
- 6 tablespoons butter
- 2 cups sliced mushrooms
- ¼ cup butter
- 1 cup consommé
- 1 cup dry red wine
- 1 stalk celery
- Salt and pepper
- Juice of 2 oranges, strained

Split the quail in half and rub with a cloth soaked in brandy. Dust with flour. Melt 6 tablespoons butter in a flameproof casserole, add quail, and cook until brown, about 10 minutes. Sauté the mushrooms in ¼ cup butter and add to casserole. Add the consommé, red wine, celery stalk, salt, and pepper. Cover and simmer for 30 minutes or until the quail are tender. Discard the celery stalk and add the strained orange juice. Serve piping hot with wild rice and asparagus. SERVES 6.

Baked Deviled Eggs

Because supper dish recipes are sometimes hard to find, I have included a number of them in this main dish chapter. Usually a salad completes the meal. With these Baked Deviled Eggs, you might also serve hot baking powder biscuits.

Incidentally, I have said that this recipe will serve 5 or 6. It is very difficult, however, to tell how many servings can be expected from a basic recipe, since it depends in part on whether the dish is to be a part of a large meal or the main dish of a relatively light meal. Then too, people's appetites vary so much that the same amount could feed three or six. We don't plan elaborate meals at our house—for instance, when we have oyster stew, it's just that, with warmed crackers, and fruit for dessert; so we use a lot more oyster stew than you would if you plan other dishes. I have tried to hit a happy medium in this collection of recipes in telling approximately how many a recipe will serve, but you will have to use your own judgment in accordance with your family's appetites.

- 6 hard-cooked eggs
- ½ teaspoon dry mustard
- ¼ teaspoon salt
- Dash of Cayenne pepper
- 5 tablespoons butter *or* margarine
- 1 tablespoon vinegar
- ¼ cup flour
- 2 cups milk
- 3 tablespoons grated Cheddar *or* Swiss cheese

Cut the eggs in half lengthwise. Remove the yolks and mash and mix them thoroughly with mustard, salt, Cayenne, 1 tablespoon butter, and vinegar. Fill the egg whites with the yolk mixture and place them in a greased shallow casserole. Melt the remaining 4 tablespoons (1/4 cup) butter, add the flour, and mix thoroughly. When the flour mixture is bubbly, add the milk and continue to cook over low heat until thickened, stirring constantly. Add the grated cheese and mix well. Pour the cheese sauce over the eggs and bake in a moderate (375° F.) oven for 45 minutes. SERVES 5 OR 6.

Deviled Eggs Delmonico

- 2 tablespoons butter *or* margarine
- 2 tablespoons flour
- 2 cups milk
- 2 tablespoons grated onion
- 1/2 cup grated sharp cheese
- 2 cups cooked macaroni
- 5 hard-cooked eggs
- Minced onion
- Mayonnaise
- Mustard
- Tabasco sauce
- Paprika
- Parsley sprigs

Make a thin white sauce of the butter or margarine, flour, and milk. Add the grated onion, sharp cheese, and cooked macaroni; place in a greased 1-quart shallow casserole. Cut the eggs in half lengthwise. Remove the yolks and mash them with minced onion, mayonnaise, a little mustard, and a touch of Tabasco. Replace in the whites and dust with paprika. Press the deviled eggs into the macaroni and cheese mixture, cover the casserole, and bake in a hot (400° F.) oven for 20 minutes. Garnish with parsley sprigs and serve with additional grated cheese (optional). SERVES 4 TO 5.

Eggs Mornay

- 6 hard-cooked eggs, cut in half lengthwise
- Mayonnaise
- 2 to 3 slices ham, finely minced
- Mustard
- Salt and pepper
- 4 tablespoons butter *or* margarine
- 4 tablespoons flour
- 2 1/2 cups milk
- 1/2 cup grated Cheddar *or* Parmesan cheese

Mash the egg yolks and moisten them with a little mayonnaise. Add finely minced ham and season to taste with mustard, salt, and pepper. Fill egg whites with this mixture and arrange, stuffed side up, in a lightly greased, shallow casserole. Melt the butter in a saucepan, stir in the flour, and gradually add milk to make a rich white sauce. Stir until smooth and glossy, then stir in the grated cheese. Heat the sauce until the cheese is well blended, then pour it over the eggs in the casserole and brown in a hot oven, 450° F. More grated cheese may be sprinkled over the top, if you like; or you can dust the top of the casserole with grated cheese and pop it under the broiler to brown. SERVES 4.

Huevos Rancheros

- 2 tablespoons minced onion
- 2 tablespoons bacon drippings
- 1 can green chilies, chopped
- 2½ cups (No. 2 can) solid-pack tomatoes
- ¼ pound sharp Cheddar cheese, cubed
- 6 eggs
- Salt to taste

Fry the onion in the bacon drippings, add chilies and tomatoes, and let simmer until almost dry. Add cheese cubes and when they are almost melted, drop in whole eggs, one at a time. Add salt to taste. Cover the skillet and cook until the eggs are the desired consistency. Allow 2 eggs to a serving. SERVES 3.

Another way to serve these eggs is to make the sauce and use it as a base for hot scrambled eggs. They are served this way at the Del Prado Hotel in Mexico City.

Scrambled Eggs de Luxe

- 1 avocado
- Salt
- 8 eggs
- ½ cup commercial sour cream
- 1 teaspoon prepared mustard
- 1 teaspoon salt
- ¼ teaspoon pepper
- ¼ teaspoon Worcestershire sauce
- 1 tablespoon butter

Cut the avocado into halves and remove the seed and skin. Cut the fruit into cubes and sprinkle with salt. Beat the eggs with the sour cream, mustard, 1 teaspoon salt, pepper, and Worcestershire. Melt the butter in a frying pan, add the egg mixture, and cook over low heat, stirring occasionally. When almost set, add the avocado and fold in carefully. Serve with rounds of plump, highly seasoned sausage. SERVES 6.

Spanish Luncheon Eggs

This is a recipe for an electric skillet.

- 3 tablespoons butter
- 1 onion, finely chopped
- 1 cup tomatoes, finely chopped
- 1 green pepper, finely chopped
- 1/4 cup pimientos, finely chopped
- 4 eggs
- 1 tablespoon chopped parsley
- Salt
- Butter

Heat the pan to 320° F., melt the butter, add the onion, and let it soften about 5 minutes. Add tomatoes, green pepper, and pimientos; cook 5 minutes longer. Reduce heat to 275° F. and open the eggs, one at a time, into the pan. Sprinkle with parsley and salt, dot with butter, cover pan, and let cook until eggs are set, about 3 minutes. Serve with rice. SERVES 3 OR 4.

Swiss Egg Pie

Mrs. Arthur Levi of Corsicana, Texas, was another winner in the recipe contest with this wonderful supper dish.

- 12 slices crisp bacon, crumbled
- 1/4 pound natural Swiss cheese, grated
- Unbaked 9-inch pie shell, well chilled
- 4 eggs
- 2 cups light cream
- 3/4 teaspoon salt
- 1/8 teaspoon pepper

Sprinkle the bacon bits and grated cheese in the bottom of the pie shell. Combine the eggs, cream, salt, and pepper; beat well with a rotary beater and pour over the bacon and cheese. Bake in a hot oven, 425° F., for 15 minutes. Reduce oven heat to 300° F. and continue baking for 40 minutes or until a knife inserted in the center comes out clean. Cut in wedges and serve at once. SERVES 4 TO 5.

This also makes a delightful hot hors d'oeuvre. A 9-inch pie, cut in small wedges, will serve 16.

Apple–Sweet Potato–Sausage Casserole

- 1 pound small link sausages *or* sausage patties
- 1 tablespoon prepared mustard
- 2 cups mashed sweet potatoes
- 2 tablespoons sausage fat
- 1 teaspoon salt
- 1/8 teaspoon pepper
- 2 1/2 cups apples, peeled and sliced
- 2 tablespoons lemon juice
- 1/3 cup brown sugar

Cook the sausages over low heat until lightly browned. Spread each link or patty with mustard. Whip the cooked sweet potatoes with sausage fat, salt and pepper; spread this mixture over the bottom and sides of a buttered 1-quart casserole. Add apples, sprinkled with lemon juice and sugar. Top with sausage links or patties. Bake 30 minutes in a preheated moderate oven, 350°F. SERVES 4.

Baked Ham and Macaroni Casserole

- ½ pound elbow macaroni
- 2 tablespoons butter *or* margarine
- 4 teaspoons minced onion
- 1 tablespoon flour
- ¼ teaspoon dry mustard
- ½ teaspoon salt
- Dash of pepper
- 2 cups milk
- 1½ cups slivered, cooked ham
- 2 cups grated sharp Cheddar cheese
- 4 teaspoons melted butter *or* margarine
- ¾ cup fresh bread crumbs

Cook the macaroni according to the directions on the package. In a double boiler melt the 2 tablespoons butter, add onion, flour, dry mustard, salt, and pepper. Slowly stir in the milk and cook until smooth and thickened, stirring constantly. Add ham and 1½ cups of the cheese; continue to cook and stir until the cheese is melted. Arrange the macaroni in a greased 2-quart casserole, pour on the ham sauce, and toss lightly with a fork until all the macaroni is coated with the cheese sauce. Sprinkle the remaining cheese over the top, then blend the 4 teaspoons melted butter with the bread crumbs and sprinkle the crumbs over cheese. Bake for 20 minutes in a hot (400° F.) oven. SERVES 4 TO 6.

Border Casserole

- 1½ pounds ground beef
- 3 tablespoons salad oil
- ¾ cup chopped onion
- 1 clove garlic, minced
- 1½ tablespoons chili powder
- 2 teaspoons paprika
- ½ teaspoon orégano
- 1½ teaspoons salt
- ½ teaspoon pepper
- 2½ cups tomato purée
- 3 cups cooked kidney beans
- 1 cup crushed corn chips
- ½ cup grated American cheese

Brown the beef in the salad oil, stirring with a fork to break it up. Add the onion and garlic and cook for 5 minutes. Stir in the chili powder, paprika, orégano, salt, pepper, tomato purée, beans, and corn chips. Pour into a greased baking dish and top with the cheese. Bake in a moderate oven, 325° F., for about 50 minutes. SERVES 6.

California Supper Casserole

- 6 slices bacon, chopped
- 1 large onion, chopped
- 1 green pepper, chopped
- 1 can condensed tomato soup
- ½ cup Burgundy *or* claret wine
- 1 4-ounce can mushrooms with liquid
- 2 cups cream-style corn
- ½ pound American cheese, grated
- Salt and pepper
- ½ pound spaghetti, cooked and drained

Fry the bacon, onion, and green pepper together, stirring frequently, until the bacon is done and the onion and pepper are soft. Add the condensed tomato soup, wine, mushrooms and liquid, corn, 1 cup cheese, and salt and pepper. Add cooked spaghetti, mix well, and turn the mixture into a 2-quart greased casserole. Sprinkle with the remainder of the cheese and bake in a moderate (350° F.) oven for 1 hour. Serve from the casserole. SERVES 4.

Chicken-Shrimp-Rice Casserole

- 2 pounds chicken breasts
- 2 tablespoons salt
- 2½ cups chicken broth
- 1 pound shrimp
- 2 3-ounce packages chive cream cheese
- 1 cup light cream
- 2 tablespoons cornstarch
- ¼ teaspoon pepper
- 4 cups cooked rice
- 2 tablespoons minced parsley
- 2 tablespoons minced pimiento
- ⅓ cup halved, blanched almonds
- ⅛ teaspoon paprika

Cook the chicken breasts in 1 quart water and 1 tablespoon salt until tender, about 30 minutes. Drain, reserving 2½ cups chicken broth. Remove skin and bones and cut the meat into thin slices. Cook the shrimp in 1 quart water and 1 tablespoon salt until tender, about 10 minutes. Drain, clean and devein. Cut large shrimp in half lengthwise. Soften the cream cheese, blend in the cream, and beat until smooth. Blend the cornstarch and chicken broth, and add to the cheese and cream mixture. Add the pepper and cook over moderate heat until thick, stirring constantly. Spread half the rice in the bottom of a buttered 12 x 8-inch baking dish. Arrange half the chicken, shrimp, parsley, pimiento, and almonds over the rice and pour half the sauce over this layer. Repeat layers, then sprinkle with paprika. Bake in a moderate (350° F.) oven until bubbly and lightly browned, about 30 minutes. SERVES 8.

Corn and Sausage Casserole

- 1 pound pork sausage
- 2 cups (No. 303 can) cream-style corn
- 2 eggs, slightly beaten
- ¼ teaspoon salt
- 2 tablespoons chopped green pepper
- 1 cup soft bread crumbs
- 2 tablespoons butter, melted

Brown the sausage until crumbly, stirring occasionally to break it up. Meanwhile, combine the corn with the eggs and add the salt and green pepper. Put half the corn mixture in a greased casserole, cover with all the browned sausage, and then add the rest of the corn. Sprinkle with bread crumbs mixed with melted butter. Bake in a moderate (350° F.) oven for 30 to 35 minutes. SERVES 4.

Danish Blue Cheese and Beef Casserole

- 2 tablespoons butter *or* olive oil
- 1 to 2 onions, finely minced
- 3½ cups (No. 2½ can) Italian-style tomatoes
- 1 6-ounce can tomato paste
- ½ cup raisins
- 1 teaspoon salt
- ½ teaspoon orégano
- ¼ teaspoon allspice
- ½ teaspoon paprika
- ¼ teaspoon ground black pepper
- 1 pound ground beef
- ½ cup Blue cheese
- Unbaked 9-inch pie shell
- Fresh tomato wedges for garnish

Melt the butter or oil in a deep skillet, add the onions, and cook until the onions are soft and yellow but not browned. In a large saucepan, combine the tomatoes, tomato paste, raisins, and seasonings. Add the onions to this mixture and cook over low heat. Brown the beef in the same skillet in which onions were cooked, stirring until all is well browned. Add to the tomato and onion mixture. Cook over low heat for two or more hours. This may be prepared a day ahead of time.

Fill the pie shell with the mixture and bake in a hot oven,

425° F., for 20 minutes or until the pie shell is crisp on the edges. Garnish with thin wedges of tomato and serve hot. SERVES 5 TO 6.

If you prefer, you may bake the pie shell ahead of time and fill it with the hot mixture; or you may use toasted English muffins or two slices of buttered toast for individual sandwiches.

Olive-Noodle Casserole

- 1 8-ounce package noodles
- 3 tablespoons butter *or* margarine
- ¼ cup chopped onion
- 1 cup chopped celery
- 2 tablespoons flour
- Salt and pepper
- 1 cup milk
- 2 tablespoons anchovy paste
- 1 cup ripe olives, cut in large pieces
- ½ cup grated American cheese

Cook the noodles in boiling salted water according to package directions; drain. In a saucepan, melt the butter, add the onion and celery, and cook over low heat until the onion is tender and yellow. Stir in the flour and add salt and pepper to taste. Blend in milk and anchovy paste and cook until thickened, stirring constantly. Add the noodles and olives. Turn the mixture into a greased casserole, top with the cheese, and bake in a moderate oven, 350° F., about 20 minutes or until browned on top.

Baked Cheese Fondue

- 1 cup milk
- 1 cup soft bread crumbs
- ½ cup grated Cheddar cheese
- 2 tablespoons butter *or* margarine
- ½ teaspoon salt
- ⅛ teaspoon pepper
- 3 eggs, separated

Scald the milk in a double boiler, add the crumbs, cheese, butter, and seasonings. Stir in unbeaten egg yolks. Beat egg whites until stiff and fold them into the mixture. Pour into a greased baking dish or 1½-quart soufflé dish, set the dish in a pan of hot water, and bake in a moderate (325° F.) oven for 30 to 45 minutes or until firm. SERVES 6.

Marye Dahnke's Cheese Soufflé

Don't shy away from trying soufflés. Just remember that a soufflé is like a lady with her hat on: she doesn't want to be kept waiting. A soufflé waits for no one; it rises up to peak of perfection and then, if you dawdle, it loses its prestige and falls down flat. Time your soufflé so that it will come out of the oven and go right to the table.

Marye Dahnke is probably one of the best-loved women in the food industry. For more years than she will probably admit, and more years than I can remember, she has been the connecting link between food editors and the Kraft Foods Company. This is her own special soufflé recipe that we pass around like tickets to the Cotton Bowl game, it is that popular. Marye is now spending most of her time on her ranch, and I'll bet the cows and horses have learned to say KRAFT CHEESE.

- ½ pound processed Cheddar cheese, sliced or grated
- 4 tablespoons margarine
- 4 tablespoons flour
- 1½ cups milk
- 1 teaspoon salt
- Dash of Cayenne pepper
- 6 egg yolks, beaten
- 6 egg whites, stiffly beaten

Make a sauce with the margarine, flour, milk, and seasonings. When the sauce is thickened and smooth, add the cheese and stir until cheese is melted. Remove from heat, add the beaten egg yolks, and mix well. Cool the mixture slightly, then pour it slowly onto the stiffly beaten egg whites, cutting and folding the mixture together thoroughly. Pour into an ungreased 2-quart casserole. Run the tip of a teaspoon around the mixture 1 inch from the edge of the casserole, making a light track or depression. This forms a "top hat" on the soufflé as it bakes and puffs up. Bake 1¼ hours in a slow oven, 300° F. Serve immediately. SERVES 4 TO 6.

Cheese-Tomato Pie

Mrs. Joseph C. Snow of Abilene, Texas, was one of the winners in a recipe contest we held at the *Dallas Morning News.* This is a supper type of pie, and a very good one. In fact, the judges liked it so well that they ate the whole pie.

- 1 8-inch unbaked pie shell
- Egg white
- 4 medium tomatoes
- Salt and pepper
- 2 small onions, finely chopped
- 2 eggs
- 1 cup milk
- ½ cup grated cheese
- 2 or 3 slices bacon

Brush the inside of the unbaked pie shell with a little egg white and allow to set. Skin the tomatoes, slice them thickly, and arrange the slices in the pie shell. Season well with salt and pepper and sprinkle with the chopped onions. Beat together the eggs and milk, add salt and pepper to taste, and pour over the tomatoes. Top with grated cheese. Bake in a moderate oven, 350° F., for 1 hour or until set. Grill the bacon slices until crisp and arrange them on top of the pie. SERVES 4.

Quiche Lorraine

Quiche Lorraine is a very popular Sunday night supper dish at our house. In fact, I keep frozen unbaked pie shells in the freezer for just this purpose. If you use a frozen pie shell, allow it to stand at room temperature until it softens, which is only a matter of minutes. I use this pie as a main dish for four and serve a mixed green salad with a garlicky French dressing with it. When unexpected guests drop in and I want to do a quick hot snack, I cut it into tiny pie-shaped pieces and serve it with drinks.

- 4 slices bacon, chopped fine
- ¼ onion, chopped fine
- 1 8-inch unbaked pie shell
- 1 cup grated sharp cheese
- 3 eggs
- 1 cup milk
- Salt and pepper to taste

Fry the bacon until very crisp and brown the onion in the bacon drippings. Spread the bacon and onions in the pie shell. Cover with the cheese. Beat the eggs slightly, add the milk and seasonings, and pour over the cheese and bacon. Bake in a moderate oven, 350° F., for approximately 30 minutes or until the crust is golden brown and completely done. SERVES 4 TO 6.

Quick Macaroni and Cheese

- 6 ounces elbow macaroni
- 1 tablespoon salt
- ¼ cup butter *or* margarine
- 5 tablespoons flour
- ¼ teaspoon salt
- ¼ teaspoon paprika
- Dash of pepper
- 2¼ cups milk
- 2 cups shredded processed pimiento American cheese
- Fine buttered bread crumbs
- ½ teaspoon crumbled tarragon leaves
- ⅛ teaspoon orégano

Add the macaroni and 1 tablespoon salt to 4½ cups boiling water; boil rapidly, stirring constantly, for 2 minutes. Cover, remove from heat, and let stand for 10 minutes. Meanwhile, melt the butter or margarine in a saucepan and blend in the flour and seasonings. Add milk gradually and cook until thickened, stirring constantly. Remove from heat and blend in the cheese. Rinse the macaroni with warm water and drain well. Fold the macaroni into the cheese sauce and turn into a greased 1½-quart casserole. Combine the buttered bread crumbs, tarragon leaves, and orégano; sprinkle this mixture over the top of the casserole. Bake in a moderate oven, 350° F., for 25 minutes. SERVES 4.

Swiss Cheese Pie

½ pound Swiss cheese, grated
1 tablespoon flour
Unbaked 9-inch pie shell
3 eggs
1 cup milk *or* cream
Salt and pepper to taste

Dredge the cheese with the flour and distribute evenly in the pie shell. Beat the eggs well, mix with the milk, season lightly, and pour over the cheese. Bake 15 minutes in a hot oven, 400° F., then reduce the heat to 325° F. and bake an additional 30 minutes or until a knife inserted in the center of the pie comes out clean. Serve at once. SERVES 4.

This pie may be made ahead of time and reheated just before serving.

Curried Spaghetti

3 cans condensed chicken soup
2 cans condensed mushroom soup
1 cup milk
¾ cup warm water
4 teaspoons curry powder
2 4-ounce cans whole mushrooms
1 tablespoon minced onion
½ teaspoon thyme
¼ teaspoon basil
¼ teaspoon orégano
2 7-ounce cans tuna
1 pound thin spaghetti, cooked

Combine the soups (undiluted), milk, and ½ cup water; simmer over low heat. Combine ¼ cup warm water, curry powder, mushrooms, onion, thyme, basil, and orégano; add to the soup mixture and simmer for 10 minutes. Add the tuna and pour the sauce over hot cooked spaghetti and toss lightly with forks until the spaghetti is coated with sauce. SERVES 8 TO 10.

Mexitalian Spaghetti

- 1 pound ground beef
- 1½ cups chopped onion
- ¾ cup chopped green pepper
- 3 cloves garlic, chopped
- 3 8-ounce cans tomato sauce
- 1 6-ounce can tomato paste
- ⅓ cup hot water
- 2 teaspoons Worcestershire sauce
- 1½ teaspoons salt
- Dash of pepper
- 1 16-ounce package spaghetti, cooked

Brown the meat and drain off excess fat. Add the onion, green pepper, and garlic; cook 1 minute. Add the tomato sauce, tomato paste, ⅓ cup water, Worcestershire sauce, salt, and pepper. Cover and simmer for 2 hours. Serve the sauce over hot spaghetti. SERVES 8 TO 10.

Spaghetti Gastronome

- 2 teaspoons salt
- 4 ounces vermicelli *or* thin spaghetti
- 1 pound chicken livers
- 3 tablespoons butter *or* margarine
- ½ cup sliced celery
- 1 cup pieces and stems of mushrooms
- 1 cup chicken broth
- 1 cup tomato sauce
- ¼ teaspoon onion salt
- ½ teaspoon paprika
- Dash of pepper
- ½ cup bread crumbs
- 2 tablespoons grated Parmesan cheese
- 1 tablespoon melted butter *or* margarine

Add 2 teaspoons salt to 3 cups boiling water. Break spaghetti into 2-inch lengths and add to the boiling salted water. Boil rapidly, stirring constantly. Cover, remove from heat, and let stand for 10 minutes. Meanwhile, rinse the chicken livers with cold water, drain, and cut into pieces. Melt 3 tablespoons butter in skillet, add the celery and mushrooms and cook, stirring occasionally, for about 5 minutes. Add chicken livers and brown lightly. Stir in the chicken broth, tomato sauce, onion salt, paprika, and pepper; bring to boiling. Reduce heat and simmer for 5 minutes. Rinse spaghetti with warm water and drain well. Fold into liver mixture and turn into a greased 1½-quart casserole. Combine bread crumbs and cheese, mix in melted butter or margarine, and sprinkle the mixture over the casserole. Bake in a moderate oven, 375° F., for 15 minutes. SERVES 6.

Alpine Rice Ring with Turkey

- 2 cups (No. 303 can) canned tomatoes
- 1 cup water
- 1½ teaspoons salt
- Dash of pepper
- 3 cups packaged pre-cooked rice
- ½ cup finely chopped onion
- ½ cup finely chopped green pepper
- 3 tablespoons fat
- 1½ cups grated Swiss cheese
- 3 cups creamed turkey

Heat the tomatoes and 1 cup water to boiling. Add salt and pepper, stir in rice, cover, and remove from heat. Let stand 5 minutes. Sauté the onion and green pepper in the fat until tender. Add the rice mixture and cheese. Mix well and pack into a 1½-quart ring mold. To keep the ring hot, place it in a shallow pan with about an inch of hot water, cover, and place over low heat until ready to use. Just before serving, unmold and fill the center with hot creamed turkey. SERVES 8.

Baked Italian Rice

- 1 medium onion, chopped
- ½ pound Italian sausage, skinned and chopped fine
- ¼ cup butter
- 1 8-ounce can hearts of artichokes, drained and sliced thin
- ½ package frozen peas *or* 1 cup fresh peas
- 3 tablespoons diced mushrooms
- ¾ cup meat stock *or* beef bouillon
- 3 cups cooked rice
- ⅓ cup grated Parmesan cheese

Sauté the onion and sausage in the butter until lightly browned. Add artichoke slices and peas and continue cooking until these are brown. Add mushrooms. Pour in ¼ cup of the meat stock or bouillon and simmer about 10 minutes. Add the rice and turn the mixture into a greased casserole. Add the rest of the stock and sprinkle the top with Parmesan cheese. Bake in a moderate oven, 375° F., until the cheese is bubbly brown, 15 to 20 minutes. SERVES 4.

Fresh Mushrooms and Chicken Livers on Wild Rice

- 1 cup wild rice, washed
- 1 pound mushrooms
- 1 pound chicken livers
- ¼ cup butter
- 4 tablespoons flour
- 2 cups chicken broth
- ½ teaspoon salt
- ¼ teaspoon pepper
- ¼ cup sherry wine

Boil the rice briskly in 4 cups water 30 to 40 minutes; do not stir. Drain off water and steam until the rice is dry and fluffy. Sauté the mushrooms and chicken livers in butter, sprinkle with flour and mix well. Add chicken broth and cook until thickened. Season with salt and pepper, add sherry, and stir. Serve over wild rice. SERVES 4.

Fried Rice with Pork

- ¼ cup olive oil
- 1 cup cooked pork, cut in small shreds
- 2½ cups cold boiled rice
- 1 green pepper, diced
- 6 water chestnuts, diced
- 2 tablespoons soy sauce
- 2 eggs, slightly beaten
- 4 green onions, finely minced

Heat the oil and add the cooked pork and rice. Cook over medium heat, stirring, for 3 to 4 minutes or until hot, then add the green pepper, water chestnuts, and soy sauce; cook for 4 minutes longer. Pour in the eggs, stir constantly over the heat for 2 or 3 minutes, sprinkle with the finely minced green onions and serve. SERVES 4.

Rice with Green Chilies and Sour Cream

Mrs. James M. Rose of Dallas, Texas, was one of the winners in a recent recipe contest in which there were eleven thousand entries. Her Rice with Green Chilies and Sour Cream was one of the most wonderful blends of flavors I have ever tasted.

- ¾ cup rice
- 2 cups commercial sour cream
- Salt
- ½ pound Jack cheese (a mild white cheese)
- 1 6-ounce can peeled green chili peppers
- Butter
- ½ cup grated Jack cheese for topping

Cook rice according to directions on package (quick-cooking rice may be used). Combine cooked rice with sour cream and season to taste with salt. Arrange half the mixture in the bottom of a greased casserole. Cut the ½ pound Jack cheese into domino-sized pieces and wrap them in strips of green chili peppers. Place these on top of the rice in the casserole, add the remaining rice mixture, and dot with butter. Cover with the grated Jack cheese. Bake in a moderate (350° F.) oven for 30 minutes and serve hot. SERVES 4 TO 6.

Rice Mexicana

- 1 pound sausage meat
- 1 medium onion, chopped
- 1 clove garlic, mashed, *or* ¼ teaspoon garlic purée
- ½ cup diced celery
- 1 tablespoon chopped parsley
- ½ cup uncooked rice
- 1½ cups water
- ¼ teaspoon powdered cumin
- 1 tablespoon chili powder
- 1 can tomato soup
- ½ cup currants
- ½ cup chopped salted peanuts

Cook sausage meat over medium heat until it breaks into small pieces. Add onion, garlic, celery, and parsley. Cook, stirring frequently, until vegetables are tender. Add rice, all remaining ingredients except peanuts, and 1½ cups water. Mix well. Cook 5 minutes longer. Pour into a greased 2-quart casserole. Cover and bake in a moderate oven, 350° F., for 35 to 40 minutes. Remove the cover and sprinkle the top with peanuts. Bake 10 minutes longer. SERVES 4 TO 6.

3

That heavenly low-budget beef

WHAT WOULD A LADY DO without the so-called "hamburger" to make the food budget go further? I have always resented ground beef being called "hamburger," although I realize that, as the story goes, it was named after Hamburg, Germany. I think it's time we called it "beefburger" or just ground beef.

One of the primary things to remember when you are handling ground beef is that you should handle it with care. The more you pound down meat balls, the harder they are packed and the less delicate the flavor.

Another most important thing to remember about ground beef is to use it the same day you buy it, or certainly not later than the next day. The reason for this is that when the meat is ground at the market, all the tissues in the meat are broken down to make a tender mix for you. With the tissues exposed to the air, it's best to use it as quickly as possible. Most meat markets grind their beef as often as three times a day, making small amounts at a time. This is to keep the fresh red look and to give you the opportunity of having the best flavor in your meat.

Many of the recipes in this chapter are new; some are old favorites. Some have come to me from young homemakers who early in their new career as buyer and shopper and keeper of the family food budget have found this "heavenly low-budget beef."

Spaghetti Extravaganza

- 6 tablespoons olive oil
- 6 cloves garlic
- 6 onions, chopped
- 2 green peppers, chopped
- 2 pounds lean ground beef
- 4 8-ounce cans tomato sauce
- 3 cans tomato paste
- 2 paste cans water
- 1/4 teaspoon garlic powder
- 1/2 teaspoon onion salt
- 1 teaspoon parsley flakes
- Tabasco sauce
- 1 1/2 teaspoons salt
- 1/4 teaspoon freshly ground pepper
- Cayenne pepper to taste
- Paprika to taste
- Pinch of orégano
- 1 1/2 pounds *or* 2 8-ounce cans mushrooms
- 4 tablespoons butter
- 2 pounds spaghetti
- Grated Parmesan cheese

Pour the oil into a large skillet. Put the garlic cloves through a garlic press; add to the oil with onions and peppers. Fry them until limp, and remove from skillet. Add meat to skillet and brown. Put the vegetables back into the skillet, and add tomato sauce, tomato paste, 2 paste cans of water, and seasonings. Cook over medium heat until the sauce comes to a boil. Simmer for about 45 minutes. Wash and slice the mushrooms and fry them lightly in butter for about 12 minutes, or add the canned mushrooms at the same time you set the mixture to simmering. If fresh mushrooms are used, add them to the sauce and simmer about 45 minutes longer, stirring occasionally. Meanwhile, cook spaghetti as directed on package. When tender, remove from heat, drain, and turn it into a 6-quart casserole. Add sauce, and mix thoroughly. Sprinkle cheese on top and bake the mixture in a hot (400° F.) oven for 15 minutes. SERVES 12.

This sauce may be made ahead of time and frozen. If you have any of the spaghetti and meat sauce left over, you may freeze it and, when you use it the second time, bake it in a moderate (350° F.) oven, adding fresh Parmesan cheese.

Beef Rounds

- 1 1/2 pounds ground beef
- 1 cup grated American cheese
- 4 saltines, finely crumbled
- 3 tablespoons finely cut chives
- 1/2 cup water
- 1 1/2 teaspoons salt
- 1/8 teaspoon pepper
- 6 ounces wide noodles
- 1/4 cup chopped parsley
- 2 tablespoons butter *or* margarine
- 1 tablespoon diced pimiento

Lightly but thoroughly combine beef, cheese, saltines, chives, ½ cup of water, salt, and pepper. Spoon mixture into 6 custard cups and place cups in shallow baking pan. Bake in a moderate (350° F.) oven for 30 minutes or until done. Cook noodles as directed on package, drain, and toss with parsley, butter, pimiento. Season to taste. Spoon the noodles onto a heated platter and arrange meat cups on top. SERVES 4 TO 6.

Lasagne

- 1 clove garlic, chopped
- 2 tablespoons finely chopped onion
- 3 tablespoons olive oil
- 1 pound ground beef
- 1 large can plum tomatoes, finely mashed
- 1 teaspoon dried basil leaves *or* 6 fresh basil leaves, chopped
- Salt and pepper to taste
- ½ teaspoon orégano *or* marjoram
- ½ pound lasagne noodles
- 1 teaspoon salad oil
- 1 pound Ricotta (Italian pot cheese)
- 3 ounces grated Parmesan *or* Romano cheese
- ½ pound Mozzarella cheese (optional)

Combine garlic, onion, and olive oil in a large saucepan and sauté over medium heat about 7 minutes, stirring occasionally. Mix in beef and cook about 10 minutes. Add tomatoes, basil, salt, and pepper. Stir and bring to a boil. Add the orégano or marjoram, cover the pan, lower the heat, and simmer for 1 hour. Stir occasionally to prevent sticking and burning. If the sauce is a little acid to the taste, add 1 teaspoon sugar.

When the sauce is almost done, boil the noodles according to instructions on the package, adding the salad oil to the boiling water. When the noodles are done, drain and rinse under cold water to cool them.

In a baking dish about 10 inches square, pour a little sauce to cover the bottom of the dish thinly. Over this, place a layer of noodles; dot here and there with bits of Ricotta. Sprinkle some grated cheese over this and add another thin layer of sauce. Repeat this process until the dish is filled. Top with sauce and grated cheese and bake in a hot (400° F.) oven for about 15 to 20 minutes or until the top is nicely browned but not too dry. Remove from the oven, cut into serving pieces, and serve with more sauce and grated cheese while still hot. If you use Mozzarella, slice it thin and place a few pieces between the layers and on the top layer over the sauce. SERVES 6.

Beef Pinwheels

- 1 pound ground beef
- 1½ teaspoons salt
- Pepper
- 1 egg
- 2 tablespoons melted fat
- ⅓ cup bread crumbs
- 2 tablespoons tomato juice *or* milk
- 1½ cups seasoned mashed potatoes
- 1½ cups cooked peas, mashed and seasoned

Combine all ingredients except potatoes and peas. Pat mixture out on waxed paper to form a 7 x 9-inch rectangle ½ inch thick. Spread potatoes over half of the meat, and spread peas over the other half. Roll the meat firmly, jelly roll fashion, starting with the end with the peas. Wrap in waxed paper and chill. When ready to cook, cut into slices with a sharp knife and bake, pan fry, or broil. SERVES 4 TO 6.

Meat Balls and Noodles

- 2 tablespoons olive oil
- 1½ cups finely chopped onion
- 1 green pepper, finely chopped
- 1 cup sliced mushrooms
- 1 cup canned tomatoes
- 1 pound ground beef
- Salt and pepper
- Butter for browning
- 2 8-ounce packages noodles
- Grated Parmesan cheese

Heat the oil; add onions, green pepper, and mushrooms and cook together for about 7 minutes. Add the canned tomatoes and let simmer while you prepare the meat. Season the chopped beef with salt and pepper and form into tiny meat balls. Brown the meat balls in butter, rolling them around in the pan so that they will keep their shape and will be browned on all sides. Cook the noodles in boiling salted water until tender; drain. In a lightly greased casserole, arrange a layer of noodles; cover with half of the meat balls. Add another layer of noodles and the rest of the meat balls. Top with a third layer of noodles, pour the sauce over all, and sprinkle with grated Parmesan cheese. Cover the casserole and bake in a moderate (375° F.) oven for 30 minutes. Remove the cover, add a little more grated cheese, and bake the uncovered casserole for 10 minutes. Serve with big slices of tomato and thin rings of Bermuda onions. SERVES 8 TO 10.

Italian Meat Balls

- ¾ pound ground chuck
- ¼ pound ground pork
- ½ cup ready-to-use bread stuffing
- 1 egg
- 1 tablespoon chopped parsley
- 1 clove garlic, finely chopped
- ½ teaspoon salt
- 3 tablespoons butter *or* margarine
- 2 8-ounce cans tomato sauce
- ¼ teaspoon sweet basil
- ½ teaspoon orégano
- 4 tablespoons water
- 4 cups cooked and seasoned noodles
- ¾ cup grated Parmesan cheese

Lightly mix together the chuck, pork, stuffing, egg, parsley, garlic, and salt until well blended. Shape into 1-inch balls and brown them in butter. In a bowl, mix the tomato sauce, basil, orégano, and 4 tablespoons of water. Pour this mixture over the meat balls, cover, and simmer for 25 minutes. Uncover the saucepan and simmer for 10 more minutes. To serve, heap the meat balls and sauce onto the cooked noodles and sprinkle with cheese. SERVES 6 TO 8.

Beef-Stuffed Tomatoes

- 1 tablespoon fat
- 1 pound ground beef
- ¼ cup chopped onion
- 1 clove garlic, minced
- 2 teaspoons salt
- ¼ teaspoon pepper
- 6 medium-size ripe tomatoes
- 1 cup uncooked rice
- ¼ cup chopped green pepper
- ½ teaspoon thyme
- ½ teaspoon steak sauce
- 3 cups water

Melt the fat in a skillet just wide enough and deep enough to hold the six tomatoes when the lid is on. Add the meat, onion, garlic, ½ teaspoon salt, and ⅛ teaspoon pepper; cook until the meat is very brown. While the meat is cooking, core the tomatoes and scoop out most of the pulp. Fill them with the browned meat. Leave any leftover meat in the skillet. Pour the rice over the bottom of the skillet. Chop the tomato pulp into fine pieces and place them over the rice. Sprinkle the green pepper, thyme, steak sauce, 1½ teaspoons salt, and ⅛ teaspoon pepper over the rice. Add 3 cups water, but do not stir. Cover and bring to a vigorous boil; lower the heat and simmer for 20 minutes. Remove the lid and stir the rice on top into any remaining liquid. If the mixture is almost dry, add a small amount of water. Place the stuffed tomatoes in the rice, cover, and simmer for 15 minutes or until rice and tomatoes are tender and most of the water is absorbed. If you find it necessary to add water from time to time to keep the rice from sticking, be sure to stir from the bottom. To serve, spoon the rice mixture onto a platter and top with the tomatoes. Serve immediately. SERVES 3 OR 4.

Hamburger Viennese

- 1½ pounds ground beef
- 1 cup water
- 6 crumbled gingersnaps
- 3 tablespoons brown sugar
- 2 teaspoons catsup
- 2 teaspoons vinegar
- 1 bay leaf
- Several peppercorns
- 4 whole cloves

Season the meat, shape it into 6 patties; lightly brown them on both sides in a little hot fat, but do not cook until done. To make the sauerbraten sauce, mix water, gingersnaps, brown sugar, catsup, vinegar, bay leaf, peppercorns, and whole cloves. Cook until the gingersnaps have completely dissolved, about 5 minutes. Add the sauce to the browned patties and simmer for ½ hour. Serve the sauce as a gravy with the patties. Buttered noodles and a green salad are the perfect accompaniments. SERVES 3.

Tomato Burger Bake

- 8 slices white bread, lightly buttered
- ¼ cup butter *or* margarine
- 1 cup sliced fresh mushrooms
- ⅓ cup finely chopped onion
- ¼ cup finely chopped green pepper
- ¾ pound ground beef
- 1 teaspoon salt
- 1 can tomato soup
- 2 eggs, beaten
- 1 cup milk

Arrange 4 slices of lightly buttered bread in the bottom of a greased, 8-inch square baking dish, and toast lightly in a moderate oven, 350° F., about 15 minutes. While the bread is toasting, melt the butter in a skillet, add mushrooms, and cook about 3 minutes. Add onion and green pepper and cook gently for 5 more minutes. Meanwhile, mix the ground beef with the salt. Remove the vegetables from the skillet and mix with the tomato soup. Add the meat to the skillet and brown, stirring frequently. Mix the browned meat with the soup mixture and spread over toasted bread, and cover with the remaining bread slices. Combine eggs and milk and pour over the bread. Bake in a moderate (350° F.) oven for about 35 minutes. Serve with celery sticks, pickles, and olives. SERVES 4.

Noodles Strogonoff

- 1/4 cup sliced green onions
- 1 clove garlic, minced
- 1/2 pound mushrooms, sliced *or* 2 4-ounce cans pieces and stems
- 1/4 cup butter *or* margarine
- 1 pound ground beef
- 3 tablespoons lemon juice
- 3 tablespoons Burgundy wine
- 1 can condensed consommé
- 1 teaspoon salt
- 1/4 teaspoon pepper
- 1/4 pound medium noodles
- 1 cup commercial sour cream
- Chopped parsley

Sauté the onions, garlic, and mushrooms in hot butter until lightly browned. Add the meat and, stirring the mixture, cook until red color disappears from the meat. Stir in lemon juice, Burgundy, consommé, salt, and pepper; simmer, uncovered, for 15 minutes. Stir in the uncooked noodles and then cook, covered, for 5 minutes or until noodles are tender. Mix in sour cream and heat quickly but do not boil. Sprinkle with chopped parsley and serve at once. A pineapple and cream cheese salad goes well with this main dish. SERVES 6.

Creole Macaroni and Beef

- 6 ounces shell macaroni
- 1/2 pound ground beef
- 1 tablespoon shortening
- 1 onion, chopped
- 1 small clove garlic, crushed
- 2 1/2 cups (No. 2 can) tomatoes
- 1/2 teaspoon Worcestershire sauce
- 1 teaspoon salt
- 1/8 teaspoon pepper
- 2 tablespoons chopped parsley
- Grated Parmesan cheese

Cook macaroni according to directions on package; drain. Brown beef in shortening with onion and garlic; add tomatoes, seasonings, and macaroni. Cover, and simmer for about 20 minutes, stirring occasionally. Season to taste with salt and pepper, and stir in parsley just before serving. Serve with grated Parmesan cheese. SERVES 4.

Chili Burger

1 pound ground beef
1 can chili
1 clove garlic, chopped fine
Salt and pepper
6 to 8 hamburger buns
Prepared mustard
Chopped onion

Brown the ground beef and drain off any excess fat. Add chili and garlic; salt and pepper to taste. Cook only until chili is hot. Spread hamburger buns with mustard and top with meat-chili mixture and chopped onion.

Buffet Casserole

1 pound ground beef
1 cup sliced onions
1 teaspoon salt
¼ teaspoon pepper
2 cups cooked sliced potatoes
1 can whole kernel corn
1 can tomato soup
½ cup milk

Brown the meat in a little fat; then push it to one side of the pan and lightly brown the onions. Add salt and pepper. In a greased 2-quart casserole arrange layers of meat, potatoes, and corn. Pour tomato soup diluted with milk over all, lifting up the layers to moisten all ingredients thoroughly. Bake in a moderate oven, 375° F., for 25 minutes. SERVES 6.

Deviled Hamburgers

1 pound ground beef
4 to 6 bacon slices (optional)
2 tablespoons catsup
1 teaspoon salt
1 teaspoon horseradish
1 tablespoon minced onion
1 teaspoon Worcestershire sauce
1 teaspoon prepared mustard
Grated Parmesan cheese (optional)

Mix all ingredients lightly and shape into 4 to 6 patties. If you like, wrap a bacon slice around each patty and fasten with a toothpick. Grill on outdoor grill or broil in oven. Serve hot in heated or toasted hamburger buns. For wiener style, form meat into finger shapes that fit into frankfurter rolls. To make them extra special, sprinkle with grated Parmesan cheese immediately after cooking. SERVES 6 TO 8.

Texas Burger

1 pound ground beef	2 tablespoons flour
2 tablespoons fat	1 can condensed onion soup

Brown the meat in fat, mix in the flour, add onion soup, and cook over low heat for 30 minutes. Serve in warmed hamburger buns. SERVES 8.

Stuffed Hamburgers

Shape ground beef into large thin patties and put together sandwich fashion with a slice of onion and cheese between, pressing edges together to keep filling from cooking out while broiling. Serve in warm hamburger buns. For variations in the filling, combine crumbled Blue cheese to taste, 1 tablespoon Worcestershire, ½ teaspoon dry mustard, and mayonnaise to moisten; or combine 1 cup grated processed American cheese, 1 tablespoon Worcestershire, and ¼ cup chili sauce.

Beef Skillet Bake with Parsley Muffins

2 tablespoons fat *or* drippings	1 can cream of celery soup
¼ cup chopped onion	¾ cup milk
½ pound ground beef	1 cup cooked diced carrots
½ teaspoon salt	Parsley muffin batter
Dash of pepper	

Melt the fat in a heavy skillet; add the onion and beef and brown well. Season with salt and pepper, and then stir in celery soup and milk. Add carrots and mix well. Drop parsley muffin batter by spoonfuls around the edge of the skillet and bake in a hot oven, 425° F., about 20 minutes. SERVES 4.

Parsley Muffins

1½ cups sifted flour	⅔ cup milk
2 teaspoons baking powder	1 tablespoon melted shortening
½ teaspoon salt	2 tablespoons chopped parsley
1 tablespoon sugar	
1 egg, beaten	

Sift together the flour, baking powder, salt, and sugar. Mix together the egg, milk, shortening, and parsley. Add the liquid to the flour mixture, stirring only until the flour is moistened. Drop by spoonfuls around the edge of the skillet onto beef mixture.

Hamburger Upside-Down Pie

- ½ pound ground beef
- 1 tablespoon fat
- ¾ cup chopped onion
- ¾ cup chopped green pepper
- ¾ cup chopped celery
- ½ can tomato soup
- 1 teaspoon barbecue sauce
- ½ teaspoon salt
- Dash of pepper
- 2 cups biscuit mix
- ⅔ cup milk
- 1 tablespoon chopped parsley
- ½ teaspoon celery seed

Brown the meat in hot fat; add the onion, green pepper, and celery, and cook until the onion is golden. Stir in the tomato soup, barbecue sauce, salt, and pepper. Turn the mixture into an 8-inch skillet or a round pan at least 1½ inches deep. Make biscuit dough with mix and milk. Stir in parsley and celery seed and roll into a circle to fit your pan. Place the dough over the meat mixture and bake in a hot oven, 450° F., for 15 minutes. Turn upside down on a platter when ready to serve. SERVES 6.

Barbecued Beans and Burgers

- 6 cups (3 No. 303 cans) baked beans
- 5 cups (2 No. 2 cans) kidney beans, drained
- 1 package frozen lima beans, slightly thawed
- ¼ cup brown sugar, packed
- 3½ teaspoons dry mustard
- 5 teaspoons salt
- ¾ teaspoon pepper
- 10 small white onions
- 2 pounds ground beef
- 1 small onion, minced
- ¼ cup water
- 1 cup catsup
- 2 tablespoons vinegar
- 1 tablespoon brown sugar
- 1 tablespoon butter *or* margarine

In a 3-quart casserole, mix the beans, ¼ cup brown sugar, 3 teaspoons dry mustard, 2 teaspoons salt, and ¼ teaspoon pepper. Bake in a hot (400° F.) oven for 45 minutes. Boil onions until tender-crisp. Lightly mix meat with 3 teaspoons salt, ½ teaspoon pepper, minced onion, and ¼ cup water. Form into 16 balls and brown in a skillet in hot fat. Remove balls from skillet and clean skillet. Add catsup, vinegar, 1 tablespoon brown sugar, ½ teaspoon dry mustard, and butter, and simmer for about 15 minutes. Arrange the meat balls and boiled onions on top of the beans, spoon on the sauce, and bake 15 minutes more or until bubbly. French bread with garlic butter and a green salad complete this meal. SERVES 8.

Dad's Favorite

- 1 pound ground beef
- 2 tablespoons salad oil
- 1 cup chopped onions
- 1½ teaspoons salt
- ¾ teaspoon chili powder
- 2 cups (No. 303 can) tomatoes
- 1 tablespoon Worcestershire sauce
- ½ teaspoon Ac'cent
- ¼ pound medium noodles
- 1 package thawed frozen succotash
- 1½ cups grated American cheese

Sauté the beef in salad oil until lightly browned; stir in the onions, salt, chili powder, tomatoes, Worcestershire, and Ac'cent. Combine the uncooked noodles and succotash with meat mixture. Turn the mixture into a 2-quart casserole, cover, and bake for 45 minutes in a moderate (350° F.) oven. Uncover, sprinkle with grated cheese, and bake 15 minutes longer or until golden. SERVES 8.

Skillet Dinner

- ½ pound ground beef
- 1 egg, beaten
- ¼ cup milk
- ¼ cup fine dried bread crumbs
- 1½ tablespoons minced onion
- 1 teaspoon salt
- ¼ teaspoon dry mustard
- 2 tablespoons flour
- 2 tablespoons salad oil
- 1 can tomato soup, undiluted
- ¾ cup milk
- 1½ cups cooked vegetables *or* 1 package thawed, frozen mixed vegetables
- ¼ teaspoon Ac'cent

Combine the meat, egg, milk, bread crumbs, onion, ½ teaspoon salt, and dry mustard. Shape into twelve 1-inch balls and sprinkle them with flour. In a skillet, heat the oil and brown the balls well on all sides. Arrange the balls around the sides of the skillet. Combine the soup with the milk; gradually pour the mixture into the center of the skillet. Top with vegetables, ½ teaspoon salt, and Ac'cent. Cover and simmer for 15 minutes. Buttered poppy seed noodles and oven toast are a nice accompaniment to this meal. SERVES 4.

Dutch Oven Dinner

- 1 pound ground meat
- 3 tablespoons fat *or* salad oil
- 1½ teaspoons salt
- ¼ teaspoon pepper
- ¼ teaspoon Ac'cent
- 1 cup diced onions
- 1 green pepper, chopped
- 1 can whole kernel corn
- 1 4-ounce can pieces and stems mushrooms with liquid
- ½ pound medium noodles
- 1 cup grated American cheese
- 3⅓ cups (No. 2½ can) tomatoes
- Grated Parmesan cheese

Cook the beef in fat in a Dutch oven, stirring until the meat is no longer red. Stir in salt, pepper, Ac'cent, onions, green pepper, corn, and mushrooms. Spread the uncooked noodles over the top, sprinkle with grated cheese, and pour tomatoes over all. Cover, and simmer on top of the stove for 1 hour. At serving time, sprinkle the top with grated Parmesan cheese. Green salad with garlic dressing and French brown-and-serve rolls go well with this dinner. SERVES 6.

Italian Casserole

- ½ cup butter *or* margarine
- 6 medium onions, chopped
- 1½ pounds ground beef
- 1½ teaspoons salt
- ¼ teaspoon garlic salt
- ⅛ teaspoon pepper
- 1 pound shell macaroni
- 1 pound sharp cheese, grated
- 2 8-ounce cans tomato sauce
- 2 3-ounce cans chopped mushrooms with liquid
- ¼ cup Burgundy wine (optional)

In a large skillet, using ¼ cup butter, sauté the onion, meat, salt, garlic salt, and pepper. Meanwhile, cook the macaroni as directed on package until it is barely tender; drain and toss with the remaining ¼ cup butter. Place in two 2-quart casseroles. Add two thirds of the cheese to the meat mixture and stir until the cheese melts; add 1 can tomato sauce and mushrooms and pour the mixture over the macaroni. Top with the second can of tomato sauce and sprinkle with remaining cheese. Bake uncovered casseroles for 1 hour and 40 minutes in a moderate (325° F.) oven. When ready to serve, pour on wine if desired. SERVES 8.

Individual Pizza Pies

Use split English muffins for a base. Brown well-seasoned hamburger meat in a skillet. Grate onion and shred American cheese. Tomato catsup will do but chili sauce is better. Toast muffin halves lightly. Place a teaspoon of grated onion and a generous portion of the cooked meat on each half. Over this, sprinkle shredded cheese and add a tablespoon of chili sauce; then top with grated Parmesan cheese. Broil until bubbly and serve immediately.

Tallerine

- 2 onions, minced
- 1½ pounds ground meat
- 1 can tomato soup
- ½ cup catsup
- 1 can ripe olives, pitted
- 1 cup water
- 1 8-ounce package noodles
- 1 teaspoon salt
- 1 can whole kernel corn
- 1 cup grated American cheese

Sauté the onions until they are tender but not brown; add the meat, and brown. Add soup, catsup, juice from olives, and 1 cup of water. To this mixture add the noodles, broken up, and the salt, corn, and olives. Cook about 30 minutes in a moderate (350° F.) oven. Remove from oven, sprinkle with cheese, then return to oven just until the cheese melts. SERVES 8.

Mushroom-Stuffed Meat Loaf

- ¼ cup butter *or* margarine
- 1 pound mushrooms
- 1 teaspoon lemon juice
- 1 medium onion, minced
- 4 cups soft, fresh bread crumbs
- 4 teaspoons salt
- ¼ teaspoon pepper
- ¼ teaspoon dried thyme
- ¼ teaspoon Ac'cent
- ¼ cup minced parsley
- 3 pounds ground beef
- 2 eggs, beaten
- ¼ cup milk
- ⅓ cup catsup
- 1½ teaspoons dry mustard

To make stuffing, cut into slices all but 7 of the mushrooms and sauté them in butter with the lemon juice and onion for about 3 minutes. Toss in bread crumbs, 1 teaspoon salt, ⅛ teaspoon pepper, thyme, Ac'cent, and parsley. With a fork, lightly mix the meat with the eggs, 3 teaspoons salt, ⅛ teaspoon pepper, milk, catsup and dry mustard. Pack half the meat mixture into a 10 x 5 x 3-inch loaf pan and pack the stuffing on top. Top with the remaining meat mixture and press down firmly. Press the 7 whole mushrooms into the top and bake in a hot (400° F.) oven for 1 hour. Baked potatoes go well with this loaf. SERVES 8.

Creole Meat Loaf

- 6 tablespoons shortening
- 3 onions, minced
- 2 cloves garlic, minced
- 2 bay leaves
- 2 tablespoons minced parsley
- 3 tablespoons minced sweet pepper
- 1/4 teaspoon thyme
- 2 tablespoons chopped celery
- 1/2 teaspoon pepper
- 2 1/2 pounds ground beef
- 2 tablespoons flour
- 2 1/2 cups (No. 2 can) tomatoes
- 1 teaspoon sugar

Melt the shortening in a frying pan and brown the onions and garlic. Add the bay leaves, parsley, sweet pepper, thyme, celery, and pepper and cook slowly for 5 minutes. Take half of the mixture out of the pan and mix well with the meat. Put the meat in a baking pan and shape into a loaf. Brown the flour in the frying pan with remaining onion mixture, add tomatoes, and stir over heat for 10 minutes. Add sugar and pour the mixture over the meat. Bake in a moderate (350° F.) oven for 45 minutes to 1 hour, depending on how well done you want the loaf. SERVES 8 TO 10.

Hamburger Steak with Water-Fried Onions

- 2 pounds ground beef
- 2 cups soft bread crumbs
- 1/2 cup milk
- 2 eggs, slightly beaten
- 2 teaspoons salt
- 1 teaspoon Ac'cent
- 1/8 teaspoon pepper
- 1/4 cup catsup
- 3 pounds onions

Combine all ingredients in a bowl except the onions. Mix well. Shape into an oval loaf 1 1/2 inches thick. Broil for 15 to 20 minutes with the surface of the meat 4 inches below source of heat. Watch to see that it doesn't get too brown on top. If it begins to brown too much before cooking time is up, move broiler pan farther away from heat. Do not turn. Remove to hot platter and serve with water-fried onions, prepared as follows:

Slice large, sweet onions very thin and place in deep, heavy frying pan. Sprinkle with salt, pepper, and Ac'cent. Place over low heat. When onions begin to carmelize on bottom, stir them with a fork. Continue this process until all are lightly browned. Add 1/4 cup water, cover pan, and cook over low heat, stirring occasionally, until onions are soft and brown and the water has evaporated. SERVES 6 TO 8.

Tiny Meat Balls Norwegian

- 2 pounds ground beef
- 1/4 pound ground pork
- 2 eggs
- Salt and pepper
- 1/4 teaspoon mace
- 1/4 teaspoon ginger
- 2 slices stale bread
- Butter *or* margarine for frying
- Onion, sliced
- 4 tablespoons flour

Have the meats ground together very fine. Add eggs and seasonings. Remove the crust from the bread; moisten under faucet and add to the meat. Knead the mixture thoroughly in a mixing bowl, and then wet your hands with cold water and roll the meat into tiny balls. Fry the balls in butter until they are brown on all sides; shake the pan frequently to keep balls round. Add sliced onion for flavor while the meat balls are browning, but remove after the balls are done. Spoon the meat balls into a casserole. For gravy, add flour to the meat juices and thin with hot water. Be sure to scrape all the brown particles from the skillet. Pour gravy over meat balls and bake in a moderate oven, 350° F., for 45 minutes. Serve with noodles or rice. SERVES 10 as a hot smorgasbord. SERVES 6 as a main course.

Sherry Little Meats

- 1 egg, beaten
- 1 cup fresh bread crumbs
- 1 1/2 pounds ground beef
- 2 tablespoons minced onion
- 1 1/2 teaspoons salt
- 1/4 teaspoon pepper
- 1/2 teaspoon Ac'cent
- 1 cup tomato sauce
- 1 tablespoon cornstarch
- 2 tablespoons brown sugar
- 3/4 cup sherry
- 1 tablespoon vinegar
- 1 teaspoon prepared mustard
- 1 beef bouillon cube
- 3/4 cup hot water

Combine lightly but thoroughly the egg, bread crumbs, meat, onion, salt, pepper, Ac'cent, and 1/2 cup of the tomato sauce. Shape this mixture into 4 individual loaves and place in a shallow baking dish. Bake the loaves for 40 minutes in a moderate (350° F.) oven and then pour off most of the juices. Meanwhile, combine the cornstarch and brown sugar and then add the other 1/2 cup tomato sauce, sherry, vinegar, mustard, and bouillon cube dissolved in hot water. Cook until thickened, stirring frequently. Pour this over the meat loaves. Bake, basting often, for an additional 30 minutes. SERVES 4.

Party Meat Loaf

1 pound ground veal
1 pound ground beef
1 pound ground pork
2 eggs, well beaten
1/3 cup onion, chopped
2 teaspoons salt
1/4 teaspoon dry mustard
1/8 teaspoon seasoning salt (optional)
1/8 teaspoon celery salt
1/8 teaspoon paprika
1/4 teaspoon black pepper

Have the meat ground only once with a coarse blade. Combine the meats thoroughly in a large mixing bowl; add the eggs, onion, and other seasonings and mix again, kneading until blended. Pack into an oiled bread-loaf pan and then turn it out onto a flat baking pan. Bake in a moderate (350° F.) oven for 1½ hours or until well done. SERVES 20.

Barbecued Meat Loaves

1 pound ground beef
2 tablespoons minced onion
1 teaspoon salt
1/4 teaspoon pepper
1/4 cup soft bread crumbs
1/4 cup milk
1/4 cup catsup
2 tablespoons vinegar
1 teaspoon Worcestershire sauce
1/2 teaspoon chili powder

Mix together thoroughly but lightly the beef, 1 tablespoon minced onion, salt, pepper, bread crumbs, and milk Shape into 4 individual loaves and arrange them in a shallow pan. Combine the catsup, vinegar, 1 tablespoon minced onion, Worcestershire, and chili powder and spoon this over the loaves. Bake in a moderate (350° F.) oven for 45 minutes, basting occasionally with sauce in the bottom of the pan. SERVES 4.

Fritos Tamale Loaf

2 beef bouillon cubes
2 cups boiling water
2 cups finely crushed corn chips (Fritos)
1/4 cup chopped onions
3/8 teaspoon pepper
1 1/4 teaspoons salt
3 eggs
1 pound ground beef
1 tablespoon chili powder
1/2 cup tomato sauce

Dissolve the bouillon cubes in 2 cups of boiling water; add the corn chips, onions, 1/8 teaspoon pepper, 1/4 teaspoon salt, and 2 beaten eggs. Pour half of this mixture into a greased 8-inch square baking dish. Mix the ground beef with 1 teaspoon salt, ¼ teaspoon pepper, chili powder, tomato sauce, and the remaining egg to form a second layer in the baking dish. Top with the remainder of the first mixture and bake in a moderate (350° F.) oven for 1 hour. SERVES 6 TO 8.

Chili Rice Casserole

- 1 cup uncooked rice
- 3 tablespoons olive oil
- ½ pound ground beef
- 2 onions, sliced paper thin
- 1 can green chilies, diced
- 1 cup ripe olives, cut into chunks, leaving a few whole
- ½ pound Cheddar cheese, cut in strips
- 2 cups beef bouillon
- 1 cup tomato juice

Stir the rice in olive oil over low heat until golden but not brown, about 3 minutes. Remove rice from skillet. In the same oil, cook the meat until it loses its red color. Place in a greased casserole, in layers, half of the rice, onions, chilies, ripe olives, meat, and cheese. Sprinkle with salt and pepper. Repeat layers. Heat bouillon and tomato juice to the boiling point and pour over the mixture. Cover tightly and bake in a moderate oven, 350° F., until rice is tender, about 40 minutes. Serve with a tossed green salad and crisp bread sticks. SERVES 4.

Meat Balls in Sour Cream Gravy

- 1 clove garlic, minced
- 1½ teaspoons salt
- 1½ pounds ground veal *or* beef *or* combination
- 2 eggs, beaten
- ½ cup milk
- 1 cup fine dry bread crumbs
- ¼ teaspoon pepper
- 3 tablespoons salad oil
- 3 tablespoons minced onion
- 3 tablespoons flour
- 1 pint commercial sour cream
- 1 tablespoon Worcestershire sauce
- 1 3-ounce can sliced mushrooms with liquid
- 4 cups broad noodles
- 3 tablespoons poppy seeds

Combine the garlic, salt, meat, eggs, milk, bread crumbs, and pepper in a mixing bowl and shape into 16 large balls or 32 small ones. In a skillet, brown the meat balls in hot salad oil. Remove them from the pan and sauté the onion in the same skillet for 3 or 4 minutes. Stir in the flour, and then add the sour cream, Worcestershire, and mushrooms. Cook, stirring constantly, until thickened. Add the meat balls, turning them to coat them with the gravy. If the gravy is too thick, add 3 or 4 tablespoons of boiling water. Cook the noodles according to the package directions and drain. Make a ring or bed of noodles on a large platter and heap the meat balls and gravy onto the center. Sprinkle with poppy seeds. SERVES 8.

Swedish Meat Balls

- 1 cup soft bread crumbs
- 1 cup milk
- 1 pound ground beef
- 1 egg, well beaten
- 1 tablespoon minced onion
- 1/4 teaspoon ground mace
- 1/8 teaspoon ground allspice
- 1 teaspoon salt
- 1/8 teaspoon pepper
- 3 tablespoons bacon drippings
- 4 tablespoons flour
- 1 can condensed consommé
- 1 cup sauterne wine
- 1/2 cup evaporated milk
- 2 tablespoons chopped parsley

Soak bread crumbs in milk for 10 minutes. Add the beef, egg, onion, mace, allspice, salt, and pepper and mix thoroughly. With wet hands, shape the mixture into tiny meat balls about the size of a walnut. Heat bacon drippings in a large heavy skillet, and brown the meat balls on all sides. Remove the meat balls. Add flour to the drippings and blend well. Add the consommé, wine, and evaporated milk. Stirring constantly, cook until the mixture is thick and smooth. Add the parsley and salt and pepper to taste. Return the meat balls to the gravy, cover the skillet, and simmer them gently for about 20 minutes. These are delicious served over buttered large noodles. SERVES 5 OR 6.

Claret Meat Balls

- 1 pound ground beef
- 1 onion, minced
- 1/2 green pepper, minced
- 1 small garlic clove, minced
- 1 cup cracker crumbs
- 1 1/2 teaspoons salt
- 1/4 teaspoon pepper
- 2 eggs, slightly beaten
- 2 tablespoons butter
- 2 tablespoons salad oil
- 3/4 cup claret wine
- 3/4 cup tomato juice
- 2 teaspoons flour

Mix together the meat, onion, green pepper, garlic, crumbs, salt, and pepper. Work the eggs into the mixture. Shape into 12 to 14 small balls. Place in a covered dish in the refrigerator to chill. To cook, heat the butter and oil in a chafing dish pan over direct heat or on your range. Flatten each ball slightly as you place it in the pan, and brown well. Add the wine and tomato juice, cover pan, and cook for 15 to 30 minutes or until the meat is well done. Push the meat balls to one side of the pan, stir the flour smoothly into the juices, and cook till slightly thickened. Serve the sauce over the meat balls. Noodles go well with this main dish. SERVES 4.

Continental Meat Balls with Horseradish Sauce

- 3 tablespoons chopped onion
- 1 tablespoon butter *or* margarine
- 20 saltine crackers
- 1¼ cups milk
- ½ pound ground beef
- ½ pound ground pork
- 1 egg
- 2 teaspoons salt
- ¼ teaspoon pepper

Sauté the onion in butter until golden. Crumble the crackers into milk and let them stand for 5 minutes. Combine with the onion and remaining ingredients. Shape mixture into 24 balls then sauté in butter until browned on all sides. SERVES 4.

Horseradish sauce

- Pan drippings
- 1 tablespoon flour
- 1½ cups milk
- 1 tablespoon horseradish
- ½ teaspoon salt
- Pepper

Blend together the pan drippings and flour in a frying pan. Gradually stir in the milk; mix in the horseradish, salt, and pepper. Cook over medium heat, stirring constantly, until the mixture thickens and boils. Serve with meat balls.

Spaghetti with Meat Balls

- ¼ cup olive oil
- 1 clove garlic, minced
- 1 onion, chopped
- ½ green pepper, chopped
- 2½ cups (No. 2 can) tomatoes
- 1 8-ounce can tomato sauce
- 1½ teaspoons seasoned salt
- ¼ teaspoon pepper
- ½ teaspoon orégano
- ¼ cup grated Parmesan cheese
- ½ pound spaghetti
- ½ cup fresh bread crumbs
- 2 tablespoons milk
- 1 pound ground beef
- 1 teaspoon seasoned salt
- 2 tablespoons olive oil
- Grated Parmesan cheese

In olive oil in a large skillet sauté the garlic, onion, and green pepper for about 5 minutes or until tender. Add tomatoes, tomato sauce, 1½ teaspoons seasoned salt, pepper, orégano, and ¼ cup Parmesan cheese. Simmer, uncovered, for 15 minutes. Meanwhile cook the spaghetti in boiling salted water until tender, about 8 minutes. Drain. Soften bread crumbs in milk; mix them with the beef and 1 teaspoon seasoned salt. Shape into 24 balls. In 2 tablespoons of hot oil in a skillet, brown the meat balls. Add the meat balls with the pan drippings to the sauce and cook about 10 minutes longer. Serve the meat sauce over the drained spaghetti and sprinkle with more Parmesan cheese. Or you can serve the spaghetti, sauce, and cheese separately, allowing everyone to help himself. Crisp bread sticks and a tossed garlic salad go well with it. SERVES 4.

4

Vegetables

VEGETABLES ARE THE STEPCHILDREN of creative cooking. We just keep right on preparing our favorites in the same old recipes, when really it could be an adventure to try one new recipe for a vegetable dish each week. The family won't like all of them, but in the course of a year you'll find some new favorites to add to your collection.

If you are using frozen vegetables, follow the directions on the package and don't overcook them. These vegetables have been picked at the peak of their goodness and flavor, and it's a shame to cook and cook them until they lose their personality and become just another badly prepared dish. I like to use frozen vegetables because there isn't an ounce of waste; you eat all you buy. Then too, in some parts of the country, it's difficult to get really fresh produce, and there is a loss of nutritional value if produce lays in a bin for a day or so. I disagree, however, with the number of servings that the frozen food people say you can get out of one ten-ounce box. Either we are pigs at our house or the number is wrong, because one box serves two healthy portions or three small ones at my table.

You'll find that I have used a lot of rice recipes in this vegetable chapter. There are two reasons: first, it's good for you; and second, it's good tasting. Of course, you never have to use rice or any other product just as it comes from the box—you can use your imagination and dream up delightful ways of serving rice. And you'll find that rice is served on most low cholesterol menus, and that rice oil, which soon will be sold throughout the country, is very low in cholesterol. More about this in a special chapter.

Green Rice I

- 1½ cups rice
- 2 tablespoons finely chopped onion
- ¼ teaspoon minced garlic
- 3 tablespoons olive oil *or* butter
- ½ cup ground *or* finely chopped parsley
- 1 cup milk
- 1 teaspoon salt
- 1 teaspoon Worcestershire sauce
- 1 cup grated Cheddar cheese
- 2 eggs, slightly beaten

Cook the rice according to the directions on the package. Sauté the onion and garlic in olive oil or butter. Combine the cooked rice and parsley in a mixing bowl, then add milk, salt, Worcestershire sauce, Cheddar cheese, and slightly beaten eggs. Add the sautéed onion and garlic. Mix thoroughly and pour the mixture into a buttered baking dish. Bake in a moderate oven, 350° F., for about 40 minutes. SERVES 6.

Green Rice II

Mrs. J. C. Oglesby of Fort Worth won first place in our recent recipe contest with this most unusual recipe.

- 2 cups cooked rice
- 1 large can evaporated milk
- ¼ pound Old English cheese, grated
- ¾ cup finely chopped parsley
- Salt and pepper
- 2 eggs, beaten
- 1 small onion, grated
- 1 clove garlic *or* ⅛ teaspoon garlic powder
- ⅓ cup cooking oil

Combine all ingredients, pour into an oiled baking dish and bake in a pan of water for 1 hour in a moderate (350° F.) oven. SERVES 4.

Roedkaal (*Red Cabbage*)

- 1 medium head *or* 2 jars red cabbage
- 2 to 4 tablespoons butter
- 2 tablespoons sugar
- 1 tablespoon vinegar
- 2 tablespoons caraway seeds *or* 2 medium apples, peeled and sliced
- ½ cup currant jelly

Shred, wash, and drain the fresh cabbage. If jars of cabbage are used, no preparation is necessary. Melt the butter in a large skillet and add sugar. Add the cabbage and vinegar. Cover and simmer until tender, stirring occasionally. Add caraway seeds or apples and the currant jelly. SERVES 4 TO 6.

Creole Okra

Creole Okra is a delightful recipe for preparing a vegetable that is sometimes overlooked. Frozen okra, cooked and served with highly seasoned butter, is a favorite Southwestern recipe; but Creole Okra leans more to the New Orleans method of preparing vegetables. Try it once, and then you can adjust it to suit your taste.

- 2 medium onions, sliced
- 8 tablespoons (1 stick) butter *or* margarine
- 6 medium-size fresh tomatoes, peeled and quartered
- 2 10-ounce boxes frozen okra pie, partially thawed
- Salt and pepper
- Ac'cent
- Tabasco sauce

Sauté the onions in the butter or margarine. Add the tomatoes and the okra. Blend well, cover, and let the mixture cook until the tomatoes cook down and the okra is tender. This should take about 20 to 25 minutes. Add the salt, pepper, Ac'cent, and Tabasco to taste (I use about 5 shakes). If you have too much liquid in the skillet, uncover the skillet and allow some of the liquid to cook away. Creole okra is even more delicious when it is reheated on the second day—and it freezes wonderfully well. SERVES 8.

Eggplant Parmegiana

- 1 eggplant (about 1 pound)
- ½ cup flour
- 1 teaspoon salt
- ¼ teaspoon pepper
- 1 egg, slightly beaten
- 2 tablespoons of milk
- ½ cup salad oil
- 2 8-ounce cans tomato sauce
- 1 teaspoon orégano
- ¾ cup grated Parmesan and Romano cheese

Peel the eggplant and cut it into ½-inch slices. Combine the flour, salt, and pepper. Combine the beaten egg and milk. Dip the eggplant slices into flour, then into the egg mixture, and then into the flour again. Fry it in oil, turning it to brown both sides. Drain on absorbent paper. Place alternate layers of eggplant, tomato sauce, orégano, and Parmesan and Romano cheese in greased baking dish. Repeat. Bake in a hot (400° F.) oven for 20 minutes or until cheese is very lightly browned. SERVES 4.

Sweet Potatoes Hawaiian

4 cups mashed cooked sweet potatoes
1 cup drained crushed pineapple
½ cup brown sugar, packed
3 tablespoons butter *or* margarine
Dash of ground cloves

Combine all ingredients and turn the mixture into a 1½-quart casserole. Bake in a moderate (350° F.) oven for 25 minutes or until bubbly hot. SERVES 6 TO 8.

Green Onion Pie

3 cups sliced green onions, including tops
3 tablespoons butter *or* margarine
1 8-inch unbaked pie shell
2 eggs
½ cup light cream
1 teaspoon salt
Dash of pepper

Sauté the sliced green onions in butter until tender. Arrange in the unbaked pie shell. Beat the eggs until just blended. Stir in the cream, salt, and pepper and pour over the onions in the pie shell. Bake in a hot (425° F.) oven for 18 to 20 minutes or until well browned; a knife inserted in the center of the pie should come out clean when the pie is done. SERVES 4.

Yellow Rice

½ to 1 teaspoon curry powder
2 cups chicken broth
1 cup long grain rice
¼ cup chopped onion
¼ cup diced green pepper
10 to 12 drops yellow food coloring

Combine the curry powder with 2 tablespoons of chicken broth to make a smooth paste. Stir in remaining broth and heat to a boil. Add the rice, onion, green pepper, and yellow food coloring. Place in a greased 1½ quart casserole. Cover and bake in a moderately hot oven, 350° F., till rice is tender, about 45 minutes. Stir once or twice during the baking time. This rice goes well with fried chicken or shrimp. SERVES 4 OR 5.

Yams with Rum and Walnuts

Boil yams or sweet potatoes, allow them to cool, and remove the skins. Slice into ½-inch slices. Arrange a layer in a buttered baking dish, sprinkle with salt and a little brown sugar, and dot with plenty of butter. Add another layer of potatoes and season the same way. Sprinkle broken walnut meats over the top layer and pour Jamaica rum over all, using 1 jigger for each pound of potatoes. Bake in a moderate (350° F.) oven until potatoes are hot and have a shiny brown glaze. Baste occasionally during the baking. If you wish, you may heat more rum and pour it over the yams, touch a match to it, and serve the yams flaming.

Scalloped Potatoes

- 7 medium potatoes, pared and sliced
- 3 medium onions, sliced thin
- 5 tablespoons flour
- Salt
- 1½ teaspoons pepper
- 5 tablespoons butter
- 1 cup crumbled Blue cheese
- 1½ cups milk
- Paprika
- Chopped parsley

In a greased casserole, place a layer of potatoes and a layer of onions. Sprinkle with flour, salt, and pepper; dot with butter and a few crumbles of Blue cheese. Repeat until all potatoes and onions are used. Pour milk almost to the top of the potatoes, and top with remaining cheese. Cover and bake in a slow (300° F.) oven for 2 hours or until the vegetables are soft. Remove the cover during the last half hour of cooking. Garnish with paprika and chopped parsley. SERVES 6.

Sour Cream Potato Casserole

- 5 medium potatoes *or* 4 cups sliced cooked potatoes
- 2 tablespoons butter *or* margarine
- ½ cup finely chopped onion
- ¼ cup dry bread crumbs
- ¼ cup grated American cheese
- 2 well-beaten eggs
- 1 cup commercial sour cream
- 1 teaspoon salt
- Dash of pepper

Cook the potatoes in boiling, salted water until tender; drain and peel. When cool, cut in thin slices. Melt the butter; add the onion to the butter and cook until tender but not brown. Put the potatoes in a 1-quart casserole. Sprinkle the onion, bread crumbs and cheese over them. Combine the eggs, sour cream, salt, and pepper; pour this mixture over the potatoes. Top with additional grated cheese if desired. Bake in a moderate oven, 350° F., for 20 minutes. SERVES 3 OR 4.

Sauterne Peanut Rice

- ½ cup sauterne wine
- 1 cup chicken broth
- ½ cup water
- 1 cup rice
- ½ cup grated Cheddar cheese
- 2 tablespoons melted butter
- ½ cup chopped salted peanuts
- Salt and pepper

Combine the sauterne, chicken broth, and ½ cup water; bring to boiling. Add rice and stir with a fork to blend well. Reduce heat to low, cover tightly, and cook slowly until tender, about 20 to 25 minutes. When the rice is done, remove the cover and stir in the cheese, butter, and peanuts. Season to taste with salt and pepper. SERVES 4 OR 5.

If you use precooked rice, use 2 cups instead of 1 cup, and cook for only 5 minutes.

Spinach Rockefeller

Spinach Rockefeller is a specialty of the house at the Imperial Club at the Baker Hotel in Dallas. I am giving it to you in a quantity recipe to serve 25 because it makes such a delightful vegetable for a large buffet supper. Men who didn't eat spinach when they were little boys order this vegetable dish every time they have luncheon at the Club. It goes especially well with pork or poultry.

- 5 pounds frozen spinach, cooked and drained
- 1 quart (4 cups) fine bread crumbs
- 1 tablespoon thyme
- 2 tablespoons Ac'cent
- 2 tablespoons garlic powder or minced garlic
- 1 teaspoon Cayenne pepper *or* Tabasco sauce to taste
- 2 teaspoons black pepper
- Salt to taste
- 1 cup Parmesan cheese
- 1 dozen green onions and tops, chopped
- 2 cups melted margarine
- 1 dozen eggs, unbeaten
- 25 thick tomato slices
- Garlic salt

Cook the spinach and drain well; chop fine. Add the bread crumbs, seasonings, and cheese. Sauté the onions in the margarine until they are transparent; add to the spinach. Add the eggs and mix well. Put the spinach mixture into a shallow baking pan and bake for 25 minutes in a moderate (350° F.) oven. Meanwhile, arrange the tomato slices on buttered baking pans and season them with garlic salt. Broil until the tomatoes are partially done. Using an ice-cream scoop, place one scoop of spinach onto each tomato slice. Serve on a warmed platter. SERVES 25.

Scalloped Eggplant

- 1 medium eggplant
- 1 egg, beaten
- ½ cup milk
- 2 tablespoons melted butter
- 1 small onion, chopped
- 1 cup dry bread crumbs
- ½ cup buttered bread crumbs *or* cracker crumbs

Pare eggplant, cut it into 1-inch cubes and cook them in boiling salted water for 8 minutes. Drain. Add egg, milk, butter, onion, and dry bread crumbs. Place in a greased baking dish, and top with buttered crumbs. Bake in a moderate (350° F.) oven for 30 minutes. SERVES 6.

Spanish Eggplant

Substitute 1½ cups canned tomatoes for the milk and sprinkle American cheese over the top.

Peas Parisienne

- 1 can peas
- 2 tablespoons butter *or* margarine *or* bacon fat
- 3 or 4 slices onion, ¼-inch thick
- ½ teaspoon salt
- 2 cups coarsely cut Romaine or lettuce

Drain the peas and add them to melted butter in a skillet. Separate the onion slices into rings or chop them coarsely. Add the onion and salt to the peas. Lay the Romaine or lettuce on top; cover, and heat slowly over low heat for just 5 minutes. Toss lightly and serve at once. Both onions and lettuce will be quite crisp. If you prefer them more thoroughly cooked, heat them an additional 5 minutes. SERVES 4.

Potato Soufflé

½ cup hot milk
½ cup grated Cheddar cheese
2 tablespoons butter *or* margarine
1 tablespoon finely chopped parsley
1 teaspoon salt
2 cups hot mashed potatoes
4 eggs, separated

Beat the hot milk, grated cheese, butter, parsley, and salt into the mashed potatoes. Beat the egg yolks until thick and lemon colored, and beat the whites until stiff but not dry. Fold the yolks into the potato mixture and then fold in the whites. Pile the mixture lightly into a greased baking dish and bake in a hot oven, 400° F., for 25 minutes. Serve this light, puffy soufflé immediately. SERVES 4.

Parsleyed Cheese Noodles

8 ounces noodles
1 cup cream style cottage cheese
½ cup crumbled Blue cheese
¼ cup melted butter
¼ cup chopped parsley
¼ cup minced onion
3 eggs, well beaten
¾ teaspoon garlic
Salt and pepper

Cook the noodles until tender in 3 quarts of rapidly boiling salted water. Drain. Combine remaining ingredients, add noodles, and toss well. Turn the mixture into a greased 1½-quart casserole and bake in a moderate oven, 350° F., for 30 minutes. SERVES 4.

Potatoes au Gratin with Sherry

2 tablespoons butter
2 tablespoons flour
1 cup milk
1⅓ cups grated American *or* Cheddar cheese
¼ cup medium dry sherry wine
Salt and pepper
4 cups diced cooked potatoes
Paprika

Melt the butter in a saucepan; stir in the flour. When well blended, add the milk and cook, stirring constantly, until the mixture is thick and smooth. Then add 1 cup grated cheese and stir over low heat until the cheese is melted. Remove from heat and add the sherry; season with salt and pepper to taste. Blend the whole, then add the potatoes. Turn the mixture into a greased casserole and top with ⅓ cup cheese and a generous sprinkling of paprika. Bake in a hot oven, 400° F., for about 20 minutes or until bubbly and brown. SERVES 4 TO 6.

Party Green Beans

- 1 3-ounce can sliced mushrooms, drained
- 1 tablespoon butter *or* margarine
- 2 cups cooked green beans
- ½ cup commercial sour cream
- ½ teaspoon salt
- ½ teaspoon dried, crushed mint leaves

In a heavy skillet, sauté the mushrooms in the butter. Add the green beans and heat thoroughly. Add the sour cream and salt and heat again, but do not boil. Add the crushed mint leaves and toss until well mixed. SERVES 4.

Orange Candied Sweet Potatoes

Slice cooked sweet potatoes and put them in a greased 7 x 13-inch casserole. If you like, put orange slices around the edge of the casserole. Pour orange sauce over potatoes and bake in a moderate (350° F.) oven for 30 minutes. SERVES 6.

Orange Sauce

- 1 cup brown sugar
- 2 tablespoons cornstarch
- ½ teaspoon salt
- 2 tablespoons grated orange peel
- ¼ cup butter *or* margarine
- 2 cups orange juice

Put all ingredients in a saucepan and cook until thick. This sauce can be made days ahead of time and kept in the refrigerator.

Noodles Romanoff

- ⅔ cup uncooked noodles
- 1 cup cottage cheese
- 1 cup commercial sour cream
- ¼ cup finely chopped onion
- 1 clove garlic, finely cut
- 2 teaspoons Worcestershire sauce
- Dash of Tabasco sauce *or* red pepper sauce
- ½ teaspoon salt
- ½ cup grated American cheese

Cook the noodles according to directions on the package; drain. Add the cottage cheese to the drained noodles, then add sour cream, onion, garlic, Worcestershire sauce, Tabasco sauce, and salt. Place the mixture in a greased 8-inch baking dish and bake in a moderate oven, 350° F., for 30 minutes. Remove the dish from the oven, sprinkle with grated cheese, and return it to the oven for 10 minutes. Serve with crusty French rolls and a pineapple and avocado salad. SERVES 5 OR 6.

Noodles Florentine

- 2 pounds noodles
- ½ cup olive oil
- 2 cloves garlic, finely chopped
- ½ cup grated Swiss cheese
- ½ teaspoon freshly ground black pepper
- 3 packages frozen chopped spinach
- 2 teaspoons tarragon
- 2 tablespoons lemon juice
- ¼ pound butter *or* margarine
- Salt to taste
- Buttered toasted crumbs
- Parmesan cheese

Boil the noodles in salted water according to the directions on the package, but do not overcook. Drain. Mix the noodles with olive oil, garlic, grated Swiss cheese, and freshly ground black pepper. Cook the spinach according to directions on the package and drain. Add the tarragon, lemon juice, and butter; add salt to taste. Make a bed of spinach on the bottom of a lightly greased baking dish. Place the noodles on top and sprinkle liberally with buttered toasted crumbs and Parmesan cheese. Place the dish under the broiler for just 5 minutes. Serve at once. SERVES 10 TO 12.

Herbed Rice

- 3 tablespoons butter *or* margarine
- 1 cup chopped onion
- 1 cup uncooked rice
- ½ teaspoon marjoram
- ½ teaspoon summer savory
- 1 teaspoon rosemary
- ½ teaspoon salt
- 3 chicken bouillon cubes
- 2 cups water

Melt the butter in a 2-quart saucepan. Add the onion and rice, and cook until the onion turns yellow and the rice begins to brown. Add the marjoram, summer savory, rosemary, salt, chicken bouillon cubes, and 2 cups water. Bring the mixture to a vigorous boil, stirring it to dissolve the bouillon cubes. Turn the heat as low as possible; cover the pan and cook over low heat for 14 minutes. Remove the saucepan from the heat but leave the lid on for 10 minutes more or until you are ready to serve. SERVES 6.

Herbed Mushrooms

- 2 pounds fresh mushrooms
- 2 small onions, finely chopped
- Few sprigs parsley, finely chopped
- ¼ cup butter *or* margarine
- 1 teaspoon salt
- Dash of pepper
- ¾ teaspoon tarragon

Wipe the mushrooms with a damp cloth and cut all large ones into quarters. Cook the chopped onions and parsley in melted butter until the onions are limp. Toss in the mushrooms, cover, and cook over moderate heat 5 to 8 minutes. Sprinkle with salt, pepper, and tarragon. SERVES 8 TO 10.

Green Beans Amandine

- 1 pound green beans
- 3 tablespoons butter *or* margarine
- ⅓ cup slivered, blanched almonds

Rinse the beans; remove the ends and strings, and slit the beans lengthwise. Cook them in a small amount of boiling salted water until they are barely tender, 20 to 30 minutes. Drain. Meanwhile, combine the butter and almonds in a small skillet; cook over moderate heat, stirring frequently, until the butter and almonds are lightly browned. Pour this mixture over the beans and mix lightly. Serve at once. SERVES 3 OR 4.

One package of frozen green beans may be used in place of the fresh ones. Cook them according to the directions on the package, but stop short of the full cooking time so that the beans are just barely tender.

Delmonico Potatoes

- 2 tablespoons butter
- 1½ tablespoons flour
- 1 cup milk
- ½ teaspoon salt
- ¼ teaspoon pepper
- 1 quart boiled potatoes, sliced
- 3 hard-cooked eggs, chopped
- ¾ cup grated American cheese
- 1 pimiento, chopped (optional)
- 2 tablespoons butter

Make a white sauce with the butter, flour, and milk. Add the salt and pepper. Arrange layers of potatoes, eggs, ½ cup cheese, pimiento, and white sauce in a buttered 2-quart baking dish. Dot each layer with butter; sprinkle with salt and pepper to taste. Cover top with the remaining ¼ cup cheese. Bake in a moderate oven, 350° F., for 30 to 35 minutes. SERVES 6 TO 8.

Chili Corn Bake

- 2 eggs, beaten
- 1 cup cream-style corn
- 1 cup commercial sour cream *or* thick buttermilk
- 1 cup yellow corn meal
- 3 teaspoons baking powder
- 1½ teaspoons salt
- ¼ cup melted bacon drippings
- 1⅓ cups grated, aged, natural Cheddar cheese
- 1 small can green chilies
- 1 small can ripe olives, sliced

Mix together the eggs, corn, and sour cream or buttermilk. Combine the dry ingredients and stir them and the bacon drippings into the mixture. Spread half of this batter in a greased 9-inch square pan. Cover with half the cheese. Rinse the chilies and remove their seeds. Cut them into strips and lay them over the cheese. Drain the olives and sprinkle them over the chilies. Cover with the rest of the batter and cheese. Bake in a moderate oven, 350° F., for 1 hour or until lightly browned. Cut into squares and serve warm. Delicious when reheated. SERVES 4.

Cheese Onion Pie

- 1 unbaked 9-inch pie shell
- 1 cup thinly sliced onions
- 2 tablespoons butter *or* margarine
- ¾ cup grated American cheese
- 3 eggs, slightly beaten
- 1½ tablespoons flour
- 2 teaspoons mustard
- 1 can condensed cream of mushroom soup
- ½ cup milk

Place the pastry in a pie plate and flute the edges. Sauté the onions in butter until tender. Spread them over the bottom of the pie shell and sprinkle with grated cheese. Blend the eggs with the flour and mustard, stir in the condensed soup and milk, and pour over the onions. Bake for 45 to 60 minutes in a moderate (350° F.) oven. Let stand for 10 minutes before serving. A green salad is all that is needed with this dish. SERVES 6.

Cauliflower Soufflé

- 3 tablespoons butter
- 3 tablespoons flour
- 1 cup milk
- ½ teaspoon salt
- 3 egg yolks, beaten
- ½ cup American cheese, grated
- 1 cup cauliflower, cooked and coarsely chopped
- 3 egg whites, stiffly beaten

Make a white sauce with the butter, flour, milk, and salt. Add the egg yolks and cheese, and stir until the cheese is melted. Add the cauliflower. Fold in the beaten egg whites, and then pour the mixture into a buttered casserole. Sprinkle the top with an additional bit of cheese. Set the casserole in hot water and bake in a moderate oven, 350° F., for 50 to 60 minutes. Serve immediately. SERVES 4.

Broccoli Soufflé

- 2 tablespoons margarine
- 2 tablespoons flour
- 1 cup milk
- 1 teaspoon salt
- ¼ teaspoon pepper
- 1 cup chopped cooked broccoli
- 6 eggs, separated

Make a cream sauce with the margarine, flour, and milk; cook until thick, stirring constantly. Add seasoning and the broccoli. Separate the eggs; beat the egg whites until stiff and beat the yolks until lemon colored. Stir the broccoli mixture into the yolks, and then gently fold into the beaten egg whites. Turn the mixture into a greased casserole and bake in a preheated moderate (375° F.) oven until firm and brown on top, about 40 minutes. SERVES 4.

Crisp Cabbage Medley

- 2 tablespoons butter *or* margarine
- 1 onion, chopped
- 1 green pepper, chopped
- 1 cup thinly sliced celery
- 3 cups shredded cabbage
- ½ cup sauterne wine
- 2 teaspoons salt
- Pepper

Melt the butter in a large saucepan. Add all ingredients and mix well; cover, and let steam for five minutes. Serve immediately. SERVES 4.

Cabbage with Sour Cream

1 medium head cabbage
1 teaspoon salt
1 cup commercial sour cream
¼ cup cabbage liquid
1 tablespoon chopped fresh chives

Wash the cabbage and cut it into wedges. Place it in a saucepan with 1 inch of boiling water and ½ teaspoon salt. Cook the cabbage, uncovered, for 5 minutes. Cover and cook until crisp-tender, about 8 to 10 minutes. Place the wedges on a warm serving platter. Heat the sour cream with the cabbage liquid and ½ teaspoon salt. *Do not boil.* Pour this sauce over the cabbage; garnish with chives. SERVES 6.

Baked Noodles Ricotta

1 8-ounce package medium noodles
1 pound Ricotta cheese
½ cup commercial sour cream
3 eggs, slightly beaten
1 teaspoon salt
⅛ teaspoon white pepper
Dash of nutmeg
¼ cup fine bread crumbs
2 tablespoons melted butter *or* margarine

Cook the noodles according to directions on the package, drain, and rinse with hot water. Combine the cheese, sour cream, eggs, and seasonings. Mix this with the noodles and place in a greased 2-quart soufflé dish. Sprinkle the top with bread crumbs and melted butter. Bake in a moderate oven, 350° F., for 40 to 45 minutes or until crumbs are lightly browned and the custard is set. SERVES 6.

Brandied Carrots

1 pound (about 5) large carrots
4 tablespoons butter
3 tablespoons water
Salt
2 tablespoons brandy
Minced parsley

Scrape the carrots and cut them into very thin diagonal slices. Put them into the blazer pan of your chafing dish or in an electric skillet with 3 tablespoons butter, 3 tablespoons water, a little salt, and the brandy. Cover and cook until the liquid is absorbed and the carrots are tender but still crisp. Add the remaining butter and a sprinkling of minced parsley. Serve with barbecued spareribs. SERVES 4.

Baked Onions and Peas

12 small onions
2 tablespoons butter
3 tablespoons flour
1¼ cups milk
Salt and pepper
2 cups cooked peas
1 cup corn flakes, buttered

Cook the onions in salted water until tender; drain. Place them in a buttered baking dish. Make a white sauce with the butter, flour, milk, and ¼ cup of liquid from the peas. Season, add the peas, and pour the sauce over the onions. Cover with corn flakes and bake in a moderate oven, 375° F., for 25 minutes. SERVES 4 TO 6.

To butter corn flakes, add melted butter to them and toss lightly.

Green Beans Parmesan

2 cups cooked green beans
¼ teaspoon salt
½ teaspoon Ac'cent
2 tablespoons grated onion
½ cup coarsely cut toasted almonds
Grated Parmesan cheese
1 can condensed cream of mushroom soup
Milk
Buttered crumbs

Combine the drained cooked beans, salt, Ac'cent, onion, and almonds. Put half the mixture in a buttered baking dish and sprinkle generously with cheese. Pour in half the soup, add a second layer of the bean mixture, and sprinkle with cheese. Fill the half-emptied soup can with milk, mix well, and pour it over the vegetables. Sprinkle with more cheese. Top with buttered crumbs and bake in a moderate (350° F.) oven until the top is browned and the contents bubbling hot, 20 to 25 minutes. SERVES 4.

Mexican Fried Rice

4 tablespoons butter *or* oil
1 cup uncooked rice
2 tomatoes, chopped, *or* 1 cup tomato juice
2 onions, chopped
4 cloves garlic *or* 1 teaspoon garlic purée
1 teaspoon salt
2 cups hot broth *or* bouillon (any kind)

Melt the butter or heat the oil in a large skillet that has a tightly fitting lid. Add the rice and stir until each grain is coated with the fat. Cook over low heat until the rice begins to brown. Add the tomatoes or tomato juice, onions, garlic, salt, and broth; bring to a boil. Cover the skillet, turn the heat as low as possible, and cook until all the liquid has been absorbed, about 30 minutes. Do not stir while the rice is cooking. SERVES 4.

If you like, you may add bits of diced ham, chicken, beef, or pork to this dish to make it more filling.

Asparagus Almond

- 2 pounds asparagus *or* 2 boxes frozen cut pieces of asparagus
- 1 can condensed cream of mushroom soup
- ½ cup half and half *or* light cream
- 1 teaspoon lemon juice
- 1 beaten egg yolk
- Salt and pepper
- ½ cup slivered blanched almonds
- Toast points *or* patty shells
- Thin strips of pimiento

Cook the asparagus in boiling salted water until tender, about 10 minutes. Mix the mushroom soup, cream, lemon juice, and egg yolk; season with salt and pepper, and heat thoroughly. Add the almonds and then add the asparagus. Serve on toast points or in patty shells. Garnish with thin strips of pimiento. SERVES 4 TO 6.

Asparagus Divan

- 1 package frozen asparagus spears
- 3 tablespoons melted butter *or* margarine
- 4 thick slices cooked chicken *or* turkey
- 4 tablespoons grated Parmesan and Romano cheese
- 2 tablespoons flour
- ½ teaspoon salt
- ¼ teaspoon pepper
- 1 cup milk
- 2 egg yolks, beaten

Cook the asparagus spears according to the directions on the package. Drain. Place them in a greased, shallow, oblong baking dish and sprinkle with 1 tablespoon melted butter. Arrange the chicken or turkey on top. Sprinkle with 1 tablespoon grated cheese. Meanwhile, make a white sauce of the remaining 2 tablespoons butter, flour, salt, pepper, and milk. Heat, stirring constantly, until thickened. Pour the hot sauce over the egg yolks, again stirring constantly. Pour this sauce over the chicken and asparagus; top with the remaining cheese. Bake in a moderate oven, 350° F., for 15 minutes or until the cheese is delicately browned. SERVES 4.

Sweet Potato Scallop

6 medium sweet potatoes
4 medium apples
¼ cup brown sugar
3 tablespoons butter
¼ cup water

Pare and slice the potatoes. Pare, core, and slice the apples. Arrange potato and apple slices in alternate layers in a greased casserole, sprinkling each layer with brown sugar and dotting with the butter. Pour ¼ cup water over all, cover, and bake in a moderate oven, 350° F., for 1 hour.

Sherry-Glazed Sweet Potatoes

3 large sweet potatoes *or* yams
6 slices canned pineapple
4 tablespoons butter *or* margarine
½ cup brown sugar
½ cup sherry wine

Boil the sweet potatoes in their jackets for 20 to 30 minutes or until tender. Peel them and cut them in halves lengthwise. Arrange a single layer of pineapple slices in a shallow baking dish, and then place a potato half, cut side down, on top of each pineapple slice. Heat the butter, sugar, and sherry together until the sugar is dissolved; pour this mixture over the potatoes and pineapple. Bake in a moderate (375° F.) oven for 30 minutes, basting often with the syrup from the pan. SERVES 6.

Curried Scalloped Potatoes

2 quarts pared, thinly sliced potatoes
1⅓ cups minced onion
¼ cup flour
2 teaspoons salt
1 teaspoon curry powder
¼ teaspoon pepper
¼ cup butter *or* margarine
3 cups scalded milk

Arrange a layer of potatoes in a greased 3-quart casserole and cover with some of the onion. Combine the flour, salt, curry powder, and pepper; sprinkle some of this mixture over the onion. Dot with some of the butter. Repeat layers until all ingredients are used, ending with butter. Pour the scalded milk over all and sprinkle paprika on the top. Cover the casserole and bake in a moderate (350° F.) oven for 1 hour. Uncover, and bake an additional 15 minutes or until the potatoes are tender. SERVES 8.

Scalloped Tomatoes

4 cups (2 No. 303 cans) peeled tomatoes
8 slices bread, cut into fourths
3 tablespoons butter *or* margarine
Salt and pepper to taste
1 tablespoon sugar
3 tablespoons bacon drippings (optional)

Place all ingredients in a casserole and bake in a moderate (350° F.) oven for about 30 minutes. Serve in vegetable side dishes. If you like a sweeter mixture, you may add more sugar. SERVES 8.

Mexican Beans

5 slices bacon
½ cup finely chopped onion
¼ cup finely chopped green pepper
½ teaspoon powdered mustard
1 teaspoon curry powder
1 tablespoon hot water
2½ cups (No. 2 can) tomatoes, drained
2 16-ounce cans pork and beans

Cut one slice of bacon into small pieces; fry them in a skillet over moderate heat until crisp. Remove the pieces. Add the onion and the pepper to the bacon drippings and cook these over low heat for 5 minutes. Combine the mustard, curry powder, and 1 tablespoon hot water; stir this into the onion mixture and then add the browned bacon pieces. Stir in the tomato pulp and baked beans. Heat thoroughly. Pour the mixture into a casserole and top with 4 slices of bacon. Bake in a hot (400° F.) oven for about 25 to 30 minutes. SERVES 6 TO 8.

Red Kraut Sweet and Sour

3 pounds red cabbage, shredded
1 large onion, shredded
4 apples, peeled and cut into wedges
¼ cup vinegar
5 tablespoons shortening, margarine *or* butter
Sugar
Salt

Cook all ingredients together in a covered saucepan over low heat for about 30 minutes or until the cabbage is tender. Do not add water. The quantity of salt and sugar is governed by your own personal preference. SERVES 6.

Cucumbers in Sour Cream

- 3 cucumbers
- 1½ teaspoons salt
- ⅛ teaspoon pepper
- 3 tablespoons minced chives *or* scallions
- 1 cup commercial sour cream
- 2 tablespoons lemon juice

Pare and then thinly slice the cucumbers. Add salt, pepper, minced chives, sour cream, and lemon juice. Chill about 30 minutes. This makes a wonderful side dish. SERVES 6.

Curried Rice

- 2 cups cooked rice
- 1 green pepper, diced
- 1 onion, minced fine
- 2 cups (No. 303 can) tomatoes
- 4 tablespoons melted fat
- 1½ teaspoons curry powder (or more to taste)

Mix all the ingredients together and bake in a greased casserole in a moderate (325° F.) oven for about 30 minutes. SERVES 6.

Rice Mexicano

- ¼ cup fat *or* drippings
- ¾ cup chopped onion
- ¼ cup chopped minced celery
- ¼ cup chopped green pepper
- 1¼ cups uncooked rice
- 2½ cups (No. 2 can) tomatoes
- 2 beef bouillon cubes
- 1 teaspoon salt
- ¼ teaspoon pepper
- ½ teaspoon chili powder
- 1½ cups grated or cubed American cheese
- ⅔ cup chopped, cooked ham (optional)

Heat the fat in a saucepan; add the onions, celery, and green pepper and cook until soft but not brown. Remove them from the pan. Brown the rice lightly; combine it with the onion-pepper mixture and turn all into a large greased casserole. In the same saucepan, combine the tomatoes, bouillon cubes, salt, pepper, and chili powder and bring to a quick boil. Be sure bouillon cubes are dissolved. Add this to the casserole. Sprinkle with cheese (and ham if you use it). Bake, uncovered, in a moderate oven, 350° F., until the rice is grainy and tender but not mushy, about 25 minutes. SERVES 4.

Banana Fritters

- Salad oil *or* melted fat
- 2 to 3 firm bananas
- ¼ cup flour
- Fritter batter

Heat the salad oil or fat to 375° F. To deep fry, have at least 3 inches of fat in the kettle. Otherwise, use 1½ to 2 inches of oil in a frying pan. Peel the bananas; cut each one into 3 or 4 diagonal pieces and roll them in flour. Dip them into fritter batter, making sure each piece is completely coated. Fry for about 6 minutes or until golden brown, turning them once or twice. Drain the pieces on paper towels. Serve hot with the main course or as a dessert either with a shaking of powdered sugar over them or with a hot fruit sauce. SERVES 4 TO 6.

Fritter Batter

- 1 cup sifted flour
- 2 teaspoons baking powder
- ½ teaspoon salt
- ¼ cup sugar
- 1 egg, well beaten
- ⅓ cup milk
- 2 teaspoons melted shortening

Sift the flour, baking powder, salt and sugar into a mixing bowl. Combine the egg, milk, and shortening; add to the dry ingredients, and mix until the batter is smooth. This is a stiff batter, but do not thin it.

Sweet-Sour Cabbage

- 5 cups shredded cabbage
- 4 slices bacon, diced
- 2 tablespoons brown sugar
- 2 tablespoons flour
- ⅓ cup vinegar
- Salt and pepper
- ½ cup water
- 1 small onion, sliced

Cook the cabbage in boiling salted water for 7 minutes. Fry the bacon; remove it from the pan and blend flour and sugar into the bacon drippings. Add the vinegar, seasonings and ½ cup of water, and cook until thick. Add the onion, bacon, and cabbage; heat through. SERVES 4 TO 6.

Asparagus Soufflé

- 2 tablespoons butter *or* margarine
- 2 tablespoons flour
- 1 teaspoon salt
- ¼ teaspoon pepper
- 1 cup milk
- 1 cup cooked asparagus cut into 1-inch pieces
- 6 eggs, separated

Melt the butter; add the flour, salt, pepper and milk. Cook over low heat until thickened, stirring constantly. Add the asparagus.

Separate the eggs; beat the whites until stiff and the yolks until lemon colored. Stir the white sauce into the yolks and then gently fold in the whites. Turn the mixture into a greased casserole or soufflé dish and bake in a preheated moderate (375° F.) oven until firm and brown on top, about 40 minutes. SERVES 4.

5

Salads, salad dressings, and sauces

EVERY MEAL SHOULD HAVE one conversation-piece dish. You may have a favorite main course that you serve for guests or for the family, but you can always change the look of a menu by changing the salad or a sauce.

When food looks good, appetites are better, so I have given different ideas for garnishing salad plates. Oftentimes you can change the whole look of a plain green salad with vinegar and oil dressing by serving toasted Parmesan cheese croutons on top of it.

If your main course is a hearty one, then use a light salad or a tossed green salad with an unusual dressing. If you are planning a "pick up" supper or a one-dish casserole, make your salad hearty.

Asparagus Vinaigrette

- 2 pounds cooked asparagus
- ¼ cup red wine
- ¼ cup red wine vinegar
- ¾ cup olive oil
- 1 teaspoon salt
- ½ teaspoon freshly ground pepper
- 2 teaspoons finely chopped shallots *or* green onions
- 1 tablespoon capers
- 1 tablespoon chopped green olives
- ½ teaspoon finely chopped thyme

Place the asparagus in a bowl. Combine all other ingredients to make a marinade and pour over the asparagus. Chill for 24 hours before serving. SERVES 6 TO 8.

Cucumbers Vinaigrette

- 4 long, slender cucumbers
- 3 chicken bouillon cubes
- ⅔ cup salad oil
- ⅓ cup vinegar
- 1 teaspoon salt
- ½ teaspoon sugar
- ⅛ teaspoon Cayenne pepper
- ¼ teaspoon dry mustard
- 3 tablespoons finely chopped green onions
- 3 tablespoons minced green onion tops
- 3 tablespoons minced green pepper
- 6 tablespoons finely chopped sweet pickle
- 4 tablespoons finely chopped pimiento
- 1 hard-cooked egg, finely chopped

Peel the cucumbers as thinly as possible and cut each one into 6 lengthwise strips. Cover the strips with boiling water, add the chicken bouillon cubes, and boil over high heat for 10 minutes. Drain. Combine in a jar the salad oil, vinegar, salt, sugar, Cayenne, and dry mustard; shake well to blend. Add the chopped onions, onion tops, green pepper, sweet pickle, pimiento, and hard-cooked egg. Mix well and pour over the cucumbers in a relish bowl. Store in the refrigerator for at least 2 hours before serving.

Potato Salad

- 6 potatoes, boiled and peeled
- 6 hard-cooked eggs
- 2 medium onions
- Mayonnaise
- Salt and pepper

Cut the potatoes in fairly large dice and chop the eggs. Combine all ingredients, using just enough mayonnaise to hold the salad together. Chill thoroughly. Before serving, taste the salad and add more seasonings and mayonnaise if necessary. SERVES 4 TO 6.

Kidney Bean Salad

- 2½ cups (No. 2 can) kidney beans, drained
- 1 cup thinly sliced celery
- ½ cup chopped dill pickles
- 2 tablespoons chopped pimiento
- 2 tablespoons chopped green pepper
- 1 tablespoon minced onion
- 1 teaspoon salt
- Dash of pepper
- ⅓ cup mayonnaise *or* salad dressing

Combine the kidney beans, celery, pickles, pimiento, green pepper, onions, salt, and pepper. Toss this lightly with the salad dressing and chill well. Serve on crisp lettuce on individual salad plates and top with additional salad dressing. SERVES 6.

Stuffed Lettuce Salad

- ½ cup shredded, blanched almonds
- 2½ cups cooked peas
- 1 cup cubed sharp American cheese
- 1 tablespoon finely chopped pimiento
- ¼ cup chopped dill pickle *or* pickle relish
- ½ teaspoon prepared mustard
- ½ teaspoon salt
- Dash of pepper
- ⅓ cup mayonnaise
- 1 large, firm head iceberg lettuce
- 8 deviled egg halves

Combine the almonds, peas, cheese, pimiento, pickle, mustard, salt, pepper, and mayonnaise. Cut the lettuce almost through into 8 wedges, leaving the head joined at the stem end. Pull the wedges apart gently and fill the center with the salad. Garnish the platter with deviled egg halves. Chill well before serving. SERVES 8.

Macaroni-Cheese Salad

- ½ pound shell macaroni, cooked
- ¾ cup sliced celery
- ½ cup sliced green onions
- 6 radishes, sliced
- 1 cup slivered sharp American cheese
- 2 tablespoons chopped parsley
- ½ cup mayonnaise
- 2 tablespoons lemon juice
- 2 teaspoons prepared mustard
- ½ teaspoon celery seeds
- 2 teaspoons salt
- ⅛ teaspoon pepper
- 1 head iceberg lettuce

Combine all ingredients except the lettuce. Chill in the refrigerator for at least 2 hours to blend the flavors thoroughly. Serve in a large salad bowl lined with crisp lettuce. Garnish the top of salad with parsley sprigs and radish roses. SERVES 8.

Hot Mustard Slaw

- 4 cups shredded cabbage
- ½ cup mayonnaise
- 1 teaspoon vinegar
- 1 tablespoon mustard with horseradish
- ½ teaspoon sugar
- Salt to taste

Place the cabbage in a skillet. Combine the rest of the ingredients and toss with the cabbage. Cook the mixture over very low heat until hot, stirring frequently. SERVES 4.

This can be served cold, too, by combining the ingredients as above and not heating. Let it stand 15 minutes before serving it as a cold slaw.

Hot Potato Salad

- ½ cup minced onion
- 2 tablespoons salad oil
- 2 teaspoons flour
- 1 tablespoon sugar
- 2½ teaspoons salt
- Freshly ground pepper to taste
- ⅓ cup vinegar
- ⅓ cup water
- 1 teaspoon celery seed
- 5 cups sliced, cooked potatoes
- 1 tablespoon finely chopped green pepper
- 1 tablespoon finely chopped pimiento
- 1 tablespoon chopped dill pickle
- 1 tablespoon minced parsley

Sauté ¼ cup minced onion in oil until tender. Combine the flour, sugar, salt, and pepper. Slowly add the vinegar and ⅓ cup water. Mix well. Add this to the cooked onion and simmer until slightly thickened. Add the remaining onion and all other ingredients and toss lightly until all are well coated with the dressing. Serve hot or cold. Plain boiled franks are delightful with it. SERVES 6.

Wilted Spinach

- Fresh spinach
- 1 hard-cooked egg, chopped
- 3 or 4 slices bacon, diced
- ⅓ cup vinegar
- 1 teaspoon sugar
- Pepper
- ½ teaspoon salt
- ¼ teaspoon dry mustard
- ½ cup water

Wash and dry the spinach; cut it into half-inch shreds and pile it into a large bowl. Add the chopped egg. Fry the bacon until crisp; pour off all but 2 tablespoons of the fat. Mix the vinegar, sugar, pepper, salt, mustard, and ½ cup of water and add this to the bacon in the skillet. Bring to a boil and then pour it hot over spinach in the bowl. Toss and serve immediately. SERVES 4 TO 6.

Wilted Lettuce Salad Bowl

1 large head lettuce
½ cup minced green onion (including some of the tops)
½ teaspoon salt
Dash of pepper
4 slices bacon, diced
¼ cup vinegar

Shred lettuce coarsely into a salad bowl. Add the onion, salt, and pepper. Fry the bacon bits until crisp and drain them on a paper towel. Add the vinegar to the bacon fat, heat to boiling, and pour over the lettuce, tossing the salad well. Sprinkle the top with crisp bacon bits. SERVES 4.

Molded Chicken Mousse

I especially like this recipe for molded chicken mousse. For a wedding luncheon or anniversary buffet, you can make what appear to be entwined wedding rings. Make the mousse in two small molds; unmold both on one large platter. Cut a section from one of the rings and, using a spatula, very gently place the cut-out section within the whole ring so that the cut edges touch the inside edge of the whole ring. Bring the remainder of the cut ring close to the whole one, so that the cut edges touch the outside of the whole ring. It will look like interlocking rings and will be quite a conversation piece.

3 envelopes unflavored gelatine
½ cup cold water
1 can condensed cream of mushroom soup
2½ cups chicken broth
2 teaspoons salt
¼ teaspoon pepper
1 cup mayonnaise
5 cups finely diced cooked chicken
1½ cups finely diced celery
1 teaspoon Worcestershire sauce
1½ tablespoons grated onion
2 tablespoons lemon juice
2 tablespoons chopped parsley
1 cup heavy cream, whipped stiff
Fresh water cress for garnish

Sprinkle the gelatine on ½ cup cold water to soften. Combine the soup, chicken broth, salt, and pepper in a saucepan and cook until blended and hot. Dissolve the gelatine in this hot mixture. Allow to cool, then blend in the mayonnaise. Add the chicken, celery, Worcestershire sauce, onion, lemon juice, and parsley. Fold in the whipped cream. Rinse a 3-quart ring mold or two 3-pint molds in cold water and spoon the mixture into them. Chill until set, at least 5 hours or overnight. Unmold on crisp lettuce and garnish with fresh water cress. Serve with French dressing. SERVES 16.

Chop Suey Salad

- 2 cups bean sprouts
- French dressing
- 2 cups cooked meat, cubed
- 2 cups cooked red kidney beans
- 1/4 cup diced pimiento
- 1 cup diced celery
- 1/2 cup diced onion
- Soy sauce to taste
- Salt and pepper to taste
- 1/2 cup mayonnaise

Marinate the bean sprouts in French dressing. Add all other ingredients in the order listed and mix thoroughly. This is a good way to use leftover meat. SERVES 6 TO 8.

Hot Turkey Salad

- 2 cups cubed cooked turkey
- 1/2 cup chopped toasted almonds
- 2 cups sliced celery
- 1/2 teaspoon salt
- 2 teaspoons grated onion
- 2 tablespoons lemon juice
- 1 cup mayonnaise *or* cooked salad dressing
- 1/2 cup grated American cheese
- 1 cup crushed potato chips

Combine all ingredients except the cheese and potato chips. Toss lightly. Pile lightly in individual bakers or custard cups and sprinkle with the grated cheese and crushed potato chips. Bake in a hot oven, 450° F., for 10 minutes. Serve hot, garnished with a sprig of parsley. SERVES 4 TO 5.

Cabbage Pineapple Slaw

- 3 cups shredded, crisp cabbage
- 1 cup (9-ounce can) pineapple tidbits, drained
- 1 cup diced apples
- 1/2 cup chopped celery
- 1 cup (10) marshmallows, cut in eighths, *or* 1 cup miniature marshmallows
- 1/2 cup mayonnaise
- Apple wedges, unpeeled

Combine all ingredients except the apple wedges and toss until well coated with mayonnaise. Line a salad bowl with garden lettuce, fill with salad, and garnish with apple wedges. SERVES 4.

You may use the chunk-style pineapple, but cut each chunk in half.

Green Goddess Salad

The recipe for Green Goddess Salad was first heard of on the West Coast, and it became so popular that many variations of it were invented by people who traveled back to their homes with the idea of whipping up their own version of this most delightful salad. This one is, I think, the original Green Goddess Salad and Dressing.

I am also giving you another version of the dressing, which can be used on any type of greens and to which fresh crabmeat, lobster, or shrimp can be added to make a hearty summer salad.

- ½ head Romaine
- 1 stalk chicory
- 1 bunch leaf lettuce
- 1 cup cooked shrimp
- 3 medium tomatoes, peeled and quartered
- ½ cup julienne-style beets

Tear the Romaine, chicory, and lettuce into bite-sized pieces. Heap on individual salad plates. Arrange shrimp, tomato wedges and beets on top. SERVES 4 TO 6. Serve with the following dressing:

Dressing

- 1 clove garlic, grated *or* ¼ teaspoon garlic purée
- ¼ to ½ teaspoon salt
- ½ teaspoon dry mustard
- 1 teaspoon Worcestershire sauce
- 2 tablespoons anchovy paste
- 1 cup mayonnaise
- 2 to 3 tablespoons finely chopped chives *or* green onions
- 2 tablespoons finely chopped, cooked shrimp

Combine garlic, salt, mustard, Worcestershire, and anchovy paste; blend well. Add the mayonnaise, chopped chives, and shrimp and mix well. MAKES ABOUT 1½ CUPS.

Green Goddess Salad Dressing

- 1 cup mayonnaise
- 1 clove garlic, crushed
- 3 anchovy fillets, finely minced
- ¼ cup finely chopped chives *or* green onion tops
- ¼ cup chopped parsley
- 1 tablespoon lemon juice
- 1 tablespoon tarragon vinegar
- ½ teaspoon salt
- Coarsely ground pepper
- ½ cup commercial sour cream

Combine all the ingredients, pour into a covered container, and store in the refrigerater until you are ready to use it. At serving time, tear salad greens into bite-sized pieces and add the dressing after shaking it well. Toss lightly to blend. Serve plain as an appetizer salad or salad course, or add fresh crabmeat, lobster, or shrimp and serve as a summer main dish. MAKES ABOUT 2 CUPS.

Baked Seafood Salad

- 1 cup cooked, cleaned shrimp
- 1 cup flaked fresh crabmeat
- ¼ cup grated onion
- 1 cup sliced celery
- ½ cup chopped pecans
- 1 cup mayonnaise
- 1 tablespoon lemon juice
- 1 tablespoon Worcestershire sauce
- ½ teaspoon salt
- Dash of pepper
- ½ cup buttered fine bread crumbs

Split the shrimp lengthwise and combine them with the rest of the ingredients except bread crumbs. Spoon the mixture into individual baking shells or a 10 x 6 x 2-inch baking dish and sprinkle with the buttered bread crumbs. Bake in a moderate (350° F.) oven for 30 minutes. SERVES 4 TO 6.

For luncheon, serve this salad with spiced watermelon pickle or other pickled preserve, potato chips, and tiny hot biscuits.

Jellied Tuna Salad

- 2 cans chunk-style tuna
- 2 hard-cooked eggs, chopped
- ½ cup chopped olives
- 2 tablespoons capers
- 1 tablespoon chopped chives *or* minced onion
- 1 envelope unflavored gelatine
- ¼ cup cold water
- 2 cups mayonnaise
- Crisp salad greens
- Tomatoes, skinned and quartered
- 1 avocado, pared and sliced
- French dressing

Combine the tuna, eggs, olives, capers, and chives or onion. Soften the gelatine in ¼ cup cold water in a measuring cup. Set the cup in a pan of boiling water, stirring occasionally until the gelatine is dissolved. Stir in the mayonnaise, then mix well with tuna mixture. Pour into a 1¼-quart ring mold which has been rinsed with cold water. Chill until firm. Unmold, garnish with crisp greens, and fill the center with tomato quarters and avocado slices seasoned with French dressing. SERVES 6 TO 8.

Heavenly Salad

- 1 envelope plain gelatine
- 3/4 cup cold water
- 3/4 cup syrup from canned pineapple
- 1/4 cup sugar
- 1/8 teaspoon salt
- 1/4 cup lemon juice
- 1 3-ounce package cream cheese
- 1 medium-sized avocado
- 1 cup canned pineapple chunks

Soften the gelatine in 1/4 cup cold water. Combine 1/2 cup water with the pineapple syrup, sugar, and salt. Heat. Dissolve the softened gelatine in the hot liquid, blend in the lemon juice, and allow to cool until the mixture is the consistency of unbeaten egg white. Cut the cream cheese into small cubes. Cut the avocado into halves, remove the seed, and skin and dice the fruit. Fold the cheese cubes, avocado cubes, and pineapple chunks into the gelatine. Turn the mixture into individual molds and chill until firm. To serve, unmold onto salad greens. SERVES 6.

Angel Salad

We can always tell in our kitchen office when women are beginning to think about Spring parties, because requests for Angel Salad come pouring in. This is a large recipe that will serve 12 generously. The salad is a beautiful pale green, and it makes a lovely luncheon plate for a bridge party or a book review club meeting. Garnish the salad with water cress, add a spiced peach and tiny hot buttered baking powder biscuits, and stand back and wait for the compliments.

- 2 packages lime-flavored gelatin
- 2 cups hot water
- 2 3-ounce packages cream cheese
- 1 small can crushed pineapple, drained
- 1 2-ounce jar pimientos, chopped
- 1 cup celery, diced
- 1 cup pecans, chopped
- 1/2 pint whipping cream

Mix the gelatin into 2 cups hot water; let cool. Mash the cream cheese and add the pineapple, pimientos, celery, and pecans. Fold this mixture into the cooled gelatin and refrigerate until it becomes thick but not firmly congealed. Whip the cream and fold it in. Rinse a mold in cold water, pour in the mixture, and chill until firm. SERVES 12.

Crunchy Pineapple-Cranberry Mold

- 2½ cups (No. 2 can) crushed pineapple
- 2 packages lemon-flavored gelatin
- ½ cup lemon juice
- 3 tablespoons shredded *or* chopped orange peel
- 3 cups whole cranberry sauce
- ⅓ cup chopped walnuts
- Canned pineapple slices

Drain the syrup from the pineapple and add enough water to make 1½ cups liquid. Heat the liquid to boiling, pour it over the gelatin, and stir until the gelatin is completely dissolved. Stir in the crushed pineapple and all the remaining ingredients except pineapple slices. Turn the mixture into a rinsed 10-inch ring mold and chill until firm. Dip the mold in hot water for about 15 seconds, then invert it over the serving plate to unmold. Garnish with pineapple slices and serve with a fluffy dressing. SERVES 8 TO 10.

Frosted Cranberry Salad

- 1 package lemon-flavored gelatin
- 1½ cups canned orange juice, heated
- 1 1-pound can whole cranberry sauce
- ½ cup chopped celery
- ½ cup chopped nuts
- 1 cup cottage cheese
- 2 tablespoons mayonnaise

Dissolve the gelatin in the hot orange juice. Add the cranberry sauce and stir until blended. Chill until the mixture begins to thicken. Add the celery and nuts, put into a mold that has been rinsed in cold water, and chill until firm. Unmold onto crisp greens and frost the top with a mixture of the cottage cheese and mayonnaise. SERVES 6.

Holiday Cranberry Salad

- 1 package lemon-flavored gelatin
- 1 cup hot water
- ½ cup pineapple juice
- 2 cups fresh cranberries
- 1 medium apple
- ½ cup sugar

Dissolve the gelatin in 1 cup hot water; add the pineapple juice and chill until partially set. Grind the cranberries and apple, mix with the sugar, and add to the partially set gelatin. Pour into a

1½-pint mold or 6 individual molds and chill until firm. Unmold onto lettuce. SERVES 6.

Bing Cherry Ring

3½ cups (No. 2½ can) bing cherries, pitted
2 cups orange juice
1½ cups sherry wine
1 cup sugar
3 tablespoons unflavored gelatine
1 cup nut meats

Drain the juice from the cherries, measure, and add enough water to make 2 cups. Combine with 1½ cups orange juice, wine, and sugar; bring to a boil. Meanwhile, soak the gelatine in the remaining ½ cup orange juice, then dissolve it in the hot fruit syrup. When the mixture begins to set, stir in the pitted, well drained cherries and the nut meats and pour into a mold which has been rinsed in cold water. Chill until firm. Unmold and serve with cream cheese dressing, made by thinning cream cheese with light cream or half and half until it is pourable.

Pear Snowdrift Salad

6 ripe Anjou pears
Salad greens
1 cup commercial sour cream
½ teaspoon nutmeg
1 teaspoon sugar
Few grains of salt
1 teaspoon lemon juice
¼ cup toasted almonds

Cut the pears in half, remove the cores, and arrange the halves on a bed of salad greens. Combine the sour cream, nutmeg, sugar, salt, and lemon juice. Fill the pear centers with the seasoned cream and sprinkle with the toasted almonds. SERVES 6.

Frosted Grapes

Dip small bunches of grapes into undiluted frozen lemonade concentrate and then into granulated sugar. Chill the grapes thoroughly before using as a garnish on molded salads.

Garnish for Fruit Plate

Roll cream cheese into balls. Roll the cheese balls in finely chopped nuts or chopped water cress.

Bali Hai Poppy Seed Dressing

At the Bali Hai Restaurant in Dallas, Mr. Tony Bifano serves a most delightful salad as a separate course before the main course. Served in a bowl, the salad consists of diced fresh fruit, including watermelon, fresh blueberries, fresh pears, and any other fruit that is in season, with this dressing. On the very top of the salad is a lovely cluster of fresh grapes, frosted in bright blue sugar.

You'll find that this poppy seed dressing is good either on a fruit platter or on greens.

- 2 cups sugar
- 1 tablespoon salt
- 1 tablespoon dry mustard
- ½ teaspoon paprika
- 1 cup cider vinegar
- ½ cup onion juice
- 3 cups salad oil (*not* olive oil)
- 1 tablespoon poppy seeds

Combine the sugar, salt, dry mustard, and paprika; add the vinegar and onion juice gradually while mixing at slow speed in a mixer. When it is well mixed, very slowly add the salad oil in the same manner. Continue beating until the dressing thickens, then fold in the poppy seeds. Keep under refrigeration. MAKES ABOUT 4 CUPS.

Sour Cream–Roquefort Dressing

- 1¼ ounces Roquefort cheese
- ½ cup commercial sour cream
- 2 tablespoons lemon juice
- ¼ teaspoon salt
- Dash of pepper

Crumble the cheese and combine it with the other ingredients. Serve with salad greens, lettuce and sliced tomatoes, lettuce wedges, or just plain sliced tomatoes. MAKES ABOUT 1 CUP.

Sour Cream Dressing

- 1 tablespoon flour
- 2 teaspoons sugar
- ½ teaspoon salt
- ½ teaspoon paprika
- Dash of Cayenne pepper
- ½ cup commercial sour cream
- 2 tablespoons vinegar

Mix the dry ingredients in top of double boiler, slowly stir in sour cream, and cook over boiling water until thick, about 8 minutes, stirring constantly. Remove from the heat, stir in the vinegar, and let cool. This dressing can be used with almost any vegetable or green salad. MAKES ABOUT ¾ CUP.

Caviar Salad Dressing

1 tablespoon horseradish
½ cup mayonnaise
Dash of lemon juice
1 small jar black caviar

Stir the horseradish into the mayonnaise and mix well. Add the lemon juice, then fold in the caviar. Serve on hearts of lettuce. MAKES ENOUGH FOR 4 SALADS.

Deep-Sea Salad Dressing

½ cup mayonnaise
4 tablespoons catsup
2 tablespoons lemon juice
2 hard-cooked eggs, chopped

Combine all ingredients. Mix with fresh or canned salmon or tuna or serve in a side dish. MAKES 1¼ CUPS.

This is excellent for a hearty salad—the kind the men prefer.

Orange Chutney French Dressing

This recipe uses one of the dehydrated salad dressing mixes. These mixes are wonderful sources of change for the four basic types of salad dressings using salad oil and vinegar. Try mine, and then make up your own favorite the next time you use a salad dressing mix. This is one of the new convenience foods that are such great fun to use. And it gives you the opportunity to have all of your herbs and spices in one little foil package.

1 package Old-Fashioned French dressing mix
½ cup orange juice
½ cup salad oil
1 tablespoon honey
1 tablespoon finely chopped chutney
2 tablespoons finely chopped pecans (optional)

Empty the contents of the package of mix into a pint jar that has a screw top. Add the orange juice, salad oil, honey, chutney, and pecans. Shake well for about 30 seconds. Chill. Serve over fruit salads. This is also delicious with water cress. MAKES 1¼ CUPS.

Tomato Juice French Dressing

1 package Old-Fashioned French dressing mix
1½ cups tomato juice
¼ cup vinegar
¼ cup salad oil
¼ teaspoon liquid nonnutritive sweetener (optional)

Empty the contents of the package of mix into a quart jar that has a screw top. Add the tomato juice, vinegar, salad oil, and liquid sweetener. Shake well for about 30 seconds. Chill. Serve with mixed green salads. MAKES 2 CUPS.

This is a low-calorie dressing—1 tablespoon contains only 16 calories.

Pitcairn Salad Dressing

- 1 quart mayonnaise
- ½ pound Roquefort cheese, crumbled
- 1 tablespoon Worcestershire sauce
- 1 cup vinegar
- 4 tablespoons chopped chives
- ½ cup sugar

Mix all ingredients thoroughly and serve cold. Leftover dressing can be stored in a tightly covered jar in the refrigerator.

Lemon Cocktail Sauce

- 6 tablespoons mayonnaise
- 1 teaspoon horseradish
- ½ teaspoon grated onion
- 1 teaspoon prepared mustard
- 2 tablespoons lemon juice

Combine all ingredients and mix well. MAKES ½ CUP.

This is a tart sauce for shrimp or crabmeat cocktails, wholly different from the usual red sauce.

Sour Cream–Caper Sauce

- ½ cup commercial sour cream
- ½ cup mayonnaise
- 2 tablespoons finely chopped capers
- 2 teaspoons caper juice
- 1½ teaspoons onion juice
- ¼ teaspoon salt
- Dash of pepper
- 2 tablespoons catsup

Combine all ingredients and blend well. Serve with shrimp, lobster, or crab cocktail, or with hors d'oeuvres of fish, eggs, or vegetables. MAKES ABOUT 1¼ CUPS.

Hollandaise Sauce

There are many ways you can whip up a quick hot Hollandaise sauce for vegetables or fish. One way is to heat mayonnaise in a saucepan and add a little Cayenne pepper and lemon juice.

Another quick version is to combine equal parts of mayonnaise and commercial sour cream and add lemon juice to taste and a little salt. But I'd like you to try a *real* Hollandaise sauce so you'll know that it isn't done by magic. It isn't difficult, and it's a good workable recipe.

3 egg yolks
½ cup (1 stick) butter
¼ teaspoon salt
1 tablespoon lemon juice

Put the egg yolks, butter, and salt in the top of a double boiler over hot, but not boiling, water. Stir until thickened, and then add the lemon juice gradually. If the temperature is too high, the sauce may separate. If it does, remove it from the heat and add to the mixture a few drops of the hot water from the lower part of the double boiler. Beat well. SERVES 4.

Tabasco Cocktail Sauce

1 cup tomato catsup *or* chili sauce
¼ teaspoon Tabasco sauce
2 tablespoons lemon juice
¼ teaspoon salt
1 tablespoon horseradish
2 tablespoons finely minced celery
1 teaspoon grated onion (optional)

Mix all ingredients and chill before serving. MAKES 1¼ CUPS.

Hot Cucumber Mayonnaise Sauce

¾ cup chopped cucumber
½ cup mayonnaise
¼ cup commercial sour cream
2 tablespoons milk
2 tablespoons chopped parsley
4 stuffed olives, chopped
¾ teaspoon salt
1 tablespoon lemon juice

Sauté the cucumber in 2 tablespoons mayonnaise. Blend the remaining 6 tablespoons mayonnaise with the rest of the ingredients, add to the cucumbers, and heat slowly until thickened. An excellent sauce to serve with fish. MAKES 1½ CUPS.

Butter 'n' Nutmeg Sauce

Put 3 tablespoons butter or margarine into a hot frying pan and add fish. When the fish is brown, turn it and add a mixture of ⅓ cup soft butter or margarine, 3 tablespoons lemon juice, and 1 teaspoon nutmeg. Brown and serve the fish on a deep platter with the sauce poured over it. Garnish with lemon wedges. This is a new and unusual flavor, excellent with all fish fillets.

Lemon Butter

- 2 tablespoons fresh lemon juice
- 3 tablespoons butter
- 1/4 teaspoon salt
- 1/4 teaspoon paprika
- 1 tablespoon finely chopped parsley

Blend all ingredients thoroughly and serve on hot steak, chops, or fish. A garnish of lemon quarters provides more tartness, if desired.

Tabasco Tartare Sauce

- 1/2 teaspoon Tabasco sauce
- 1 teaspoon vinegar
- 1 cup mayonnaise
- 1 tablespoon minced onion
- 1 tablespoon chopped parsley
- 1 tablespoon chopped green olives
- 2 tablespoons chopped pickle

Stir the Tabasco and vinegar into the mayonnaise, then add the remaining ingredients and mix well. MAKES ABOUT 1 1/3 CUPS.

Hot Tartare Sauce

- 1 cup mayonnaise
- 2 tablespoons finely chopped parsley
- 2 tablespoons capers *or* 2 tablespoons chopped bread and butter pickles
- 1/2 teaspoon grated onion
- 2 tablespoons lemon juice
- 1/4 cup water
- 1/8 teaspoon salt
- Dash of pepper

Blend all ingredients and heat in the top of a double boiler for 5 minutes. An excellent sauce over baked, broiled, or fried fish. MAKES ABOUT 1 CUP.

Tomato Sauce for Fish or Meat

- 3/4 cup tomato juice
- 2 tablespoons chopped parsley
- 1 bay leaf
- 1/4 cup mayonnaise
- 2 tablespoons flour
- 1 cup milk
- 1/4 teaspoon salt
- Dash of pepper
- Pinch of sugar
- 2 tablespoons tomato catsup

Combine the tomato juice, parsley, and bay leaf; simmer for 15 minutes. Remove the bay leaf. Blend the mayonnaise and flour, add the milk, and stir until the mixture is smooth. Add the mayonnaise mixture to the tomato juice with the salt, pepper, sugar, and catsup. Cook, stirring constantly, until thickened. MAKES ABOUT 1⅓ CUPS.

Whipped Horseradish Sauce

Whip ½ cup heavy cream until stiff, then fold in ¼ cup well-drained prepared horseradish sauce. Serve immediately. Delicious with ham, corned beef, or pork and sauerkraut.

Salsa Fria

- 2½ cups (No. 2 can) solid-pack tomatoes
- 1 onion, finely chopped
- 1 can green chilies, chopped
- 1 teaspoon orégano
- 2 tablespoons wine vinegar
- 1 tablespoon oil
- Salt and pepper to taste
- 1 teaspoon coriander

Chop the tomatoes finely; mix all the ingredients together and serve as a cold meat sauce instead of catsup or chili sauce.

Wine Sauce for Fish, Chicken, or Meat

- 3 tablespoons flour
- ¼ teaspoon salt
- ¾ cup light cream
- 1 cup hot rich chicken stock *or* 2 bouillon cubes in 1 cup boiling water
- 3 tablespoons butter
- ¼ cup sherry *or* sauterne wine

Combine the flour and salt; gradually add the cream and stir until smooth. Place over low heat, add the hot bouillon, and cook over low heat, stirring constantly, until the sauce is smooth and thickened. Add butter and sherry or sauterne. MAKES 2 CUPS.

Lemon Tartare Sauce

- 1 cup mayonnaise
- ½ teaspoon onion juice *or* 1 tablespoon chopped chives
- 2 tablespoons chopped green relish *or* green pepper
- Fresh lemon juice

Combine all ingredients in the order listed, thinning the sauce to the desired consistency with lemon juice. To vary the sauce, add chopped celery, chili sauce, or Worcestershire sauce.

Steak Barbecue Sauce

- ¼ cup vinegar
- 2 tablespoons sugar
- 1 tablespoon prepared mustard
- ¼ teaspoon coarsely ground black pepper
- 1½ teaspoons salt
- ⅛ teaspoon Tabasco sauce
- 1 lemon, thickly sliced
- 1 medium onion, sliced
- ¼ cup butter *or* margarine
- 2 tablespoons Worcestershire sauce
- ½ cup Taylor N.Y. State Burgundy wine

Combine all but the last three ingredients and simmer for 20 minutes. Add butter, Worcestershire, and wine; bring to a boil. Strain. Use to brush steaks while grilling. MAKES ABOUT 1½ CUPS.

Wine Vinegar Barbecue Sauce

- 1 cup catsup
- ½ cup wine vinegar
- ¾ cup water
- 3 tablespoons brown sugar
- 2 tablespoons Worcestershire sauce
- ½ teaspoon salt
- 1 teaspoon dry mustard
- 1 teaspoon chili powder
- Generous dashes Cayenne pepper *or* Tabasco sauce
- 1 onion, grated
- 1 teaspoon celery seed
- Liquid smoke *or* smoked salt

Combine all ingredients thoroughly and use as a basting sauce for spareribs, pork chops, or beef ribs.

Barbecue Sauce

- 3 tablespoons butter *or* margarine
- ⅓ cup minced onion
- 1 cup catsup
- ⅓ cup vinegar
- 2 tablespoons brown sugar
- ½ cup water
- 2 teaspoons prepared mustard
- 2 tablespoons Worcestershire sauce
- ⅛ teaspoon salt

Melt the butter in a saucepan, add the onion, and sauté until tender but not brown. Add the rest of the ingredients, cover, and simmer for 10 minutes. An excellent basting sauce for charcoal-broiled chicken. MAKES ABOUT 2½ CUPS.

Jetton's Barbecue Sauce

Walter Jetton and his two sons, of Fort Worth, Texas, have the most fabulous barbecue catering service in the world. They can feed five or twenty-five thousand, and they have traveled all over the country to set up parties and furnish the food and service. Mr. Jetton has specially built trucks with baking ovens on the back to bake Texas biscuits and rolls, and refrigerated space in the middle to furnish the best cole slaw I have ever tasted. He was nice enough to give me his barbecue sauce recipe, which I am passing along to you—although, of course, Mr. Jetton makes it in five gallon quantities! The sauce can be used on ribs, beef, pork, or chicken.

- 1 cup tomato catsup
- ½ cup cider vinegar
- 1 teaspoon sugar
- 1 teaspoon chili powder
- ⅛ teaspoon salt
- 1½ cups water
- 3 stalks celery, chopped
- Dash of black pepper
- 3 bay leaves
- 1 clove garlic
- 2 tablespoons chopped onion
- 4 tablespoons (⅛ pound) butter
- 4 tablespoons Worcestershire sauce
- 1 teaspoon paprika

Combine all ingredients and bring to a boil. Reduce heat and simmer for 15 minutes; strain. MAKES ABOUT 2½ CUPS.

6

Breads and rolls

TEA BREADS AND QUICK ROLLS are fun to make, and often they will lift a routine meal out of the ordinary. I'm sure you know that tea breads should be wrapped in foil after they are cold and allowed to "ripen" for at least a day. They will cut better and the flavor is improved.

For an afternoon tea, an assortment of tea breads with either orange marmalade and cream cheese filling, or raspberry jam and cream cheese, or just butter, makes a delightful platter of small sandwiches. Put two slices together with your filling, and then make two diagonal cuts, one from each upper corner to the lower center, making three small triangular sandwiches.

In this chapter you'll find our Southwestern recipe for hush puppies, those hearty little deep-fried chunks of goodness to eat along with fish. From Betty Crocker, bless her heart, comes the recipe for butter dips, a rich little piece of biscuit dough that is especially fine with chicken. And the popover recipe is "unsinkable."

I can't let this chapter go by without mentioning the wonderful frozen coffee cakes and rolls and breads that are now available in the frozen food case at your grocery store. They are delicious products.

Popovers

Grease 8 custard cups and set them on a pan (not in water) in a hot (425° F.) oven while you mix the batter.

- 2 eggs
- 1 cup milk
- 1 cup sifted flour
- ½ teaspoon salt

Combine all ingredients and beat until smooth with a rotary beater. Pour into sizzling hot cups and bake until golden brown in a hot (425° F.) oven, 35 to 40 minutes. Serve immediately with butter, preserves and bacon curls, for a very special breakfast hot bread.

Cheddar Apple Bread

- 1 to 2 Winesap apples (1 cup chopped apples)
- 2 cups sifted flour
- 1 teaspoon baking powder
- 1 teaspoon baking soda
- ½ teaspoon salt
- ½ cup shortening
- ⅔ cup sugar
- 2 eggs, well beaten
- ½ cup grated Cheddar cheese
- ¼ cup chopped nuts

Peel and chop the apples to measure 1 cup. Combine the sifted flour with the baking powder, soda, and salt; sift again. Cream together the shortening and sugar. Add the beaten eggs, apples, and juice from apples. Gradually add the dry ingredients to the creamed mixture. Stir in the cheese and nut meats. If the apples are not very juicy, a tablespoon of milk may be added. Spoon into a greased 5 x 9-inch loaf pan and bake in a moderate oven, 350° F., for 1 hour or until bread tests done in the center. (To test, press the bread lightly with your fingertip; if the bread is done it will spring back.)

Pineapple-Nut Bread

- 2 cups sifted flour
- ½ cup sugar
- 1 teaspoon baking powder
- ½ teaspoon salt
- 1 cup raisins
- ½ cup walnuts, coarsely chopped
- 1 egg, beaten
- 1 teaspoon vanilla
- 2 tablespoons melted shortening
- 1 teaspoon baking soda
- 1 small can crushed pineapple, not drained

Sift the flour, sugar, baking powder, and salt into a large mixing bowl. Add the raisins and nuts. Combine the egg, vanilla, and shortening; add to the dry mixture. Dissolve the soda in the pineapple, add, and stir until just blended. Pour the batter into a greased 8 x 4-inch loaf pan and bake in a moderate (350° F.) oven about 1 hour or until done. Allow to cool on a rack. Serve buttered or spread with cream cheese.

Toasted Almond Anise Loaf

- 3/4 cup blanched almonds, chopped fine
- 2 1/4 cups sifted flour
- 2 teaspoons baking powder
- 1/2 teaspoon salt
- 1/2 cup butter *or* margarine
- 1 cup sugar
- 1/2 to 1 teaspoon anise seeds
- 1/4 teaspoon almond extract
- 5 eggs

Toast the blanched almonds in a hot (450° F.) oven for 5 minutes or until they are golden brown, stirring occasionally to prevent burning. Remove them from the oven and allow them to cool. Sift together the flour, baking powder, and salt. Cream the butter or margarine and gradually add the sugar, anise seeds, and almond extract. Add the unbeaten eggs, one at a time, beating well after each addition. Blend in the dry ingredients and toasted almonds, and mix thoroughly. Grease a 9 x 5 x 3-inch loaf pan thoroughly, and lightly flour the bottom only. Turn the batter into the pan and bake in a moderate oven, 350° F., for 50 to 60 minutes. Serve warm or cold, plain or with butter.

Spicy Orange Buns

- 2 cups sifted flour
- 3 teaspoons baking powder
- 1/2 teaspoon salt
- 4 tablespoons shortening
- 3/4 cup milk (approximately)
- 2 tablespoons sugar
- 1 teaspoon cinnamon
- 4 tablespoons butter *or* margarine
- 1/2 cup sugar
- 1 6-ounce can orange juice concentrate, thawed

Sift together the flour, baking powder, and salt. Cut in the shortening until the mixture is the consistency of corn meal. Stir in milk to form a smooth dough. Knead on lightly floured board for one-half minute. Roll out lightly to form a rectangle about 1/2 inch thick. Blend together 2 tablespoons sugar and cinnamon and sprinkle over dough. Roll up like a jelly roll, from the long side of the rectangle and cut the roll in 9 equal slices. In a small saucepan over moderate heat, combine butter or margarine with 1/2 cup sugar and undiluted orange concentrate; stir just until the butter is melted. Pour this mixture into an 8-inch square baking pan and place the buns in the pan, cut side down. Bake in a hot oven, 425° F., for 20 to 25 minutes. This is a delicious brunch bread.

Poppy Seed Tea Bread

- 3 cups sifted flour
- 3½ teaspoons baking powder
- 1 teaspoon salt
- ⅓ cup poppy seeds
- ¾ cup sugar
- 2 tablespoons shortening
- 2 eggs
- 1 teaspoon grated lemon rind
- 1⅓ cups milk

Sift together the flour, baking powder, and salt. Mix in the poppy seeds. Beat together the sugar, shortening, and eggs; add grated lemon rind. Add the flour mixture alternately with the milk. Turn the batter into a well-greased, lightly floured 9 x 5 x 3-inch loaf pan. Bake in a preheated moderate (350° F.) oven for 1 hour or until well done.

Paprika Dumplings

- 1 cup sifted flour
- 1½ teaspoons baking powder
- ½ teaspoon salt
- 2 tablespoons melted shortening
- ½ cup milk

Sift together the flour, baking powder, and salt. Add the shortening and milk, blending very lightly. Drop the fluffy dough from a teaspoon into chicken broth or hot goulash, sprinkle with paprika, cover, and let them steam for 15 minutes. SERVES 4 TO 6.

Orange Nut Bread

- 2 tablespoons butter *or* margarine
- ½ cup boiling water
- 2 cups sifted flour
- 1 teaspoon baking soda
- 1 teaspoon baking powder
- ½ teaspoon salt
- ½ cup orange juice
- 2 tablespoons grated orange rind
- 1 cup sugar
- 2 teaspoons vanilla
- 1 egg, slightly beaten
- ½ cup coarsely chopped walnuts

Melt the butter or margarine in boiling water. Sift together the flour, baking soda, baking powder, and salt. Add the orange juice, grated orange rind, sugar, and vanilla to the butter and water. Add the egg. Sift the dry ingredients over the orange mixture, then add the nuts and stir until all of the flour is dampened. The batter will be lumpy. Bake in a moderate (350° F.) oven for 1 hour or until a wooden pick comes out clean when inserted in the center of the loaf. Remove the bread from the pan and allow to cool on a wire rack. Wrap the cold loaf in waxed paper and store it in the breadbox. It slices better the day after baking. Orange nut bread sandwiches with orange marmalade filling or cream cheese filling are delicious.

Olive Cheese Biscuits

For this recipe, you may use the salad pack of pimiento-stuffed green olives. They are less expensive and can be used in any recipe that calls for chopped pimiento-stuffed olives.

- 2 cups sifted flour
- 2½ teaspoons baking powder
- ¼ teaspoon salt
- ½ cup grated processed Cheddar cheese
- ¼ cup shortening
- ½ cup finely chopped pimiento-stuffed green olives
- ¾ cup milk

Sift together the flour, baking powder, and salt. Add the cheese and mix lightly. Cut in the shortening with a pastry blender or two knives. Add the olives and milk and mix only until the ingredients are moistened. Turn out the dough on a lightly floured surface and knead lightly about 10 times. Roll or pat out the dough to ½ inch thickness. Cut with a floured 2½-inch biscuit cutter. Place on an ungreased baking sheet and bake in a very hot oven, 450° F., for 8 to 10 minutes or until the biscuits are golden brown. MAKES ABOUT 16 BISCUITS.

Onion Shortcake Biscuits

- 1 tablespoon instant minced onion *or* 2 tablespoons finely chopped raw onion
- ⅔ cup milk
- 2 tablespoons shortening
- 2 cups prepared biscuit mix
- ½ cup grated American cheese

Stir the onion into the milk. Cut the shortening into the biscuit mix and add the cheese and liquid mixture, forming a moderately stiff dough. Turn out the dough on a lightly floured board and roll it about ¼ inch thick. For each biscuit, cut two 3½-inch rounds; put the two rounds together (one on top of the other); cut a 1-inch round and place it on top (an added topknot for decoration). Bake in a very hot oven, 450° F., until golden brown, about 15 minutes.

Split open and serve with creamed fish, meat, chicken, eggs, or vegetables. MAKES 4 OR 5 SHORTCAKE BISCUITS.

For plain biscuits, roll the dough about ½ inch thick and cut with a 2-inch biscuit cutter. Bake in a hot oven, 450° F., for 10 to 12 minutes. MAKES ABOUT 1 DOZEN BISCUITS.

Holiday Braid

- 1 cup candied fruits and peels
- ½ cup light or dark raisins
- ¼ cup California sherry wine
- 2 cakes or packages yeast
- ⅓ cup lukewarm water
- 1⅔ cups very hot milk
- ½ cup sugar
- 2 teaspoons salt
- 2 eggs, beaten
- 7 cups sifted flour
- ½ cup soft shortening
- Sherry glaze (sherry and powdered sugar)

Chop the candied fruits and peels coarsely. Rinse, drain, and chop the raisins. Combine the fruits with sherry and let stand several hours or overnight. Soften the yeast in ⅓ cup lukewarm water. Combine the hot milk, sugar, and salt; let cool to lukewarm. Stir in yeast, beaten eggs, and 3½ cups flour; beat until smooth. Add the remaining 3½ cups flour and the soft shortening. Mix to form a moderately stiff dough. Turn out the dough on a floured board and knead it until smooth. Place in lightly greased bowl, cover, and let rise until doubled in bulk, about 1½ hours. Turn out the dough onto a lightly floured surface and pat or roll into an oblong about ½ inch thick. Spread the surface of the dough with the fruits. Fold the dough and knead *very lightly,* just until fruits are distributed. Cover and let rest 15 minutes. Divide the dough in half to make 2 large loaves or into thirds for 3 medium loaves. Divide each piece of dough into 3 equal portions and roll each one with your hands to form ropes about 12 inches long. Braid the 3 ropes loosely together, tucking both ends under to seal them. Place the loaves on lightly greased baking sheets, brush the tops with melted shortening, and let the loaves rise until light and almost doubled in bulk, about 30 to 40 minutes. Bake in a hot oven, 400° F., about 25 minutes. While the loaves are still warm, brush them with sherry glaze, made by mixing powdered sugar with sherry wine to make a thick paste. Decorate with glacé fruit if desired. Let the bread cool 4 to 5 hours or overnight before cutting.

The loaves may be kept in an even shape by enclosing the

shaped dough in a small collar of foil. Place the foil loosely around the braid after it is shaped and arranged on the baking sheet for the final rising.

Holiday Doughnuts

- 1 pound shortening for deep frying
- 1 egg, beaten
- ½ cup milk
- 1 teaspoon vanilla
- 1⅓ cups sifted flour
- 2 teaspoons baking powder
- ¼ teaspoon salt
- ⅓ cup sugar
- 1 tablespoon melted shortening, cooled

Heat the shortening slowly in a small kettle to 365° F. (or, if you don't have a deep fat thermometer, until a cube of bread browns in 60 seconds). Beat together the egg, milk, and vanilla. Add the sifted dry ingredients and blend thoroughly but do not beat. Stir in the cooled melted shortening. Dip a teaspoon into the hot shortening then dip up a spoonful of batter. Quickly immerse the spoon in the hot shortening and drop off the batter. Turn the doughnut balls when they come to the surface and fry them about 3 minutes or until they are delicately browned. Do not crowd the kettle. Drain the doughnuts well over the kettle and then place them on absorbent paper. They may be iced when cool, if desired. They may also be served plain or rolled in confectioners' sugar.

Hush Puppies

- 2 cups corn meal
- 1 tablespoon flour
- ½ teaspoon baking soda
- 1 teaspoon baking powder
- 1 teaspoon salt
- 3 tablespoons chopped onion
- 1 cup buttermilk
- 1 egg, beaten

Mix the dry ingredients together. Add the onion, then the milk, and finally the beaten egg. Drop by spoonfuls into a pan or kettle where fish is frying and fry to a golden brown. Drain on paper toweling. Serve on hot platter with fish. SERVES 4.

Cheesed Melba Toast

Cut thin slices of white or rye bread, brush with soft butter or margarine, and sprinkle with grated Parmesan cheese and paprika. Toast in a slow oven, 250° F., until crisp and nicely browned.

Cheese Pimiento Biscuits

- 2 cups sifted flour
- 1 tablespoon baking powder
- 1 teaspoon salt
- ¼ cup shortening
- 1 cup shredded American cheese
- 3 tablespoons minced pimiento, drained
- ⅔ to ¾ cup milk

Sift together the flour, baking powder, and salt. Cut or rub in the shortening until the mixture is crumbly. Stir in the cheese and pimiento. Add enough milk to make a soft dough. Turn out the dough onto a lightly floured board or pastry cloth and knead gently for 30 seconds. Roll out, cut with a biscuit cutter, and place on an ungreased baking sheet. Bake in a hot oven, 450° F., for 10 to 12 minutes. MAKES 18 BISCUITS.

Chili Hard Rolls

- ⅓ cup butter *or* margarine
- 1½ teaspoons chili powder
- 8 hard rolls

Soften the butter and blend in the chili powder. Split the rolls and spread them with the chili-butter mixture. Wrap the rolls in foil and heat in a moderately hot (375° F.) oven about 10 minutes or until hot. Serve with salads or casserole dishes.

Blueberry Scones

- 2 cups sifted flour
- ½ teaspoon salt
- 2 teaspoons baking powder
- ¼ teaspoon baking soda
- ¼ cup butter
- 1 cup blueberries, rinsed
- ½ cup buttermilk *or* sour milk
- 1 tablespoon unsulphured molasses

Sift together the flour, salt, baking powder, and soda. Cut in the butter until the mixture forms coarse crumbs the size of peas. Add the blueberries and mix lightly. Make a hollow in the center of the mixture and gradually pour in the buttermilk or sour milk mixed with the molasses. Stir well. Pat the dough with your hands —gently, to avoid crushing berries—to ½-inch thickness. Cut the dough into triangles, place on a baking sheet, and bake in a hot oven, 425° F., for 12 to 15 minutes. Split, spread with butter, and serve hot. MAKES 6 TO 8 SCONES.

Blueberry Tea Cake

¼ cup shortening
1 cup plus 2 tablespoons sugar
1 egg
2 cups sifted cake flour
2 teaspoons baking powder
¼ teaspoon salt
¾ cup milk
1 teaspoon vanilla
¾ cup blueberries, washed and drained
Butter

Cream the shortening. Add 1 cup sugar gradually, and continue creaming until well blended. Add the egg and beat until the mixture is light and fluffy. Sift together the cake flour, baking powder, and salt. Add to the creamed mixture alternately with the milk and vanilla. Turn the batter into a greased 9-inch square cake pan and cover with the blueberries. Sprinkle the top with the remaining 2 tablespoons sugar, dot with butter, and bake in a moderate oven, 350° F., for about 1 hour. SERVES 6 TO 8.

Quick Coffee Cake

1½ cups sifted flour
2½ teaspoons baking powder
½ teaspoon salt
½ cup sugar
¼ cup shortening
1 egg, well beaten
½ cup milk

Sift the flour, baking powder, salt, and sugar into a mixing bowl. Cut in the shortening. Combine the egg and milk and mix quickly with the other ingredients. Turn the mixture into a well-greased ring pan and sprinkle with topping. Bake in a preheated moderate (375° F.) oven for 20 minutes.

Topping

3 tablespoons flour
1 tablespoon grated orange rind
¼ cup chopped nuts
¼ cup sugar
2 tablespoons melted butter

Mix all ingredients and spread over unbaked coffee cake.

French Toast–Banana Sandwich

Bread slices, crusts removed
Soft butter
Banana slices
Egg batter
Maple syrup
Canadian bacon slices, broiled

Spread the bread with soft butter and make sandwiches, using the sliced bananas as filling. Place each sandwich on a spatula, dip it into the egg batter, place it in a greased skillet, and brown lightly on both sides. Turn the sandwich only once. Serve hot with syrup and broiled Canadian bacon.

Egg Batter

To each beaten egg, add 3 tablespoons milk and a pinch of salt. Beat well.

Baked Olive French Loaf

- 1 small loaf French bread
- 3 tablespoons butter *or* margarine
- 3 tablespoons flour
- ½ teaspoon salt
- 1½ cups milk
- ½ teaspoon Worcestershire sauce
- 1 egg, beaten
- 2 cups grated American cheese
- 1 cup ground cooked ham
- 1 cup chopped ripe olives
- 1 clove garlic
- 2 tablespoons melted butter *or* margarine

Break open the French loaf along the seam. Remove the soft center and crumble it. Melt 3 tablespoons butter, blend in the flour and salt, and add the milk slowly, stirring and cooking until smooth and thick. Remove from heat, add Worcestershire sauce, beaten egg, cheese, ham, olives and crumbled bread. Stir until the mixture is well blended. Refill the loaf and press the edges together. Rub the outside of the loaf with the cut clove of garlic and brush with melted butter. Bake in a moderately hot oven, 375° F., for 25 to 30 minutes. SERVES 6.

I wrap this bread in foil. I find that the crust is plenty crunchy and yet it doesn't get too hard.

Cranberry-Banana Bread

- ⅓ cup shortening
- ⅔ cup sugar
- 2 eggs
- 1¾ cups sifted flour
- 2 teaspoons baking powder
- ½ teaspoon salt
- ¼ teaspoon baking soda
- ½ cup coarsely chopped walnuts
- 1 cup (3 or 4) mashed ripe bananas
- 1 cup drained cooked fresh cranberry sauce *or* canned whole cranberry sauce

Cream the shortening with the sugar. Add the eggs, one at a time, beating well after each addition. Sift the dry ingredients together and add the nuts. Add the flour mixture alternately with the mashed bananas to the creamed mixture, beating well after each addition. Fold in the cranberries. Pour into a greased 8 x 4 x 2-inch loaf pan. Bake in a moderate oven, 350° F., for 60 to 65 minutes or until done. Allow to cool on a rack before slicing.

Cheese-Cranberry Bread

- 2 cups fresh *or* frozen cranberries
- 2 cups sifted flour
- 1 tablespoon baking powder
- ½ teaspoon salt
- 1 cup sugar
- ½ cup coarsely chopped pecans or walnuts
- 1 cup milk
- 1 egg, slightly beaten
- Grated rind of 1 orange
- ¼ cup butter, melted
- 1½ cups shredded Cheddar cheese

Halve the cranberries and set them aside. Sift together the sifted flour, baking powder, salt, and sugar. Add the cranberries and nuts to the dry ingredients and mix until they are well coated. Combine milk, egg, orange rind, and melted butter; add to the dry ingredients along with the shredded cheese. Stir only enough to moisten the ingredients. Pour the batter into a buttered 9 x 5 x 3-inch loaf pan. Spread the batter evenly in the pan, making the corners and sides slightly higher than the center. Bake in a preheated moderate oven, 350° F. Turn the loaf out of the pan onto a rack to cool. The bread slices more easily if it is stored overnight before cutting.

Herbed French Bread

- 2 loaves French bread
- 2 cloves garlic
- ½ pound butter *or* margarine
- 1 cup chopped parsley
- 1 cup chopped chives *or* green onion tops
- ¼ cup fresh *or* 1 tablespoon dried basil, crumbled
- Toasted sesame seeds

Cut the loaves in half lengthwise. Grate the garlic or put it through a garlic press. Cream the butter or margarine, add the garlic, parsley, chives, and basil; cream all together. Spread this seasoned butter on the bread and sprinkle with toasted sesame seeds. Press the two halves of the loaf together, wrap in foil, and heat in a moderate (350° F.) oven for 20 minutes. Cut in thick slices through the loaf.

Butter Dips

1/3 cup butter	3 1/2 teaspoons baking powder
2 1/4 cups sifted flour	1 1/2 teaspoons salt
1 tablespoon sugar	1 cup milk

Heat the oven to hot, 450° F. Melt the butter in the oven in an oblong pan, 13 x 9 x 2 inches. Remove the pan from the oven when the butter is melted. Sift the dry ingredients into a bowl. Add the milk and stir slowly with a fork until the dough just clings together, about 30 strokes. Turn out dough onto a well-floured board and knead it lightly about 10 times. Roll out the dough into a rectangle 8 x 12 inches, 1/2 inch thick. Cut it in half lengthwise, then crosswise into 16 strips. Dip each strip into melted butter, so that the butter coats both sides. Place the strips close together in two rows in a pan. Bake 15 to 20 minutes, or until golden brown. Serve piping hot. MAKES 32 BUTTER DIPS.

Christmas Tree Coffee Cake

2 cups biscuit mix	2 tablespoons evaporated milk
1/3 cup evaporated milk	2 tablespoons finely chopped citron
1/3 cup water	1/3 cup halved candied cherries
1 cup confectioners' sugar	

Place the biscuit mix in a bowl, add 1/3 cup evaporated milk and 1/3 cup water, and stir with a fork until the mix is thoroughly moistened. Grease a baking sheet in a Christmas tree shape about 12 inches long. Using a generous tablespoonful at a time, drop the dough on the greased sheet to form a tree. Start with one spoonful at the top, then continue with touching rows of 2, 3, 4, 5, and 6 spoonfuls, using the last of the dough to form a trunk at the bottom of the last row. Bake in a hot oven, 400° F., until lightly browned, from 12 to 15 minutes. Leave on baking sheet and set on cooling rack. For the topping, blend the confectioners' sugar with 2 tablespoons evaporated milk until smooth; spoon over the coffee cake while it is still hot. Decorate the top with chopped citron and candied cherries. Do not slice; break with two forks. Serve hot with butter. SERVES 8.

Streusel Coffee Cake

- 1½ cups sifted flour
- 3 teaspoons baking powder
- ¼ teaspoon salt
- ¾ cup sugar
- ¼ cup shortening
- 1 egg, well beaten
- ½ cup milk
- 1 teaspoon vanilla

Sift the dry ingredients. Cut or rub in the shortening until the mixture is the consistency of fine corn meal. Mix the egg with the milk and blend into the dry mixture. Add the vanilla and beat just enough to mix well. Pour half the batter into a floured and greased 7 x 11-inch pan and sprinkle with half the streusel mixture. Add the remaining batter and sprinkle the rest of the streusel on top. Bake in a moderately hot oven, 375° F., for 25 to 30 minutes.

Streusel Filling and Topping

- ½ cup brown sugar
- 2 tablespoons flour
- 2 teaspoons cinnamon
- 2 tablespoons melted butter
- ½ cup nuts, chopped

Mix the dry ingredients and blend in melted butter and nuts.

Applesauce Nut Bread

- 2 cups sifted flour
- ¾ cup sugar
- 1 tablespoon baking powder
- 1 teaspoon salt
- ½ teaspoon baking soda
- ½ teaspoon nutmeg
- 1 cup coarsely chopped walnuts
- 1 egg, well beaten
- 1 cup canned unsweetened applesauce
- ¼ cup salad oil

Mix the sifted dry ingredients and nuts together. Combine the egg, applesauce, and oil; add to dry ingredients and stir until just blended. Pour the batter into a greased loaf pan and bake in a moderate oven, 350° F., for 50 minutes. Allow to cool on a rack. When the bread is cold, wrap it in foil. It will slice more easily and have better flavor if you let it stand for a day or two before cutting it.

7

Desserts and dessert sauces

THIS CHAPTER HAS BEEN my downfall. I love desserts and, ironically enough, this is the one type of food that I have to guard against, because I need only look at a piece of chocolate cake to gain five pounds!

Often a routine meal can become something very special with a lovely dessert.

I have always felt that there should be one conversation piece in every meal that you serve for company, and dessert is the easiest course in which to have it. This makes friends and foes leave your house with the creative urge to "outdo" you when next you come to dinner. In fact, we had a very funny feud between two wonderful Texas homemakers. They were very close friends, but jealous of each other's culinary ability. All of us who were fortunate enough to be guests in their homes enjoyed the feud, because the most heavenly desserts were served, each in an effort to top the last one. Gastronomically, it was a delight; calorie-wise, it was fatal.

Here in our part of the country men love cheese, fresh fruit, and crackers. Apple pie is also a great favorite, and I understand that it is the most popular American dessert with men all over the country.

In this chapter you'll find the most simple but delicious desserts, and also some that are more complicated. But I am sure that by this time, as you use this book, you realize that I am not a "gourmet-type" cook. I cook the way most homemakers do, and I'll be delighted if you find some brand-new recipes here that you will add to your favorite recipe file. Let's start with a universal favorite, strawberry shortcake. You'll find that I make my biscuits and shortcake "shorter" than usual, but it gives a lovely flaky delicate flavor to them.

Strawberry Shortcake

- 2 cups flour
- 3 teaspoons baking powder
- 1 teaspoon salt
- ⅔ cup shortening
- ¾ cup milk
- Butter
- 1 tablespoon sugar
- Crushed strawberries
- Whipped cream

Sift together the flour, baking powder, and salt. Cut in the shortening, and then add the milk. Turn the dough onto floured board or pastry sheet and knead about 10 times. Roll it out into a rectangular or oval shape and bake in a hot (450° F.) oven for 15 to 20 minutes. Dot with butter and sprinkle with the sugar while still hot. Split through the middle, cover the bottom half with strawberries and whipped cream, add the top half, and top with berries and whipped cream. SERVES 8.

Chocolate Fancy

- 2 squares unsweetened chocolate
- ⅔ cup sugar
- ⅓ cup hot water
- ½ teaspoon salt
- 4 eggs, separated
- 1½ teaspoons unflavored gelatine
- 1 tablespoon cold water
- 1 teaspoon vanilla
- ½ cup heavy cream, whipped stiff
- ½ cup finely chopped walnuts
- Lady fingers *or* sponge cake

Melt the chocolate over hot water in a double boiler. Add the sugar, ⅓ cup hot water, and salt; stir and cook until smooth. Beat the egg yolks lightly, stir them slowly into the chocolate mixture, and cook and stir until the mixture thickens. Soften the gelatine in 1 tablespoon cold water and dissolve it in the hot chocolate mixture.

Remove from heat, blend in vanilla, and allow to cool. Fold in the stiffly beaten egg whites, whipped cream, and walnuts. Line a loaf pan with wax paper or foil and arrange lady fingers or strips of sponge cake over the bottom and around the sides. Fill the pan with alternate layers of the chocolate mixture and lady fingers. Chill overnight. Unmold and slice to serve.

Meringue Torte

While we're on the subject of strawberries, fresh or frozen, let's talk about a *new* method of baking a meringue torte (this same recipe can be divided into six or eight individual meringue shells and baked in the same manner).

Very often ovens get out of adjustment and are either too hot or too cold; and meringue, being of a delicate nature, suffers from overexposure or underexposure. If you will preheat the oven to 400° F. and then turn off the heat as soon as you put the meringue shells or torte into the oven, the meringue comes out snowy white. Don't let your curiosity get the best of you, and don't open the oven door for at least three hours.

4 egg whites
Dash of salt
½ teaspoon vinegar
1 cup sugar
1 teaspoon vanilla
1 pint heavy cream, whipped
1 box frozen strawberries *or* 1 box fresh strawberries, sliced and sweetened

Combine the egg whites, salt, and vinegar, beat until soft peaks are reached, and then gradually add sugar and vanilla; beat until the mixture is very stiff. Cover a cooky sheet with a piece of brown paper. Draw a circle, 8 or 9 inches in diameter, to make it easy for you to build this meringue shell. Start building the shell by piling the meringue in the center of the circle. With the back of a spoon, pull the meringue up into a shell form. Be sure there is an indentation in the center. Put the shell into a preheated hot (400° F.) oven and *turn off the heat immediately*. Let it stay (*don't peek*) until the oven is cold, or at least 3 hours. You'll find that the meringue is snowy white, instead of an ecru color. When ready to serve, fill the shell with a mixture of whipped cream and berries. Or you may fill it with scoops of vanilla ice cream and use the berries for topping. Cut in wedges. SERVES 6.

Wine-Baked Bananas

- 4 ripe bananas, cut lengthwise in halves
- Apricot or pineapple-apricot jam
- 2 tablespoons sherry wine
- 2 tablespoons melted butter
- 1 tablespoon lemon juice
- 2 tablespoons brown sugar

Arrange the bananas, cut side up, in a shallow baking dish and spread thinly with jam. Mix the sherry, butter, lemon juice and brown sugar; spoon the mixture over the bananas. Bake in a moderate oven, 350° F., for 20 to 25 minutes, basting occasionally with the sauce. Serve warm, not hot. SERVES 4.

Vanilla Cream

- 1 envelope unflavored gelatine
- ¼ cup milk
- 4 egg yolks
- ½ cup sugar
- ¼ teaspoon salt
- 2 cups milk, scalded
- 1 cup heavy cream, whipped stiff
- 1 teaspoon vanilla

Soften the gelatine in ¼ cup milk. Beat the egg yolks in a saucepan and gradually beat in sugar and salt. Slowly blend in the scalded milk. Cook over low heat until the mixture boils. Remove from heat, stir in softened gelatine, and allow to cool. When the mixture is partially set, beat it with a rotary beater and fold in the whipped cream and vanilla. Pour the mixture into an oiled 1-quart mold and chill for about 4 hours. Unmold on large serving dish and garnish with sweetened whipped cream and fresh berries in season.

Bananas au Rhum

- 6 large ripe bananas
- ½ cup olive oil
- ½ teaspoon vanilla
- 3 tablespoons rum
- ¼ cup powdered sugar

Peel the bananas and cut crosswise into thin slices. Sauté the slices in hot oil. When they are browned lightly, remove them from the oil and drain them on brown paper. When the banana slices are cool, place them in shallow serving dish. Combine the vanilla and rum; sprinkle over the bananas. Sieve powdered sugar over the top and serve cold. SERVES 6.

Baked Fresh Bananas

- 6 ripe bananas
- ½ pound butter *or* margarine
- 1 4-ounce glass rum
- ½ pound brown sugar
- 2 tablespoons Cointreau
- 1 teaspoon cinnamon

Peel the bananas and put them in a baking dish. Combine all the other ingredients and pour the mixture over the bananas. Bake in a moderate (350° F.) oven for 30 minutes and serve warm. SERVES 6.

Snowmist Pudding with Custard Sauce

This is a versatile recipe I picked up in Jamaica. You can add grated coconut to make a delicious, light coconut pudding. The cold custard sauce can be used for floating island or for any dessert that requires a cool, smooth sauce.

- 1 envelope unflavored gelatine
- ¼ cup cold water
- 1 cup boiling water
- 1 cup sugar
- ¼ cup lemon *or* lime juice
- 3 egg whites
- Grated lemon *or* lime rind

Soak the gelatine in ¼ cup cold water and dissolve it in 1 cup boiling water. Add the sugar and juice. Set the mixture aside in a cool place; or set it in a pan of cracked ice to cool it down quickly, stirring occasionally. When the mixture will hold the print of a spoon or when it is the consistency of unbeaten egg white, whip it with a wire whisk or wire spoon to incorporate lots of air and bubbles and make it froth up. Beat the egg whites until they are stiff; beat them into the gelatine mixture with the wire whisk, and continue beating until the mixture is about stiff enough to hold a peak. If you get tired, use your electric mixer for the last 3 or 4 minutes. Turn the pudding into a mold that has been rinsed with cold water. Chill. To serve, unmold onto a platter, sprinkle with grated rind, and cut into wedges. Serve with cold custard sauce.

Custard Sauce

- 3 egg yolks
- ¼ cup sugar
- ⅛ teaspoon salt
- 2 cups scalded milk
- 1 teaspoon vanilla

In the top of a double boiler, beat the egg yolks and mix in the sugar and salt. Gradually add the scalded milk, stirring constantly. Cook and stir over hot, but not boiling, water until the mixture coats a spoon, about 7 minutes. (This custard will not be thick, but it will thicken slightly during the cooking and still more during the cooling.) Strain the custard into a bowl, add the vanilla, and chill thoroughly. This custard is wonderful served over fresh cake or dabs of sweetened meringue.

Crème Brulée Banana

When the test kitchens of the large food companies send out new recipes to food editors throughout the country, it's like a breath of spring coming into the room. All of us are deeply indebted to the home economists who work out these recipes to give us a "change of pace" to pass along to our readers. This is a brand-new luxury-type dessert coming from the test kitchens of General Foods, using one of the cooked pudding mixes that are truly convenience foods.

- 1 small package vanilla pudding mix
- 1¾ cups milk
- 1 teaspoon rum extract
- 1 cup heavy cream, whipped
- ⅓ cup brown sugar
- 2 teaspoons cinnamon
- 4 ripe bananas

Prepare the cooked pudding mix according to package directions, using 1¾ cups of milk instead of 2 cups. Cool the mixture. Add the rum extract and fold in the whipped cream. Pour into a casserole dish that can withstand broiler heat. Set in the refrigerator to chill. Mix the sugar and cinnamon; sprinkle over the top of the pudding. When ready to serve, set the casserole in a pan of ice cubes and place it in the broiler, as far away from the heat as possible. Broil 5 minutes or until the sugar is melted and makes a crust. Slice the bananas into dessert dishes and spoon the sauce over the top. (The chilled cream will remain cold because the casserole was set in the ice.) You can also use this Crème Brulée plain, or over sliced sweetened strawberries. SERVES 6.

Black Cherry Whip

- 2 cups (No. 303 can) pitted black Bing cherries
- 1 package black cherry-flavored gelatin
- ¼ cup dry sherry
- ½ teaspoon grated lemon rind
- 1 tablespoon lemon juice
- 1⅓ cups ice-cold evaporated milk

Drain the cherries thoroughly, saving the juice. Combine the juice with enough boiling water to make 1 cup liquid. Place the gelatin in a large mixing bowl, add the boiling water and juice mixture, and stir until the gelatin is dissolved. Stir in the sherry, lemon rind, and lemon juice. While the mixture is cooling, cut the cherries in halves, saving out 8 halves for garnish, if desired. Add the cherries to the gelatin mixture and chill to the consistency of unbeaten egg white. Whip the cold evaporated milk until it is stiff and will hold a peak. (To whip evaporated milk, place the milk in a bowl or in the ice cube tray in the refrigerator freezing compartment. When ice particles have formed around the edge, turn the milk out into a chilled bowl and beat quickly with chilled beaters until light and thick. The secret of great volume is to have the milk, beaters, and bowl icy cold.) Fold the whipped milk quickly but thoroughly into the gelatin mixture. Spoon immediately into sherbet glasses or dessert dishes and garnish with cherry halves. Chill until set, which should take 2 to 3 hours. SERVES 8.

Baked Carrot Pudding with Bourbon Sauce

The bourbon sauce used here with carrot pudding is also an excellent sauce to use over pound cake, hot gingerbread, or any uniced cake. This unusual recipe for an old-fashioned type of pudding came from the test kitchens of the Bourbon Institute.

- 1¼ cups flour
- 1 teaspoon baking powder
- ½ teaspoon nutmeg
- ½ teaspoon cinnamon
- ½ teaspoon baking soda
- ½ cup shortening
- ½ cup dark brown sugar
- 2 eggs, slightly beaten
- 1 cup grated raw carrots
- 2 tablespoons candied lemon peel
- ½ cup seedless raisins
- 1 cup currants
- ¼ cup bourbon whiskey

Butter a 1-quart ring mold. Sift together the dry ingredients. Cream together the shortening and brown sugar; add beaten eggs, carrots, fruit, and bourbon. Stir in the sifted dry ingredients. Put the mixture into the mold and cover with foil. Bake in a moderate (350° F.) oven for approximately 35 minutes. Allow to cool for 15 minutes, unmold, and serve with bourbon sauce.

If you make this pudding ahead of time, steam it over hot water before serving. Just set it on a cooling rack, put the rack on top of a saucepan with boiling water in it, and put the top of the pan over the pudding. It will heat through in about 30 minutes.

Bourbon Sauce

4 eggs, separated	¼ cup bourbon whiskey
1½ cups powdered sugar	

Beat the egg yolk until thick and lemon colored. Slowly add ½ cup sugar. Beat egg whites until they form peaks; add the remaining 1 cup sugar. Fold the whites into the yolks, add the bourbon slowly, and mix well. Serve over the warm carrot pudding or any pudding or cake.

Individual Chocolate Soufflés

It's a well-known fact that soufflés wait for no one, and for years I have been trying recipes to find an individual soufflé that would hold up if it were baked ahead of time. This is it. For the best taste possible, serve this soufflé hot, with ice-cold whipped cream and thin chocolate sauce; but if you want to bake them ahead of time, you can still have lovely soufflés that won't fall. They settle slightly, but they don't sink in the middle.

Just to see if this batter could be made ahead and used even the next day, I combined half of the batter with two beaten egg whites and baked it. Then I refrigerated the other half of the batter overnight and baked it the next day, after adding two beaten egg whites to it. Both batches looked exactly the same as to color, shape, and texture. If you want to try this recipe for two desserts on two separate days, divide the soufflé batter (before you add the egg whites) and put 1¼ cups of it in the refrigerator.

I am perfectly happy with this recipe because now I know that I don't have to jump up from the dinner table, while my guests are eating, to put together a soufflé.

4 ounces German's sweet chocolate	½ teaspoon salt
2 cups milk	2 tablespoons butter
½ cup sugar	1 teaspoon vanilla
½ cup flour	4 eggs, separated

Add the chocolate to the milk and heat in a double boiler. When the chocolate is melted, beat the mixture with a rotary beater until it is well blended. Combine the sugar, flour, and salt. Add a small amount of the chocolate mixture to the dry ingredients and stir until smooth. Return this to the double boiler with the remaining chocolate mixture and cook, stirring constantly, until thickened. Continue cooking for 5 minutes. Remove from heat, add butter and vanilla, and allow to cool slightly. Beat the egg yolks until they are thick and lemon colored, add, and mix well. When you are ready to bake the soufflés, beat the egg whites until stiff and gently fold them into the soufflé batter. Turn the batter into greased and sugared individual bakers or custard cups. Place them in a pan of *hot* water and bake in a moderate over, 350° F., until they are dry on the top and puffy, 25 to 30 minutes. Serve at once with ice-cold whipped cream and a thin chocolate sauce. SERVES 12.

Lemon Soufflés

1 cup sugar
1 tablespoon butter
1 lemon, juice and grated rind
2 unbeaten egg yolks
2 tablespoons flour
1 cup milk
2 egg whites, stiffly beaten

Cream together the sugar and butter. Add the lemon rind and juice, then egg yolks, one at a time. Add the flour and milk and fold in the stiffly beaten egg whites. Pour into buttered custard cups, place in a pan of hot water, and bake in a moderate (350° F.) oven for 25 to 30 minutes. Serve cold with whipped cream, whipped topping, or vanilla ice cream. SERVES 4 TO 6.

Cranberry Relish Ice Cream Bombe

Relish

1 pound (4 cups) fresh cranberries
2 oranges, quartered and seeded
2 cups sugar

Put the cranberries and oranges, including the rind, through a food chopper; add the sugar and chill. This relish keeps in the refrigerator for weeks. It can be made in large quantities and frozen in small containers so that you can defrost it as you need it. MAKES 1 QUART.

Bombe

1 recipe cranberry-orange relish
½ gallon vanilla ice cream

Add relish to ice cream which has been softened in the electric mixer so that it is workable but not entirely melted. Blend in relish and pour into a large mold and freeze. Use a mold with plain sides and line it with foil which makes it simple to turn out. If you prefer a fancy mold, then apply warm cloths or sponges so that it releases itself. Immediately put it back in the freezer so the top won't liquefy too much. SERVES 16.

You can also use this same amount to make 3 or 4 small molds, each of which will serve 4 to 6.

Topsy-Turvy Peach Cobbler

- 3½ cups (No. 2½ can) peach slices
- ⅓ cup brown sugar, packed
- Dash of salt
- 1 tablespoon cornstarch
- 1 teaspoon nutmeg
- 1½ tablespoons butter
- 1 tablespoon lemon juice
- 1 can refrigerated pan-ready cinnamon rolls

Drain the syrup from the peaches and add enough water to make 1 cup of liquid. Heat to boiling. Blend together the sugar, salt, cornstarch, and nutmeg; stir into the syrup. Cook, stirring, until the sauce boils and thickens. Add butter and lemon juice. Put the drained peaches in a round, 8- or 9-inch glass cake pan. Cover with the cinnamon rolls, scroll side up. Pour the hot sauce over them. Bake in a hot oven, 400° F., about 25 minutes. Serve warm with sweet or sour cream or a scoop of ice cream.

Spicy Pear Macaroon

- 4 ripe Anjou pears, peeled
- 1 tablespoon quick-cooking tapioca
- 2 tablespoons orange juice
- 1 tablespoon grated orange rind
- 1 egg
- ⅔ cup sugar
- 2 tablespoons flour
- 1 teaspoon baking powder
- ⅛ teaspoon salt
- ⅛ teaspoon nutmeg
- ⅛ teaspoon ginger
- ¼ teaspoon almond extract
- ¼ cup chopped nuts

Slice the pears into a greased 1-quart casserole or 8-inch square baking pan. Sprinkle with tapioca, orange juice, and grated rind. Beat the egg, then add the sugar, flour, baking powder, salt, spices and extract; spread this mixture over the pear slices. Sprinkle with the nuts and bake in a moderate oven, 325° F., for 40 to 45 minutes or until a macaroon-like crust develops. Serve warm or cold. SERVES 5 OR 6.

Surprise Peach Dumplings

- 2 cups rich biscuit dough
- 6 canned peach halves, drained
- Brown sugar
- Cinnamon
- 1 3-ounce package cream cheese
- Grated orange rind
- 1½ cups apricot nectar
- ½ cup sugar
- 1 tablespoon lemon juice
- 1 tablespoon butter

Roll out the biscuit dough about ¼-inch thick and cut it into six 6-inch squares. Top each square with a peach half and sprinkle with brown sugar and cinnamon. Divide the cheese among the dumplings and sprinkle each one with a little orange rind. Pinch the corners of the dough together, over the fruit, to seal. Place the dumplings in a greased, shallow pan and bake in a very hot oven, 450° F., for about 10 minutes. In a saucepan, combine nectar, sugar, and ½ teaspoon orange rind; heat to boiling. Add the lemon juice and butter, pour this over the dumplings, and bake about 15 minutes longer. Serve hot. SERVES 6.

Rice Bavarian

- ½ cup uncooked rice
- 1 teaspoon salt
- 4 cups milk
- ½ cup sugar
- Nutmeg *or* cinnamon
- ½ teaspoon vanilla
- 1 tablespoon unflavored gelatine
- ¼ cup water
- 2 egg whites, beaten stiff but not dry

Combine the rice, salt, and milk; cook over hot water, stirring frequently, until the rice is soft and the mixture is thick, about 45 minutes. Add the sugar, spice, and vanilla. Soak the gelatine in ¼ cup water for a few minutes, then stir it into the hot rice mixture. Let the mixture cool. When it is nearly set, beat the egg whites until stiff, but not dry, fold them into the rice mixture, and turn it into a mold. Chill. Serve with whipped cream or a dessert sauce. SERVES 6.

Orange-Honey Sauce

½ cup honey
¼ cup orange juice
1 teaspoon grated orange rind
Few grains salt

Mix ingredients until well blended. MAKES ¾ CUP.

Ring of Hearts Cobbler

2 cups (No. 303 can) pitted tart red cherries
1½ cups pitted cooked prunes
⅔ cup sugar
¼ cup red cinnamon candies
2 tablespoons cornstarch
2 tablespoons water
1 tablespoon butter
Topping

Drain the cherries, measure the juice and add water or liquid from cooking the prunes to make 1½ cups liquid. Blend the juice with the sugar and cinnamon candies, bring to a boil, reduce heat, and simmer until candy dissolves. Blend in the cornstarch combined with butter, and 2 tablespoons water; simmer 2 to 3 minutes longer. Add the drained cherries and prunes. Turn the mixture into a shallow baking dish and place in a hot oven, 425° F., while you make the topping.

Topping

1 cup sifted flour
1½ teaspoons baking powder
½ teaspoon salt
1 tablespoon sugar
3 tablespoons shortening
1 egg, beaten
¼ cup milk

In a mixing bowl, sift together the flour, baking powder, salt, and sugar. Cut in the shortening, add the egg and milk, and mix to a moderately stiff dough. Roll out on floured board to ¼-inch thickness. Cut in heart shapes (or any other desired shapes) and arrange on top of the filling. Bake in a hot oven, 425° F., until golden brown, about 15 to 20 minutes. SERVES 8.

Quick Chocolate Soufflé

1 package Royal Dark 'n' Sweet Chocolate Pudding
1 cup milk
1 tablespoon margarine
4 eggs, separated

Empty the pudding into a saucepan and add the milk and margarine. Bring to a boil over low heat, stirring constantly. Remove from heat. Beat the egg yolks until thick, then gradually add pudding mixture to them, beating steadily until the mixture cools. Beat the egg whites until stiff and lightly fold them into the pudding, mixing just enough to combine ingredients. Pour the pudding into a greased and sugared 1½-quart baking dish and bake in a hot oven, 450° F., for 20 minutes. Serve with light or whipped cream. SERVES 6 TO 8.

Pecan Torte

- 4 egg whites
- 1 whole egg
- ½ cup sugar
- 6 ounces pecan meats
- ¼ teaspoon salt
- 1 teaspoon vanilla
- 1 teaspoon baking powder

Put the egg whites into a mixing bowl. Put the remaining ingredients, in the order listed, into the container of an electric blender, cover, and turn the motor to high speed. Uncover and stir the surface of the mixture with a rubber spatula, pulling the paste from the sides of the container into the center until it is smoothly blended, about 40 seconds. Beat the egg whites until very stiff and carefully but thoroughly fold them into the nut paste. Spoon the mixture into a 7-inch spring form pan and bake in a moderate oven, 300° F., for 1 hour. Run a knife blade around the side of the cake and let it cool and settle in the pan. When it is cool, slice it into two layers and put the layers together with French butter cream or your favorite frosting.

French Butter Cream

- 1 6-ounce package chocolate bits
- ¼ cup boiling water
- 4 egg yolks
- ½ cup soft butter
- 1 teaspoon vanilla

Put the chocolate pieces into the dry container of an electric blender. Cover and blend on high speed for 6 seconds. Turn off the motor and scrape the chocolate away from the sides of the container with the blade of a knife. Add ¼ cup boiling water, cover, and blend at high speed for 6 seconds. Add the egg yolks, butter, and vanilla; cover and blend for 15 seconds longer or until the frosting is smooth. In warm weather, chill the frosting until it is the right consistency to spread.

Peaches Anisetta

- 3½ cups (No. 2½ can) cling peach halves
- 2½ cups (No. 2 can) Bing cherries, pitted
- 1 tablespoon butter
- 1 cup California port wine
- 3 tablespoons sugar
- 1 teaspoon grated lemon rind
- 1 2-inch stick cinnamon
- ¼ teaspoon anise seeds
- ⅓ cup toasted almond slivers

Drain the peaches and cherries, saving ½ cup syrup from each. Put the peaches in shallow baking dish, dot each half with butter, and put a cherry in each. Pour the rest of the cherries around the peaches. Mix the wine, sugar, lemon rind, fruit syrup, cinnamon, and anise seeds; boil for 2 or 3 minutes and pour the mixture over the fruit. Bake in a moderate oven, 350° F., for 25 minutes or until bubbly hot. Baste the peaches frequently with the sauce. Let cool till just warm, spooning the sauce over the fruit from time to time. Sprinkle with the almonds and serve with very cold whipped or sour cream. SERVES 4.

Pecan Gingerbread

Pecan gingerbread is a very good brunch dessert, or a nice hot bread to serve with butter at the end of a supper. There are wonderful gingerbread mixes on the market, and you may want to use one of them. If you do, then just add the ½ cup chopped pecans to the prepared mix.

- ¼ cup shortening
- ½ cup sugar
- 1 egg
- ½ cup molasses
- 1¾ cups sifted flour
- ½ teaspoon salt
- 1 teaspoon baking soda
- 1 teaspoon ginger
- 1 teaspoon cinnamon
- ½ cup buttermilk
- ½ cup chopped pecans

Cream the shortening, add the sugar, and blend thoroughly. Add the egg and beat until fluffy. Add the molasses and mix well. Sift together the sifted flour, salt, soda, and spices; add to the batter alternately with the buttermilk. Fold in the pecans. Pour the batter into a well-greased 8-inch square pan and bake in a moderate oven, 350° F., for 30 to 35 minutes. Cut in squares. Serve warm or cold with whipped cream, cream cheese, applesauce, or fresh fruits in season.

Praline Ice Cream Ring

Praline ice cream ring is a "fun" dessert, and teen agers love it. It is crunchy, good tasting, and not at all difficult to make.

Don't crush the cornflakes; you want the whole flakes to combine with the butter-sugar mixture and nuts.

- ½ cup butter *or* margarine
- 1 cup brown sugar, firmly packed
- 2¼ cups corn flakes
- ½ cup coarsely chopped pecans
- Vanilla ice cream

Combine the butter and sugar in a saucepan, bring to boiling, and boil for just 2 minutes. Add the nuts and corn flakes; toss with a fork to coat with the sugar-butter mixture. Press the mixture lightly into a chilled ring mold and chill for 10 minutes. Unmold on a serving dish and spoon ice cream, rounded side up, into the center of the ring. Cut through the ring to serve. SERVES 6.

Pistachio Brown Betty

- 2 tablespoons butter
- 2 cups dried bread cubes
- ¼ cup white sugar
- ¼ cup brown sugar
- ⅛ teaspoon salt
- ½ teaspoon cinnamon
- Dash of nutmeg
- 1 teaspoon grated orange peel
- 1 cup canned applesauce

Heat the chafing dish pan over direct heat. Melt the butter in the pan and add the bread cubes, turning them until they are slightly browned. Mix together the sugar, salt, cinnamon, nutmeg, and grated orange peel. Add this mixture to the browned bread cubes in the chafing dish. Add the applesauce and mix well. Fill dessert cups with this tangy pudding and top with sweetened cinnamon whipped cream and salted pistachio nut meats for accent. SERVES 4.

Orange Marshmallow Dessert

- 2 oranges, chilled
- ¼ pound marshmallows
- ½ cup orange juice
- ½ cup heavy cream, whipped

Peel the oranges and divide them into sections. Remove all the white membrane, then halve the sections. Place the marshmallows and orange juice in a saucepan and cook over low heat, stirring occasionally until the marshmallows are melted. Remove the pan from the heat and stir in the diced orange sections. Chill until the mixture is the consistency of unbeaten egg whites. Fold in whipped cream, spoon into dessert dishes, and chill until firm. If desired, garnish with additional whipped cream and orange sections. SERVES 4.

Orange Soufflé with Eggnog Sauce

- 3 egg whites
- 1/4 teaspoon cream of tartar
- Dash of salt
- 3 tablespoons granulated sugar
- 1 teaspoon orange extract
- 2 tablespoons finely cut orange marmalade

This soufflé is cooked in a 2-quart double boiler. Grease the top well with butter. Beat together until stiff the egg whites, cream of tartar, and salt. Beat in gradually, a little at a time, the granulated sugar and orange extract, then fold in the marmalade. Pour the mixture into the top of the double boiler and steam for 1 hour. Do not lift the cover. When the hour is up, remove the top of the double boiler and keep in a warm place for a moment. Carefully turn out the soufflé into a *hot* serving dish. Garnish with shaved almonds and serve with eggnog sauce. Serve immediately. SERVES 4.

Eggnog Sauce

- 2 egg yolks
- 1/2 cup sifted confectioners' sugar
- 2 tablespoons rum *or* sherry flavoring
- 1/2 cup cream, whipped stiff

Beat the egg yolks until thick and lemon colored, then beat in the confectioners' sugar and flavoring. Fold into the whipped cream.

Old-Fashioned Plum Pudding

- 1 cup coarsely chopped walnuts
- 3/4 cup coarsely chopped blanched almonds
- 1/2 pound candied fruit, diced
- 2 cups seedless raisins
- 2 cups fine dry bread crumbs
- 6 ounces suet
- 2 cups plus 2 tablespoons sifted flour
- 2 tablespoons sugar
- 1/2 teaspoon baking soda
- 1/2 teaspoon salt
- 1 1/2 teaspoons cinnamon
- 1 1/4 teaspoons nutmeg
- 3/4 teaspoon cloves
- Pinch of allspice
- 1/2 cup plus 2 tablespoons firmly packed brown sugar
- 4 eggs, slightly beaten
- 1/2 cup molasses
- 1/2 cup milk
- 1/4 cup double-strength coffee

Grease a mold or molds and add the chopped nuts to the fruits, raisins, and bread crumbs. Set aside. Break apart the suet, discarding the membrane that coats it, finely chop it, and set it aside. Sift together in a large bowl the sifted flour, sugar, baking soda, salt, cinnamon, nutmeg, cloves and allspice; blend in the brown sugar. Blend the fruit-and-nut mixture and the suet into the dry ingredients. Set this mixture aside. Blend together thoroughly the eggs, molasses, milk, and coffee. Add the liquid ingredients to the dry ingredients and mix until they are well blended. Put the batter into the mold, filling it about two-thirds full. Cover the mold tightly with a greased lid or tie on aluminum foil. Place a trivet or rack in a steamer or a deep kettle with a tight-fitting cover. Pour boiling water into the bottom of the steamer, enough to continue boiling throughout the whole steaming period (or you may quickly add more boiling water during the steaming period). Tightly cover the steamer and steam for 3 hours. Keep the water boiling at all times. Remove the pudding from the steamer and immediately loosen edges of the pudding with a knife. Unmold the pudding onto a serving plate and serve with hard sauce or foamy sauce. MAKES TWO 1-QUART MOLDS OR ONE 2-QUART MOLD.

Foamy Sauce

1 egg
1 cup sifted confectioners' sugar
½ cup soft butter
1 tablespoon vanilla

In the top of a double boiler over hot water, beat the egg and blend in sugar, butter, and vanilla. Keep the sauce over hot water until serving time.

Nut Soufflé

4 eggs, separated
¼ cup sugar
⅓ cup pecans
1 teaspoon orange *or* lemon extract

Put all the ingredients except the egg whites into the container of your electric blender. Cover and turn the motor on high speed. Uncover and stir the surface of the mixture with a rubber spatula until the ingredients are smoothly blended. Beat the egg whites until stiff and carefully but thoroughly fold them into the nut paste. Turn the mixture into a 1-quart soufflé dish and bake in a moderate

(350° F.) oven for 30 to 40 minutes. Serve immediately with chilled whipped cream or an orange-flavored sauce. SERVES 4 TO 6.

Lime Cake Pudding

- 2 tablespoons butter *or* margarine
- 3/4 cup sugar
- 3 eggs, separated
- 1/4 cup flour
- 1/8 teaspoon salt
- 1/3 cup lime juice
- 1 tablespoon grated lime rind
- 1 1/2 cups milk

Cream butter and sugar together. Stir in slightly beaten egg yolks, flour, salt, lime juice, rind, and milk. Fold in stiffly beaten egg whites. Turn the mixture into a buttered and sugared 1 1/2-quart baking dish or 4 individual baking dishes. Place the dish in a shallow pan, pour boiling water into the pan to half the depth of the casserole, and bake in a moderate oven, 350° F., for 45 minutes. Serve warm or hot with chilled whipped cream. SERVES 4.

Linzer Torte

Linzer torte is a traditional Viennese dessert that we have adopted for our American recipe files. This is a fairly standard recipe, although I have seen one or two variations of it. If you don't have a spring-form pan, save enough from your household budget—they are not expensive—and treat yourself to one. They are invaluable in making cheese cakes, tortes, and molded gelatin tortes. If you are buying only one (they come in sizes from 6 inches in diameter up to 12 inches) then buy the 8-inch size; it will be the most useful for you.

- 1 cup butter *or* margarine
- 2 cups sifted flour
- 1/4 teaspoon salt
- 1 heaping cup confectioners' sugar
- 1 cup ground almonds
- 1/2 teaspoon cinnamon
- 1/4 teaspoon allspice
- 1 teaspoon cocoa
- Juice and grated rind of 1/2 lemon
- 3 egg yolks
- Raspberry jam
- 1 egg white, slightly beaten

Knead together the butter, flour, salt, sugar, almonds, cinnamon, allspice, cocoa, lemon juice and rind, and egg yolks. When all ingredients are thoroughly blended, chill. Then roll out two-thirds of the dough 1/4 inch thick and line a spring-form cake pan, making a turned-up edge at least 1 inch deep. Spread the dough generously with raspberry jam. Roll the remaining dough into strips ¼ inch wide; crisscross these strips over the jam. Then place 1 wide strip around the edge of the cake. Paint the dough with egg white. Bake in a moderate oven, 350° F., about 45 to 55 minutes. When the torte is cool, fill the squares formed by the lattice with more jam. Sprinkle with confectioners' sugar. Serve in the bottom of the spring-form pan; don't try to turn it out. SERVES 6 TO 8.

Holiday Pineapple Sherbet

1 envelope unflavored gelatine
1 cup syrup drained from 1 No. 2 can crushed pineapple
½ cup sugar
1 teaspoon grated lemon rind
2 tablespoons lemon juice
Dash of salt
2 cups cold milk
¾ cup crushed pineapple, drained

Sprinkle the gelatine over the pineapple syrup and allow to soften. Set the bowl containing the gelatine in a pan of hot water and stir until the gelatine dissolves. Stir in the sugar, lemon rind, lemon juice, and salt; remove from heat. Gradually stir this mixture into the cold milk. Pour into an ice-cube tray and freeze at the coldest setting of the refrigerator until partially firm. Turn the sherbet into a chilled bowl and beat with an electric mixer or rotary beater until it is smooth but not melted. Fold in the pineapple. Quickly return the mixture to the ice-cube tray and freeze until it is just firm enough to spoon out. Don't forget to reset the temperature control to normal. SERVES 6.

Hershey Frozen Mousse

1 (8½-ounce) Hershey bar with almonds
¼ cup water
2 eggs, beaten
½ pint whipping cream, whipped stiff

Put the chocolate and ¼ cup water into the top of a double boiler over hot water. When the chocolate is melted, blend smoothly and rapidly stir in the beaten eggs. Stir and cook for about 2 minutes over boiling water. Remove from heat, stir the chocolate mixture into the whipped cream, and turn into 2 small or 1 large refrigerator ice trays. Freeze. Turn the freezing unit to cold until the mousse is frozen, then return freezer control to normal. This mousse can be cut into small triangles or into squares. Or it can be made in stiff, waxed, individual soufflé cups.

Glazed Doughnut Puffs

- 2 tablespoons butter *or* margarine
- ½ cup sugar
- 2 eggs, well beaten
- 2 cups sifted flour
- 2 teaspoons baking powder
- ½ teaspoon salt
- ¼ teaspoon nutmeg
- ½ teaspoon mace
- ½ cup milk

Cream the butter and sugar together until light and fluffy. Add the eggs and beat well. Sift the dry ingredients together and add them alternately with the milk to the first mixture. Chill the dough thoroughly. Drop by rounded teaspoonfuls into deep hot fat, 375° F. Turn the doughnuts as they rise to the top and again as necessary to brown evenly. Drain the puffs on absorbent paper and, while they are still warm, drizzle the glaze over them. MAKES 2½ DOZEN PUFFS.

Glaze

- 2 teaspoons light corn syrup
- 1 teaspoon rum extract
- 1½ cups sifted confectioners' sugar

Combine all ingredients with just enough hot water (about 2 tablespoons) to make a thin glaze.

Frozen Eggnog Pudding

- 3½ cups (No. 2½ can) fruit cocktail, drained
- ½ cup maraschino cherries, quartered
- 2 3-ounce packages cream cheese, softened
- ⅛ teaspoon salt
- 1 teaspoon vanilla
- 1 cup commercial eggnog
- 1 cup whipping cream, stiffly beaten
- 2 cups miniature marshmallows *or* about 24 regular marshmallows, cut in small pieces
- Red vegetable food coloring

Blend the softened cream cheese with salt, vanilla, and eggnog until smooth. Fold in the stiffly beaten cream, marshmallows, drained fruit cocktail and cherries. Tint the mixture a delicate pink with red food coloring and turn it into a ring mold, small angel food pan, or any container that will fit into the freezing unit of your refrigerator or freezer. Freeze the pudding until firm, at least 8 hours or overnight. Unmold it onto a cold platter and decorate as desired. Serve at once. SERVES ABOUT 16.

If you line the mold first with Saran Wrap it will unmold much more easily and you won't have to liquefy the top of your dessert.

Frozen Lemon Tarts

- 3 eggs, separated
- 1/4 cup lemon juice
- 2/3 cup sugar
- 1/4 teaspoon salt
- 1 teaspoon grated lemon rind
- 1 teaspoon vanilla extract
- 1 cup heavy cream, whipped
- 1/2 cup fine vanilla wafer crumbs

Place the egg yolks in the top of a double boiler and beat them thoroughly. Add the lemon juice, sugar, and salt; beat well and cook over hot, not boiling water until the custard coats a metal spoon. Chill the custard thoroughly. Stir in the lemon rind and vanilla extract. Beat the egg whites until stiff peaks form; fold the whites into the lemon mixture, then fold in the whipped cream. Place 12 fluted paper baking cups in muffin tins (if you are using the muffin type of paper cups, use them double; soufflé cups can be used singly). Sprinkle the bottom of each cup with 1 teaspoon wafer crumbs, then fill the cups with the lemon mixture. Sprinkle the top with the remaining crumbs. Place in freezer until firm. SERVES 6.

Easy Creamy Pineapple Ice Cream

- 2 eggs
- 1 1/4 cups sugar
- 1 tablespoon cornstarch
- 1 cup milk
- 1 1/2 cups unsweetened pineapple juice
- 1 cup (1/2 pint) heavy cream
- 2 drops lemon extract

Turn the freezer control on your refrigerator to its coldest setting. In the top of a double boiler, mix together the eggs, sugar, cornstarch, milk, and pineapple juice; cook, stirring constantly, until smooth and thickened. Chill thoroughly. Whip the cream, adding the lemon extract, then fold it into the chilled pineapple custard. Pour the mixture into a refrigerator tray and freeze until it is very firm. Turn the ice cream into a bowl and beat it with a rotary beater or electric mixer until it is creamy. Return it to the tray and refreeze. MAKES MORE THAN 1 QUART of smooth, delicately flavored pineapple ice cream.

Glorified Pears

- 1 cup cooked rice
- 8 marshmallows cut into eighths or about 60 miniatures
- 8 maraschino cherries, coarsely chopped
- 3 fresh Anjou pears
- 2 tablespoons lemon juice
- ½ cup whipping cream
- ¼ cup sugar

Place the cooked rice in a large bowl. Add the marshmallows and cherries. Wash, peel, and dice the pears; sprinkle them with the lemon juice. Add the pears to the rice and toss lightly. Whip the cream and add the sugar. Fold the cream into the rice mixture and mix together lightly. Chill and serve in dessert dishes. SERVES 4 TO 6.

Date-Nut Torte

- 2 egg whites
- ⅓ cup instant dry milk
- ¼ cup water
- 1 cup sugar
- 1 cup fine soda cracker crumbs
- ½ cup cut pecans
- ½ cup cut dates

With electric mixer at high speed, beat the egg whites, instant dry milk and ¼ cup water in a large bowl until the mixture is stiff. Beat in the sugar, a tablespoon at a time, to make a thick, glossy, meringue-like mixture. Fold in all at once the cracker crumbs, pecans, and dates. Spread evenly in a greased 9-inch pie pan. Bake near the center of a moderate (325° F.) oven for 45 to 50 minutes or until the top is light brown. Cool the torte, cut it into 6 to 8 wedges, and top with whipped cream or vanilla ice cream.

To vary this recipe, use ½ cup coconut in place of the nuts. Or, to make a chocolate nut torte, use ½ cup semisweet chocolate pieces in place of the dates.

Date-Whip Ice Cream Tarts

- 1 cup fresh California dates
- 1 cup whipping cream
- 1 tablespoon sugar
- 1 teaspoon instant powdered coffee
- 6 large baked tart shells
- 1 quart vanilla ice cream

Snip the dates into small pieces and combine them with the cream, sugar, and coffee. Let this mixture stand for several hours in the refrigerator, then whip it with a rotary beater until stiff. Fill the tart shells with ice cream and spread each one with whipped date mixture. Serve immediately.

These tarts may be made in advance and frozen. Remove them from the freezer about 10 minutes before serving time to "soften."

Delicate Orange Crêpes

- 1 cup cream-style cottage cheese
- 1 cup thick commercial sour cream
- 1 tablespoon sugar
- ¾ teaspoon salt
- 1 tablespoon grated orange rind
- 3 tablespoons orange juice
- 4 eggs, well beaten
- 1 cup sifted flour

Beat the cottage cheese with an electric mixer or press it through a sieve until it is very fine grained; add sour cream, sugar, salt, grated orange rind, and orange juice. Blend in the eggs and flour; beat until smooth. Pour the batter, ¼ cup at a time, onto a lightly greased, medium-hot skillet. Tilt the skillet to form a thin, round, 6-inch pancake. Brown lightly, 1 to 2 minutes on each side. Roll up the warm pancakes as they are baked. Serve 3 or 4 pancakes per serving, with hot orange honey sauce.

The pancakes may be made ahead of time, then rolled and reheated in a moderate (350° F.) oven for 5 to 8 minutes before serving.

Orange Honey Sauce

- ½ cup honey
- ⅓ cup butter *or* margarine
- ¼ teaspoon cinnamon
- 2 teaspoons grated orange rind
- 2 tablespoons orange juice

Blend all ingredients and heat them thoroughly in a saucepan, stirring constantly. Serve hot over the crêpes.

Coconut Soufflé

- 2 tablespoons butter
- 3 tablespoons flour
- ¼ teaspoon salt
- 1 cup milk
- 3 egg yolks
- ¼ cup sugar
- 3 egg whites, stiffly beaten
- ¾ cup flaked coconut
- 1 teaspoon vanilla

Melt the butter in a saucepan, add the flour and salt, and stir until smooth. Add the milk gradually, stirring constantly. Cook over low heat, stirring constantly, until the mixture is smooth and thickened. Remove from heat. Beat the egg yolks slightly, add the sugar gradually, and continue beating with a rotary beater until the eggs are thick and lemon colored; then add the flour mixture and mix well. Fold in the beaten egg whites. Carefully fold in the coconut and vanilla and turn the batter into a greased 1-quart baking dish. Place the dish in a pan of hot water and bake in a moderate oven, 350 F., for 50 to 60 minutes. Serve hot with fresh or canned fruit or fruit sauce. SERVES 6.

Christmas Pudding-Cake

- 1 cup soft dried figs
- 2 cups light *or* dark raisins
- 1½ cups coarsely grated citron
- 1 cup candied cherries, quartered
- 1 cup candied pineapple, sliced into tidbits
- 1 cup sauterne wine
- ¾ cup butter *or* margarine
- 1½ cups sifted powdered sugar
- 2 teaspoons vanilla
- 3 eggs, well beaten
- 1 cup coarsely chopped English walnuts
- 2 cups sifted flour
- 1½ teaspoons baking powder
- 1½ teaspoons salt

Clip the stems from the figs and cut the figs into small pieces. Rinse and dry the raisins. Combine the fruits, peels, and wine, mixing well. Let stand for several hours or overnight. Cream the butter, powdered sugar, and vanilla until fluffy. Beat in the eggs and add the fruits and nuts. Sift together the flour, baking powder, and salt; add to the fruit mixture, stirring until well blended. Spoon the mixture into a well-greased mold (about 2½-quart size) and bake in a slow oven, 300° F., for about 1 hour and 45 minutes. Let the pudding stand for 10 minutes, then turn it out of the mold and cool thoroughly before storing.

To serve as a pudding, cut the cake while hot into slices and serve warm with sherry-cream sauce or your favorite pudding sauce. The cake may be made ahead of time, cooled, stored, and then reheated before it is served as a pudding. Cut as much cake as is needed, either in one large piece or in individual slices. Wrap in foil and heat in a moderately hot oven, 375° F., for 15 to 20 minutes.

To serve as a fruit cake, the cake may be cut after 24 hours or it may be aged longer if desired.

Sherry-Cream Sauce

- 2 cups light cream
- 1/4 cup cornstarch
- 1/2 teaspoon salt
- 1/3 cup sugar
- 2 egg yolks
- 1/4 cup sherry wine
- 1 teaspoon vanilla

Blend together the cream, cornstarch, salt, and sugar. When the mixture is smooth, cook it over moderate heat, stirring constantly, until it boils and thickens, about 10 minutes. Beat the egg yolks, beat in a little of the hot mixture, and then blend in remaining cornstarch mixture. Cook slowly, stirring, for 2 or 3 minutes longer. Allow to cool. Blend in the wine and vanilla and beat with a rotary beater until smooth. SERVES 8.

Coconut Bavarian Cream

- 1 envelope unflavored gelatine
- 2 tablespoons cold water
- 4 egg yolks, beaten
- 1/2 cup sugar
- 1 cup milk
- 1 teaspoon vanilla
- 1 cup Angel Flake coconut
- 1 cup heavy cream, whipped
- 2 cups melon balls or other fruit in season
- Mint sprigs

Soften gelatine in 2 tablespoons cold water. Mix the egg yolks with the sugar until smooth and creamy. Scald the milk, gradually add it to the egg yolk mixture, and cook over boiling water or very low heat, stirring constantly, until smooth and thick. Add the softened gelatine and stir until it dissolves. Remove from heat, add the vanilla, and allow to cool. When the mixture begins to thicken, add the coconut. Fold in the whipped cream, pour the mixture into a 1-quart mold, and chill until firm. Unmold onto a large serving plate and surround with melon balls and mint sprigs or other fruit in season.

Cranberry-Apple Parfait

- 1 1-pound can cranberry sauce
- 1/4 cup mincemeat
- 1/2 cup chopped, peeled apple
- 1/4 cup chopped nut meats
- 1 cup heavy cream, whipped stiff

Crush the cranberry sauce with a fork. Add the mincemeat, apple, and walnuts; mix well. Fold in the whipped cream and freeze the parfait in the refrigerator freezing compartment. Cut into triangles. SERVES 6.

Cherry Bubble Dessert

Cherry bubble dessert is only one of the many desserts that you can make with ready-to-bake biscuits. All you have to do is to put your thinking cap on, sit down, look off into space, and bingo! you've dreamed up fried pies with fruit filling, or polka-dot biscuits with dabs of currant jelly in the middle, or even chutney biscuits for a pork dinner. These biscuits are fun to work with and quick as a wink if you are pressed for time in preparing dinner.

- 2½ cups (No. 2 can) sour cherries
- ½ cup sugar
- ½ teaspoon salt
- 4 teaspoons cornstarch
- 2 tablespoons butter *or* margarine
- ⅛ teaspoon almond extract
- 1 package ready-to-bake biscuits
- Whipped cream (optional)

Drain the cherries, reserving the juice. Place the cherries in an 8-inch square pan. Combine the sugar, salt, and cornstarch in a saucepan, stir in the cherry juice, and cook until thick and clear, stirring constantly. Remove from the heat and add butter or margarine and almond extract. Arrange 10 ready-to-bake biscuits on top of the cherries, pour the cherry sauce over the biscuits, and bake in a moderately hot oven, 400° F., about 25 minutes. Serve warm. If desired, top with whipped cream.

Baked Pears in Cranberry Sauce

Baked pears in cranberry sauce is probably one of the most delicious of all fresh fruit combinations. If Anjou pears are not available in your market when the mood strikes you to try this recipe, use Bartlett pears. And of course you know that you can freeze fresh cranberries and have them in your freezer the year round. Don't wash them, and don't take them out of the cardboard carton; just put them in your freezer and forget them until the next time cranberries come up in your menu planning. If you will cook the cranberries without thawing them first, they won't lose their fresh flavor.

1 pound fresh cranberries	½ teaspoon cinnamon
2 cups sugar	8 fresh Anjou pears
2 cups water	2 tablespoons lemon juice

Wash and sort the cranberries. To prepare the cranberry sauce, add the sugar to 2 cups water, bring to a boil, cook for 5 minutes, and add the cranberries. Continue cooking until the skins pop, about 5 minutes. Remove from heat, stir in the cinnamon, and set the sauce aside.

Wash the pears, core from the blossom end to preserve the shape of the tips, peel, and dip in lemon juice. Stand the pears in a casserole and pour the cranberry sauce over them. Bake in a moderate oven, 350° F., for 30 minutes or until tender, basting occasionally. Serve warm in individual dishes, spooning the hot cranberry sauce over them. Or, if you prefer, chill the dish and serve cold. SERVES 8.

Apricot-Coconut Cream

1 cup apricot whole fruit nectar	Few grains salt
½ cup milk	½ cup whipping cream
3 tablespoons lemon juice	¼ teaspoon almond extract
½ cup sugar	¼ cup toasted coconut

Combine the nectar, milk, lemon juice, sugar, and salt; stir until the sugar is dissolved. Turn the mixture into a refrigerator tray, place the tray in the freezing compartment with the control set at the lowest temperature. Freeze until firm. Remove the mixture to a chilled bowl and beat until it is smooth and fluffy. Whip the cream until stiff, add almond extract, and fold it into the frozen mixture with the coconut. Return the dessert to the freezing compartment and freeze to the desired consistency. Reset the temperature control to normal. MAKES ABOUT 1 PINT.

Baked Ambrosia

Once upon a time, ambrosia dessert meant orange segments and sliced bananas with coconut. Now ambrosia is any combination of fruits that you like. This baked ambrosia is delicious when served either piping hot or just warm.

- 2½ cups (No. 2 can) fruit cocktail
- 3 sliced ripe bananas
- 6 quartered marshmallows *or* ½ cup miniatures
- 1 cup crushed pineapple
- 2 tablespoons orange juice
- 1 cup shredded coconut
- Cream

Drain the fruit cocktail and place the fruit in a shallow oblong baking dish, 6 x 10 inches. Lightly stir in the bananas, marshmallows, pineapple, and orange juice. Sprinkle with coconut. Bake in a moderate oven, 350° F., for about 20 minutes, until coconut is toasted and marshmallows have melted. Serve piping hot with cream. Crisp peanut butter cookies are wonderful with this dessert. SERVES 5 OR 6.

Apricot Nectar Mousse

- 1½ cups apricot whole fruit nectar
- 8 marshmallows
- 5 tablespoons sugar
- 1 tablespoon lemon juice
- ⅛ teaspoon salt
- ½ cup whipping cream, whipped

Combine ¼ cup nectar and the marshmallows; heat over hot water until the marshmallows are melted. Blend in the remaining 1¼ cups nectar, sugar, lemon juice, and salt. Pour the mixture into a refrigerator tray, place the tray in the freezing compartment with the control set at the lowest temperature, and chill for about 30 minutes. Turn the mixture out into a bowl and fold in the whipped cream. Return the mousse to the freezing compartment and freeze, stirring two or three times during the freezing process. When the mousse is firm, reset the temperature control to normal. SERVES 6.

German Apple Strudel

- ½ cup water
- 4 cooking apples, peeled and quartered
- ½ recipe pie-crust dough (the amount for a 1-crust pie)
- 1 cup raisin bran cereal
- ¼ cup sugar
- ¼ teaspoon cinnamon
- 2 tablespoons butter
- Melted butter
- 1 tablespoon sugar

Place the apples in a saucepan, add ½ cup water, and place over low heat. Steam the apples, uncovered, just long enough to soften them slightly; allow to cool. Meanwhile, roll out the pie dough, thin, to about 10 inches in diameter. Sprinkle the cereal over the dough, then slice the quartered apples in half lengthwise and arrange them on top of the cereal. Combine ¼ cup sugar and the cinnamon; sprinkle this over the apples and dot with butter. Carefully roll the filled pie crust as for jelly roll. Brush the roll with melted butter and sprinkle it with 1 tablespoon sugar. Place the strudel on a cooky sheet or in a shallow oblong baking pan. Bake in a moderate oven, 375° F., for 35 to 40 minutes or until the strudel is lightly browned. SERVES 8.

German's Sweet Chocolate Refrigerator Pudding

- 1 4-ounce package German's sweet chocolate
- 1 tablespoon water
- Dash of salt
- 2 egg yolks
- 1 cup whipping cream, whipped
- 32 vanilla wafers

Place chocolate and 1 tablespoon water in a saucepan over low heat and stir until the chocolate is melted. Add salt. Add the egg yolks, one at a time, beating well after each addition. Remove from heat and allow to cool. Fold in the whipped cream. Line the bottom and sides of an 8 x 4 x 3-inch loaf pan with waxed paper, letting the paper extend over the edges of the pan. Arrange a layer of vanilla wafers on the bottom of the pan. Add about one fourth of the chocolate mixture and arrange more vanilla wafers on top of it. Repeat until all ingredients are used, topping with chocolate mixture. Chill for 8 to 12 hours in the refrigerator. Unmold and serve in slices, plain or with whipped cream topping. SERVES 6 TO 8.

Baked Bananas with Coconut Cream

This recipe for baked bananas with coconut cream has a very romantic story connected with it. Jerry Haynes, who is my "man in the kitchen" on television, came into my office one day and said, "Julie, I've met *the* girl. She's coming to dinner tonight and I want to impress her. What can I do for dessert that will just bowl her over?" Helen Haycraft, my assistant, and I put our heads together and decided that, with Jerry's limited experience in doing "gourmet-type" desserts, this would be best, because it's simple and he just couldn't get into any trouble with it. So that night Jerry Haynes broiled a steak, baked potatoes, and made this lovely dessert for his beautiful Doris. He proposed, she accepted him, and he says that he feels the dessert had a great deal to do with the fact that she thought he would make a good husband. They now have two beautiful children, Doris is one of the most popular models in Dallas, and Jerry is still my man in the kitchen. So it's a story with a happy ending.

6 firm bananas, peeled	Brown sugar
Melted butter *or* margarine	Rum

Arrange the bananas in a greased shallow baking dish. Brush them with melted butter; then sprinkle them generously with brown sugar and sparingly with rum. Bake in a moderately hot oven, 375° F., for 15 to 20 minutes, until the bananas are tender. Serve warm with coconut cream. SERVES 6.

Coconut Cream

1 cup heavy cream, whipped	1 cup shredded coconut
2 tablespoons sugar	½ teaspoon vanilla

Sweeten the whipped cream with sugar then fold in coconut and vanilla. Chill.

Chocolate Roll

This chocolate roll is adaptable for a frozen ice cream roll. Instead of spreading with sweetened whipped cream, spread with softened pistachio or chocolate ice cream, and roll up like a jelly roll. Then put in the freezer, and if you plan to keep it for more than a day in the freezer, be sure it is wrapped in freezer wrap. It takes about 20 minutes at room temperature to bring this frozen chocolate roll back to "eating softness."

5 egg yolks	1 teaspoon vanilla
1 cup confectioners' sugar	5 egg whites, stiffly beaten
¼ cup flour	Sweetened whipped cream for filling
½ teaspoon salt	
3 tablespoons cocoa	

Beat the egg yolks until thick and lemon colored. Sift together the sugar, flour, salt, and cocoa; add to eggs and blend well. Add the vanilla and fold in the egg whites. Spread the batter in a greased, waxed-paper-lined jelly roll pan and bake in a moderately hot oven, 375° F., for 15 to 20 minutes. Turn out the cake onto a towel sprinkled with additional confectioners' sugar. Remove the paper, cut off the crisp edges, and roll up for 1 minute. Unroll and allow to cool. Spread the cake with sweetened whipped cream, then roll it like jelly roll. Dust with more confectioners' sugar, or coat with whipped cream and sprinkle with chipped chocolate. You can chill this roll or freeze it, if you wish. SERVES 6.

Zabaglione

This is a liquid dessert that is served in sherbet glasses and eaten with a spoon.

6 egg yolks
6 tablespoons sugar
Few grains of salt
6 tablespoons sherry wine

Combine the egg yolks, sugar and salt in the top of a cold double boiler. Beat with a rotary beater until the eggs are thick and lemon colored, then gradually beat in the sherry wine. Place over hot, not boiling, water and beat until the zabaglione is thick and fluffy, which should take 4 to 6 minutes. Remove from heat and serve immediately in sherbet glasses. SERVES 4 TO 6.

Hot Fudge Pudding

1 cup sifted flour
½ teaspoon baking soda
¼ teaspoon salt
¾ cup sugar
6 tablespoons cocoa
2 tablespoons vinegar plus milk to make ½ cup
2 tablespoons shortening, melted
1 cup chopped nuts
1 cup brown sugar
1¾ cups boiling water

In a mixing bowl, sift together the flour, baking soda, salt, sugar, and 2 tablespoons cocoa. Add vinegar and milk, melted shortening, and nuts; stir until well blended. Turn the mixture into a greased 8-inch square pan. Mix together the brown sugar and the remaining 4 tablespoons cocoa; sprinkle this over the batter. Pour 1¾ cups boiling water over the batter. Bake in a moderate oven, 350° F., for 40 to 45 minutes. Cut into squares, invert the squares on serving plates, dip some sauce from the pan over each square, and serve warm. SERVES 6 TO 9.

Frozen Grape Mousse

Mrs. Gordon Rupe, one of the most popular hostesses in Dallas, "invented" this recipe because of a diet problem in her family. With this recipe you can also make frozen apricot mousse, frozen peach mousse, or any other flavor that you want, using puréed fruit or the fruit juice. This low-calorie whipped topping—just 17 calories to the average serving—is one of the fine new convenience foods that we are so fortunate to have.

- 2 packages Dream Whip low-calorie topping
- 1 cup milk
- 1 teaspoon vanilla
- 2 teaspoons sugar (optional)
- 1¾ cups grape juice

Prepare Dream Whip according to the directions on the package, adding sugar if a little sweeter taste is desired. Turn your mixer to low speed and add the grape juice. Pour the mixture into freezer pans and freeze until it is mushy around the edges, then beat again in the electric mixer. Return the mousse to freezer pans and freeze until it is solid. Scoop out the mousse with an ice cream scoop or cut it into triangles. Place 1 or 2 candied violets on top of each serving. SERVES 8.

Holiday Applesauce Cake

- 1 cup light *or* dark raisins
- 1 cup fresh dates, pitted
- 3 cups sifted flour
- 2½ teaspoons baking soda
- ¾ teaspoon salt
- 1 teaspoon cinnamon
- 1 teaspoon nutmeg
- 1 teaspoon allspice
- ¾ cup shortening, part butter
- 1½ cups sugar
- 3 eggs
- 2¼ cups canned applesauce
- ¼ cup orange marmalade
- 1½ cups coarsely chopped pecans
- 1 tablespoon brandy
- 1 teaspoon vanilla

Rinse the raisins and dry them on paper towels. Cut the dates into small pieces. Sift together the flour, soda, salt, and spices. Cream the shortening and sugar together till fluffy and smooth. Beat in the eggs, one at a time. Add alternately, blending in each time, the flour mixture and applesauce. Stir in the raisins, dates, marmalade, nuts, brandy and vanilla. Turn the batter into two greased 9 x 5 x 3-inch loaf pans and bake in a moderate oven, 350° F., for 1 hour and 15 minutes or until done when tested. Remove the cakes from the pans and cool them on wire racks. If you wish, frost with hard sauce frosting and decorate with nuts and candied cherries.

Hard Sauce Frosting

Cream butter with confectioners' sugar and add rum or vanilla for flavoring. Use cream to soften the frosting just enough to spread.

Strawberry Floating Island

- 2 cups sliced strawberries
- 1/4 cup sugar
- 1 tablespoon flour
- 1/8 teaspoon salt
- 1 1/2 cups milk
- 2 egg yolks, slightly beaten
- 1 teaspoon vanilla

Place the strawberries in a serving bowl and chill them thoroughly.

Combine the sugar, flour, and salt in the top of double boiler; blend in milk and egg yolks. Cook over boiling water, stirring constantly, for 7 to 9 minutes or until the custard thickens. Pour it at once into a bowl, stir in the vanilla, and allow to cool; then chill the custard in the refrigerator. At serving time, pour the custard over the berries and top with meringue.

Meringue

- 2 egg whites
- 1/4 cup sugar
- 1/8 teaspoon almond extract

Beat the egg whites until foamy. Add the sugar, a little at a time, and beat until stiff; then fold in the almond extract.

Bourbon Cake

Time after time I tried recipes for bourbon cake and found them to be dismal failures. Then one day, in the television kitchen where the staff comes to eat what is made in the cooking show, Bernice Dean, a most attractive executive secretary, said, "I have a recipe, Julie, but you may have to do a little work on it." She brought it and we had great fun making six cakes in different ways for the staff to taste. This recipe was the most popular of the six, and I hope you like it. The cake keeps wonderfully well and freezes perfectly.

- 2 8-ounce bottles maraschino cherries
- 2 cups shortening (½ butter *or* margarine)
- 2 cups sugar
- 6 eggs
- 3 cups flour
- 1 teaspoon baking powder
- ½ teaspoon salt
- ½ teaspoon nutmeg
- 2 teaspoons cinnamon
- 2 cups pecans *or* English walnuts
- ½ cup plus 1 ounce bourbon whiskey
- Red food coloring

Drain the cherries, reserving ⅓ cup juice, and cut them in halves. Cream together the shortening and sugar until fluffy. Add the eggs one at a time, beating after each addition; add the ⅓ cup cherry juice. Sift together the dry ingredients and add them to the creamed mixture a little at a time. Mix thoroughly. Stir in the nuts, ½ cup bourbon, and cherries. Use your discretion about the amount of red food coloring, depending on the color you want your cake. Bake in a 10-inch angel cake pan in a slow oven, 325° F., for 1 hour and forty minutes. When you remove the cake from the oven, let it cool in the pan on a cake rack; while it is still hot, pour over it 1 ounce of bourbon. This brings back all the flavor that you have baked out of the batter in the long baking time. MAKES ONE 4-POUND CAKE.

Daisy's Icebox Cake

Mrs. Bert Wilson of Irving, Texas, is one of the most creative cooks I know. Her homemade bread is indescribably wonderful, and her desserts are the kind that one just can't resist. This is one of her best.

- ½ pound butter
- 3 cups confectioners' sugar
- 4 eggs, beaten
- 1 flat can grated pineapple, drained
- 1 4-ounce bottle maraschino cherries, drained
- ½ pint whipping cream
- 3½ dozen lady fingers

Cream together the butter and sugar, add eggs, and mix well. Combine the pineapple and cherries. Whip the cream until it is stiff. In a 10-inch spring form pan, spread a layer of lady fingers and line the sides with more lady fingers that have been split open. Spread a layer of the butter-egg mixture over the lady fingers, then a layer of the mixed fruits, and then a layer of whipped cream. Repeat until all the ingredients are used. The top layer should be of lady fingers. Let stand overnight in the refrigerator. When ready to serve, remove the sides of the pan and slice the cake. Serve with whipped cream.

Pumpkin Cake with Raisin Icing

- ½ cup shortening
- 1¼ cups sugar
- 2 eggs, well beaten
- 2¼ cups sifted cake flour
- 3 teaspoons baking powder
- ½ teaspoon salt
- ½ teaspoon cinnamon
- ½ teaspoon ginger
- ½ teaspoon nutmeg
- 1 cup cooked or canned pumpkin
- ¾ cup milk
- ½ teaspoon baking soda
- ½ cup chopped nuts

Cream the shortening, add the sugar gradually, cream thoroughly, and blend in the beaten eggs. Sift together the flour, baking powder, salt, and spices. Combine the pumpkin and milk and stir in the soda. Add the flour mixture and pumpkin alternately to the creamed mixture. Blend in the nuts. Pour the batter into two well-greased and floured 8-inch layer cake pans and bake for 30 to 35 minutes in a moderate (350° F.) oven. When cool, spread raisin icing between the layers and over the top and sides of the cake.

Raisin Icing

- 2 large egg whites
- 2 cups brown sugar, packed
- 6 tablespoons water
- ½ cup seeded raisins, cut in half

In the top of a double boiler, combine the egg whites, sugar, and 6 tablespoons water. Beat together just enough to blend ingredients. Place over rapidly boiling water and beat with a rotary beater until the mixture is light and fluffy and will hold a peak, 5 to 7 minutes. Remove from hot water and carefully fold in the raisins. (The raisins cause the icing to soften a little so be sure that it is cooked until very thick before adding them.) This makes enough icing for the two-layer cake.

Helen's Fabulous Frosting

- 1 6-ounce package semisweet chocolate bits
- ½ cup commercial sour cream
- Pinch of salt

Melt the chocolate bits over hot water. Remove from heat and combine with sour cream and salt; stir until smooth.

Cream Cheese Frosting

2 3-ounce packages cream cheese
2 tablespoons milk
5 cups sifted confectioners' sugar
2 teaspoons vanilla

Blend together the cheese and milk. Gradually blend in the sifted sugar. Add the vanilla and beat until smooth. This makes enough frosting for a good thick filling and frosting for two layers.

Lemon Refrigerator Cake

1 envelope unflavored gelatine
¼ cup cold water
Hot water
1 cup sugar
4 egg yolks, beaten
Rind of 1 lemon
Juice of 2 lemons
4 egg whites, stiffly beaten
1 pint heavy cream, whipped
18 fresh lady fingers, split

Dissolve the gelatine in ¼ cup cold water. When the gelatine has softened, fill the cup with hot water, stir, and allow to cool. Combine the sugar and egg yolks, then add the lemon rind and juice. Add the gelatine mixture, then fold in the beaten egg whites and stiffly whipped cream. Line a spring-form pan with lady fingers. Turn the rounded sides of the lady fingers to the outside and trim off bottom round edges straight. (In making the bottom layer of lady fingers, be sure to fill up all the little chinks so that the lemon mixture won't seep through.) Pour the lemon mixture over the lady fingers. Make crumbs of remaining lady fingers, brown them lightly, and sprinkle them over the top. Place the dessert in the refrigerator to set. To serve, remove the sides of the pan, leaving the bottom of the spring form under the cake, and serve on a cake server. SERVES 10 TO 12.

Vanilla-Poppy Seed Cake

2 cups sifted cake flour
⅛ teaspoon salt
2 teaspoons baking powder
½ cup poppy seeds
1½ cups vanilla sugar (see recipe below)
½ cup butter *or* margarine
1 cup milk
4 large egg whites
Confectioners' sugar *or* creamy vanilla frosting

Sift together the flour, salt, and baking powder; mix with poppy seeds and set aside. Gradually blend 1¼ cups of the vanilla sugar with butter or margarine, mixing well after each addition. Stir in ¼ cup of the milk. Add the flour mixture alternately with the remaining ¾ cup milk. Beat the egg whites until they stand in soft peaks, beat in the remaining ¼ cup of vanilla sugar, and fold into the cake batter. Turn the batter into a well-greased, lightly floured 9-inch tube cake pan. Bake in a preheated moderate oven, 350° F., for 50 minutes or until a cake tester or toothpick inserted in center comes out clean. Allow to cool in the pan for 10 minutes. Remove the cake from the pan to a wire rack and finish cooling. If desired, dust with sifted confectioners' sugar or frost with your favorite butter cream vanilla frosting.

Vanilla Sugar

Use 2 vanilla beans for 5 pounds sugar. Split the vanilla beans down the center, tuck them into the sugar, and let stand for two weeks before using.

Orange Cake

If you like a cake without frosting, then this is the recipe for you to try. It is an elegant cake with wonderful keeping qualities and it goes well with lemon or pineapple sherbet. Another version of this orange cake follows, this time with chopped black walnuts added to the batter.

- 1 cup sugar
- ½ cup shortening
- 2 eggs
- ⅔ cup buttermilk
- 2 cups sifted flour
- 1 teaspoon soda
- Pinch of salt
- 2 tablespoons grated orange rind

Cream together the sugar and shortening, add the eggs, and beat until the mixture is creamy and light. Add the buttermilk. Sift together the dry ingredients and add them to the shortening mixture. Fold in the orange rind. Turn the batter into a greased 9-inch stem cake pan and bake for 35 to 40 minutes in a moderately hot (375° F.) oven. After cake is baked, leave it in the pan and, while still hot, slowly pour over it a mixture of the juice and grated rind of 1 orange and ½ cup sugar. Let it soak into the cake, and allow the cake to cool completely before turning it out of the pan.

If you want an even more scrumptious taste to this blend of sugar and orange juice, add 2 or 3 tablespoons Cointreau (orange liqueur).

Orange-Nut Cake

- 1½ cup sugar
- ½ pound butter *or* margarine
- 3 eggs, separated
- 2 cups flour
- Pinch of salt
- 1 teaspoon baking powder
- 1 teaspoon baking soda
- ¾ cup commercial sour cream
- Grated rind and juice of 1 orange
- Grated rind and juice of 1 lemon
- 1 cup chopped black walnuts

Cream together the 1 cup sugar and butter; add egg yolks. Sift together the flour, salt, baking powder, and baking soda; add to the creamed mixture alternately with the sour cream. Add lemon and orange rind and nuts. Beat the egg whites until stiff and fold them into the batter. Turn the batter into a stem cake pan and bake in a moderate oven, 325° F., for 1 hour. Mix the remaining ½ cup sugar with the lemon and orange juices; pour this over hot cake in pan. Let the cake stand in the pan until liquid is absorbed and the cake is just warm, then turn it out onto a cooling rack. This cake keeps well when wrapped in foil.

Lemon Icebox Cake

- 1 cup finely crushed chocolate cookie crumbs
- 6 tablespoons sugar
- 2 tablespoons melted butter *or* margarine
- 2 eggs, separated
- 1 can sweetened condensed milk
- 1 tablespoon grated lemon rind
- ½ cup lemon juice
- ¼ teaspoon almond extract

Combine the crumbs, 2 tablespoons of the sugar, and the butter; mix well. Press 1 cup of the mixture onto the bottom and sides of a buttered refrigerator tray; chill. Reserve the remaining crumbs for the top. Beat the egg yolks until thick and add the sweetened condensed milk. Add the rind, juice, and almond extract and stir until thickened (don't cook). Beat the egg whites until they begin to hold soft peaks, add remaining sugar, and continue beating until the whites are stiff. Fold them into the milk and lemon mixture.

Pour the mixture over the crumbs in the ice tray, top with remaining crumbs, and freeze until firm, about 4 to 6 hours. Cut into triangular serving pieces. This dessert has a lovely creamy consistency, with no ice crystals. SERVES 6.

Cranberry-Pineapple Upside-Down Cake

- 3 tablespoons butter *or* margarine
- ¼ cup brown sugar, packed
- 1 1-pound can jellied cranberry sauce
- 4 or 5 slices pineapple
- Walnut halves
- 1 package spice cake mix

Preheat the oven to moderate, 350° F. Grease a 10-inch round cake pan or a 10-inch round skillet. Melt the butter and brown sugar together and spread the mixture on the greased pan. Arrange slices of jellied cranberry sauce, pineapple slices, and walnuts in a pretty design on top of the sugar mixture. Prepare the spice cake mix as directed on the package and pour the batter gently and evenly over the fruit. Bake for 55 to 60 minutes, or until the surface of the cake springs back when it is pressed gently. Let the cake set for about 10 minutes in the pan before turning it out onto a cooling rack. Serve hot or cold, plain or with whipped cream. SERVES 8 TO 10 GENEROUSLY.

Black Walnut Cake

- ½ cup butter *or* margarine
- 1½ cups sugar
- 2 cups sifted flour
- 4 teaspoons baking powder
- ½ teaspoon salt
- 1 cup milk
- 1 cup finely ground black walnuts
- 1 teaspoon vanilla
- 4 egg whites
- ¼ teaspoon cream of tartar

Cream the butter or margarine. Add the sugar gradually, beating with spoon until light and fluffy. Sift the flour with the baking powder and salt and add to the butter-sugar mixture alternately with the milk, mixing well after each addition. Add the ground nuts and vanilla. Beat the egg whites with cream of tartar until stiff but not dry, and fold them into the batter. Cover bottom of a 9-inch tube pan with waxed paper and oil the sides. Pour in the batter and bake in a slow moderate oven, 325° F., for 15 minutes, then increase the heat to 350° F. and bake about 30 to 40 minutes longer, or until the top springs back when lightly pressed with a finger. SERVES 12 TO 14.

Cream Cheese Cake

- 2 cups fine zwieback *or* graham cracker crumbs
- 1 cup sugar
- ½ cup melted butter *or* margarine
- 2 tablespoons flour
- ¼ teaspoon salt
- 2 8-ounce packages cream cheese
- ½ teaspoon vanilla
- 1 tablespoon lemon juice
- 1 teaspoon lemon rind, grated
- 4 egg yolks
- 1 cup cream
- 4 egg whites, stiffly beaten

Combine the crumbs, ½ cup sugar, and melted butter; mix thoroughly and press onto the bottom of a 9-inch spring form pan. Combine the remaining ½ cup sugar, flour, salt, and cream cheese. Add the vanilla, lemon juice, and lemon rind. Add, one at a time, the 4 egg yolks, blending well after each addition. Add the cream and fold in the stiffly beaten egg whites. Pour this mixture on top of the crumbs and bake in a moderate oven, 325° F., for 1 hour or until the cake is set in the center. Cool the cheese cake by turning off oven, opening door, and letting it stand until cold. Then remove the rim of the pan and chill. Do not invert. SERVES 12 TO 16.

Fruit Icebox Cake

- 2 cups milk
- 1 pound marshmallows
- 1 cup whipping cream
- 1 teaspoon vanilla
- 2½ cups (No. 2 can) pineapple tidbits, drained
- ½ cup nutmeats, chopped
- 2 cups graham cracker crumbs

Bring the milk to a boil in the top of a double boiler, add the marshmallows, and stir until melted. Let cool. Whip the cream, flavor it with the vanilla, and fold it into the marshmallow mixture. Add the pineapple and nuts. Sprinkle a 7 x 11-inch pan with graham cracker crumbs, pour in the mixture, and top with another layer of crumbs. Chill overnight. Serve plain or topped with whipped cream. SERVES 12.

German's Sweet Chocolate Cake

This is the fabulous German's sweet chocolate cake that swept through the country like an epidemic of gossip. One of my viewers first sent the recipe to me, and we sent out over seventy thousand copies of it to homemakers. Texas homemakers wrote to North Dakota homemakers, and they in turn wrote to English homemakers, and finally the recipe came back to me from Karachi. Now the recipe appears on the wrappers of German's Sweet Chocolate bars. If you want a simply scrumptious cake, this is it.

- 1 cup shortening (I use margarine)
- 2 cups sugar
- 4 egg yolks
- 1 4-ounce bar German's Sweet Chocolate, melted
- 2½ cups sifted flour
- ¼ teaspoon salt
- 1 teaspoon baking soda
- 1 cup buttermilk
- 4 egg whites, beaten stiff
- 1 teaspoon vanilla

Cream the shortening and sugar, add the egg yolks, and stir in the melted chocolate. Sift together the dry ingredients and add to the first mixture alternately with the buttermilk. Fold in the egg whites and vanilla. Bake in three greased layer cake pans (or two layer pans and one 9 x 5 x 2-inch pan) in a moderate oven, 350° F., for 30 to 35 minutes. Allow the cake to cool in the pans, and then turn it out onto racks for further cooling. Put together with filling and frosting.

Filling and frosting

- ½ pint whipping cream
- ¼ pound butter
- 3 egg yolks
- 1 cup sugar
- 1 cup chopped pecans
- 1 cup coconut

Mix the cream, butter, egg yolks, and sugar in a saucepan and cook until the mixture begins to thicken, about 12 minutes. Remove from heat, add nuts and coconut, and set aside to cool. (It will thicken as it cools.) This frosting and filling requires little or no beating. There is enough for a filling for two layers and a frosting. Use the third layer or the little sheet cake with a different kind of frosting for another time or serve it with a puff of whipped cream.

Pineapple Upside-Down Cake

1 package yellow cake mix
2 tablespoons butter *or* margarine
½ cup brown sugar
5 pineapple slices, drained
5 maraschino cherries, cut in half
½ cup nut meats

Make the cake batter according to the directions on the package. Melt the butter in a heavy 10-inch skillet and stir in the brown sugar. Arrange the pineapple slices in a design in the sugar-butter mixture with cherry halves centered in the rings; sprinkle nuts between the pineapple rings. Pour the cake batter on top and bake in a moderate oven, 375° F., for 45 minutes. Remove the cake from the oven, let it stand in the skillet for 5 minutes, and then turn out, upside down, on a cake platter. Cut in wedges.

Light Applesauce Cake

1 cup sugar
¾ cup butter
1 egg, beaten
1 cup canned applesauce
1 teaspoon baking soda
2 cups flour
½ teaspoon cinnamon
½ teaspoon cloves
½ teaspoon nutmeg
1 cup chopped dates *or* raisins
1 cup pecans, broken

Cream together the sugar and butter; add egg. Mix the applesauce and soda. Sift together the flour and spices. Combine the sugar and butter mixture with the applesauce, flour and spices, dates or raisins, and nuts. Bake in a moderate oven, 350° F., about 40 minutes either in a long pan or in a loaf pan. I prefer this cake unfrosted, but you may use a creamy frosting or whipped cream slightly sweetened. Try a little mocha flavoring instead of vanilla.

Banana Chiffon Cake

2¼ cups sifted cake flour
1½ cups sugar
1 tablespoon baking powder
1 teaspoon salt
½ cup cooking *or* salad oil
5 medium egg yolks, unbeaten
1 cup (2 to 3) mashed ripe bananas
1 tablespoon fresh lemon juice
½ teaspoon cream of tartar
1 cup (7 to 8) egg whites

Sift together the flour, sugar, baking powder, and salt. Make a well in the dry ingredients and add in order the oil, egg yolks, bananas, and lemon juice. Beat until smooth. Add the cream of tartar to the egg whites and beat until they form very stiff peaks. Do not underbeat. Gradually and gently fold the banana mixture into the egg whites until just blended. Do not stir. Pour the batter into an ungreased 10-inch tube pan that is 4 inches deep. Bake in a moderate oven, 325° F., about 1 hour and 5 minutes or until the cake is done. Immediately turn upside down, placing the tube part of the pan over a small necked bottle or funnel so that the pan is elevated above the surface of the table. Let the cake hang until it is cold. Loosen the cake from the sides and tube of the pan with a spatula, turn the pan over, and rest the cake on a cooling rack. SERVES 16 TO 20.

Jelly Roll

- 3 large eggs
- 1 cup sugar
- 1 teaspoon vanilla
- 5 tablespoons water
- 1 cup sifted flour
- 1 teaspoon baking powder
- ¼ teaspoon salt
- Confectioners' sugar
- 1 cup jelly or jam

Grease and flour a 15 x 10-inch jelly roll pan or line the pan with greased paper (waxed, plain, or foil) and turn up the edges. With a rotary beater, beat the eggs until thick, then gradually beat in sugar. Mix and beat in the vanilla and 5 tablespoons water. Sift together the flour, baking powder, and salt; add the dry ingredients to the eggs all at once, then beat until smooth. Pour the batter into a pan and bake in a moderate oven, 375° F., for 12 to 15 minutes. Turn the cake upside down on a towel sprinkled with sifted confectioners' sugar. Quickly remove the paper and cut off the hard edges of the cake. Spread the cake with the jelly or jam and gently roll it up, beginning at short end. If the cake starts to break, keep right on rolling. Wrap the cake in a towel and allow to cool for about half an hour. Then sprinkle the jelly roll with powdered sugar and serve in slices, plain or with whipped cream or ice cream.

To make an ice cream roll, don't spread the cake with jelly but roll it up loosely and wrap it in a towel until it cools. When the cake is cold, open it out, spread it with softened ice cream, and roll it up into jelly roll shape again. Wrap it in foil and store it in the freezer until the ice cream is firm. Slice and serve with chocolate sauce.

Carrot Cake

- 3 cups flour
- 2 teaspoons baking powder
- 2 teaspoons baking soda
- 2 teaspoons cinnamon
- 2 cups sugar
- 1½ cups salad oil
- 4 eggs
- 2 cups finely grated carrots
- ½ cup chopped pecans

Sift together into a mixer bowl the flour, baking powder, soda, cinnamon, and sugar. Start the mixer at low speed and add the salad oil. Break the eggs, one at a time, into the batter, then add the carrots and nuts. Turn the batter into an ungreased stem cake pan and bake in a moderate oven, 350° F., for 65 to 70 minutes. Serve plain or, if desired, with cream cheese icing.

Cream Cheese Icing

- 3 ounces cream cheese
- 1½ cups sifted confectioners' sugar
- 1 teaspoon vanilla

Cream all ingredients together until fluffy and of a good spreading consistency.

Macaroon Cake

- 3 tablespoons butter *or* margarine
- 1½ cups sugar
- 3 egg yolks
- 1 cup sifted flour
- ½ teaspoon salt
- 2 teaspoons baking powder
- ¼ cup milk
- 3 egg whites
- Pinch of cream of tartar
- 1 cup finely chopped pecans
- 1 cup heavy cream, whipped

Heat the oven to moderate, 375° F. Grease and flour 2 8-inch layer cake pans. With the back of a spoon, work the butter until it is creamy. Gradually add ½ cup sugar, beating with the spoon until blended. Add the egg yolks and mix until light and fluffy. Sift together the flour, ¼ teaspoon salt, and baking powder; add to the egg yolk mixture alternately with the milk. Spread the batter in layer pans and set aside. Beat the egg whites with cream of tartar and remaining ¼ teaspoon salt until the whites are stiff. Gradually add the remaining 1 cup sugar, beating constantly until the meringue forms stiff peaks. Fold in the nuts. Spread the meringue over the batter in the pans. Bake about 20 minutes or until lightly browned. Remove the cakes from the oven, loosen them carefully from the pans, and turn them out onto racks to cool. Place one layer, cake side down, on a cake plate and spread whipped cream over the meringue. Cover with the second layer, cake side down, and top with more whipped cream if desired.

Grandmother's Jam Cake

This cake recipe was given to me by one of my readers. She paid $150.00 for it at one of the leading hotels in New York, and she has had more than $150.00 worth of fun and pleasure giving the recipe to her friends. A spicy, heavy-type cake, it stays fresh and moist and is really better after the second day.

- 1 cup butter
- 2 cups sugar
- 3 eggs
- 1 cup blackberry jam
- 3 cups flour
- ½ teaspoon salt
- 1 teaspoon cinnamon
- 1 teaspoon nutmeg
- 1 teaspoon allspice
- 1 teaspoon ginger
- 1 teaspoon baking soda
- 1 cup buttermilk
- 1½ cups pecans
- 1 cup raisins

Cream the butter and sugar, add the eggs, and cream well. Blend in the jam. Sift together the flour, salt, and spices. Add the soda to the buttermilk. Add the sifted dry ingredients to the creamed mixture alternately with the buttermilk, ending with the dry mixture. Fold in 1 cup pecans and the raisins. Turn the batter into 4 greased and floured 8-inch pans and bake in a moderate oven, 350° F., for 35 to 40 minutes. Cool the layers on racks and use the frosting recipe below for filling and for frosting only on the top of the cake, leaving the sides plain. Sprinkle with the remaining ½ cup chopped nuts.

Frosting

- 2 cups sugar
- ½ cup cream
- 1 cup butter

Combine all ingredients and cook without stirring until the mixture reaches the soft-ball stage, or 230° F. on a candy thermometer. Beat until spreadable.

Valentine Cherry Pie

- 2 cups (No. 2½ can) pitted, sour cherries and their juice
- ¾ cup sugar
- 4 tablespoons flour *or* 2½ tablespoons cornstarch
- Dash of salt
- 2 tablespoons butter *or* margarine
- Few drops red food coloring (optional)
- Pastry for double-crust pie

Drain the cherries, reserving ½ cup of the juice. Combine the juice, ½ cup sugar, flour or cornstarch, and salt; cook until thickened. Add butter, remaining sugar, and red food coloring, if desired. Pour the syrup over the cherries in an 8-inch pastry-lined pie pan. Attach the top crust and make vents, or use a lattice top crust. Bake in a hot oven, 400° F., for 45 minutes to 1 hour. Serve with vanilla ice cream.

Sweet Potato Pie

- ¼ cup butter
- ½ cup brown sugar, packed
- 1 cup cooked mashed sweet potatoes
- 3 eggs, slightly beaten
- ⅓ cup corn syrup
- ⅓ cup milk
- ½ teaspoon salt
- 1 teaspoon vanilla
- 1 unbaked 9-inch pie shell

Cream the butter and sugar together well, add mashed potatoes and eggs, and mix well. Combine with syrup, milk, salt, and vanilla. Turn the filling into the pie shell. Bake in a hot oven, 425° F., for 10 minutes, then reduce the heat to 325° F. and continue to bake for 35 to 45 minutes longer. Allow the pie to cool before serving. This pie is especially good when it is served with a dab of tart jelly such as grape or currant.

Southern Cashew Pie

- 2 eggs, beaten
- 1 cup dark corn syrup
- 1 teaspoon vanilla
- 1 cup sugar
- 2 tablespoons melted butter *or* margarine
- 1 cup salted cashew nuts
- 1 unbaked 8-inch pie shell
- Additional pie dough for decoration

Combine the beaten eggs, corn syrup, vanilla, sugar, and melted butter; blend thoroughly. Stir in the salted cashews and pour the filling into the unbaked pie shell. Bake in a moderate oven, 350° F., for 45 minutes to 1 hour. Cut the additional pie dough into strips or crescents and bake on a cookie sheet. They brown quickly, so watch them. Place the baked pastry bits on top of the pie when you remove it from the oven.

Rich Coconut Pie

- 4 eggs
- 1½ cups sugar
- 1½ cups dark corn syrup
- ¼ cup melted butter *or* margarine
- 1½ teaspoons vanilla
- ¼ teaspoon salt
- 2 cups flaked coconut
- 1 10-inch unbaked pie shell

Combine the eggs, sugar, corn syrup, butter or margarine, vanilla, and salt; beat until well blended. Stir in the coconut and turn the filling into the pie shell. Bake in a hot oven, 400° F., for 50 minutes. Allow to cool. At serving time, garnish with whipped cream if desired.

Rum Chiffon Pie

- 2 cups graham cracker crumbs
- ¼ cup melted butter *or* margarine
- 2 teaspoons granulated sugar
- 1½ cups milk
- ¾ cup brown sugar
- 3 egg yolks
- Pinch of salt
- 1 envelope unflavored gelatine
- 4 tablespoons white wine
- 3 tablespoons Jamaica rum
- 3 egg whites, stiffly beaten
- ½ cup heavy cream, whipped
- Grated sweet chocolate

Combine crumbs, melted butter or margarine, and sugar. Spread the mixture in a lightly greased 9-inch pie pan and set in a moderate (350° F.) oven for 10 minutes. Chill the crust before adding the filling.

In the top of a double boiler over boiling water, combine and cook the milk, brown sugar, egg yolks, and salt until the custard coats the spoon. Soak the gelatine in the white wine and dissolve it in the hot custard. Stir the custard over cracked ice until it is cool and thick. Stir in the rum and fold in the stiffly beaten egg whites and the whipped cream. Turn the filling into the chilled pie shell and sprinkle with grated sweet chocolate. Chill the pie thoroughly before serving.

Peach Praline Pie

- 4 cups sliced canned peaches
- 2 tablespoons cornstarch
- 1 tablespoon grated lemon rind
- 2 tablespoons lemon juice
- ½ teaspoon almond extract
- 1 baked 9-inch pie shell

Drain the peaches thoroughly, reserving 1¼ cups of the peach syrup. Combine this syrup with the cornstarch and cook over low heat stirring constantly, until clear and thickened. Add the peaches, rind, juice, and almond extract. Continue to cook slowly for 10 minutes, stirring occasionally. Allow the filling to cool slightly, then pour it into the baked pie shell. Chill. Sprinkle with praline topping.

Praline Topping

- ½ cup butter *or* margarine
- ½ cup brown sugar
- ½ cup coarsely broken walnuts
- 1 cup corn flakes

Melt the butter or margarine and brown sugar in a saucepan. Bring the mixture to a boil and cook about 1½ minutes. Remove from heat, add broken walnuts and corn flakes, and toss lightly with a fork. Allow the topping to cool, then sprinkle it over the peach pie.

Pineapple Chiffon Pie

- 1 envelope plain gelatine
- ¼ cup cold water
- 3 eggs, separated
- ¾ cup sugar
- ¾ cup crushed pineapple (not drained)
- 1 teaspoon grated lemon peel
- 3 tablespoons lemon juice
- ¼ teaspoon salt
- ½ cup heavy cream, whipped
- 1 baked 9-inch pie shell

Add the gelatine to ¼ cup cold water and let stand. In the top of a double boiler stir together the egg yolks, ¼ cup sugar, the crushed pineapple, lemon peel, and juice; cook over hot water, stirring constantly, until smooth and thickened. Add the softened gelatine and stir until it is dissolved. Remove from heat. Add the salt to the egg whites and beat until stiff, gradually beating in the remaining ½ cup sugar. Fold in the hot pineapple mixture. Heap the filling into the baked pie shell and chill about 3 hours or until set. At serving time spread the pie with whipped cream and decorate each serving with a spoonful of thoroughly drained crushed pineapple.

Pecan Pie

1 unbaked 8-inch pie shell
2 eggs
½ cup sugar
½ cup dark corn syrup
2 tablespoons melted butter *or* margarine
½ teaspoon vanilla
1½ cups pecans

Line pie pan with pastry and chill it while you make the filling. Preheat the oven to moderate, 375° F. Beat the eggs slightly, add the sugar, corn syrup, butter, and vanilla, and stir in the pecans. Pour the filling into the pie shell and bake 45 minutes or until lightly browned. Serve cold or warm, not hot. Wonderful with vanilla ice cream.

Osgood Pie

½ cup butter *or* margarine
1 cup sugar
2 egg yolks, slightly beaten
½ cup chopped pecans
½ cup raisins *or* chopped dates
1½ teaspoons vinegar
2 egg whites
Unbaked 8-inch pie shell

Cream the butter, then add the sugar and cream together well. Add the egg yolks and mix well. Add the pecans, raisins or dates, and vinegar. Beat the egg whites until they are stiff and fold them into the mixture. Pour the filling into the unbaked pie shell and bake in a moderate (325° F.) oven for about 1 hour or until it tests done.

Orange Meringue Pie

1 envelope unflavored gelatine
1¼ cups milk
¾ cup sugar
2 large eggs, separated
1 tablespoon cold milk
1 6-ounce can orange juice concentrate, thawed
½ cup heavy cream, whipped stiff
1 9-inch baked pie shell
Cinnamon

In a small pan, soften the gelatine in ¼ cup milk. Combine the remaining 1 cup milk and ½ cup sugar in the top of a double boiler. Stir over direct heat until the mixture is hot and the sugar is dissolved. Remove from heat. Beat the egg yolks with 1 tablespoon cold milk. Add the hot milk-sugar mixture slowly to the yolks, beating constantly with rotary beater. Return the mixture to the top of the double boiler and stir over hot, not boiling, water until the mixture thickens and coats a spoon. Remove from heat. Stir the gelatine mixture over low heat until it is just dissolved, then blend it into the egg mixture. Stir in the thawed and undiluted orange juice concentrate. Allow the mixture to cool at room temperature. When it is cool but not set, fold in the whipped cream. Pour the filling into the pie shell and chill it in the refrigerator for 3 or 4 hours. Before serving, prepare the meringue by beating the egg whites with the remaining ¼ cup sugar until very stiff. Pipe the meringue around the edge of the pie and dust with a little cinnamon.

Nesselrode Pie

- 2 envelopes unflavored gelatine
- 4 cups cold bottled eggnog
- ¼ cup sugar
- ¼ teaspoon nutmeg
- 4 teaspoons rum flavoring
- 1 cup heavy cream, whipped
- ¼ cup maraschino cherries, chopped
- ½ cup chopped nuts
- 1 baked 10-inch pie shell

Add the gelatine to 1 cup eggnog and place in the top of a double boiler over hot water. Add the sugar and stir until the gelatine and sugar are dissolved. Add this mixture to the remaining 3 cups eggnog, nutmeg, and rum flavoring. Chill the mixture until it is the consistency of unbeaten egg whites, then whip it until it is light and fluffy. Fold in the whipped cream, cherries, and chopped nuts. Turn the filling into the pie shell and chill the pie thoroughly before serving. Garnish with additional whipped cream, shaved chocolate, and chopped maraschino cherries.

Lemon Chiffon Pie

- 1 envelope unflavored gelatine
- ¼ cup cold water
- 3 egg yolks
- ⅓ cup sugar
- ½ cup lemon juice
- ½ teaspoon salt
- 1 teaspoon grated lemon rind
- 3 egg whites
- ½ cup sugar
- 1 baked 9-inch pie shell

Soften the gelatine in ¼ cup cold water. Beat the egg yolks slightly and add ⅓ cup sugar, lemon juice, and salt. Place in the top of a double boiler and cook over hot water, stirring constantly, until the mixture is of custard consistency. Remove from the heat, add the softened gelatine, and stir until it is dissolved.

Add the lemon rind and chill to the consistency of unbeaten egg white. Beat the egg whites until stiff and gradually add ½ cup sugar. Fold the gelatine mixture into the beaten egg whites. Pour the filling into the pie shell and chill until the filling is firm. Garnish with whipped cream and maraschino cherries.

Key Lime Chiffon Pie

- 1 envelope unflavored gelatine
- ¼ cup cold water
- ½ cup lime juice
- 4 eggs, separated
- ¾ cup sugar
- ½ teaspoon salt
- 1 9-inch baked pie shell

Soften the gelatine in ¼ cup cold water. Combine lime juice, ½ cup sugar, and salt. Beat the egg yolks and blend them into the lime juice mixture. Cook in the top of a double boiler over hot water, stirring constantly, until the mixture is thick and coats a spoon. Remove from heat, add gelatine, and stir until it is dissolved. Allow the mixture to cool until it is slightly thickened. Beat the egg whites until stiff but not dry. Gradually add the remaining ¼ cup sugar, beating constantly. Fold the lime mixture into the egg whites. Pile the filling into the pie shell and chill until it is firm. If you like, you may add a few drops of green food coloring to give the filling a deeper green color.

Fresh Cranberry Pie

- 2 cups fresh cranberries
- 1½ cups sugar
- ½ cup chopped walnuts *or* pecans
- 2 eggs
- 1 cup sifted flour
- ½ cup butter *or* margarine, melted
- ¼ cup shortening, melted

Grease a 10-inch pie plate well. Spread the cranberries over the bottom of the plate and sprinkle with ½ cup sugar and the nuts over them. Beat the eggs well, add the remaining 1 cup sugar gradually, and beat until thoroughly mixed. Add the flour, melted butter, and shortening to the egg-sugar mixture; beat well. Pour the batter over the cranberries. Bake in a moderate oven, 325° F., for 60 minutes or until crust is golden brown. Cut into wedges and serve either warm or cold with generous scoops of vanilla ice cream.

Fresh Coconut Bavarian Lemon Pie

- 1 envelope unflavored gelatine
- 1/4 cup cold water
- 4 eggs, separated
- 1 cup sugar
- 1/2 cup lemon juice
- 1/2 teaspoon salt
- 1 teaspoon grated lemon rind
- 1/3 cup heavy cream, whipped
- 3/4 cup grated coconut
- 9-inch baked pie shell, chilled
- 1/2 cup heavy cream, whipped, for garnish
- 1/3 cup grated coconut for garnish

Soften the gelatine in 1/4 cup cold water and set aside. Beat the egg yolks until thick and lemon colored; gradually beat in 1/2 cup sugar, lemon juice, and salt. Cook over hot water or very low heat, stirring constantly, until the custard coats a metal spoon, about 10 minutes. Remove from the heat and add the softened gelatine; stir the mixture until the gelatine is dissolved. Blend in the lemon rind. Chill until the mixture is the consistency of unbeaten egg white. Beat the egg whites until they stand in soft, stiff peaks, then gradually beat in the remaining 1/2 cup sugar. Fold the whites into the lemon mixture. Quickly fold in the whipped 1/3 cup cream and the 3/4 cup grated coconut. Turn the filling into the pie shell and chill until firm and ready to serve. Garnish with the additional whipped cream and grated coconut.

Fudge-Nut Pie

- 2 eggs, beaten
- 1 cup dark corn syrup
- 1/8 teaspoon salt
- 1 teaspoon vanilla
- 1 cup sugar
- 1 cup pecan meats
- 2 tablespoons melted butter *or* margarine
- 2 squares unsweetened chocolate
- 1 unbaked 9-inch pie shell

Melt the chocolate with the butter. Add the eggs, corn syrup, salt, vanilla, sugar, and pecans. Pour the filling into the pie shell. Bake in a hot oven, 400° F., for 15 minutes, then reduce the heat to moderate 350° F., and bake 30 to 35 minutes longer or until a silver knife inserted in the center of the pie comes out clean. Allow to cool before serving. You may use almonds, peanuts, or walnuts instead of the pecans, but if you use salted nuts, omit the salt from the recipe.

Eggnog Chiffon Pie

- 1 envelope unflavored gelatine
- ½ cup sugar
- ½ teaspoon salt
- 1¼ cups milk
- 3 egg yolks, slightly beaten
- 2 teaspoons rum flavoring
- ½ cup heavy cream, whipped stiff
- 3 egg whites
- ¼ teaspoon cream of tartar
- 6 tablespoons sugar
- 1 baked 9-inch pie shell
- ¼ teaspoon nutmeg

Soften the gelatine in ¼ cup cold water. In a saucepan, combine ½ cup sugar, salt, and milk. Cook over low heat, stirring constantly, until the milk is scalded. Remove from the heat. Slowly stir half the hot mixture into the egg yolks, then blend this into the remaining hot mixture in the saucepan. Cook over low heat, stirring, until the custard just comes to boiling; *immediately* remove from heat. Stir in the softened gelatine and allow to cool. When the mixture is partially set, beat it with a rotary beater until smooth. Blend in the rum flavoring and gently fold in the whipped cream. Combine the egg whites with cream of tartar and beat until foamy. Gradually add 6 tablespoons sugar. Gently fold the rum mixture into the meringue mixture. Pile the filling into the pie shell, sprinkle with nutmeg, and chill until set (about 2 hours). Remove the pie from the refrigerator 20 minutes before serving.

Cranberry Surprise Pie

This is an unusual pie in that the batter makes its own crust.

- 2 cups fresh cranberries
- 1½ cups sugar
- ½ cup chopped walnuts
- 2 eggs, well beaten
- 1 cup sugar
- 1 cup sifted flour
- ½ cup butter *or* margarine, melted
- ¼ cup shortening, melted

Grease well a 10-inch pie plate and spread the cranberries over the bottom. Sprinkle ½ cup sugar and the chopped walnuts over the berries. Beat the eggs and add the remaining 1 cup sugar gradually, beating until thoroughly mixed. Add the flour, butter, and shortening; beat well. Pour the batter over the cranberries and bake in a moderate oven, 325° F., for 1 hour or until the crust is golden brown.

Cream Cheese Pie

1 pound cream cheese
3 eggs
⅔ cup sugar
½ teaspoon almond extract
½ pint commercial sour cream
3 tablespoons sugar
1 teaspoon vanilla
Slivered Brazil nuts (optional)

Beat together thoroughly the cream cheese, eggs, ⅔ cup sugar, and almond extract until the mixture is smooth, thick, and lemon-colored. Pour this into a greased 9-inch deep pie plate or a 10-inch regular-depth pie plate. Bake in a moderate (350° F.) oven for 25 minutes, then allow to cool for 20 minutes. While the cheese pie is cooling, combine the sour cream, 3 tablespoons sugar, and vanilla; beat thoroughly. Pour the sour cream mixture over the top of the cooled cream cheese pie. Return the pie to a moderate (350° F.) oven and bake 10 minutes longer. Allow the pie to cool before serving. Sprinkle the top with slivered Brazil nuts before serving, if desired.

Chess Pie

2 eggs
1½ tablespoons flour
⅔ cup brown sugar, firmly packed
½ teaspoon salt
1 teaspoon vanilla
1 cup heavy cream
½ cup seedless golden raisins
1 cup pitted dates, cut up
1 cup broken walnut meats
1 9-inch unbaked pie shell

Beat the eggs until thick and lemon-colored. Combine the flour, brown sugar, and salt; add this mixture to the eggs while continuing to beat. Stir in the vanilla, cream, raisins, dates, and walnuts. Spoon the filling into the pie shell and bake in a moderate oven, 350° F., for 50 to 60 minutes or until a knife inserted in the middle of the pie comes out clean. Serve warm (not hot) or cold.

Cranberry Chiffon Pie

1 envelope unflavored gelatine
¼ cup cold water
1 1-pound can jellied *or* whole cranberry sauce
⅛ teaspoon salt
1 teaspoon grated lemon rind
2 teaspoons lemon juice
2 egg whites
2 tablespoons sugar
8-inch baked pie shell

Place the gelatine in a custard cup, add ¼ cup cold water, and let stand 2 minutes. Put the cup in a pan of boiling water until the gelatine dissolves. Place the cranberry sauce in a bowl and crush it with a fork. Add the gelatine, salt, lemon rind, and lemon juice. Chill until the mixture begins to set. Beat the egg whites until stiff, beat in the sugar, and fold into the cranberry mixture. Pour the filling into the baked pie shell and chill until firm. Garnish with whipped cream, if desired.

Pumpkin Ice Cream Pie

- 1 cup canned *or* mashed cooked pumpkin
- ½ cup brown sugar, packed
- ½ teaspoon salt
- ½ teaspoon cinnamon
- ½ teaspoon ginger
- ¼ teaspoon nutmeg
- 1 quart vanilla ice cream, softened
- 1 9-inch graham cracker pie shell
- Pecans, sliced

Combine the pumpkin, brown sugar, salt, and spices. Stir and fold in the softened ice cream. Spoon the filling into the graham cracker crust and freeze until it is firm. Arrange sliced pecans in a design on top of the filling.

Graham Cracker Crust

- 1½ cups fine graham cracker crumbs
- ¼ cup butter *or* margarine

Combine the crumbs and butter, mix well, and press firmly into a buttered 9-inch pie pan. Chill the crust about 45 minutes or until it is set.

Black Cherry Chiffon Pie

- 1 8-ounce can pitted Bing cherries
- 3 egg yolks, slightly beaten
- 1 cup water
- ¼ cup sugar
- 1 package black cherry-flavored gelatin
- 3 tablespoons lemon juice
- Dash of salt
- 3 egg whites
- 4 tablespoons sugar
- 1 baked 9-inch pie shell
- Sweetened whipped cream

Drain the cherries, reserving the juice. Set aside five cherries and cut the remainder in halves. In a saucepan, combine the egg yolks and 1 cup water. Add ¼ cup sugar and cook over low heat, stirring constantly, until the mixture coats a silver spoon, then cook 1 minute longer. If the mixture curdles, beat it with a rotary beater. Remove from heat. Add the gelatin and stir until it dissolves. Add the cherry juice and enough water to make ½ cup; add lemon juice. Chill until the mixture is slightly thickened. Add the salt to the egg whites and beat until foamy. Gradually add 4 tablespoons sugar, beating after each addition until well blended; then continue beating until mixture stands in peaks. Beat the gelatin mixture slightly, fold it into the meringue, and again beat the mixture very slightly. Fold in the cherry halves. Chill until the mixture begins to hold its shape, then spoon it into the pie shell and chill the pie until firm. Just before serving, top with the whipped cream and garnish with the whole cherries.

Chocolate Brownie Pie

- 2 squares unsweetened chocolate
- 2 tablespoons margarine
- 3 large eggs
- ½ cup sugar
- ¾ cup dark corn syrup
- ¾ cup pecan halves
- 9-inch unbaked pie shell

Melt together over hot water the chocolate and margarine. Combine and beat with a rotary beater the eggs, sugar, chocolate mixture, and corn syrup; then mix in the pecan halves. Pour the filling into the pie shell and bake in a moderately hot oven, 375° F., for 40 to 50 minutes or until just set. Serve slightly warm or cold, garnished with ice cream or whipped cream.

The pie may also be made with cocoa. Omit the chocolate, sift ½ cup cocoa with the sugar, and then add ¼ cup melted margarine to the eggs and sugar mixture. The cocoa provides the chocolate flavor and the melted margarine gives the oiliness of the chocolate.

Ice Cream Pie with Caramel Sauce

- 1½ cups graham cracker crumbs
- ⅓ cup brown sugar
- ⅓ cup melted butter
- 1 quart butter brickle ice cream

Combine crumbs, brown sugar, and melted butter; press into a greased 9-inch pie pan. Bake in a moderate oven, 350° F., for 10 minutes. Soften the ice cream slightly and spoon it over the crust. Freeze, wrap, and return to freezer. To serve, drizzle with caramel topping.

Caramel Topping

Melt ½ pound caramels with 2 to 3 tablespoons water in the top of a double boiler. If the sauce is too thick for your taste, thin it with a little more water.

Macaroon Pie

- 14 Saltine crackers (14 squares)
- 12 dates, cut fine
- ½ cup finely cut pecans
- 1 cup sugar
- 3 egg whites
- ¼ teaspoon salt
- 1 generous teaspoon almond extract

Roll out the crackers to make fine crumbs. Combine the crumbs, dates, pecans, and sugar. Beat the egg whites until stiff, adding the salt and almond extract. Fold the whites into the first mixture and turn it into a buttered 9-inch pie pan. Bake for 45 minutes in a slow (300° F.) oven. Serve warm or cold with whipped cream, ice cream, or plain or whipped topping.

Chocolate Chiffon Pie

- 4 squares unsweetened chocolate
- ¾ cup water
- 1 envelope plain gelatine
- 1 cup sugar
- 4 eggs, separated
- 1 teaspoon vanilla
- 9-inch baked pie shell
- Whipped cream
- Grated German's sweet chocolate

Melt the chocolate in ½ cup water over low heat. Soften the gelatine in ¼ cup cold water, then add it to the chocolate and stir until the gelatine is dissolved. Mix ½ cup sugar with the egg yolks, add to the chocolate mixture, and then add the vanilla. Allow to cool thoroughly. Beat the egg whites with the remaining ½ cup sugar until stiff, and fold into the cooled chocolate mixture. Pour the filling into the pie shell and chill for at least 2 hours. Cover with whipped cream and top with grated German's sweet chocolate.

Busy Day Lemon-Cream Cheese Pie

This pie is a combination of the fine products of Borden's and General Foods' Jello. The recipe has appeared in all of the women's magazines, but I include it here because you may have failed to clip it, and it's a recipe well worth saving.

- 1½ cups graham cracker crumbs
- ¼ cup melted margarine
- 2 teaspoons sugar
- 1 8-ounce package cream cheese
- 2 cups milk
- 1 package lemon-flavored instant pudding

Combine the graham cracker crumbs with the melted margarine and sugar and press into a buttered 9-inch pie pan. Bake in a moderate oven, 350° F., for 10 minutes and allow to cool, or place the pan in the refrigerator for 30 minutes until the crust is set. Combine the cream cheese with ½ cup milk and mix until smooth, then add the remainder of the milk and the instant pudding. Immediately pour the filling into the graham cracker shell, sprinkle additional graham cracker crumbs over the top, and refrigerate for at least 1 hour before serving. SERVES 6 TO 8.

Chocolate Almond Bar Pie

- 12 pieces sweetened zwieback
- ¼ cup butter *or* margarine
- ¼ cup sugar
- ¼ teaspoon cinnamon
- 7 small (10 cent) chocolate almond bars
- ¼ cup blanched toasted almonds
- 16 large marshmallows
- ½ cup milk
- Pinch of salt
- ½ pint whipping cream

Roll the zwieback into fine crumbs. Mix the crumbs thoroughly with the butter, sugar, and cinnamon and pat into a 9-inch pie pan. Bake in a hot oven, 400° F., for 10 minutes, then allow the crust to cool. Meanwhile, put the chocolate bars, almonds, marshmallows, milk, and salt in the top of a double boiler over hot water and stir until the chocolate and marshmallows are melted. Allow to cool thoroughly. Whip the cream until stiff and fold it into the chocolate mixture. Pour the filling into the pie shell and chill until firm. If desired, sprinkle a slivered chocolate bar over the top or sprinkle with sliced almonds. SERVES 8.

Old-Fashioned Pumpkin Pie

- 1 cup evaporated milk *or* light cream
- 3/4 cup brown sugar
- 1 1/2 cups cooked mashed pumpkin
- 1 tablespoon molasses
- 1/2 teaspoon ginger
- 3/4 teaspoon cinnamon
- 1/4 teaspoon mace
- 1/4 teaspoon ground cloves
- 3/4 teaspoon salt
- 2 eggs
- 9-inch unbaked pie shell

Combine the evaporated milk or cream, sugar, and pumpkin; mix well. Add the molasses, spices, and salt. Beat the eggs and add them to the pumpkin mixture. Pour the filling into the pie shell and bake in a very hot oven, 450° F., for 20 minutes. Reduce the heat to 325° F. and bake for 45 minutes longer or until a silver knife inserted in center of the pie comes out clean. Top with dabs of whipped cream or arrange walnut halves around the outer edge of the pie.

Brazil Nut Holiday Fruit Cake

You'll find many fruit cake recipes in this dessert section because our readers and television viewers tell us that cookbooks rarely provide an assortment of different types of fruit cakes. This is strictly a seasonal cake for use during the Christmas holiday season, but I'm sure that among the recipes in this chapter you will find a new favorite.

- 3 cups Brazil nuts (2 pounds unshelled or 1 pound shelled)
- 1 pound pitted dates
- 1 8-ounce jar maraschino cherries, drained
- 3/4 cup sifted flour
- 3/4 cup sugar
- 1/2 teaspoon baking powder
- 1/2 teaspoon salt
- 3 eggs
- 1 teaspoon vanilla

Put the nuts, dates, and cherries into a large bowl. Sift the flour, sugar, baking powder, and salt over the nuts and fruits; mix with your hands until the nuts and fruits are coated with the dry ingredients. Beat the eggs until they are foamy, then add the vanilla. Stir the eggs into the nut-fruit mixture until well mixed. Turn the batter into a pan that has been greased and lined with waxed paper. (This will make one 9 x 5 x 3-inch loaf or 2 loaves in the smaller fruit cake pans.) Spread the batter evenly. Bake in a slow oven, 300° F., for 1 hour and 45 minutes. The cake must be cooled thoroughly before cutting. It keeps very well when wrapped in foil.

California Fruit Cake

4 cups light *or* dark raisins
1 cup dried apricots
1½ cups dried figs
2½ cups sliced citron
2 cups sliced candied cherries
1 cup thinly sliced pitted fresh dates
1½ cups thick orange marmalade
½ cup orange juice
2 teaspoons nutmeg
2 teaspoons mace
1 teaspoon cardamom
½ teaspoon white pepper
2 cups butter *or* margarine
2½ cups sugar
8 eggs, beaten
4½ cups sifted flour
2 teaspoons salt
3 teaspoons baking powder
3 teaspoons rum flavoring
3 cups coarsely chopped blanched almonds

Rinse, drain, and dry the raisins thoroughly. Pour hot water over the apricots and let stand about 20 minutes; drain, dry thoroughly, and cut very fine. Rinse, drain, and dry the figs; clip off the stems and slice the figs thin. Combine raisins, apricots, figs, citron, cherries, dates, and marmalade. Blend the orange juice, spices, and pepper; pour over the fruit mixture and stir to blend. Cover and let stand overnight. Cream the butter, add the sugar, and cream thoroughly. Blend in the beaten eggs. Sift the flour with the salt and baking powder and stir into the creamed mixture. Add the fruit mixture, flavoring, and nuts; stir until the fruits are well distributed. Pour the batter into 2 greased and paper-lined pans (one 10-inch tube pan and one loaf pan, 10 x 5 x 3 inches). Smooth the tops of the batter. Bake in a slow oven, 275° F., 3¾ to 4 hours for tube pan, and 3 to 3¼ hours for loaf pan. This cake may be used as soon as it is cool, or it may be allowed to ripen before slicing.

Company Pound Cake

Butter *or* margarine
1 cup slivered almonds
2 packages (1 pound 1 ounce each) pound cake mix
2 teaspoons grated orange rind

Butter a 10-inch tube pan and sprinkle the almonds on the bottom and all around the inside of the pan. Prepare the cake batter according to package directions for using 2 packages cake mix. Stir in the orange rind and spoon the batter into the tube pan. Bake in a moderate oven, 325° F., until the cake tests done, about 1½ hours. Allow to cool for ½ hour before removing the cake from the pan. Then turn out gently onto a wire rack and allow to cool completely.

Dark Holiday Fruit Cake

- 1½ cups fresh California dates
- ¾ cup dried figs
- 1½ cups light *or* dark raisins
- ½ cup halved candied cherries
- ½ cup cut preserved orange peel
- 1 cup cut citron
- ½ cup thick orange marmalade
- 2 tablespoons molasses
- 1 cup chopped or ready diced blanched almonds
- ¾ teaspoon cloves
- 1 teaspoon cinnamon
- ½ teaspoon mace
- 1 teaspoon allspice
- ¼ teaspoon ginger
- 1 teaspoon salt
- 1 tablespoon brandy flavoring
- 1 teaspoon vanilla
- ¼ cup apricot whole fruit nectar
- 1 cup shortening
- 1¼ cups sugar
- 4 eggs
- 2 cups sifted flour
- ½ teaspoon baking soda
- 1 teaspoon baking powder

Pit and slice the dates. Cover the figs with water and simmer them for 10 minutes; drain thoroughly. Clip the stems from the figs and cut the figs into thin strips. Rinse and drain the raisins. Combine all fruits, peels, citron, marmalade, molasses, almonds, spices, salt, flavorings, and nectar. Blend thoroughly and let stand while preparing the batter and the pans. Cream the shortening, add the sugar gradually, and cream together thoroughly. Add the eggs, one at a time, and beat after each addition. Sift together the flour, soda, and baking powder; add half of the mixture to the creamed mixture and beat well. Stir in the fruit mixture. Add the remainder of the flour mixture and mix until very well blended. Pour the batter into a 9-inch tube pan lined with 2 thicknesses of greased brown paper. Bake in a slow oven, 300° F., about 3 hours. Place a shallow pan of water on the bottom of the oven during baking. Test the cake with a pick before removing it from oven. MAKES ABOUT 4 POUNDS CAKE.

Coconut Fruit Cake

- 1 package yellow cake mix
- ½ cup applesauce
- 4 eggs, unbeaten
- 1 teaspoon salt
- 1 teaspoon orange extract
- 2 cups (about 1 pound) cut-up pitted dates
- ½ pound candied pineapple, cut in narrow strips
- ½ pound whole candied cherries
- 1⅓ cups Angel Flake coconut
- 1 pound (4 cups) coarsely chopped walnuts
- ¾ cup sifted flour

Line two 8 x 4 x 3-inch loaf pans with triple thicknesses of waxed paper and grease well. Empty the cake mix into a bowl and add the applesauce, eggs, salt, and orange extract. Beat until the mixture is smooth and creamy, about 3 minutes. Combine the fruits, coconut, and nuts; add the flour, mix well, and stir into the batter. Pour the batter into the pans. Bake in a very slow oven, 275° F., about 2 hours and 45 minutes. Place the pans on cake racks and allow to cool thoroughly. Remove the cakes from the pans, leaving the paper attached to the cakes. Wrap the cakes and store them in the refrigerator for 2 to 4 weeks before using, to allow fruits to mellow and flavors to blend. (The reason for refrigerator storage is the large amount of dates used.) This cake can be frozen and thawed to room temperature before serving.

Fabulous Fruit Cake

- 1¼ cups sifted flour
- ½ teaspoon baking powder
- ½ teaspoon salt
- ⅛ teaspoon allspice
- ⅛ teaspoon cinnamon
- ⅛ teaspoon cloves
- ⅛ teaspoon nutmeg
- ¼ pound raisins
- ¼ pound diced dates
- ¾ pound diced mixed candied fruits
- ⅓ cup salad oil
- ¼ cup brown sugar
- ½ cup light *or* dark corn syrup
- 2 eggs, well beaten
- 2 tablespoons orange juice

Mix and sift the dry ingredients. Dredge the fruit with ¼ cup dry ingredients. Combine the oil and sugar, add the syrup, and mix well. Add ½ cup dry ingredients; beat until smooth. Add the eggs and beat well. Add the orange juice, mix well, and add the fruit mixture. Fold in the remaining dry ingredients. Turn the batter into a well-greased, paper-lined loaf pan and bake in a slow oven, 250° F., for 4 to 5 hours, until cake tests done. Place a shallow pan of water on the bottom rack of the oven during baking; remove during the last hour. Allow the cake to cool on a rack. Wrap the cake in foil and store it in a covered container in a cool place. It keeps well.

Jubilee Fruit Cake

1½ cups seedless raisins
¾ cup golden raisins
1½ cups dried figs
1½ cups cut citron
1 cup cut candied cherries
3 teaspoons cinnamon
1 teaspoon cloves
⅛ teaspoon black pepper
2 teaspoons rum flavoring
½ cup thick orange marmalade
¼ cup sweet wine
1⅓ cups butter *or* margarine
1½ cups sugar
4 eggs, well beaten
3½ cups sifted flour
1 teaspoon baking powder
½ teaspoon baking soda
1½ teaspoons salt
¾ cup chopped roasted unblanched almonds
¾ cup chopped walnuts

Topping

½ cup golden raisins
½ cup chopped roasted unblanched almonds
½ cup chopped walnuts
½ cup finely cut citron
½ cup sliced candied cherries
4 tablespoons honey
¼ teaspoon cloves

Rinse, drain, and dry the raisins. Pour boiling water over the figs, let stand 10 minutes, drain, and dry. Clip off the stems and slice the figs thin. Combine the dried fruits, citron, cherries, spices, flavoring, marmalade, and wine; blend well. Cover and let stand several hours or overnight. Cream butter and sugar together thoroughly and stir in the well-beaten eggs. Sift the flour with baking powder, soda, and salt. Add a portion of the flour mixture to the creamed mixture, beating well. Mix in the fruits, nuts, and remaining flour; stir until well blended. Pour the batter into 2 greased 1½-quart casseroles. Combine the topping ingredients and spread them over the batter. Cover the casseroles and bake in a slow oven, 250° F., about 3½ hours. Place a shallow pan of water on the bottom shelf of the oven while baking. Test the cake with a toothpick or cake tester before removing it from the oven. Baked weight is ABOUT 5½ POUNDS.

Old-Fashioned Fruit Cake

1 pound sausage meat
2 cups sugar
7 cups sifted flour
1 tablespoon baking soda
1 tablespoon cinnamon
1 tablespoon nutmeg
1 tablespoon cloves
2 cups boiling water
1 pound raisins
1 pound dates, chopped
1 pound candied fruit, diced
1 pound nuts, chopped

Pan fry the sausage. Combine the fried sausage and drippings with the sugar. Sift together the flour, soda, and spices. Add the dry ingredients alternately with 2 cups boiling water to sausage-sugar mixture. Stir in the fruits and nuts. Pour the batter into 2 loaf pans (9 x 5 x 3 inches) lined with brown paper. Bake in a slow oven, 275° F., for 2½ to 3 hours.

Skillet Fruit Cakes

1 cup sifted flour
1 cup sugar
1 teaspoon salt
½ teaspoon baking powder
½ teaspoon cinnamon
½ teaspoon nutmeg
1½ cups (½ pound) seeded raisins
1 cup (½ pound) candied pineapple
2¼ cups (¾ pound) unblanched almonds
2½ cups (1 pound) pitted dates
1½ cups (½ pound) candied cherries
4 large eggs
1 tablespoon vanilla

Sift together the flour, sugar, salt, baking powder, and spices. Rinse and drain the raisins; then place them in a colander over boiling water, cover, and steam until soft, about 10 minutes. Cut the pineapple into wedges; leave the other fruits and almonds whole. In a large bowl, combine the flour mixture with the fruits and nuts and mix until the fruits and nuts are well coated. Beat the eggs with the vanilla and pour them over the fruits and nuts, mixing until the fruits and nuts are evenly moistened and covered with a thin film of batter. Spoon the batter into three 6-inch iron skillets which have been lined with two layers of greased brown paper and one layer of waxed paper for insulation. Bake in a very slow oven, 275° F., for 1 hour and 15 minutes. Allow to cool in the pans. Wrap the cakes in foil or plastic film and refrigerate until ready to use. MAKES 3 CAKES (ABOUT 4 POUNDS).

White Fruit Cake

- ½ pound citron, chopped
- ½ pound whole candied cherries
- ¾ pound orange and lemon peel, chopped
- 2 pounds white raisins, washed and drained
- ¾ pound candied pineapple, cut up
- ¼ cup fruit juice
- 1 pound butter
- 2 cups sugar
- 10 eggs
- 4 cups sifted flour
- 1½ pounds whole pecans

Place the fruits in a large bowl, pour the fruit juice over them, and let stand while you are preparing the rest of the batter. Cream the butter and add the sugar gradually. Then add the eggs, one at a time, beating well after each addition. Add the flour and mix well, then add the nuts and fruits. Pour the batter into 3 loaf pans that have been buttered, lined with waxed paper, and buttered over the waxed paper. Bake in a slow (250° F.) oven for 2 hours. Allow to cool on racks.

Yuletide Fruit Cake

- 4 cups seedless raisins
- 1 cup seeded raisins
- 1 cup fresh California dates
- 2 cups uncooked prunes
- 2 cups halved candied cherries
- 2 cups diced candied pineapple
- 2 cups sliced preserved orange peel
- 2 cups sliced citron
- 3 teaspoons cinnamon
- 2 teaspoons allspice
- 1 teaspoon cloves
- 1 cup apricot whole fruit nectar
- 2 cups butter *or* margarine
- 1 cup brown sugar, packed
- 2 cups granulated sugar
- 10 eggs, well beaten
- 4½ cups sifted flour
- 1 teaspoon baking soda
- 1 teaspoon salt
- 1 teaspoon baking powder
- 1½ cups coarsely chopped unblanched almonds
- 1½ cups coarsely chopped walnuts
- 2 tablespoons rum flavoring

Rinse, drain, and dry the raisins thoroughly. Chop the seeded raisins. Pit and slice the dates. Pour boiling water over the prunes, cover, and let stand 10 minutes; drain, dry, and cut from pits into small pieces. Combine the fruits, peel, citron, spices, and nectar; cover and let stand about 1 hour. Cream the butter, add the sugars, and cream together thoroughly. Mix in the well-beaten eggs. Sift together the flour, soda, salt, and baking powder; add to the creamed mixture and blend thoroughly. Stir in the fruit mixture, almonds, walnuts, and flavoring. Mix until the fruits are well distributed. Pour the batter into 2 tube pans that have been lined with 2 thicknesses of greased brown paper and 1 of greased waxed paper. Bake in a slow oven, 300° F., about 3½ hours. MAKES ABOUT 9 POUNDS CAKE.

Dark Fruit Cake

2 cups dried prunes
½ cup dried apricots
1 cup seedless raisins
1 cup dates
½ cup sliced preserved orange peel
½ cup sliced preserved lemon peel
⅔ cup sliced candied pineapple
1 cup sliced candied *or* maraschino cherries
⅔ cup sliced citron
2 cups broken walnuts
2 teaspoons cinnamon
1 teaspoon cloves
1 teaspoon allspice
1 teaspoon salt
¾ cup honey
1 cup sugar
1 cup butter *or* margarine
6 eggs, slightly beaten
½ cup fruit juice
2 teaspoons vanilla or rum extract
4¼ cups flour
1 teaspoon baking soda
2 teaspoons baking powder
Fruit or nuts for decorating tops

Rinse the dried prunes, apricots, and raisins; drain and dry them on a cloth. Cut the prunes from the pits into small pieces. (If the prunes are very dry, boil them in sufficient water to cover for 10 minutes; drain them thoroughly before pitting.) Cut the dates and apricots into small pieces. Combine all the fruits, peels, nuts, spices, salt, and honey; mix thoroughly and let stand for 2 hours or longer. Cream together the sugar and butter. Add the slightly beaten eggs, fruit juice, and flavoring; blend well. Sift the flour with the soda and baking powder; add to the creamed mixture and beat well. Stir in the fruit mixture. Grease two 9 x 5 x 3-inch loaf pans and line them with 2 thicknesses heavy brown paper and 1 of greased waxed paper. Spoon in the batter. Bake in a slow oven, 300° F., about 2 hours, with a shallow pan of water on the bottom rack of the oven. MAKES 6 POUNDS CAKE.

Simplicity Fruit Cake

- 2 cups golden raisins
- 2 cups dark raisins
- 1½ cups butter *or* margarine
- 1¾ cups sugar
- 6 eggs, beaten
- 3¼ cups sifted flour
- 1½ teaspoons salt
- 1 teaspoon baking soda
- 1 teaspoon cloves
- 3 teaspoons cinnamon
- 2 cups walnuts, chopped
- 1 cup blanched almonds, chopped
- 1½ cups finely cut citron
- 1½ cups diced candied orange peel
- ½ cup thoroughly drained, crushed pineapple
- 2 teaspoons vanilla
- ¼ teaspoon almond extract

Rinse, drain, and dry the raisins thoroughly. Cream the butter, add the sugar, and cream thoroughly. Blend in the beaten eggs. Sift the flour with the salt, soda, and spices; add to the creamed mixture, blending well. Stir in the raisins, nuts, citron, peel, pineapple, and flavorings. Spread the batter in a greased, paper-lined, 9-inch tube pan. Bake in a slow oven, 300° F., about 3¼ hours. Test with a cake tester or pick before removing the cake from the oven. MAKES ABOUT 5¾ POUNDS CAKE.

Quick Fudge Sauce

- 1 6-ounce package semisweet chocolate pieces
- ¾ cup evaporated milk

In a saucepan over low heat, cook the chocolate pieces and milk, stirring until the chocolate is melted and the sauce is smooth. This sauce is good hot or cold. If you like a peppermint flavor, add ½ teaspoon peppermint extract after removing the sauce from the heat. MAKES 1 CUP.

Raspberry Sauce Melba

- 1 package frozen raspberries
- 2 tablespoons water
- ¼ cup sugar
- 1 teaspoon lemon juice

Heat the raspberries in a saucepan with 2 tablespoons water, sugar, and lemon juice. Boil the sauce gently for 5 minutes, then force it through a fine sieve into a jar. Cover and chill. Serve on peach melbas or over ice cream in a meringue nest.

Heavenly Hot Fudge Sauce

- ½ cup margarine
- 4 squares unsweetened chocolate
- 3 cups sugar
- ½ teaspoon salt
- 1⅔ cups (1 tall can) evaporated milk

Melt the margarine and chocolate in the top of a double boiler over boiling water. Gradually stir in the sugar, about 4 tablespoons at a time, being sure the sugar is completely moistened after each addition. The mixture will become very thick and quite dry. Add the salt and slowly stir in the evaporated milk, a little at a time. Serve warm. MAKES APPROXIMATELY 3½ CUPS.

If a thinner sauce is desired, slowly stir in an additional 1 or 2 tablespoons evaporated milk. Store the sauce in a covered jar in the refrigerator and reheat in a double boiler before using.

Hot Rum Sauce

Cook together 1 cup sugar and 1 cup water. When the syrup reaches the thread stage, 230° F., remove it from the heat. Add ½ cup butter and, when it is melted, stir in ¼ cup rum. Serve immediately.

Hard Sauce

- ½ cup butter
- 2 cups sifted confectioners' sugar
- 1 teaspoon vanilla *or* whiskey

Cream thoroughly the butter and sugar. Add vanilla or whiskey and blend well. MAKES 1⅔ CUPS.

Mincemeat Sauce

Use a good rich mincemeat, either the prepared or condensed (made according to package directions). Heat the mincemeat in a saucepan and add apple juice or other fruit juice to thin the mincemeat so that it can be spooned. When it is heated, add rum to taste and serve warm over vanilla ice cream. If you want to flambé this sauce, serve it hot, flambé it in the saucepan or server, and spoon the flaming sauce over the ice cream.

Orange-Honey Sauce

- ½ cup honey
- ¼ cup orange juice
- 1 teaspoon grated orange rind
- Few grains of salt

Mix all ingredients until well blended. MAKES ¾ CUP.

Date-Nut Ice Cream Sauce

- 1 tablespoon cornstarch
- ⅛ teaspoon salt
- 1½ cups maple syrup
- 2 tablespoons butter *or* margarine
- ½ cup diced dates
- ¼ cup chopped pecan meats

In a saucepan, combine the cornstarch, salt, syrup, and butter. Bring to a boil, then reduce heat and simmer for 3 minutes, stirring constantly. Remove the pan from the heat and add the dates. Allow to cool, then stir in the nuts. Serve on ice cream or pudding. MAKES 2¼ CUPS.

8

Cookies

DOES ANY WOMAN ever have enough cookie recipes? Because cookies are so popular, it seems to me that they deserve a chapter all to themselves.

In the past few years a new custom has sprung up in the Southwest at Thanksgiving and Christmas time: the cookie exchange party. Usually these parties are held by small clubs or neighborhood groups. Every woman bakes her own special, favorite cookie, and she bakes enough so that if there are twelve women attending the party, they can each have a dozen cookies. She comes home with eleven different kinds of cookies, and her Christmas cookie-baking problem is solved. Maybe you'd like to start this delightful custom in your neighborhood next Christmas.

All of the bar-type cookies or the moist cookies in this chapter will pack and ship easily. Use foil to wrap small quantities of cookies, and pack them in popped popcorn. This is the best packing property you can use. This first recipe for Coconut Dream Squares is one of our favorites, and it packs very well.

Coconut Dream Squares

- 1¼ cups sifted cake flour
- 1¼ cups firmly packed brown sugar
- ⅓ cup butter
- 2 eggs
- ½ teaspoon baking powder
- 1 teaspoon vanilla
- 1⅓ cups Angel Flake coconut
- 1 cup chopped walnuts

Combine 1 cup flour and ¼ cup sugar. Add the butter and mix until thoroughly blended and smooth. Press the mixture firmly into an ungreased 9-inch square pan and bake in a moderate oven, 350° F., for 15 minutes. Beat the eggs until light. Gradually add the remaining 1 cup sugar, beating until the mixture is light and fluffy. Sift the remaining ¼ cup flour and the baking powder together; fold into the egg mixture. Add the vanilla, coconut, and nuts; mix thoroughly. Spread this on top of the baked mixture and return the pan to the oven. Bake 20 to 25 minutes longer or until lightly browned. Cut in squares while still warm. MAKES ABOUT 2 DOZEN 1½-INCH SQUARES.

Basic Christmas Cookies

Of course there is no reason in the world why you shouldn't use this basic recipe for Christmas cookies at any time, but it seems that at Christmas we are always looking for a basic recipe that can be finished off in several different ways. This is the perfect answer.

- 1 cup butter *or* margarine
- 1½ cups sifted confectioners' sugar
- 1 egg
- 1 teaspoon vanilla
- 2½ cups flour, sifted
- 1 teaspoon baking soda
- 1 teaspoon cream of tartar
- ¼ teaspoon salt

Cream the butter, add the sugar gradually, and cream until fluffy. Add the unbeaten egg and vanilla; beat well. Sift together the dry ingredients and blend them into the creamed mixture. Divide the dough and prepare in any of the following variations. Use an unbuttered cookie sheet and bake in a hot (400° F.) oven.

Butter Crispies

Chill the dough and roll it out on a well-floured pastry cloth to ⅛-inch thickness. Cut with floured cookie cutters. Bake 6 to 8 minutes and allow to cool on a cake rack. Half of the basic recipe MAKES ABOUT 3 DOZEN COOKIES.

Butterfingers

To half the basic dough, add ½ cup chopped nuts and ¼ cup chopped candied cherries. Chill. Shape into oblongs the size of your little finger. Bake 8 to 10 minutes. While the cookies are hot, sprinkle them with granulated sugar; sprinkle them with sugar again when cool. MAKES ABOUT 2 DOZEN COOKIES.

Snowballs

To half of the basic dough, add ¾ cup ground walnuts. Chill. Roll the dough into balls the size of large marbles. Bake 8 to 10 minutes. MAKES ABOUT 2½ DOZEN COOKIES.

Trixie Treats

Chill half the dough, then mold it into balls the size of walnuts. Roll the balls in a mixture of 2 tablespoons sugar and 1 teaspoon cinnamon. Bake 8 to 10 minutes. MAKES ABOUT 2½ DOZEN COOKIES.

Butter Thinsies

Form the dough into a roll 2 inches in diameter. Wrap the roll in waxed paper and chill until firm. Slice ⅛ inch thick and sprinkle with finely chopped nuts or coconut. Bake 6 minutes. Half of the basic recipe MAKES ABOUT 3 DOZEN COOKIES.

Chocolate Mint Creams

To half the basic dough, add 1 square melted and cooled unsweetened chocolate. Form the dough into a roll 2 inches in diameter. Wrap the roll in waxed paper and chill until firm. Slice ⅛ inch thick. Bake 8 minutes. Allow to cool. Put the cookies together, sandwich-fashion, with mint cream filling. To make the filling, cream together 2 tablespoons butter, 1 cup sifted confectioners' sugar, 1 tablespoon cream, and mint flavoring to taste. MAKES 1½ DOZEN COOKIES.

Molasses Spice-Eez

To half the basic dough, add 2 tablespoons molasses, ½ teaspoon ginger, 1 teaspoon cinnamon, and ¼ teaspoon nutmeg. Chill for at least 1 hour. Roll out to ⅛-inch thickness on a well-floured surface. Cut into patterns. Bake 6 to 8 minutes. MAKES 3 DOZEN COOKIES.

Jewel Clusters

Drop the dough by half teaspoonfuls on a cookie sheet. Press a candied fruit into each cookie. Bake 8 minutes. Half of the basic recipe MAKES 2½ DOZEN COOKIES.

Sugar Jumbles

When you read this recipe you're going to say, "Oh-oh, that's an error. There's no moisture in that recipe." But the recipe is entirely right, and it makes a lovely crisp cookie.

- ½ cup margarine
- ½ cup sugar
- 1 egg
- 1 teaspoon vanilla
- 1⅛ cups sifted flour
- ¼ teaspoon baking soda
- ½ teaspoon salt

Mix together and beat until light the margarine, sugar, egg, and vanilla. Sift together the flour, soda, and salt; stir into the creamed mixture. Drop the dough by rounded teaspoonfuls about 2 inches apart onto a lightly greased baking sheet. Bake in a moderate (375° F.) oven for 8 to 10 minutes, until the cookies are delicately browned. Watch them carefully and don't let them get too brown. The cookies should still be soft. Allow them to cool slightly and then remove them from the baking sheet. MAKES ABOUT 3 DOZEN COOKIES.

If desired, these cookies may be sprinkled with a combination of sugar and cinnamon before baking.

Walnut Refrigerator Cookies

- 1 cup shortening
- 2 cups brown sugar, packed
- 2 teaspoons vanilla
- 2 eggs
- 3½ cups sifted flour
- 1 teaspoon salt
- 1 teaspoon baking soda
- 1 cup finely chopped walnuts

Cream together the shortening, brown sugar, and vanilla. Add the eggs and mix well. Sift together the flour, salt, and soda; add to the creamed mixture. Add the nuts and mix until well blended. Shape the dough into 2 long rolls about 2 inches in diameter. Wrap each roll in waxed paper and chill in the refrigerator until firm. Cut the chilled rolls into ⅛-inch slices. Bake on a cookie sheet in a moderate oven, 375° F., for 8 minutes. MAKES 8 TO 9 DOZEN SMALL CRISP COOKIES.

Shortbread Cookies

- 1 cup soft butter *or* margarine
- ⅝ cup (½ cup plus 2 tablespoons) sugar
- 2½ cups sifted flour
- Cinnamon and sugar for topping

Mix the butter and sugar thoroughly. Stir in the flour and mix well with your hands. Chill the dough. Roll out the dough 1/4 inch thick and cut with a floured, 2-inch, scalloped cutter. Sprinkle the cookies lightly with a cinnamon and sugar mixture. Place the cookies on an ungreased baking sheet and bake in a slow oven, 300° F., for 20 to 25 minutes. Allow to cool on racks. MAKES ABOUT 3 DOZEN COOKIES.

Spice Cookies

- 1/2 cup sugar
- 1/2 cup shortening
- 1/2 cup molasses
- 1 egg
- 1/2 teaspoon ginger
- 2 cups sifted flour
- 1/2 teaspoon cinnamon
- 1 teaspoon baking soda
- 1/2 teaspoon nutmeg

Cream together the sugar and shortening. Add the molasses and egg; blend well. Sift together the dry ingredients and gradually add them to the first mixture. Drop by teaspoonfuls onto a greased cookie sheet, using the bottom of a damp glass to press each cookie flat. Bake in a moderate oven, 350° F., for 10 minutes or until brown. Remove the cookies to a cooling rack.

Spicy Banana Bars

- 1 cup sifted flour
- 3/4 cup sugar
- 1/2 teaspoon baking powder
- 1/4 teaspoon baking soda
- 1/2 teaspoon salt
- 3/4 teaspoon cinnamon
- 1/4 teaspoon cloves
- 1/4 teaspoon allspice
- 1/4 cup shortening
- 1/3 cup mashed ripe banana
- 1 egg
- 1/4 cup milk
- 1/3 cup chopped pecans

Sift together the flour, sugar, baking powder, soda, salt, cinnamon, cloves, and allspice. Combine the shortening and banana in a mixing bowl and beat hard for 2 minutes. Add the unbeaten egg and beat 1 minute longer. Add the dry ingredients alternately with the milk, blending thoroughly after each addition. Stir in the chopped pecans and spread the batter in a well-greased and lightly floured 13 x 9 x 2-inch pan. Bake in a moderate oven, 350° F., for 22 to 25 minutes. Frost while warm.

Lemon Frosting

Combine 2 tablespoons melted butter, 1 tablespoon hot water, and 2 teaspoons lemon juice. Blend in 1 cup sifted confectioners' sugar and thin to spreading consistency with additional hot water, a few drops at a time, if necessary.

Swedish Almond Cookies

- 1¾ cups sifted flour
- 1 teaspoon baking powder
- ½ teaspoon salt
- ¼ cup butter *or* margarine
- ¼ cup shortening
- ½ cup sugar
- 1 egg
- 1 tablespoon molasses
- ⅓ cup chopped unblanched almonds

Sift together the flour, baking powder, and salt. Cream together the butter or margarine and shortening. Gradually add the sugar, creaming well. Add the unbeaten egg and molasses; beat well. Gradually blend in the dry ingredients. Turn out the dough onto a lightly floured board and add the almonds. Knead the dough into a ball to distribute the nuts evenly. Place the dough on waxed paper and shape into a roll 2 inches in diameter. Wrap the roll in waxed paper and chill at least 2 hours or overnight. Cut the dough into ⅛-inch slices and place them on ungreased baking sheets. Bake in a moderately hot oven, 400° F., for 8 to 10 minutes or until the cookies are a light golden brown.

Scotch Shortbread

- 1¼ cups fine granulated sugar
- 5 cups sifted flour
- 1 pound sweet butter
- Blanched almonds

Sift the flour and sugar together several times. Break the butter into small pieces and work it into the flour-sugar mixture. If necessary, add a little more flour. Roll out the dough to ½-inch thickness and cut it into fancy shapes. Place an almond in the center of each cookie. Bake in a moderate oven, 325° F., for 20 minutes or until the cookies are lightly browned.

Skiparoons

Skiparoons, of course, get their name from Skippy Peanut Butter. This type of cookie goes well with a cold glass of milk for the children when they come home from school hungry.

⅔ cup confectioners' sugar
½ cup peanut butter
2 egg whites, stiffly beaten

Add the sugar gradually to the peanut butter, mixing thoroughly. Fold in the beaten egg whites. Drop the dough by teaspoonfuls onto brown paper on a cookie sheet. Bake in a moderate oven, 375° F., for 10 minutes. Allow the cookies to cool on the paper; remove when cool. MAKES 2 DOZEN COOKIES.

Rolled Sour Cream Cookies

⅔ cup shortening
1⅔ cups sugar
1 teaspoon salt
1 teaspoon vanilla
2 eggs
3½ cups sifted flour
½ teaspoon baking soda
2 teaspoons baking powder
½ cup commercial sour cream

Cream the shortening well. Add the sugar gradually with the salt and vanilla; continue creaming. Add the eggs, one at a time, beating well after each addition. Sift together the flour, soda, and baking powder; add to the creamed mixture. Add the sour cream, mix well, and chill. Roll out the dough on a floured board or pastry cloth. Cut with a cookie cutter, sprinkle with sugar, and place on a cookie sheet. Bake in a moderate oven, 375° F., for about 8 minutes. MAKES ABOUT 9 DOZEN COOKIES.

These may also be made as drop cookies. Do not chill the dough. Drop it from a teaspoon into finely chopped nuts and shape into balls. Bake for about 8 minutes at 375° F.

Pecan Sticks

½ cup soft butter
1½ cups plus 2 tablespoons sifted flour
¾ teaspoon salt
1 tablespoon granulated sugar
3 eggs
2 tablespoons water
1 cup brown sugar
½ teaspoon baking powder
½ teaspoon vanilla
1 cup chopped pecans

Mix the butter, 1½ cups flour, ¼ teaspoon salt, and the granulated sugar to the consistency of a fine corn meal. Mix in 1 egg and 2 tablespoons water, press the mixture into a shallow rectangular baking dish, and bake 15 minutes in a moderate (350° F.) oven.

Beat the remaining 2 eggs. Add the brown sugar, the remaining 2 tablespoons flour, baking powder, ½ teaspoon salt, vanilla, and pecans; mix well. Spread this over the baked layer and bake 40 minutes longer. Allow to cool in dish, then cut into sticks. MAKES ABOUT 32 COOKIES.

Pecan Clusters

- ¼ cup margarine
- ½ cup sugar
- 1 egg
- 1½ teaspoons vanilla
- 1½ squares unsweetened chocolate, melted
- ½ cup sifted flour
- ¼ teaspoon baking powder
- ½ teaspoon salt
- 2 cups unbroken pecans *or* English walnuts

Mix together the margarine and sugar until well blended, add the egg and vanilla, and mix well. Mix in the melted chocolate. Sift together the dry ingredients and add them to the first mixture. Stir in the pecans. Drop the dough by teaspoonfuls, 1 inch apart, onto a cookie sheet. Bake in a moderate oven, 350° F., for just 10 minutes. Be careful not to burn them. MAKES 3 DOZEN COOKIES.

Pecan Balls I

- ¼ pound butter
- 1 cup flour
- 2 tablespoons sugar
- 1 teaspoon vanilla
- 1 cup chopped pecans
- ¼ teaspoon salt
- Confectioners' sugar

Combine all ingredients except the confectioners' sugar; shape into balls. Place on a cookie sheet and bake in a moderate (350° F.) oven for 15 minutes. Roll the balls in confectioners' sugar. Allow them to cool and roll them again in confectioners' sugar.

Pecan Balls II

- 1 cup butter *or* margarine
- ½ cup confectioners' sugar
- ½ teaspoon salt
- 2 teaspoons vanilla
- 2 cups sifted flour
- 2 cups finely chopped pecans

Cream together the butter or margarine and confectioners' sugar. Add the salt, vanilla, flour, and chopped pecans; mix well. Chill the dough for 2 hours, then shape it into 1-inch balls and place the balls on an ungreased baking sheet. Bake in a moderate oven, 350° F., for 12 to 15 minutes. While the cookies are still warm, roll them in confectioners' sugar. These may be made in advance and kept in a cookie jar; they stay fresh for days. MAKES 4 TO 5 DOZEN COOKIES.

Peanut Butter Chews

- 1 can sweetened condensed milk
- ½ cup peanut butter
- 2 cups fine graham cracker crumbs
- ½ cup chopped, pitted dates

Mix the condensed milk and peanut butter until smooth. Stir in the crumbs and dates. Drop the dough by teaspoonfuls, 1 inch apart, onto a greased cookie sheet. Bake in a moderate (350° F.) oven for about 15 minutes. MAKES 3 DOZEN COOKIES.

Peanut Butter Cookies

- ½ cup shortening
- ½ cup white sugar
- ½ cup brown sugar
- ½ teaspoon salt
- 1 egg
- ½ cup crunchy peanut butter
- 1¼ cups flour
- ½ teaspoon soda
- ½ teaspoon nutmeg
- ¼ teaspoon cloves
- ½ teaspoon cinnamon

Blend together the shortening, sugars, salt, and egg; then add the peanut butter. Sift the dry ingredients together and stir them into the first mixture. Form the dough into small balls and place the balls on a greased cookie sheet. Press them flat with a fork and bake in a moderate oven, 375°F., for 10 minutes or until brown. MAKES 3 DOZEN COOKIES.

Orange Crackle Cookies

- ¼ pound butter *or* margarine
- 1 cup sugar
- 1 6-ounce can frozen orange juice concentrate
- 3 cups sifted flour
- ½ teaspoon baking powder
- Glazed fruit for garnish

Place the butter or margarine over low heat until melted. Allow to cool slightly, then blend with the sugar. Add the orange juice concentrate directly from the can and mix well. Sift the flour with the baking powder and add gradually to the orange mixture. Knead the dough until it is well blended. Roll out the dough 1/8 inch thick and cut into rounds with a 2-inch cookie cutter. Place the rounds on greased cookie sheets and garnish with glazed fruits (optional). Bake in a moderate oven, 375° F., for 10 to 12 minutes or until golden brown. Immediately place the cookies on a cooling rack. MAKES 4 1/2 TO 5 DOZEN COOKIES.

Orange Marmalade Bars

- 2 1/2 cups sifted flour
- 3 teaspoons baking powder
- 1/2 teaspoon salt
- 3/4 cup butter
- 1 cup sugar
- 3 eggs, well beaten
- 3 tablespoons orange marmalade
- 2 tablespoons grated orange rind
- 1 cup orange juice

Mix and sift the flour, baking powder, and salt. Cream the butter until soft and smooth; gradually add the sugar and continue creaming until fluffy. Beat in the eggs, then add marmalade and grated orange rind. Add the flour alternately with the orange juice. Turn the batter into a greased shallow baking pan and bake in a moderately (350° F.) oven for 40 to 50 minutes. When cold, cut in narrow strips and spread with orange frosting. To make the frosting, cream together confectioners' sugar and butter and thin to spreading consistency with orange juice.

Old-Fashioned Sugar Cookies

- 1/2 cup butter
- 1 cup sugar
- 1 egg
- 1 teaspoon vanilla
- 3 cups sifted flour
- 3 teaspoons baking powder
- 1/2 cup milk

Cream the butter, add the sugar, and continue creaming until smooth. Add the egg and vanilla and beat well. Sift the flour and baking powder together and add to the creamed mixture with the milk. Chill the dough thoroughly. Roll it out to 1/8-inch thickness on a lightly floured board or pastry cloth and cut with a cookie cutter. Sprinkle the cookies with sugar or a cinnamon-sugar mixture. Bake on a cookie sheet in a moderate oven, 375° F., for 10 to 12 minutes. MAKES ABOUT 4 DOZEN COOKIES.

Orange Drop Cookies

- 1/2 cup margarine
- 3/4 cup sugar
- 1 egg
- 2 cups sifted flour
- 1/4 teaspoon salt
- 1/2 teaspoon baking soda
- 1/2 cup orange juice
- 1/2 cup chopped pecans *or* walnuts
- 1/2 cup chopped dates
- 1 teaspoon shredded orange peel

Cream together the margarine and sugar. Add the egg and blend well. Sift the flour, salt, and soda together; add with the orange juice to the creamed mixture. Fold in the nuts, dates, and orange peel. Drop the dough by teaspoonfuls onto a cookie sheet. Bake in a hot oven, 400° F., for about 10 to 12 minutes. MAKES ABOUT 4 DOZEN COOKIES.

Mary Alden Special

- 1 cup sifted flour
- 1/2 teaspoon salt
- 1/2 teaspoon baking soda
- 1 cup shortening
- 1/2 cup granulated sugar
- 1/2 cup brown sugar
- 1/2 teaspoon vanilla
- 1 egg
- 1 package (6 ounces) semisweet chocolate pieces
- 1 1/2 cups instant oats

Sift together the flour, salt, and soda. Add the shortening, sugars, 2 tablespoons water, vanilla, and egg; mix well and stir in the chocolate pieces and oats. Drop the dough by teaspoonfuls onto a greased cookie sheet and bake for 10 minutes in a preheated moderate (375° F.) oven.

Old-Fashioned Pepparkakor

- 3 1/2 cups sifted flour
- 1 teaspoon baking soda
- 1 1/2 teaspoons ginger
- 1 1/2 teaspoons cinnamon
- 1 teaspoon cloves
- 1/4 teaspoon ground cardamom
- 1/2 cup butter *or* margarine
- 3/4 cup sugar
- 1 egg
- 3/4 cup molasses
- 2 teaspoons grated orange rind

Sift together the flour, soda, ginger, cinnamon, cloves, and cardamom. Cream together the butter and sugar until light and fluffy. Add the unbeaten egg, then add the molasses and grated orange rind and beat well. Gradually stir in the dry ingredients, mixing until well blended. Cover and chill overnight. The dough may be used in small amounts if desired and will keep for one week. Roll out the dough on a well-floured pastry cloth or board to 1/8-inch thickness. Cut it into shapes with cookie cutters, place the cookies on greased baking sheets, and bake in a moderate oven, 375° F., for 8 to 10 minutes. If desired, a blanched almond half may be put in the center of each cookie, or you may cut the dough in animal shapes and decorate them with confectioners' sugar frosting.

Nut-Rimmed Butter Slices

- 1½ cups sifted flour
- 2 teaspoons baking powder
- ½ teaspoon salt
- ½ cup butter
- ⅔ cup sugar
- 1 unbeaten egg yolk
- 2 tablespoons light cream
- 1 teaspoon vanilla
- ½ cup unblanched almonds, chopped fine
- 3 tablespoons sugar
- 1 egg white, slightly beaten

Sift together the flour, baking powder, and salt. Cream the butter, add the sugar, and cream until well blended. Add the unbeaten egg yolk, light cream, and vanilla; beat well. Gradually blend in the dry ingredients and mix thoroughly. Divide the dough into two parts. Place it on waxed paper and shape into long rolls 1½ inches in diameter. Wrap the rolls in waxed paper and chill them for at least 1 hour. Combine the almonds and 3 tablespoons sugar; spread the mixture on a sheet of waxed paper. Brush the chilled cookie rolls with slightly beaten egg white, then roll them in the almond-sugar mixture, pressing the nuts firmly into the dough. Cut into ¼-inch slices, place the slices on a greased baking sheet, and bake in a hot oven, 400° F., for 6 to 8 minutes or until delicately browned.

Marmalade Drop Cookies

- 3 cups sifted flour
- ½ teaspoon baking soda
- ½ teaspoon salt
- ½ cup butter
- 1 cup sugar
- 2 eggs, well beaten
- ¾ cup orange marmalade

Sift together the flour, soda, and salt. Cream the butter and gradually beat in the sugar and eggs. Stir in the flour, then the marmalade. Drop the dough from a teaspoon onto a greased baking sheet, about

2 inches apart. Bake in a moderate oven, 350° F., for about 12 minutes. Remove at once from the pans. MAKES 4 DOZEN COOKIES.

Gingersnaps

- ¾ cup shortening
- 1 cup sugar
- 1 egg
- ¼ cup molasses
- 2 cups sifted flour
- ¼ teaspoon salt
- 2 teaspoons soda
- 1 teaspoon cinnamon
- 1 teaspoon cloves
- 1 teaspoon ginger

Cream the shortening and sugar until light and fluffy. Add and beat well the egg and molasses. Sift together and mix in all the dry ingredients. Chill the dough for 1 hour. Roll it out into 1-inch balls and roll the balls in granulated sugar. Place the balls 2 inches apart on an ungreased cookie sheet. Bake in a moderately hot oven, 375°F., for 8 to 10 minutes or until lightly browned. Allow to cool slightly, then remove the cookies from the sheet. These cookies have crackled tops and the sugar imparts a slight glaze. MAKES ABOUT 5 DOZEN GINGERSNAPS.

Glazed Date Bars

- ¼ cup butter *or* margarine
- 1 cup brown sugar, packed
- 1 egg
- 1 teaspoon vanilla
- 1 cup sifted flour
- 1 teaspoon baking powder
- ¾ teaspoon salt
- 1 cup pitted dates, sliced
- ½ cup pecans or other nuts, coarsely chopped

Combine the butter, sugar, egg, and vanilla; beat until smooth. Sift the flour with the baking powder and salt; blend into the butter-sugar mixture. Blend in dates and nuts. Turn the batter into a greased and floured 9-inch square baking pan. Bake in a moderate oven, 350° F., for about 20 minutes. Spread a thin layer of the glaze over the top while it is still slightly warm. Allow to cool and then cut into bars.

Glaze

- 1 tablespoon soft butter *or* margarine
- 1 teaspoon lemon juice
- 1 teaspoon orange juice
- ½ cup sifted confectioners' sugar

Combine all ingredients and beat until smooth.

Gumdrop Cookies

4 eggs
2 cups brown sugar, packed
1 teaspoon vanilla
2 cups flour
¼ teaspoon salt
1 teaspoon cinnamon
½ cup chopped nuts
1 cup small gumdrops, cut in pieces

Beat the eggs until light. Add the sugar and vanilla. Sift together the flour, salt, and cinnamon; add to the eggs, and mix well. Stir in the nuts and gumdrops. Spread the dough ¼ inch thick in a greased baking pan and bake in a moderate oven, 325° F., for 30 minutes. While still warm, cut into squares.

Gingerbread Boys

½ cup shortening
½ cup sugar
½ cup unsulphured molasses
1 egg
2½ cups sifted flour
½ teaspoon baking soda
1 teaspoon baking powder
1 teaspoon ginger
1½ teaspoons cloves
1½ teaspoons cinnamon
⅛ teaspoon nutmeg

Cream together the shortening, sugar, and molasses. Add the egg and mix well. Sift together the flour, soda, baking powder, ginger, cloves, cinnamon, and nutmeg. Add the dry ingredients to the molasses mixture, mix well, and chill in the refrigerator for 1½ hours. Roll out the dough on a lightly floured board or pastry cloth. Cut with a 6-inch gingerbread boy cookie cutter. Press cut raisins into each cookie for the features on the face and buttons on the jacket. Bake in a moderate oven, 350° F., 10 to 12 minutes. Decorate with frosting. MAKES ABOUT 1½ DOZEN.

Chewy Butterscotch Bars

½ cup butter *or* margarine
1½ cups brown sugar, packed
2 eggs
1 teaspoon vanilla
1½ cups sifted flour
2 teaspoons baking powder
1 cup chopped nuts

Melt the butter in a saucepan. Add the sugar, bring to boiling, and boil over low heat, stirring constantly, until the sugar dissolves. Allow to cool slightly. Drop in the eggs, one at a time, and mix well. Add the vanilla and sifted dry ingredients. Stir in the nuts. Pour the batter into a greased 9 x 13 x 2-inch pan. Bake in a moderate oven, 350° F., about 30 minutes. When cool, cut into bars. MAKES ABOUT 32 BARS.

Ginger Cookies

½ cup shortening
½ cup sugar
½ cup light molasses
½ tablespoon vinegar
1 egg, beaten
3 cups flour
¼ teaspoon salt
½ teaspoon baking soda
½ teaspoon cinnamon
½ teaspoon ginger

Combine in a saucepan and bring to boiling the shortening, sugar, molasses, and vinegar. Remove from heat and allow to cool, then add the egg. Sift together the dry ingredients, add them to the first mixture, and mix well. Chill. Roll out the dough on a lightly floured surface and cut it into any desired shapes. Bake on a greased cookie sheet in a moderately hot oven, 375° F., for 12 to 15 minutes. MAKES 2½ DOZEN COOKIES.

German Anise Drops

2 eggs
1 cup sugar
1 teaspoon anise seeds
1¼ cups flour

Beat together the eggs and sugar for 20 minutes. Add the anise seeds and stir in the flour gradually. Drop by half teaspoonfuls onto greased cookie sheets and let stand overnight or at least 8 hours before baking. Bake in a moderate (325° F.) oven until the cookies are pale yellow on the bottom (this should take 10 to 12 minutes). Store in a tightly covered tin. If these cookies get too hard when they are stored, put a couple of slices of white bread into the tin with them and they will soon soften. This is, however, a hard Christmas cookie. MAKES ABOUT 6 DOZEN COOKIES.

Fudge Cookies

1½ cups sifted flour
¼ cup sugar
½ teaspoon baking powder
½ teaspoon salt
½ cup semisweet chocolate pieces
½ cup chopped pecans
¼ cup soft butter
1 beaten egg
Granulated sugar

Sift together the flour, sugar, baking powder, and salt. In a double boiler, combine the chocolate, pecans, and butter. Heat over hot water until the chocolate is melted, then stir until smooth. Remove from the heat and allow to cool slightly. Add the egg and mix thoroughly. Add the flour mixture and mix well. Place the dough on waxed paper and shape it into rolls. Wrap the rolls and chill them in the refrigerator overnight. To bake, slice the dough 1/8 inch thick, place the slices on an ungreased cookie sheet, and sprinkle them with sugar. Bake in a moderate oven, 375° F., for 10 minutes. Allow the cookies to cool before removing them from the cookie sheet. MAKES 2½ DOZEN COOKIES.

French Meringues

- 1 cup sugar
- ½ cup water
- 2 egg whites
- 1/8 teaspoon almond extract
- ¼ teaspoon vanilla
- ½ cup ground, blanched almonds

Boil the sugar with ½ cup water to 265° F. on a candy thermometer or until it forms a hard, almost brittle, ball. Beat the egg whites until stiff, then add the sugar syrup in a fine stream, beating constantly. When the mixture holds its shape, fold in the flavorings and almonds. Drop the mixture by teaspoonfuls onto a well-greased cookie sheet and bake in a slow oven, 250° F., for 15 minutes. MAKES ABOUT 40 MERINGUES.

French Butter Cream Cookies

- ½ cup butter
- ½ cup shortening
- 1½ cups sifted powdered sugar
- ¼ teaspoon salt
- 1 teaspoon vanilla
- 1 egg
- 2 cups sifted flour
- 1 teaspoon baking soda
- 1 teaspoon cream of tartar

Cream together the butter and shortening. Add the powdered sugar gradually, continuing to cream. Add salt, vanilla, and egg; beat thoroughly. Add the flour, soda, and cream of tartar; mix well. Chill for at least 10 minutes. Form the dough into ½-inch balls, place them on a cookie sheet, and flatten with a fork. Bake in a moderate (350° F.) oven for 13 to 14 minutes. Allow to cool slightly before removing from the cookie sheet. These are very tender, short cookies. MAKES ABOUT 70 TO 80 COOKIES, 2 inches in diameter.

Cinnamon Nibbles

1¼ cups sifted flour
1 teaspoon baking powder
¼ teaspoon salt
½ cup soft butter
1 cup sugar
1 beaten egg
1 teaspoon vanilla
½ cup finely chopped nuts
2 teaspoons cinnamon

Sift together the flour, baking powder, and salt. Mix together until creamy the butter, sugar, egg, and vanilla. Add the dry ingredients and mix well. Chill for 1 hour. Shape level teaspoons of dough into balls, roll the balls in combined nuts and cinnamon, and arrange them on a greased cookie sheet, 2 inches apart. Bake in a moderate (375° F.) oven for 15 minutes. MAKES ABOUT 30 COOKIES.

Cranberry Chews

2 eggs
1 cup sugar
Juice of ½ lemon
1½ cups sifted flour
1½ teaspoons baking powder
½ teaspoon salt
1 cup pecans, finely chopped
Half of a 1-pound can jellied cranberry sauce

With a rotary beater, beat together the eggs and sugar until creamy. Add the lemon juice and beat about 1 minute. Sift together the flour, baking powder, and salt. Stir the dry ingredients into the egg and sugar mixture. Fold in the pecans. Chop the jellied cranberry sauce into small cubes about ¼-inch square. Add and mix only slightly. Turn the batter into a greased, shallow 10 x 15-inch pan and bake in a moderate oven, 350° F., for 30 minutes. Cut into squares while still slightly warm.

Chocolate Butter Cookies

½ cup butter
1 cup sugar
1 egg
2 squares unsweetened chocolate, melted and cooled
1 teaspoon vanilla
2 cups sifted flour
½ teaspoon salt
1 teaspoon double-acting baking powder
Mint or rum-flavored milk chocolate wafers
Bittersweet chocolate frosting
Confectioners' sugar frosting
Nuts
Tiny colored candies

Cream the butter, gradually add the sugar, and continue creaming until light. Add the egg and mix well. Add the chocolate and vanilla. Sift together the dry ingredients and stir them into the first mixture. Chill. Roll out the dough 1/8 inch thick and cut with floured cookie cutters. Bake on ungreased cookie sheets in a moderate oven, 375° F., for 8 to 10 minutes. To decorate, put a chocolate wafer on some of the cookies and return them to the oven for a few seconds. While still hot, sandwich some of the cookies (by that, I mean put two together with the creamy chocolate wafer in between). Allow to cool. Decorate others with nuts or candies or frosting.

Chocolate Puffs

- 2 egg whites
- ½ cup sugar
- ¼ teaspoon salt
- 1 teaspoon vanilla
- 1 6-ounce package chocolate pieces, melted
- 1⅓ cups shredded coconut
- ½ cup chopped walnuts

Beat the egg whites until stiff, gradually add the sugar, and continue beating until blended. Add the salt and vanilla. Fold in the melted chocolate, coconut, and nuts. Drop by teaspoonfuls onto a cookie sheet. Bake in a slow oven, 300° F., for 10 to 15 minutes. MAKES ABOUT 3 DOZEN COOKIES.

Chocolate Almond Balls

- 3 cups sifted flour
- ¾ teaspoon salt
- ¾ cup butter *or* margarine
- ¾ cup shortening
- 2½ tablespoons cream cheese
- ⅔ cup sifted confectioners' sugar
- ½ cup chocolate syrup
- 1 teaspoon vanilla
- 1 teaspoon almond extract
- 1 cup coconut, cut fine
- 1 cup chopped blanched almonds

Sift together the flour and salt. Cream together the butter and shortening, and blend in the cream cheese and confectioners' sugar. Add the chocolate syrup, vanilla, and almond extract; beat well. Stir in the coconut and almonds, then gradually blend in the dry ingredients. Chill for at least 1 hour. Shape the dough into small balls, place them on ungreased baking sheets, and bake in a slow (325° F.) oven for 18 to 20 minutes. Cookies should not brown, but they should spring back when touched lightly in the center. While they are warm, roll them in confectioners' sugar.

Chocolate Chip Cookies

½ cup shortening
½ cup brown sugar, packed
¼ cup sugar
1 egg
1 cup plus 2 tablespoons sifted flour
½ teaspoon baking powder
½ teaspoon salt
½ cup chopped nuts
1 6-ounce package semisweet chocolate pieces
½ teaspoon vanilla

Cream the shortening with the sugars. Add the egg and beat well. Sift together the flour, baking powder, and salt; add to creamed mixture. Add nuts, chocolate pieces, and vanilla, mixing thoroughly. Drop by teaspoonfuls onto a cookie sheet, keeping the cookies 2 inches apart. Bake in a moderate oven, 375° F., about 10 minutes.

Banana-Oatmeal Cookies

1½ cups sifted flour
1 cup sugar
½ teaspoon baking soda
1 teaspoon salt
¼ teaspoon nutmeg
1 teaspoon cinnamon
¾ cup shortening
1 egg, beaten
1 cup mashed ripe bananas (2 to 3 bananas)
1¾ cups quick-cooking rolled oats
½ cup chopped nuts

Sift together the flour, sugar, soda, salt, nutmeg, and cinnamon. Cut in the shortening with a pastry blender or two knives. Add the egg, bananas, oats, and nuts; beat until thoroughly blended. Drop the dough by teaspoonfuls onto a lightly greased cookie sheet and bake in a moderate (375° F.) oven for 15 minutes. MAKES ABOUT 5 DOZEN COOKIES.

Butterscotch Brownies

¼ cup melted butter
1 cup dark brown sugar
1 egg
¼ teaspoon salt
¾ cup flour
1 teaspoon baking powder
½ teaspoon vanilla
½ cup nut meats, broken in pieces

Butter a shallow 8-inch square pan. Mix all ingredients together and spread in the pan. Bake 25 minutes in a moderate (350° F.) oven. Cut into squares or strips while warm.

Black Walnut Bars

- 1 cup butter
- 3 cups brown sugar, firmly packed
- 2 cups plus 2 tablespoons sifted flour
- 4 eggs
- 2 teaspoons vanilla
- ½ teaspoon salt
- ½ teaspoon baking powder
- 3 cups black walnuts, chopped

Cream together the butter and 1 cup brown sugar until light and fluffy. Gradually add 2 cups flour, stirring until the mixture forms a ball. Grease a 9-inch square baking pan and line it with waxed paper. Pat the dough into the baking pan and bake in a moderate oven, 350° F., for 10 minutes. Remove from heat and let cool while making the topping. Beat the eggs until light and lemon-colored. Gradually add the remaining 2 cups brown sugar beating constantly. Add the vanilla. Sift together the salt, 2 tablespoons flour, and baking powder. Fold the dry ingredients into the egg mixture. Fold in the nuts. Spread the topping over the dough in the pan. Bake in a moderate oven, 375° F., for 25 to 30 minutes or until the center is firm to the touch. When cool, cut into squares. MAKES 20 TO 24 BARS.

Black Walnut Butter Wafers

- 1 cup black walnuts, chopped very fine
- ½ cup butter
- ½ cup sugar
- 2 unbeaten egg yolks
- 1½ cups sifted flour

Cream together thoroughly the butter and sugar; add unbeaten egg yolks and beat well. Gradually add the flour, mix to form a dough, and stir in the finely chopped black walnuts, minus 2 tablespoons which you reserve for the icing. Place the dough on waxed paper and shape it into a roll 2½ inches in diameter and 12 inches long. Wrap the roll in waxed paper and chill for at least 2 hours or overnight. Cut the chilled dough into ¼-inch slices and place the slices on ungreased baking sheets. Bake in a moderate oven, 375° F., 8 to 10 minutes. Allow to cool. Frost if desired.

For the frosting, combine 2 unbeaten egg whites, ⅛ teaspoon

salt, 1/4 teaspoon cinnamon, and 2 cups sifted confectioners' sugar. Beat until smooth, then stir in the reserved 2 tablespoons nuts. MAKES 4 DOZEN WAFERS.

Banana-Nut Bars

- 1 cup sifted flour
- 1/4 teaspoon baking powder
- 1/4 teaspoon salt
- 1/4 cup nonfat dry milk
- 1/3 cup soft shortening
- 1 cup sugar
- 1 unbeaten egg
- 1/2 cup mashed banana
- 1/2 cup broken, unsalted nuts

Combine and sift together the sifted flour, baking powder, salt, and nonfat dry milk. Cream together the shortening and sugar until light and fluffy. Add the egg and beat vigorously. Stir in about half the flour mixture, then stir in the mashed banana. Add the remaining flour mixture and mix well. Fold in the broken nut meats. Spread the batter evenly in a greased, 8-inch square pan and bake in a moderate (350° F.) oven about 35 minutes or until the cake pulls away from the sides of the pan. Allow to cool in the pan and then cut into bars. MAKES 1 1/2 DOZEN BARS.

Arabian Macaroons

- 1 cup Angel Flake coconut
- 1/2 cup finely cut dates *or* figs
- 1/2 cup chopped walnuts
- 1/2 cup sugar
- 1/8 teaspoon salt
- 1 egg, well beaten
- 1/2 teaspoon vanilla

Combine the coconut, dates or figs, walnuts, sugar, and salt; mix well. Add the egg and vanilla, blend, and let stand 5 minutes. Drop the dough from a teaspoon onto a greased baking sheet and bake in a moderate oven, 350° F., for 15 minutes or until golden brown. Remove at once from the baking sheet and allow to cool on a rack. MAKES ABOUT 20 MACAROONS.

Almond Snow Balls

- 3/4 cup shortening
- 1/2 cup sugar
- 1 egg, well beaten
- 2 teaspoons vanilla
- 2 cups sifted flour
- 1/2 teaspoon salt
- 2 cups ground blanched almonds
- Sifted confectioners' sugar

Cream the shortening, add the sugar, and cream well. Stir in the beaten egg and vanilla; beat until fluffy. Stir together the flour and salt and cut it into the creamed mixture. Mix in the ground almonds. This will be a very stiff dough and you will probably have to do the last mixing with your hands. Shape the dough into small balls about 2/3 inch in diameter. Place the balls on an ungreased baking sheet and bake in a moderate oven, 350° F., for 20 minutes. Allow to cool slightly on baking sheet, then roll in sifted confectioners' sugar. Store in a loosely covered container. MAKES 6 TO 7 DOZEN COOKIES.

Almond Cookies

- 1 cup sifted flour
- 1/4 teaspoon salt
- 1/3 cup butter
- 1/3 cup sugar
- 1 egg yolk
- 1 tablespoon milk
- 1/4 teaspoon almond extract
- 2 hard-cooked egg yolks, sieved
- 3 tablespoons finely chopped blanched almonds

Sift together the flour and salt. Cream the butter and sugar together until light. Add the uncooked egg yolk and milk; beat well. Add the almond extract, cooked egg yolks, and the sifted dry ingredients; stir until well blended. Add the almonds and blend well. Chill the dough. Roll out the dough 1/8-inch thick on a lightly floured board or pastry canvas and cut with a small cookie cutter. If desired, brush the tops with slightly beaten egg white and sprinkle with a few coarsely chopped almonds before baking. Bake in a moderate (325° F.) oven about 10 to 12 minutes or until the cookies are lightly browned. MAKES 2 DOZEN COOKIES.

Lebkuchen

- 2 1/4 cups sifted flour
- 1/2 teaspoon salt
- 1 teaspoon baking powder
- 1/2 teaspoon ground cloves
- 1 teaspoon cinnamon
- 1 cup broken walnuts
- 1/2 pound diced mixed candied fruits
- 3 eggs plus 1 egg yolk
- 1 1/2 cups dark brown sugar, packed
- 1/2 cup strong coffee *or* sherry wine
- 1 cup confectioners' sugar
- 2 tablespoons milk

Grease a jelly roll pan, 15 x 10 x 1 inches. Heat the oven to moderate, 375° F. Sift the flour with the salt, baking powder, cloves, and cinnamon. Add the nuts and fruits, mixing well. In large bowl, with the mixer at high speed, beat the eggs and egg yolk till thick and lemon-colored. Gradually add the brown sugar, beating well after each addition. With a spoon, blend in the coffee or sherry, then the flour mixture. Turn the batter into the jelly roll pan, spreading it evenly. Bake for 25 minutes or until a cake tester inserted in the center comes out clean and the top springs back. Allow to cool in the pan. Frost with the confectioners' sugar mixed with the milk. Cut lengthwise into eight strips, then crosswise into three strips, making 24 large bars. Store the bars in a tightly covered container with a cut apple to keep the bars soft; or, if preferred, freeze the bars. MAKES 24 BARS.

Pfeffernüsse

4 cups sifted flour
1 teaspoon baking soda
½ teaspoon salt
1 tablespoon cinnamon
1 teaspoon ground cloves
1 teaspoon nutmeg
¼ teaspoon black pepper
1 tablespoon ground cardamom
1 teaspoon anise seed
4 ounces candied orange peel
8 ounces citron
2 tablespoons butter
2½ cups very fine granulated sugar
5 eggs, separated
1½ teaspoons grated lemon rind
1½ cups confectioners' sugar
About 3 tablespoons milk

Sift together the flour, soda, salt, cinnamon, cloves, nutmeg, and black pepper. Add the cardamom and anise seed. Grind together coarsely the peel and citron; add to the dry ingredients. In large bowl, with the mixer at high speed, mix the butter with the granulated sugar; then add the egg yolks and lemon rind, mixing till well blended. With a spoon, blend in the dry ingredients. Beat the egg whites until stiff and fold them into the dough. Refrigerate for 1 hour. With floured hands, shape the dough into small balls. Place the balls on an ungreased cookie sheet and let stand uncovered, for 12 hours at room temperature. Then bake in a moderate oven, 350° F., for 15 minutes or until done. Allow to cool.

Make a glaze by blending the confectioners' sugar with milk. Dip the cookies into the mixture and drain them on a cooling rack. This leaves a hard sugar glaze. Leave the cookies in this state or toss them in sifted confectioners' sugar before the sugar glaze hardens. MAKES ABOUT 7 DOZEN COOKIES.

Old-Fashioned Tea Cakes

2 cups sugar
1 cup butter
4 cups sifted flour
1 teaspoon baking soda
1 teaspoon baking powder
1 cup commercial sour cream
1 teaspoon vanilla

Cream the butter thoroughly then gradually add the sugar. Combine the dry ingredients and add them to the butter-sugar mixture alternately with the sour cream. Add the vanilla and mix well. Turn out the dough onto a floured board, knead it, and roll it out as thin as possible. Cut into desired shapes. Bake in a hot (450° F.) oven until lightly browned.

Lemon Drop Cookies

2 cups sifted flour
½ teaspoon baking soda
½ teaspoon salt
½ cup shortening
1 cup sugar
2 eggs
¼ cup lemon juice
1 teaspoon vanilla

Sift together the flour, soda, and salt. Cream the shortening and sugar together until light and fluffy, then add the eggs and beat well. Add the flour mixture to the creamed mixture alternately with the lemon juice and vanilla. Mix well. Drop the dough by teaspoonfuls onto a greased cookie sheet, 2 inches apart. Bake in a moderate oven, 350° F., for 10 minutes. Check the cookies after 8 minutes' baking time. They are a delicate cookie and should brown lightly around the edges, but do not let them get too brown. Use a spatula to remove them from the cookie sheet and transfer them to a wire cake rack to cool. Store the cookies in a covered metal container lined with waxed paper, and put waxed paper between the layers. MAKES ABOUT 5 DOZEN COOKIES.

Best-Ever Brownies

2 squares unsweetened chocolate
¼ cup butter *or* margarine
1 cup sugar
2 eggs
¼ teaspoon salt
½ cup sifted flour
1 teaspoon vanilla
1 cup chopped walnuts

Melt the chocolate with the butter in the top of a double boiler. Remove from the heat, add the sugar and eggs, and beat well. Add salt, flour, vanilla, and ½ cup nuts. Pour the batter into a greased and floured 8-inch square pan. Scatter the remaining ½ cup nuts over the top and gently press them down with the back of a spoon. Bake in a slow (300° F.) oven for 40 minutes. Allow to cool slightly. MAKES 16 LARGE, CHEWY BROWNIES.

You can also make this into a brownie pie and slice it in wedges and serve it with whipped cream or vanilla ice cream.

9

Beverages

ALMOST EVERY HOMEMAKER has her own favorite recipes for punches and drinks, but once in a while it's fun to live dangerously and try a new punch recipe for a bridge club meeting or a small open house.

In the ten years that we have been furnishing recipes for Texas homemakers, we have found that there are some who like nonalcoholic drinks, some who like to use champagne, and others who prefer a tea-base punch.

I am very partial to our domestic champagnes for punch recipes, and I think more champagne would be used if people realized that you don't have to buy an expensive imported champagne for good flavor. There is a lovely pink champagne from California that we use for many of our parties here in Dallas, and you'll find a magnificent pink champagne with a Taylor New York State label.

Elegant Champagne Punch

1 quart champagne
1 13½-ounce can frozen pineapple chunks
½ cup sugar
⅔ cup lemon juice
¼ cup syrup from maraschino cherries

Chill the champagne thoroughly. Combine the pineapple chunks, sugar, lemon juice, and syrup from cherries; let stand in the refrigerator until the pineapple is thawed. Just before serving, add the champagne and mix lightly. Serve at once. If you are making more, don't double this recipe. Make the recipes separately, to keep the bubbly quality of the champagne.

Simple Sugar Syrup

In a saucepan, combine 3 cups sugar and 3 cups water. Bring to a boil, stirring until sugar dissolves; cover and boil for 5 minutes without stirring. Allow to cool. Pour the syrup into a clean, dry jar; cover and store in refrigerator. MAKES 4⅓ CUPS.

Keep a supply of this syrup on hand for mixing various drinks.

Orange Eggnog

- 6 egg yolks, beaten
- 1½ cups orange juice
- ¼ cup sugar
- 6 egg whites
- 3 to 4 cups milk
- Grated orange rind

Combine the egg yolks, orange juice, and 1 teaspoon sugar; beat well. Combine the egg whites and the remaining sugar; beat until stiff but not dry. Fold most of the egg white mixture into the egg yolk mixture. Pour into tall glasses, add milk to fill the glasses, and top with the remaining egg white. Sprinkle each with grated orange rind. MAKES 6 GLASSES.

Spiced Tomato Bouillon

Spiced tomato bouillon may be served in teacups or demitasse cups in the living room for a first course, along with tiny, bite-sized bread and butter sandwiches made with thinly sliced pumpernickel or rye bread.

- 3 quarts solid pack, canned tomatoes
- 2 onions, sliced
- 6 whole cloves
- ¼ teaspoon dried basil
- ½ teaspoon sugar
- 2 teaspoons salt
- ½ teaspoon garlic salt
- 3 beef bouillon cubes
- ½ lemon, thinly sliced
- Sour cream (optional)

Combine all ingredients except lemon and sour cream; simmer for 10 minutes. Strain through a fine sieve. Add lemon slices. Reheat just before serving. Top each serving with a spoonful of sour cream, if desired. SERVES 10 TO 12.

Russian Tea

Without question, this old standby Russian Tea is the favorite hot drink for club gatherings.

The favorite little sandwiches to go with this Russian Tea are chicken salad on whole wheat bread, cream cheese with minced onion on rye bread, and tuna or crabmeat on white bread. With the trend toward smaller snacks, make sandwiches of miniature size, so that your guests can have one of each.

- 4 cups sugar
- 4 sticks cinnamon
- 2 quarts water
- 8 oranges
- 6 lemons
- 4 cups (2 No. 303 cans) pineapple juice
- ⅔ cup (32 teaspoons) black tea
- 4 cups boiling water

Make a syrup by boiling together the sugar, cinnamon, and 2 quarts water for 5 minutes. Add the juice of the oranges and lemons, and the pineapple juice. Boil the orange and lemon rinds with 1 quart water. Strain and combine with first mixture. Add 5 quarts water and heat. Steep the tea in 4 cups boiling water, strain, and add just before serving. SERVES 50.

Punch Rosé

- 4 packages frozen strawberries, thawed
- 1 cup sugar
- 4 bottles rosé wine
- 4 6-ounce cans lemonade concentrate
- 2 large bottles sparkling water

Mix the thawed strawberries, sugar, and 1 bottle of wine and let stand for 1 hour. Strain. Add the lemonade concentrate and stir in the remaining wine and the sparkling water. Serve in an ice bowl or a punch bowl with cubes of ice in it. MAKES 6 QUARTS.

Pink Punch

- 2 packages fruit-flavored gelatin (strawberry, cherry, *or* raspberry)
- 2 cups hot water
- 6 cups cold water
- 1½ cups lime *or* lemon juice
- 2 cups pineapple juice
- 5 cups orange juice
- ½ to 1 cup sugar
- 5 to 6 fully ripe bananas
- 1 quart chilled ginger ale

Place the gelatin in a large mixing bowl and add 2 cups hot or boiling water. Stir until the gelatin is dissolved. Add 6 cups cold water and the fruit juices, stir in the sugar, and chill. Just before serving, mash or whip the bananas until smooth and creamy, beat them into the mixture, and add the ginger ale. Garnish with fluted slices of banana, pineapple, strawberry, lime, lemon, or orange. MAKES 1 GALLON OR 32 4-OUNCE SERVINGS.

Nonalcoholic Eggnog

- ¼ teaspoon salt
- 6 eggs, separated
- ½ cup sugar
- 2½ cups milk
- 2 cups heavy cream, whipped stiff
- 2½ tablespoons vanilla
- Nutmeg

Add the salt to the egg whites and beat until the whites are stiff but not dry. Gradually add the sugar, beating continuously. Beat egg yolks until thick and lemon-colored; fold in the egg whites. Gradually add the milk. Fold in the whipped cream and vanilla. Sprinkle with nutmeg and serve at once.

New Year's Eggnog

- 2 eggs, slightly beaten
- ½ cup sugar
- 1 tablespoon flour
- 1½ cups scalded milk
- ⅛ teaspoon salt
- ½ teaspoon vanilla
- ¼ cup brandy
- ¼ cup Jamaica rum
- ½ pint heavy cream, whipped

Mix the eggs, sugar, and flour; pour the milk slowly into the egg mixture, blending well. Cook, stirring constantly, in the top of a double boiler over simmering water (water should not touch the bottom of the upper bowl) until the mixture coats a spoon. Remove from the heat, and immediately stir in the salt and vanilla. Cool promptly by pouring the custard into a chilled bowl or by placing the pan in cold water. Cover and refrigerate overnight. Just before serving, stir in the brandy and rum and fold in the whipped cream. Sprinkle with nutmeg if desired. MAKES 1 QUART.

Hot Buttered Rum

- 2 quarts apple juice
- ½ cup brown sugar
- ¼ cup butter
- Rum

Combine the apple juice and brown sugar; heat until the sugar is dissolved and the juice reaches the boiling point. Add the butter. Keep hot while serving. Put a jigger of rum in each mug. Pour on hot apple juice mixture and stir well before serving. Sprinkle with powdered cinnamon or add a stick of cinnamon for a stirrer.

Purple Cow

1 6-ounce can frozen grape juice, partly thawed
1 pint vanilla ice cream
1 quart chilled carbonated water

Spoon 2 tablespoons concentrated grape juice, right from the can, into each of six tall glasses. Add about ⅓ cup ice cream to each glass and fill with carbonated water; stir. SERVES 6.

Milk Punch

1 tumbler sweet milk
1 jigger bourbon whiskey
1 tablespoon powdered sugar
Nutmeg

Combine all ingredients and shake well with cracked ice. Serve with a sprinkling of nutmeg on top.

Hot Mulled Wine Lemonade

2 cups boiling water
18 whole cloves
3 2-inch cinnamon sticks
2 6-ounce cans lemonade concentrate
2 bottles claret, Burgundy, *or* port wine

Place the cloves and cinnamon sticks in 2 cups boiling water and boil together for 15 minutes. Add the lemonade concentrate and wine. Heat to piping hot, but do not boil. Strain out the spices or serve with spices in, as you prefer. SERVES 12 TO 16.

Hot Buttered Cranberry Punch

¾ cup brown sugar, packed
4 cups water
¼ teaspoon salt
¼ teaspoon nutmeg
½ teaspoon cinnamon
½ teaspoon ground allspice
¾ teaspoon ground cloves
2 cans jellied cranberry sauce
1 quart canned pineapple juice
Butter
Cinnamon sticks

Bring to a boil the sugar, 1 cup water, salt, and spices. With a fork, crush the cranberry sauce. Add 3 cups water to the cranberry sauce and beat with a rotary beater until smooth. Add the pineapple juice and hot syrup; simmer for about 5 minutes. Serve hot in mugs with dots of butter and cinnamon-stick stirrers.

Frosted Eggnog

- 8 eggs
- 1 cup sugar
- ½ teaspoon salt
- 2 quarts milk
- 1 cup whipping cream
- 1 teaspoon vanilla

Beat the eggs well with a rotary or electric beater. Add the sugar and salt; blend well. Add the milk and mix thoroughly. Chill before serving unless the milk is very cold. Just before serving, whip together the cream and vanilla; top each serving with a mound of the flavored cream. SERVES 16 TO 20.

Hot Mulled Cider Punch

- 6 quarts cider
- 2 teaspoons whole cloves
- Cinnamon sticks
- ½ teaspoon nutmeg
- ¾ cup sugar

Combine the cider, cloves, cinnamon sticks, nutmeg, and sugar. Bring to a boil, then boil for 5 minutes. Strain and serve hot in punch cups. SERVES 48.

Cranberry Punch

- 1 pint cranberry juice cocktail
- 1 cup orange juice
- ½ cup pineapple juice
- 4 tablespoons sugar
- Juice of 2 lemons
- 1 to 2 cups water

Combine all ingredients and chill. SERVES 4 TO 6.

For 50 servings

- 1 12-ounce can frozen orange concentrate
- 1 6-ounce can frozen lemonade concentrate
- 2½ cups pineapple juice
- 1½ quarts water
- 6 pints cranberry juice cocktail

Add water to frozen concentrates as directed on cans. (In other words, reconstitute the fruit juice concentrates.) Combine all ingredients, add $1\frac{1}{2}$ quarts water, and mix well. Serve in a punch bowl over crushed ice or ice cubes.

Cognac Eggnog

- 8 eggs, separated
- 2 cups sugar
- 2 jiggers rum
- 1 bottle ($\frac{4}{5}$) cognac
- 1 pint heavy cream, whipped
- 1 quart milk
- Freshly grated nutmeg

Beat the egg yolks until thick. Beat the egg whites until stiff, gradually add sugar, and continue beating until the mixture stands in peaks. Gently fold the egg whites into the egg yolks. Add the remaining ingredients and chill thoroughly. Serve in cups with freshly grated nutmeg on top. SERVES 20.

Sauterne Punch

Use half chilled sauterne and half chilled dry ginger ale. Tint with a little red food coloring or add maraschino cherries and chunks of pineapple.

Champagne-Fruit Cocktail

- $\frac{1}{2}$ cup chopped fresh pineapple
- 1 orange, peeled and sliced
- $\frac{1}{2}$ cup strawberries
- 3 tablespoons sugar
- $\frac{3}{4}$ cup cognac
- 1 bottle champagne, well chilled

Chop together the pineapple, orange, and berries until very fine. Sprinkle with the sugar and pour the cognac over the mixture. Chill for at least 1 hour. Divide the mixture among 6 chilled champagne glasses, fill with the champagne, and serve immediately.

Champagne Punch

- 6 quart bottles champagne, well-chilled
- 2 bottles sauterne, well-chilled
- 6 lemons, sliced but not peeled
- 6 oranges, sliced but not peeled
- 6 fresh mint leaves
- 1 cup sugar (more or less to taste)
- 3 dozen fresh pineapple sticks (optional)
- 2 cups brandy
- 2 quarts small fresh strawberries (optional)

Into a large bowl pour the contents of 3 bottles champagne and 2 bottles sauterne. Add the lemon and orange slices, mint leaves, sugar to taste, and enough pineapple sticks to allow one for each serving. Stir well, until the sugar is completely dissolved. Place a large piece of ice in a punch bowl and add the brandy and fresh strawberries, if available. (Wild strawberries are especially nice.) Just before serving, pour in the remaining 3 quarts champagne. Serve in chilled champagne glasses or punch cups. SERVES ABOUT 35.

Creamy Coffee Punch

4 quarts cold strong coffee
1 quart cold milk
1 tablespoon vanilla
1 cup sugar
2 quarts vanilla ice cream

Combine the coffee, milk, and vanilla. Add the sugar and stir until it is dissolved. Chill thoroughly. Pour over ice cream in a punch bowl. Serve in punch cups. Top with whipped cream, if desired. SERVES ABOUT 30.

Brazilian Iced Chocolate

2 squares unsweetened chocolate
4 tablespoons sugar
1 cup strong hot coffee
4 cups milk
Ice cream (optional)
Whipping cream (optional)

Melt the chocolate in the top of a double boiler. When it is melted, add the sugar. Gradually pour in the hot coffee, stirring all the time. Scald the milk and combine it with the chocolate-coffee mixture. Cook for 10 minutes or until smooth, then remove from heat and chill thoroughly. Before serving, add ice cream or ice cubes, if desired. Sweetened whipped cream may be used as a topping. SERVES 6 TO 8.

Hot Spiced Tea

1 teaspoon whole cloves
1 1-inch stick cinnamon
3 quarts water
2½ tablespoons black tea
Juice of 3 oranges
Juice of 1½ lemons
1 cup sugar

Tie the spices loosely in a cheesecloth bag, place in 3 quarts water, and bring to a boil. Add the tea, tied loosely in another cheesecloth bag, and steep 5 minutes. Remove the bags. Heat the fruit juices and sugar and add to the tea. SERVES 25.

Hawaiian Champagne Punch

- 6 cans frozen pineapple chunks
- $3\frac{1}{3}$ cups confectioners' sugar
- ½ cup maraschino liqueur
- ½ cup Curaçao
- 2 cups lemon juice
- 2 cups brandy
- 2 cups rum
- 4 quarts chilled champagne

Place the pineapple in a large glass bowl with the sugar and let it stand for about 1 hour. Add all remaining ingredients except the champagne and let stand about 12 hours longer. Pour in a large punch bowl, add a large block of ice, and, just before serving, add the champagne. SERVES ABOUT 50.

Cider Punch

- 2 quarts apple cider *or* apple juice
- Juice of 6 oranges
- 3 limes, sliced
- Sugar to taste
- 2 cups ice water
- 1 quart ginger ale

Mix 1 quart cider with the orange juice, lime slices, and 3 to 6 tablespoons sugar. Let stand 2 hours to blend the flavors. At serving time, add 2 cups ice water, the remaining cider and the ginger ale.

Wassail Bowl

For each mug, use a teaspoonful of maple syrup (pure maple syrup is important), a marble-sized butter ball, two cloves, a slice of lemon. Fill to the brim with boiling hot apple cider and toss in a pinch of cinnamon. It is suggested that the cider in the chafing dish be replenished from the kitchen where a kettle of the boiling cider is available. Let the guests help themselves, but show them the traditional ritual of building a wassail bowl.

Royal Champagne Punch

- 4 $3\frac{1}{4}$-ounce glasses bar-le-duc
- 2 cups Taylor New York State rosé wine
- 2 bottles Taylor New York State champagne

Combine bar-le-duc and rosé. Chill several hours. Pour over a large block of ice in a small punch bowl. Just before serving, add the well-chilled champagne and garnish to taste. Serve in punch cups. SERVES 20 TO 25.

Garnishes

Feature a tray of choose-your-own garnishes near the punch bowl. Colorful suggestions are whole strawberries, sprigs of mint, lemon and lime slices, and such seasonal items as red currants or fresh cherries with stems.

Basic Milk Punch

1 teaspoon powdered sugar	½ pint (1 cup) milk
2 ounces whiskey, cognac, *or* brandy	Grated nutmeg

Combine all ingredients, shake well with cracked ice, and strain into a 12-ounce glass. Grate nutmeg over the top.

If you want to make this in a punch bowl, make it in quart quantity (4 teaspoons powdered sugar, 8 ounces whiskey, 1 quart milk). Pour over ice cubes and let stand for 10 to 15 minutes, then pour off the ice cubes so that the punch is not diluted.

10

Jams, jellies, and preserves

THIS IS A SMALL CHAPTER, because we have such magnificent jams and jellies and preserves at our fingertips on the shelves of our favorite grocery stores.

I do think, however, that there is a place for old favorites, so I am giving you some that were in my grandmother's cookbook and some new ones that I have added in recent years.

Jams, jellies, and preserves make wonderful gifts or welcome contributions to Christmas bazaars. The recipes that I am giving you here are simple ones that are especially welcome around the house during the holiday season, and such fun to make.

Rosé-Cranberry Jelly

2 cups California rosé wine
¼ cup strained lemon juice
1 cup cranberry juice cocktail
1 2½-ounce package powdered pectin
5 cups sugar

In a large kettle, combine the wine, lemon juice, and cranberry juice cocktail; stir in the pectin. Cook over high heat, stirring frequently until the mixture comes to a boil. Add the sugar at once and bring to a full rolling boil (this is a rapid boiling that can't be stirred down); boil for 1 minute, stirring constantly. Remove from heat and skim the foam from the top. Pour the jelly into hot, sterilized glasses and cover with paraffin. MAKES 5 8-OUNCE GLASSES.

Spiced Watermelon Cubes

Choose firm, ripe, top-quality fruit; wash it well and cut out any soft spots. Measure accurately and make sure all jars are sterilized and have good closures. Pare off the green skin and inner pink portions from the watermelon rind, cut it into ½-inch cubes, and measure.

- 6 cups cubed watermelon rind
- 3½ cups water
- ½ cup fresh mint leaves, firmly packed
- 2 teaspoons whole cloves
- 2 2-inch sticks whole cinnamon
- 6 cups sugar
- 1 cup cider vinegar
- 1 lemon, sliced thin
- Green food coloring

Soak the watermelon rind overnight in salt water to cover (¼ cup salt to 2 quarts water) in the refrigerator or a cool place. Drain, cover with clear water, and boil for 30 minutes. Drain again. Measure 3½ cups water into a 4-quart kettle. Tie the mint leaves, cloves, and cinnamon in a piece of clean cheesecloth, add to the water, and boil 2 minutes. Then add the sugar, vinegar, lemon slices, and cubed watermelon. Boil gently for 50 minutes, until the watermelon is transparent and the syrup is slightly thickened. Fifteen minutes before the cooking is completed, add a few drops of food coloring to tint a delicate color. Remove the spice bag, spoon the mixture into hot, sterilized jars, and seal. MAKES 6 HALF PINTS.

Spiced Plum Conserve

- 3 pounds ripe plums
- ½ cup water
- 7½ cups sugar
- 1 lemon, juice and grated rind
- 2 oranges, juice and grated rind
- 2 tablespoons mixed pickling spice
- ½ cup walnut meats
- ½ cup seedless raisins
- ½ bottle liquid pectin (Certo)

Pit the plums, but do not peel them. Chop the plums into coarse pieces, add ½ cup water, and boil for three minutes. Add the sugar, fruit juices and rind, pickling spice tied in a small cheesecloth bag, nuts, and raisins. Bring back to boiling, reduce heat, and simmer for 5 minutes, stirring constantly. Remove from heat and add the pectin. Allow the jelly to cool slightly, stirring and skimming alternately until most of the scum has been removed. Ladle the jelly into hot, sterilized jelly glasses and seal at once. MAKES 6 PINTS.

Pear Conserve

- 3 ripe Anjou pears
- 3/4 cup diced fresh tomato
- 1 cup crushed pineapple with syrup
- 1/2 lemon, quartered and thinly sliced
- 1 teaspoon cinnamon
- 1/2 teaspoon nutmeg
- 1/4 teaspoon ginger
- 1 3 1/2-ounce package powdered pectin
- 5 cups sugar

Peel, core, and dice the pears. Place the pears, tomato, pineapple with syrup, lemon, and spices in a large 5- or 6-quart saucepan. Mix the pectin with the fruit. Place over high heat and stir until mixture comes to a rolling boil. Stir in the sugar, all at once, and bring again to a rolling boil. Boil rapidly for 2 minutes—no longer—stirring constantly. Remove from heat. Stir and skim for 5 minutes to prevent floating fruit; pour into hot, sterilized jars and seal. MAKES 6 HALF PINTS.

Frozen Strawberry Preserves

We are using the Birdseye brand name because the sugar content differs among brands of frozen fruits. Also, package sizes vary in different parts of the country. This recipe came from the Birdseye test kitchens.

You may think that this is a very expensive way of making strawberry preserves, but remember that you can make small amounts of these preserves any month in the year. And if you have had sky-high strawberry prices in your home town, as we have, I think you'll welcome this recipe.

- 4 cups thawed Birdseye frozen strawberries
- 4 cups sugar

Combine the berries and sugar in a deep kettle and cook over low heat until the sugar melts, then turn the heat to high and cook for 12 minutes, skimming as the berries cook. Turn out into platters and let stand overnight. Ladle the preserves into hot, sterilized jars and seal with paraffin. MAKES 2 PINTS.

Kumquat Marmalade

- 2 pounds kumquats
- 1 lemon, thinly sliced
- 1½ quarts cold water
- 4 cups sugar

Wash and dry the kumquats, slice them thinly, and remove the seeds. Add the lemon slices and 1½ quarts cold water. Let this stand 12 hours. Heat the mixture to the boiling point and cook over a low heat until the peel is clear and tender. Let stand 24 hours. Add the sugar and cook over low heat, very slowly, until the marmalade thickens, stirring occasionally to prevent scorching. Pack in hot, sterilized jars and seal.

Vanilla Peach and Pear Jam

- 2 cups (1½ pounds) coarsely crushed fresh peaches
- 2 cups (1½ pounds) coarsely crushed fresh pears
- 1 box (2½ ounces) powdered pectin
- 6 cups sugar
- 1½ teaspoons vanilla extract

In a 6-quart saucepan, mix together the peaches, pears, and powdered pectin. Bring to a full rolling boil over high heat. (A rolling boil is one that cannot be stirred down). Boil 1 minute, stirring constantly. Add the sugar, mix well, and bring again to a full rolling boil. Boil 2 minutes. Remove the jam from the heat. Stir and skim for 5 minutes with a metal spoon to prevent the fruit from floating. Add the vanilla extract and quickly ladle the jam into hot, sterilized jars, filling them to within 1 inch of the top. Seal at once. MAKES TWELVE HALF PINTS.

Vanilla Peach Conserve

- 4 cups (3 pounds) peeled and coarsely crushed fresh peaches
- 1 box (2½ ounces) powdered pectin
- 5 cups sugar
- ½ cup diced maraschino cherries
- 1 cup chopped English walnuts
- 1½ teaspoons vanilla
- 2 teaspoons grated orange rind
- ½ teaspoon grated lemon rind

In a 6-quart saucepan, mix together the peaches and powdered pectin. Bring to a full rolling boil over high heat. (A full rolling boil is one that cannot be stirred down). Boil for 1 minute, stirring constantly. Add the sugar, again bring to a full rolling boil, and boil 1 minute. Remove from the heat and add the remaining ingredients. Skim off the foam and stir the conserve with a metal spoon for 5 minutes to prevent the fruit from floating. Quickly ladle the conserve into hot, sterilized jars and seal at once. MAKES 6 PINTS.

Green Tomato Pickle

- 5½ pounds green tomatoes
- 6 large onions, sliced
- ½ cup plus 1½ teaspoons salt
- 3 cups cider vinegar
- 8 green peppers, sliced
- 3 red peppers, sliced
- 4 cloves garlic, minced
- 1 cup brown sugar
- 3 cups dark corn syrup
- 1 tablespoon dry mustard
- 1 tablespoon whole cloves
- 1 3-inch stick cinnamon, crushed
- 1 tablespoon ginger
- 1½ teaspoons celery seed

Wash the tomatoes, remove the stems, and slice thin. Add the onions and sprinkle with ½ cup salt. Let stand 2 hours, then wash and drain. Combine the vinegar, peppers, garlic, brown sugar, and corn syrup; heat to the boiling point. Add the tomatoes, onions, spices, 1½ teaspoons salt, and celery seed. Bring back to boiling and boil gently for about 10 minutes. Place the pickle in hot, sterilized jars and seal immediately. MAKES ABOUT 8 PINTS.

Gingered Pear Preserves

These preserves just got right up and walked out of the pantry booth at my church bazaar. Everyone is mad about the flavor, and if you think that the preserves are too bland a color, add a few drops of red food coloring to the pears while they are cooking and the preserves will have a beautiful pinkish tint.

- 5 large California Bartlett pears
- 2 cups sugar
- ¼ teaspoon salt
- Grated peel and juice of 1 lemon
- ⅓ to ½ cup chopped candied *or* preserved ginger

Wash, pare, core, and quarter the pears. Add the sugar, salt, grated lemon peel, and lemon juice. Mix and let stand about 30 minutes, until enough juice is drawn out of the pears to moisten the sugar. Add the ginger. (If you have fresh ginger root, peel, slice, and chop it very fine. Use 2 tablespoons of the fresh in place of the candied or preserved ginger.) Heat to boiling, stirring constantly, and boil gently about 20 minutes or until the pears look clear and slightly glazed. Let the preserves stand in the kettle overnight. Stir occasionally while cooling to plump the fruit. Next day, lift the pears out into hot, sterilized, small jars. Reheat the syrup and boil for 5 to 10 minutes, until quite thick. Pour the hot syrup over the pears and seal with scalded lids. MAKES 3 HALF PINT JARS OF PEARS.

Seal leftover syrup in jars and use over waffles, pancakes, or ice cream.

Chablis-Apple Jelly

- 2 cups Chablis, sauterne, or other white wine
- 1½ cups bottled apple juice
- ¼ cup strained lemon juice
- 1 2½-ounce package powdered pectin
- 5 cups sugar

In a large kettle, combine the wine, apple juice, and lemon juice. Stir in the pectin. Cook over high heat, stirring frequently, until the mixture reaches a boil. Add the sugar at once, bring to a full rolling boil (this is a rapid boiling that can't be stirred down), and boil for 1 minute, stirring constantly. Remove from heat and skim the foam from the top. Pour the jelly into hot, sterilized glasses and cover with paraffin. MAKES 7 8-OUNCE GLASSES.

Apple Chutney

- 6½ pounds (16 medium) Jonathan apples, peeled and cored
- 1 pound (4 medium) onions, peeled
- ½ pound (2 medium) green peppers
- 1 4-ounce can pimientos, drained
- 1 cup seedless raisins
- 4 cups white vinegar
- 2½ cups sugar
- 1 cup brown sugar, firmly packed
- 2 tablespoons mustard seed
- 1 tablespoon salt
- 1 teaspoon ground ginger

Put the apples, onions, green peppers, and pimiento through the food chopper, using the coarse blade. Combine this mixture with the remaining ingredients in a large preserving kettle, stirring well to mix. Bring to a boil over high heat, then reduce heat to medium and cook slowly until the mixture thickens, about 20 to 30 minutes, stirring occasionally. Pour the chutney into hot, sterilized jars and seal. MAKES 6 PINTS.

This chutney is beautiful in color and simply delicious—and it will keep for a year.

Sweet Crisp Cucumber Pickles

- 7 pounds cucumbers
- 1 cup household lime
- 5 pounds sugar
- 1 quart cider vinegar
- ½ package cinnamon sticks
- 1 teaspoon mace
- 1 teaspoon turmeric
- 1 teaspoon whole cloves

First Day

Wash and slice the cucumbers in ¼-inch slices, soak in lime water for 24 hours. Use 1 cup lime (regular household lime which may be purchased at hardware stores) to 7 pounds of cucumbers, and water to cover. Do not use a metal container; use a crock or porcelain container.

Second Day

Thoroughly rinse the cucumbers twice in very cold water. Drain and soak in a mixture of the vinegar, sugar, and spices.

Third Day

Over medium heat, bring the cucumbers and the marinade to a boil. After the boiling starts, start timing a 20-minute cooking period. Let the cucumbers simmer while you are filling the jars, so the pickles will be sealed hot.

A delicious green tomato pickle can be made with this same recipe. Simply use green tomatoes in place of the cucumbers and proceed as directed.

11

Candies

I AM NOT A DEDICATED CANDY MAKER. Oh, I like to make certain favorites, but candy thermometer, kettle, and marble slab really don't stir my creative urge too much. The ten recipes in this very short chapter are ones that are often looked for and rarely found.

The praline recipe is one of the greatest I have ever tasted, and even my husband, who cut his sweet tooth on southern pralines, has told Helen Haycraft, whose recipe it is, that these are the finest he has ever tasted. Incidentally, if you are a devotee of raw peanuts, it makes a delightful peanut praline, too.

Last Christmas I made seventy pounds of Heavenly Hash for a party at a Golden Age Home for Senior Citizens. They adored it. Along with this candy, we sent fruit cakes well-laced with cognac, and one hundred pounds of Celebrity Fudge. You'll find this recipe further along in the chapter, and it has been called by many names. Supposedly it came from the White House kitchen, as a favorite of a First Lady named Mamie. It is simple and delicious.

I feel this way about candy recipes: If *I* can make them, anyone can make them.

Pralines

1 cup brown sugar
1 cup white sugar
1 tablespoon corn syrup
1 tablespoon butter
5 tablespoons water
½ pound pecans, broken up

Combine the sugars, corn syrup, butter and 5 tablespoons water. Bring to a boil, add the nuts, and cook to the soft-ball stage (238° F.). Remove from heat and beat until the mixture holds its shape when dropped from a spoon. Drop onto waxed paper and allow to harden. You must work quickly in order to finish before the pralines turn sugary.

Heavenly Hash

- 3 cups sugar
- ¾ cup cocoa
- ½ cup light corn syrup
- 1 cup milk
- 4 tablespoons butter *or* margarine
- 1 tablespoon vanilla
- 1 cup pecan meats
- ½ pound marshmallows, cut in pieces
- ½ cup chopped cherries

Combine the sugar, cocoa, corn syrup, and milk; cook over low heat until the sugar is dissolved. Continue cooking over medium heat, stirring frequently, until the mixture reaches the soft ball stage (238° F.). Remove from the heat and add butter or margarine. Allow to cool to lukewarm, add the vanilla, and beat until creamy. Stir in the pecan meats, marshmallow pieces, and cherries. Continue to beat until thick, then pour into a buttered pan. When cold, cut into squares.

Chocolate Dreams

- 12 ounces semisweet chocolate (Dot)
- 2 tablespoons butter
- 1 cup sweetened condensed milk
- 1½ teaspoons vanilla

Melt the chocolate and butter in the top of a double boiler. Add the sweetened condensed milk and cook until thick, about 15 minutes. Add the vanilla. The candy should be thick enough to drop by spoonfuls and hold its shape. After you add the vanilla, let the candy rest for 10 minutes then drop by spoonful onto a slab or cookie sheet. When it cools, you can shape it as you want—in drops, crescents, or long, bite-sized rolls. Roll some of the pieces in sweetened cocoa mix, some in ground nuts, and some in chocolate shot. Let stand until solid. Don't get impatient; this takes quite some time to harden. MAKES 50 TO 60 PIECES.

Rum Balls

- 1 cup crushed vanilla wafers
- 1 cup sifted confectioners' sugar
- 1½ cups pecans, chopped fine
- 2 tablespoons cocoa
- 2 tablespoons light corn syrup
- ¼ cup rum
- ½ cup fine granulated sugar

Combine the crumbs, confectioners' sugar, 1 cup pecans, and the cocoa. Add the corn syrup and rum, mix well, and shape into 1-inch balls. Roll half the balls in granulated sugar and the other half in the remaining ½ cup nuts. Store the balls in an airtight container; like fruitcake, they improve with age.

Bourbon or cognac may be used in place of rum for bourbon or cognac balls.

Celebrity Fudge

- 4½ cups sugar
- Pinch of salt
- 2 tablespoons butter *or* margarine
- 1 tall can evaporated milk
- 12 ounces semisweet chocolate
- 12 ounces German's sweet chocolate
- 1 pint marshmallow cream
- 2 cups nut meats

Combine the sugar, salt, butter, and milk; bring to boiling and boil 6 minutes. In a large bowl, combine the semisweet and German's sweet chocolate, marshmallow cream, and nut meats. Pour the boiling syrup mixture over the ingredients in the bowl. Beat until the chocolate is completely melted, and then pour into a greased pan. Let stand several hours before cutting. Store the fudge in a tin box, tightly covered.

Mocha Balls

- 1 7-ounce box vanilla wafers
- 2 cups confectioners' sugar
- ⅔ cup finely chopped nut meats
- 2 tablespoons cocoa
- ¼ cup heavy cream
- ¼ cup double-strength cold coffee

Crush the vanilla wafers into fine crumbs (you should have about 2 cups crumbs). Add the sugar and mix well. Stir in the nut meats and cocoa. Add the cream and coffee, mix well, and shape into balls about ¾ inch in diameter. Roll some of the balls in confectioners' sugar. Chill. MAKES ABOUT 4 DOZEN BALLS.

Pecan Brittle

2 cups sugar
1 tablespoon butter *or* margarine
1 teaspoon baking soda
2 cups broken pecans

In a heavy skillet over low heat, melt the sugar, stirring constantly. When the sugar has entirely melted, add the butter, soda, and broken pecans. Pour the mixture onto a greased cookie sheet or platter and allow to cool. Break into small pieces. MAKES 1 POUND.

Cinnamon Popcorn Balls

1½ cups sugar
1 cup water
½ cup red cinnamon candies
2 tablespoons vinegar
½ teaspoon salt
3 quarts popped unsalted corn

Combine the sugar, cinnamon candies, vinegar, salt, and 1 cup water. Cook to the hard ball stage, 250° F. on the candy thermometer. Remove from heat. With a damp cloth, wipe crystals from the pouring side of the saucepan and pour the hot syrup over the popped corn. Pour slowly and mix with a wooden spoon to cover all the corn. Mix well so that the syrup doesn't go to the bottom of the bowl. When the mixture is cool enough to handle, butter your hands and form it into twelve 4-inch balls, or smaller ones if preferred.

Crunchy Butter Nut Toffee

1 cup granulated sugar
½ teaspoon salt
½ cup butter
¼ cup water
1 cup chopped walnuts
2 6-ounce packages semisweet chocolate

Combine the sugar, salt, butter, and ¼ cup water. Cook to a light crack stage, 270° F. Add ½ cup walnuts and pour the mixture onto a well-greased cookie sheet. Allow to cool. Melt the chocolate and spread half of it over the top of first mixture. Sprinkle with ¼ cup walnuts. Allow to cool. Turn the candy over, spread the other side with the remaining chocolate, and sprinkle with the remaining ¼ cup walnuts. When the chocolate has cooled, break the toffee into pieces with a wooden mallet or small kitchen hammer. MAKES ABOUT 2 DOZEN PIECES.

Taffy Apples

6 large red apples
2 cups sugar
½ cup light corn syrup
¾ cup water
Red vegetable coloring
Oil of cinnamon (optional)

Wash and dry the apples thoroughly. Insert a wooden skewer into the stem end of each apple. Combine the sugar, corn syrup and ¾ cup water in a deep saucepan. Cook slowly, stirring constantly, until the sugar is dissolved. Add enough coloring to color the syrup a deep red. Cook slowly, without stirring, to the hard crack stage, 300° F., when a small quantity of syrup dropped into cold water becomes brittle. Remove from heat; add a few drops oil of cinnamon, if desired, stirring only enough to mix. Place the pan over boiling water. Dip the apples, one at a time, into the hot syrup, twirling each apple as you remove it from the syrup. Place the apples on waxed paper and allow them to cool.

12

Brainstorming

THIS CHAPTER CONTAINS LITTLE EXTRA HINTS or "quickies" that provide the changes in pace that can make your meals a lot more interesting. After reading the chapter through once, you can check the ones you like in the margin and refer back to them as you need them. It's like having a brainstorming session on recipes or cooking ideas with a next-door neighbor.

The busy homemaker of today has no time to dally in the kitchen. If you will make use of the many convenience foods now on the market and plan ahead for two or three days of menus, you will make fewer shopping trips and your pantry emergency shelf will be the source of many good meals.

If you'd like a snack that's different from the usual potato or corn chips, try banana chips. In a skillet, heat melted shortening or salad oil (½ inch deep). Peel and slice firm bananas into thin rounds and fry them until golden, turning once. Drain well on paper towels and sprinkle with salt. These are very popular through the Caribbean, where they use plantain slices as well as banana slices.

Little table hibachis are very inexpensive and fun to use for hot canapés. Set the hibachi on a tray, have bits of cooked food handy on a plate with bamboo spears. Provide a hot sauce or red sauce or barbecue sauce. Your guests can heat the bite of food over the hibachi, dip it in the sauce, and they're gourmets!

Two-inch pieces of celery, crisped and filled with softened liverwurst, make tasty and easy-to-do hors d'oeuvres.

To make a spread for rye bread, combine Blue cheese, cottage cheese, crisp bacon bits, and sliced stuffed olives. Use in proportions to suit your own taste.

Mr. Jean Charles Heidsick once told me that smoked salmon slices in champagne added a great deal to a collection of hors d'oeuvres. And he's right. All you do is marinate the smoked salmon slices in champagne, not long enough to lose the bubbles. It probably won't stay on your table long enough to lose the bubbles, either.

If you have as many as ten guests for cocktails, you can bet that six of them will be counting calories. Be a thoughtful hostess and have low-calorie foods. They can be filling and tasty, and your guests will appreciate your thoughtfulness. Use two-inch chunks of crisp celery, hearts of celery, carrot sticks, raw cauliflowerets, little sweet raw turnips (peeled or scraped and crisped in ice water), tiny new onions in season, and cucumber sticks made by peeling the cucumber, cutting it in sticks, and cutting away the seedy part. All of these dipping vegetables can be crisped in ice water until ready to serve. Arrange them around a bowl of low-calorie dip, made as follows:

Buy low-calorie cottage cheese and whiz it in your blender till smooth. Season it with a little Tabasco and Worcestershire sauce, salt, pepper, and Ac'cent.

For a good low-calorie drink (only about 10 calories per serving), serve canned beef bouillon on the rocks in old-fashioned glasses.

Madrilene is very low in calories and high in flavor. Chill it in a bowl and add chopped chives as it begins to jell. Serve with a slice of lemon.

A sparse dinner can be made to look like company fare if you serve a cream soup as the first course. Heat canned cream of asparagus soup, and add 1 tablespoon sherry wine. At serving time, stir tiny cubes of cheese into the hot soup, pour the soup into cups, and sprinkle each cup with slivered or chopped almonds.

Do you like oyster stew? You will need 1 quart milk, 1 pint oysters, ¼ pound butter or margarine, salt, and pepper. Scald the milk with half the butter. Heat the oysters in their own liquor with the rest of the butter and combine the two when the edges of the oysters start to curl. Season to taste and ladle into heated soup bowls. SERVES 3 OR 4.

I have always felt that women who are home alone don't eat properly during the day. They "snack" out of the refrigerator and then wonder why they are putting on a "spare tire" around the middle. Canned soups provide well-rounded, good tasting luncheons. Invite a neighbor to join you, because one can will make two hearty servings.

Colorful gelatin salads will dress up a plate for brunch or luncheon. The salads need not be large, but they should be made in fancy molds. Try lemon gelatin with grated carrot and tiny bits of peeled avocado, it makes a colorful and tasty combination. With so many people on diets today, it's well to remember that you can serve a well-rounded menu if you will but keep the portions small. A little gelatin mold, a tiny square of toast with creamed chicken, a miniature baking powder biscuit, and a small piece of lemon chiffon cake with a lemon-sugar glaze—and plenty of good fragrant coffee—is an example of a complete menu within the bounds of most diets.

For a good salad during the tomato season, combine thin slices of tomato, thin slices of cucumber, and a few onion rings. Marinate them in a mixture of half water and half vinegar. When ready to serve, drain off the marinade and serve the salad with French dressing.

A fine luncheon for the summer months is a ripe, red, juicy tomato —not peeled, not scooped out, but simply cut down into four sections. If you don't cut all the way through it will spread out like a tulip. Fill with low-calorie cottage cheese.

Dehydrated potato slices make a good potato salad. Cook the slices according to package directions and before they cool, add chopped onion, chopped hard-cooked eggs, mayonnaise, salt, pepper, and

Ac'cent to please your taste. When you make the salad with warm potatoes the flavors blend better. Chill the salad in the refrigerator before serving.

Make a salad with canned artichoke hearts. Pour a zippy Italian dressing over drained artichoke hearts and chill. Arrange wedges of tomatoes and the artichoke hearts on romaine lettuce and garnish with little anchovy fillets and ripe olives. You can pass more Italian dressing at the table.

Artichoke hearts make a fine addition to water cress salad. Tiny pickled beets, one or two cut up artichoke hearts, and a bed of water cress, served with a cole slaw dressing—and there is a conversation-piece salad.

Waldorf salad is an old standby that is always enjoyed. Combine 2 cups chopped apples, skin and all, 2 cups chopped celery, 1 cup broken walnuts, and ½ cup mayonnaise. Chill and serve in lettuce cups.

When buying stuffed olives to cut up for salads, dips, or Italian recipes, why not buy the broken olives that are called a salad pack? They are much less expensive and you cut them up anyway.

You can make a gourmet-type vegetable salad dressing by mixing instant minced onion (to your own taste), mayonnaise, a little Worcestershire sauce, salt, pepper, and a little garlic. For the vegetables, combine little whole canned beets, green beans, diced celery, and artichoke hearts.

To make an unusual and exotic French dressing, use cognac in place of vinegar in the same proportion. Combine oil, cognac, and seasonings and shake vigorously. Serve immediately over sliced tomatoes. We call this Tomatoes Jarnac.

Although there are two very fine cole slaw dressings on the market now, I still have a favorite recipe. Use ½ cup sugar, 1 teaspoon salt, ⅛ teaspoon cayenne pepper, ½ teaspoon powdered mustard, 3 eggs, 2 tablespoons butter, 1 cup tarragon vinegar, 1 cup cream. Separate the eggs and mix the yolks with the dry ingredients; then blend all together with the exception of the egg whites. Cook in the top of a double boiler until thick, then remove from the heat and allow to cool. Beat the egg whites and blend them into the dressing. This amount of dressing is enough for 6 cups chopped or shredded cabbage. The cabbage should be crisped in ice-cold water, then drained thoroughly. Incidentally, if you haven't tried shredded iceberg lettuce with this dressing, you've missed a treat.

If you get tired of using the same salad dressings all the time, make up some new combinations. Use half mayonnaise and half creamy-type French dressing; half Thousand Island dressing and half commercial sour cream; half mayonnaise and half sour cream; or half garlic-type French or Italian dressing and sour cream. The possibilities are endless—all you need is a little daring.

For a quick fruit salad dressing, combine in a mixing bowl 1/3 cup mayonnaise, 1 mashed ripe banana, 1/2 teaspoon salt, and 1 tablespoon milk. Stir until well blended. MAKES ABOUT 3/4 CUP.

For a more lavish fruit salad dressing, whip 1/3 cup heavy cream and fold in 1 mashed ripe banana, 1/4 teaspoon salt, and 1/3 cup mayonnaise. MAKES ABOUT 1 1/4 CUPS.

Vegetables are the stepchildren of cooking. We never seem to have enough original ideas for cooking them. If you like red cabbage (it's in most every market at some time of the year), here is a good recipe that goes especially well with pork. Shred 6 cups cabbage. Sauté 2 tablespoons chopped onion in 3 tablespoons butter or bacon drippings; add 6 tablespoons sugar, 3 tablespoons vinegar, and the cabbage. Cover and sauté it for 18 minutes over low heat. SERVES 6.

Carrots may not be one of your favorite vegetables, but try them this way. Slice the carrots into very thin slices. Put the slices in a saucepan with butter, salt, and about 2 tablespoons sugar. Cover the carrots with cold water and bring the water to a boil. Boil, uncovered, until all of the water has evaporated; the carrots will brown in the butter. Serve hot.

Texans eat chili the year around, and this quick supper dish is a great favorite. Combine 1 can chili without beans with 1/2 cup minced onion and 2 cups corn chips (Fritos). Sprinkle ½ cup grated Cheddar cheese over the top and bake for 20 minutes in a preheated moderate (350° F.) oven. Serve with a green salad. SERVES 3 OR 4.

It's exciting to see what can be done by combining two vegetables. I'll bet you never thought of mixing turnips and peas. Peel and cut fresh turnips into thin strips. Put the strips in a saucepan with ¼ cup liquid from a 1-pound can of peas. Season with butter, salt and pepper and cook until the turnips are almost tender, which should take about 4 minutes. Add the drained peas and heat through. SERVES 6.

Combinations of frozen vegetables are interesting if you use two vegetables of different textures or colors. Use 2 packages frozen French-cut green beans and 1 package frozen lima beans. Cook them separately, then combine them and add garlic salt and butter.

Sweet and sour lima beans are wonderful with a pork roast. Drain 2 cans dry limas and add to them 1 cup catsup, ½ cup brown sugar, ¼ cup cider vinegar, 1 tablespoon prepared mustard, salt and pepper to taste, and 2 teaspoons lemon juice. Pour into a casserole and bake in a moderate (350° F.) oven for 30 minutes.

Canned water chestnuts, sliced thin, seem to add something unusual to such vegetables as lima beans, string beans, or peas. Add them just before serving and dress with melted butter.

For a tasty vegetable, try little yellow squash, sliced and fried. Don't peel them; just wash and slice the squash ¼-inch thick. Sauté a couple of onions (the amount depends upon how well you like onions in your vegetables). When the onions are limp, add the squash. No moisture added, please. Blend together and cook in a covered skillet until the squash is done, about 30 minutes. Season to taste and serve. Leftover squash reheats well the second day. Put it in a small casserole, sprinkle buttered bread crumbs over the top, and bake for 20 minutes in a moderate (350° F.) oven.

Canned tomatoes are a versatile vegetable. I like to use the whole peeled tomatoes, because I think you get more for your money. This Creole tomato recipe is especially good with pork chops.

Drain a No. 303 can of tomatoes, saving the juice. To the juice add chopped celery, minced onion, and chopped green pepper in amounts to spark up the flavor to your taste. Cook for 15 minutes over medium heat, then add the tomatoes and a generous measure of toasted bread croutons. If you like, you may add a 4-ounce can of pieces and stems of mushrooms. Place in a casserole and bake in a moderate oven, 350° F., for 20 minutes. SERVES 4.

Most people think that tomatoes have to be red to be good. Not at all. Cut green tomatoes into thick slices, sprinkle the slices with salt and pepper, dip them into a mixture of ½ cup cornmeal, ½ teaspoon thyme, and about 1 tablespoon brown sugar. Fry the tomato slices slowly in butter until they are lightly browned and soft. These fried green tomatoes are a wonderful vegetable to serve with lamb.

If you can get little cherry tomatoes, try this. Split the tomatoes in half, brush them with salt, pepper, and butter, and place them under the broiler for just a few minutes. Serve with steak or pork.

There is a sliced almond pack now on the market that takes all the work out of making an amandine sauce. Just place the butter in a pan and let it brown—*not burn,* but brown; then add the almonds and heat through. Pour over vegetables or fish.

Here is a sauerkraut quickie dinner. Use 1 1-pound can sauerkraut and 1 1-pound can baked beans. Add 1 pound frankfurters, cut in slices, and 1 4-ounce can pieces and stems of mushrooms, drained. Season with ¼ teaspoon pepper, ¼ teaspoon onion salt, and a dash of garlic salt. Cook the mixture in a skillet over low heat for about 10 minutes. It's a wonderful combination. Serve with a tossed green salad and hot French bread. SERVES 4 TO 6.

Speaking of baked beans, you know that canned pork and beans is one of the greatest emergency-shelf foods that you could have. To dress them up, add catsup, a little brown sugar, and a little molasses. Place them in a covered bean pot or casserole and bake for about 1 hour in a moderate oven, 350° F. Then, if you are serving sausage patties with the baked bean casserole, put the cooked patties on top of the beans and serve all together. Or, if you are serving frankfurters, slit them in several places and place them, cold, on top of the beans for the last half hour of baking. Don't cover the casserole or baker after the frankfurters are added because the liquid should cook down through the beans, and you don't want to steam the franks.

A casserole of red kidney beans is another favorite at our house. You can either use the canned ones or cook the dried ones, but be sure that you add some salt pork to the dried ones and cook it until it falls apart in the beans. If you use the canned beans, dress them up with a little molasses and brown sugar, bake them in a moderate (350° F.) oven in an open casserole for about 1 hour, then cover the top of the casserole with browned rounds of pork sausage.

For a potato dish that is a little unusual and very easy to prepare, heat a can of tiny new potatoes and roll them in melted butter. Sprinkle the potatoes with salt, pepper, and Ac'cent, and roll them in grated Cheddar or Swiss cheese. Place them in a well-buttered, shallow baking dish and heat them under the broiler until lightly browned. These go well with any kind of meat or fowl.

A quick and tasty potato casserole can be made with dehydrated potato slices. Cook them in boiling water for 15 minutes or until they are done, drain and add them to a cream sauce made with 3 tablespoons butter or margarine, 3 tablespoons flour, and 2 cups milk. (If you need more cream sauce, double the recipe.) Blend well, sprinkle with grated Swiss cheese, and heat in a moderate (350° F.) oven until the cheese is bubbly. 1 package of potato slices SERVES 5 OR 6.

For au gratin potatoes, try grated Swiss cheese instead of Cheddar for a change. The flavor is bland but delicious. Make your cheese sauce in the usual manner and combine it with the cooked sliced potatoes. Put the potatoes and sauce in a casserole and heat them in the oven for about 20 minutes. A puff of paprika over the top adds to the beauty of this dish.

Canned sweet potatoes have an affinity for orange marmalade. Slice the sweet potatoes and place them in a skillet. In a little saucepan, heat some orange marmalade and, when it is melted, pour it over the sweet potatoes. Sauté the potatoes gently over low heat until they are glazed and brown.

Have you ever thought of putting pitted dates in with baked squash or candied sweet potatoes? Place the cooked vegetable in a shallow casserole and dot with butter. Sprinkle with brown sugar and chopped dates and then lightly drizzle honey onto it. Bake in a moderate oven (350° F.) for 30 minutes, basting several times with the glaze.

It's always seemed a shame not to use the pretty shells of half oranges. Here's a way we use them at our house. Scoop out all of the pulp after you have squeezed the juice out and put the shells in the refrigerator until dinner time. Then mash canned sweet potatoes, add a little brown sugar and some sliced almonds, and pile the mixture into the orange shells. Put them in a moderate (350° F.) oven and bake until the potatoes are well heated through. Serve in the orange shells.

Down through the southern part of the country, and even as southwest as Texas, rice is used for many meals each week. One favorite way to prepare it is to melt 3 tablespoons butter or margarine in a skillet and pour in 1 cup of rice, moving it about with a wooden spoon until it is golden brown. Then pour in 2 cups chicken or beef broth, add salt and pepper, cover tightly, and simmer over medium heat until the broth has been absorbed and the rice is fluffy. This should take about 15 to 20 minutes. Be careful not to scorch the rice.

Venetian Rice is a quickie that is wonderful with pork. Use ½ cup precooked Minute Rice, 1 4-ounce can sliced mushrooms, drained, 2 tablespoons butter, 1 can onion soup, ½ soup can water. Brown the uncooked rice and mushrooms lightly in the melted butter. Stir in the onion soup and water, cover, and cook over low heat until the moisture is absorbed and the rice is tender. Leave the top on the saucepan and let it steam for a while—about 10 minutes. SERVES 4.

Rice Oriental is a combination of half white rice and half wild rice. Combine the cooked rices, mix with melted butter, salt, pepper, and Ac'cent, and press the mixture into oiled ramekins. Unmold and serve with poultry or pork.

Noodles take very well to all kinds of spices. Butter the hot noodles, then sprinkle them with toasted sesame seeds, poppy seeds, celery seeds, or caraway seeds.

It's fun to spring green noodles or spinach noodles on the family. Cook the noodles in salted boiling water. Add melted butter and about ½ cup grated Parmesan cheese to 7 or 8 ounces noodles. You'll see funny looks around the table, but the smiles will come with the first bite.

You can make a mock fettucini by boiling thin egg noodles in salted water until they are nearly done. Drain but don't rinse them. Add melted butter and Parmesan cheese, toast the noodles, and serve hot. Delicious with pork.

A quick supper dish is veal cutlets in cream gravy. Dredge the veal cutlets in flour seasoned with salt, pepper, and Ac'cent. Brown them quickly in margarine or butter in a skillet. When the cutlets are browned on both sides, remove them from the skillet and pour off all but 3 tablespoonfuls of drippings. Leave the little brown crusty pieces of flour in the skillet; they give the gravy its color. To the drippings in the pan, add 3 tablespoons flour, mix well, and then 2 cups milk. Cook and stir until this cream gravy thickens. Return the cutlets to the skillet, cover, and bake in a moderate oven, 350° F., for 25 minutes. Serve over hot buttered noodles.

If you like chicken livers with an oriental flavor, dip the chicken livers in fritter batter that has been well-flavored with soy sauce. Fry in deep fat and serve with sweet and sour sauce (you can buy bottled sweet and sour sauce; in some parts of the country it's called plum sauce).

Frozen chicken pieces are the answer for a family that wants all white meat or all dark meat. Dip the chicken pieces into seasoned flour and brown them in a skillet. Arrange the pieces in a baking pan. Stir 1 teaspoon curry powder into a can of chicken soup and pour this over the chicken. Cover and bake in a moderate oven,

350° F., for 40 minutes or until the chicken is tender. Then stir in ½ cup chopped roasted almonds and ½ cup commercial sour cream. Serve with fluffy rice (use the pre-cooked type—it takes only 5 minutes to prepare). Fill canned peach halves with chutney and pop them under the broiler for 5 minutes. Chicken curry, fit for a king!

Almost every homemaker I know has an emergency shelf, on which she keeps sliced chicken in glass and an assortment of canned vegetables and fruits that she can use for a quick dinner. The small Dutch canned hams that require no refrigeration provide another "quickie" dinner. An excellent sauce for this ham can be made with a can of peach slices or fruit cocktail. Drain the fruit, mix a little cornstarch into a small amount of cold juice, and add the mixture to the remaining juice. Heat and stir until thickened. Just before serving, add the fruit.

Canned soups make wonderful quick sauces for the second appearance of meat loaf or for hot chicken or turkey sandwiches. Cream of mushroom soup seems to lead the parade of favorites. For a thin sauce, add to 1 can condensed soup, 1 soup can milk; for a thicker sauce for hot sandwiches, add to 1 can condensed soup ½ can milk.

On a Sunday night when you don't feel like going to a lot of trouble to feed the family, Heavenly Hamburgers could be the answer to your supper problem. Grind a can of peanuts and mix them with enough mayonnaise to hold them together as a spread. Broil some hamburgers, and put them into hot hamburger buns with a slice of Bermuda onion. Spread the hamburgers generously with the peanut spread. Be sure to get enough ground meat for two hamburgers apiece, because this is a dish that always calls for encores. Serve with pickles and potato chips.

Steak à la Stanley (who is Stanley?) is a good hearty beef dish. For four persons, use four beef fillets, 4 firm bananas, and lemon juice. Broil the steak on one side, season to your particular preference, then peel the bananas and brush them with lemon juice. Place the bananas on the rack for the last 10 minutes of broiling. To serve, cut the bananas diagonally in half and arrange on the platter with the steak. Serve immediately.

Have you ever wanted to show off with a rotisserie but felt that your budget wouldn't stand strip steaks? Then buy a big piece of bologna, skin it, score the sides with a knife, and place it on the spit of your rotisserie. Baste it with your favorite barbecue sauce. It's wonderful for hot bologna sandwiches and makes a fabulous meat to serve with a casserole of beans.

No matter how cold it gets in Texas, we fire up the charcoal grill and do steaks and hamburgers. A whole meal—meat, baked potatoes, and sweet corn—can be done on the grill. Salt, pepper, and butter each ear of corn, and then wrap it in foil. Wrap each potato in foil. Allow 30 minutes for an ear of corn and one hour for a medium-sized potato. Put the foil-wrapped vegetables toward the back of your grill when you start the fire and burn it down to hot coals for the meat. Add a green salad, and the meal is complete.

If you're cooking on a charcoal grill (and if you haven't, you've missed a lot of fun) try roasting bananas. Remove a strip of the peel from the banana and brush the banana meat with butter. Roast on the grill until the peel is black and glossy and the fruit is tender. Eat it with a spoon if necessary, but don't miss this wonderful taste treat.

For a sweet-sour sauce to be used with barbecued meats, you will need 3 tablespoons cornstarch, 1 cup vinegar, 1 cup sugar, 5 dashes Tabasco, 1 tablespoon Worcestershire sauce, 1 tablespoon prepared mustard, 2 green peppers, chopped, and 1 large can pineapple chunks, juice and all. Mix the cornstarch with the sugar and cook in the vinegar until clear. Add the rest of the ingredients and pour over meat or fish while it is baking or baste it with this sweet-sour sauce while cooking.

If your husband likes to go hunting and he brings home ducks, doves, and quail, don't be alarmed. They're wonderful eating and not at all difficult to prepare (but make him clean them and get them ready for the freezer).

Let's take ducks first. Defrost the birds and put half a potato and half an onion in the cavity of each one. Rub the birds well with salt and brush them with melted butter or margarine. Place them in an uncovered roaster and bake in a hot (450° F.) oven for thirty minutes. Turn down the oven heat to moderate (350° F.) then roast for another hour if they are large ducks, like mallards. If they are small, like teal, cover and cook for only thirty minutes longer.

Doves, which are all dark meat, are delicious in cream gravy. The recipe is listed in the index. Quail, which are all white meat, may be cooked in the same way. Quail can also be broiled. Strip the birds and lay them flat on the broiler pan. Brush them with seasoned butter or margarine and broil until tender.

Suppose the hunter brings home elk's meat or venison. This meat has a strong flavor and should be marinated in wine. I use a red wine and marinate the meat for about four hours in the refrigerator. How you cook it depends on the cut that you have (steak or roast). If it's a roast, treat it as a pot roast and use a covered Dutch oven with moist heat. Cook in a moderate (350° F.) oven until the meat is tender. A steak can be broiled if it is cut thin. If it's a thick cut, cook it exactly like a Swiss steak, using a moderate (350° F.) oven; cook until the meat is fork tender.

These are only a few ways of cooking game. If you have it often, invest in one of the good game cookbooks available at your local bookstore.

If you are using crabmeat for a main luncheon or light supper dish, sauté minced onion in butter, then add the crabmeat and heat through. Make a well in the center of the crabmeat and add 1/4 cup of cognac for each pound of crabmeat. Spoon through the crabmeat while still over the heat and light momentarily. The dish has a most unusual flavor and can be served as a main dish or as an appetizer.

If you like a Mornay sauce on a rolled crêpe, you will probably like this dish too. Fill the rolled pancake, or crêpe, with creamed crabmeat to which you have added thinly sliced water chestnuts. Make a light cheese sauce and spoon it over the crêpes. Set them under the broiler for just a second. Serve two to each person.

Canned tuna is one of the most versatile foods on the market today. For a tasty, quick, and easy supper, serve hot tunabergers. Mix undiluted cream of mushroom soup with ½ cup chopped ripe olives, 2 teaspoons instant minced onion, and 1 can tuna. Then add 1 teaspoon Worcestershire sauce and 1 teaspoon parsley flakes. Split hamburger buns and toast them in the broiler. Spread the olive and tuna mixture over the buns and broil for about 5 minutes. Serve as open-face sandwiches with whole ripe olives, crisp potato chips, and celery hearts.

Creamed tuna fish is an excellent Friday night supper dish, and it's simple to make. Prepare your favorite cream sauce recipe. Add flaked tuna and a bit of sliced pimiento for color or pimiento-stuffed green olives chopped into fairly big pieces. Serve in patty shells or on toast points or toasted English muffins. For a green vegetable, use the canned long green beans. Heat them in their own liquid, then drain. Add 1 tablespoon minced onion, 1 tablespoon prepared mustard, a pat of butter or margarine, and a squeeze of lemon juice. Heat again and serve.

I think that sardines have been greatly maligned. People think of them only as little fish stacked neatly in rows in a tin can that is sometimes difficult to open. For a new approach, get some of the sardines that you like, either the large ones or the tiny ones, roll them in cracker crumbs, and fry them for just a minute in some of the oil that they were packed in. Serve them on toast, garnished with a slice of lemon and accompanied by a green salad.

Frozen fish fillets come in two types, the sweet-tasting fish and the "fishier" cod type. Dip the sweet fish fillets in milk and then in flour and fry them quickly, only turning them once. Remember that fish is delicate and shouldn't be overcooked. Long cooking just dries it out. Serve with tartare sauce and French-fried potatoes.

If you are cooking fish fillets, fresh or frozen, slice lemons into thin slices and lay the fish fillets on top of the lemon slices (3 slices to a good-sized fillet). You'll find that the fish doesn't stick to the foil or the pan. When I broil fish, I line the broiler pan with foil and then simply pick up the foil and pour the butter-lemon marinade over the finished dish.

It seems to me that "gourmet cooks"—and I am not one of them—make directions a little too complicated for some people to follow. For instance, in making the fish stock for Bechamel Sauce, which is elegant-sounding in itself, you don't need fish bones, heads, fins, tails, and what not. To make a fine fish stock, just buy a 1-pound package of frozen fish fillets and boil the heck out of them.

With the new Pepperidge Farm frozen patty shells you can have a party that will look like a catered affair. These puff paste shells are large enough for a luncheon serving, depending on how much filling you put into the shell and allow to spill over. For the filling, use creamed fish, seafood, or poultry (tuna, shrimp, crab meat, chicken, turkey, etc.). Dress up the luncheon plate with a spiced peach or a slice or two of spiced watermelon pickle, two tiny hot rolls or miniature biscuits, and a few salted nuts.

A very good seafood filling for patty shells can be made with 1 can frozen cream of shrimp soup, ½ cup milk, 1 cup flaked cooked lobster or crab meat (1 6-ounce can or 8 ounces fresh), and ½ teaspoon curry powder. Combine all ingredients, heat, and stir. Serve in 4 patty shells.

For a budget filling for patty shells, use 1 can cream of celery or mushroom soup, ⅓ cup milk, 4 sliced hard-cooked eggs, and 2 tablespoons chopped pimiento. Blend the soup and milk and heat thoroughly, then gently stir in the eggs and pimiento. Serve in 4 patty shells.

For a wonderful luncheon dish, try a French-fried ham sandwich. Make a batter of eggs and milk or cream, dip the slices of bread in the batter, and fry them quickly in butter. Don't turn the slices more than once. When they are beautifully browned on both sides, put a slice of ham (or spread deviled ham) between two slices of French fried bread, cut through the middle, and serve hot with a spiced peach.

Do you realize that canned foods were our first "convenience" foods, and that these canned foods are processed with infinite care? If you are having the younger set, ages five to seven, for luncheon, try these Hot Chicken Boat sandwiches. Cut a thin strip from the top of a brown-and-serve roll and hollow out the center. Brush with melted butter. Mix some chopped celery, finely chopped onion, sliced stuffed olives, and canned boned chicken or turkey that you have cut up. Moisten with a mixture of mayonnaise and just a little mustard. Pile into the rolls and put on a baking sheet and bake in a hot (450° F.) oven for 10 to 15 minutes.

My husband is from Georgia, although he has lived most of his life in Texas. He went to school at Tulane in New Orleans, and so Poor Boy sandwiches were part of his education. We use the brown-and-serve rolls that are about 5 inches long and 3 inches wide. Bake them in a hot (450° F.) oven, split them open, pull out some of the inside and fill each roll with a half dozen big fried oysters. Serve hot and pass the catsup bottle. Always make two apiece—it's a cinch everyone will ask for seconds.

Another Poor Boy sandwich can be made with ham and cheese. Mustard is in order, and pickle relish if you think you need it. We like Polish ham and Swiss cheese on the hot brown-and-serve rolls.

This is a seafood version of the Poor Boy sandwich. Cut a 1-pound loaf of French bread in half lengthwise and scoop out the center. Brush the bread "box" that you have made with melted butter or margarine. Add a filling made by combining 2 7-ounce cans flaked tuna, ½ cup pickle relish, 1½ cups chopped hard-cooked eggs, 2 cups processed cheese cubes (cut small), and 1 cup mayonnaise. Bake in a hot oven, 400° F., for 10 minutes. Slice the loaf down into five generous servings. Serve with cups of coffee or tea for a hearty TV snack.

There are endless recipes for baked cheese sandwiches, but I like this one because it is so quick and simple. In a baking pan, arrange 6 crust-trimmed sandwiches made with ham and cheese or just cheese. Over the sandwiches pour a mixture of 4 beaten eggs, 2½ cups milk, ½ teaspoon salt, and ½ teaspoon pepper. Bake in a slow oven, 325° F., for 30 minutes or until light and golden brown. Remember that bread should be kept in your daily diet, even if you are counting calories; it's one of the four basic foods.

Nothing takes the place of a good bacon and egg sandwich. Toast the bread, scramble the eggs, and season to taste. I like a touch of Worcestershire along with salt and pepper. Fry the bacon crisp, assemble the sandwich, and there's a lunch that will hold you through the day to a late dinner.

If the middle of the afternoon brings a troop of hungry children to your kitchen, give them peanut butter sandwiches with banana slices added to the peanut butter filling. It's an unusual taste blend that goes perfectly with a glass of cold milk.

Scrambled eggs are as American as apple pie. Serve them plain, or with chili on top of them, or with bits of avocado cooked right in them. For especially delicious, light scrambled eggs, beat the eggs with cream and cook them in the top of a double boiler over hot water, stirring all the time. Serve at once.

Add an exotic touch to scrambled eggs and call them Eggs Oriental. Sauté some chopped fresh green onions in butter, add the beaten egg and milk mixture, as many sliced ripe olives as you like, salt, pepper, and a touch of soy sauce. Scramble by whatever method you prefer.

For a change, serve scrambled eggs in French toast cups. Dip slices of bread in an egg and milk mixture, just as you would if you were frying French toast. Press each softened slice of bread into a buttered custard cup. Bake in a moderate oven, 350° F., until lightly browned, or about 20 minutes. Meanwhile, make fluffy scrambled eggs. Spoon the scrambled eggs into the baked French toast cups and serve with Canadian bacon.

If you want something very special for dinner, try Eggs Benedict. Sounds difficult? Couldn't be easier. Use a half of a toasted English muffin for a base, add a round of lightly broiled Canadian bacon, place a poached egg on top of the Canadian bacon, and top it with Hollandaise sauce (the recipe is in the sauce chapter).

Refrigerator biscuits are a great help to a busy woman. One package of refrigerated biscuits, a little marmalade or jelly, and four tablespoons of melted butter are all you need for making delightful sweet rolls for breakfast. Melt the butter and dip the biscuits into it so that they are coated on both sides. Lay the biscuits flat in a pie pan. Make an indentation in the center of each biscuit and fill with marmalade or your favorite jelly. Bake in a hot oven, 450°F., for 10 minutes; serve hot.

Here is another idea for using refrigerator biscuits, but this time serve them with pork or lamb. Prepare them in the same way that you did for the sweet rolls, but in place of the marmalade or jelly, use finely chopped chutney.

If you bake your frozen yeast raised rolls in greased muffin tins they will look much more beautiful than if they are cooked on a baking sheet. Clover leaf rolls stand up like shamrocks and square rolls turn into round ones. Allow at least two hours rising time at room temperature before baking these rolls.

Sometimes Sunday brunch needs a lift, and nut-topped English muffins might be the answer. Spread butter on toasted English muffin halves. Drizzle honey over the muffins and sprinkle them with chopped walnuts or almonds. Run the muffins under the broiler to heat through, and serve warm.

Sunday morning brunch can be something special when you toast halves of English muffins, drizzle maple blended syrup onto them, and sprinkle them with sliced almonds. Serve hot, with rounds of sausage.

Poor Knights is delightful for dessert or for Sunday brunch. Use 2 to 3 slices of white bread per serving. Dip the bread into milk and sprinkle with a combination of sugar and cinnamon. Next dip the slices into beaten eggs, and then dip them quickly into dry bread crumbs. Fry the slices in plenty of butter or margarine until they are golden brown. Spread with jam or jelly and serve at once.

Sometimes just a bite of sweetness is all that is needed for the end of a meal, and here is an easy one. Use either biscuit dough or refrigerator biscuits. If you use the dough, roll it 1/4-inch thick and cut in 2 1/2-inch squares. If you use the refrigerator biscuits, elongate them with your fingers so they make ovals. Put a drained pineapple chunk on each one, sprinkle with a little brown sugar and cinnamon, and add a bit of butter. Fold the biscuits over, press the edges together, brush with melted butter, and bake on a greased cookie sheet in a hot (450° F.) oven for 15 minutes.

If you have mint in your back yard, bruise a few stalks with a mortar and pestle or with the back of a wooden spoon and add it to canned fruit. Chill the fruit, then remove the bruised pieces of mint. Serve the fruit in sherbet glasses and garnish with fresh mint leaves. Low in calories and high in flavor.

Just a touch of almond extract works miracles with cake mixes, puddings, and even frozen desserts. One day I was experimenting with ruby red grapefruit segments and toasted sliced almonds. I added a sliced banana and shredded coconut and then just a few drops of almond extract. It's a dessert that truly is elegant.

When the cupboard is bare of everything that could be used for dessert, cut grapefruit into halves, remove the seeds, and drizzle a good maple or maple-flavored syrup over the halves. Put them under the broiler and heat through.

For a fresh-tasting dessert, combine orange segments, sliced bananas, and pineapple chunks. Serve chilled with the combined juice of the fruits and sprinkled with Angel Flake coconut. You might even add a few sliced almonds to top it off.

Cut fresh pineapple into finger lengths. Sprinkle with sugar, add a sprig or two of bruised fresh mint, and pour rosé wine over all. Chill overnight before serving. Serve with thin slices of pound cake.

For a regal fruit cocktail, chill 1 can pear halves, 1 can peach halves, and 1 can pitted Bing cherries. At serving time, get out your best sherbet glasses and put into each one a peach half, a pear half, and as many cherries as you like, drained. Cover the fruit with champagne and serve at once. This would make a plain bean and frankfurter supper seem like Sunday dinner.

Many people have completely missed the fun of cooking with liqueurs. I think that Cointreau, which is an orange flavored liqueur, is one of our finest. Try this Fruit Cocktail Romanoff.

Pour ½ cup Cointreau over 1 can (2½ cups) drained fruit cocktail. Place this in the refrigerator to chill. Prepare 1 package vanilla pudding mix (the cooked type) in the usual manner, but use only 1½ cups of milk instead of 2 cups. Allow to cool. Stir the fruit-Cointreau mixture into the cooled pudding and chill. Just before serving, cut 1 pint vanilla ice cream into small cubes, fold the cubes into the pudding, and garnish with maraschino cherries. Serve at once in sherbet glasses. SERVES 6 TO 8.

I keep a supply of canned peach halves and use them for garnish, for salads, for desserts, and even for fruit for breakfast. For a quick dessert, drain canned peach halves and dust them with a combination of cinnamon and sugar (you can buy this in a little shaker bottle). Broil the peach halves until they are thoroughly heated and lightly tinged with brown. Serve them hot, two to each serving, and topped with a slightly sweetened sour cream dollop (a dollop is a large spoonful).

Here is another speedy dessert using canned peach halves. Drain 8 large peach halves and chill them thoroughly. Place a peach half in a sherbet glass or a dessert dish. Place a scoop of vanilla ice cream in each half. Sprinkle generously with toasted almonds. Or top with frozen strawberries that are just barely defrosted, or with strawberry sundae topping.

If you like the flavor of dry white wine, use it as a marinade for canned Bartlett pears or peach halves. Drain the canned fruit, cover with the dry white wine, and refrigerate in a covered dish for half a day. A very elegant dessert, served with a crisp cookie.

Pears Curaçao are made with the fine Bartlett and Anjou pears that come from the West Coast. For 12 pears, make a marinade with 2 tablespoons sugar, 2 cups freshly squeezed orange juice, the juice of ½ lemon, and ½ cup Curaçao liqueur. Place the whole, unpeeled pears in the marinade and let stand in the refrigerator to chill. At serving time, peel, core, and thinly slice the pears. Serve the marinade over them as a sauce. SERVES 10 TO 12.

In canteloupe season use the finest melons that you can get, cut them in halves, and scoop out the seeds. Fill the centers with vanilla ice cream and cover with crushed raspberries or strawberries. It's a hearty and refreshing dessert, and men like it.

It is no longer necessary to make your own graham cracker crumbs; you can buy them in a little sack. Here is a pie which we call Graham Cracker Quickie, although some people call it macaroon pie. Beat 3 eggs thoroughly, add 1 cup granulated sugar, and beat again. Fold in 1 cup finely chopped English walnuts and 1 cup graham cracker crumbs and add a dash of salt. Spread the mixture in a lightly greased 9-inch pie pan and bake in a preheated moderate oven (325° F.) for 25 to 30 minutes. Serve either warm or cold with whipped cream.

White cake mix is the base for many wonderful quick desserts. Don't ever feel you are using a substitute when you use one of the modern fine cake mixes. They're made with prescriptionlike precision in test kitchens, and the cakes will stay moist and flavorful if you keep them covered. You can make twin Boston cream pies to serve 16 persons from only two layers of white cake mix. When the layers have cooled, split them across, making two layers of each one (four layers all together). Just before serving, spread two of the half layers generously with chilled instant pudding, any flavor that you prefer. Top with the remaining cake and sprinkle the cakes with sifted confectioners' sugar. Serve side by side on a large cake server or platter.

When you know you won't have enough time before dinner to prepare a dessert, bake a cake ahead of time, using any one of the fine cake mixes. Before serving, prepare a fluffy egg-white frosting, again using a mix, and fold in ½ cup chopped dates, ½ cup chopped candied cherries, and ½ cup chopped almonds. Use this for both filling and frosting.

If you are using the time-saving method of baking two cakes at one time, using one and freezing the other, go ahead and frost the one to be frozen with the butter cream type of frosting (don't use the snowy mountain type of frosting). Cover the cake well with plastic wrap and then, when you are ready to use it, set it out about one hour before serving time. The frosting will be fresh and moist and the cake will be delicious.

Try a lemon icing: Blend 1½ cups sifted confectioners' sugar with 3 tablespoons lemon juice. Add 1 teaspoon softened butter or 1 tablespoon cream and mix well. If the icing is too thick, add a little light cream. If it is too thin, add a little more sugar.

Maraschino cherry syrup is an excellent flavoring for butter cream icings. Combine 1½ cups sifted confectioners' sugar, 3 tablespoons light cream, and 2 tablespoons maraschino cherry juice. Beat until well blended, and add a few drops of red food coloring if you wish.

The prepared frosting mixtures of the fudge type lend themselves well to variations. For an orange-flavored frosting, use the vanilla-flavored frosting mix, add orange juice instead of the water, and add a little grated orange rind. Make a lemon frosting in the same way, but use lemon juice for only half the liquid, or the frosting will be too tart. If you like a mocha flavor, use the chocolate-flavored fudge frosting mix and substitute strong cold coffee for the ¼ cup water called for in chocolate frosting.

Angel food cake mixes are marvelous things. You couldn't make a higher, finer cake if you made your own with thirteen egg whites—and then what do you do with the thirteen yolks? For a luxury dessert, bake an angel food cake from a mix. (There are several flavors now.) After the cake is cold, cut off the top about 1 inch down. Pull out the soft insides of the cake, leaving a shell that has 1-inch walls. Fill this with sweetened whipped cream (about 1½ pints) to which you have added sweetened sliced fresh strawberries or fresh blueberries; or, if you prefer a chocolate flavor, fold 1 cup grated German's Sweet Chocolate into the whipped cream. Put the top back on the cake, cover it with more sweetened whipped cream, and refrigerate until time to serve.

Don't throw away the soft inside of an angel food cake when you remove it to make a filled one. Combine the soft cake with softened pistachio or coffee ice cream, pack it into a small loaf pan lined with foil or wax paper, and freeze it. Serve with raspberry or chocolate sauce, depending on the flavor ice cream you use.

There are several very good pound cake mixes on the market and they are delightful served fresh. If you have leftover cake, a slice apiece for the family, make a new dessert out of it by serving it with this fruit sauce. Boil the syrup from a can of fruit cocktail with a little chopped candied ginger. Watch it carefully so that it does not boil away too much. When the syrup is reduced to about ½ cup, add a few drops lemon juice and the drained fruit cocktail. Continue cooking just long enough to heat the fruit. Remove from heat and serve over the pound cake.

Leftover pound cake that needs a boost may be sliced and served with sweetened whipped cream into which you have folded lovely big blueberries.

Here is a good wine sauce for pound cake that is too tired to serve plain. You will need 1 tablespoon butter, 1 teaspoon flour, 1 cup sherry wine, 2 tablespoons sugar and the yolks of 4 eggs. Melt the butter, add the flour, and blend well. Add the sherry wine, sugar, and egg yolks; stir briskly until the sauce almost comes to the boiling point. Remove from the heat and add a dash of nutmeg. This sauce is delicious when served hot over pound cake or gingerbread.

Another easy dessert is hot gingerbread, made with a mix if you like, and topped with a combination of sliced bananas and ice-cold whipped cream or ice-cold whipped topping. It must be cold, because that's what makes it wonderful with the hot gingerbread.

A simple, quick, but especially good dessert can be made by lining a glass or dessert dish with split, plain lady fingers and then filling the dish with sweetened whipped cream to which you have added vanilla and chopped maraschino cherries. Top with either chopped nuts or toasted coconut.

A Bavarian Rum Cream with lady fingers requires 1 dozen lady fingers, ½ pint whipping cream whipped stiff, rum to taste, 5 teaspoons granulated sugar, and 5 egg yolks. Beat together the yolks and sugar until light and creamy, add rum to taste, and fold in the whipped cream. Break the lady fingers in half lengthwise and line a bowl with them. Pour in half the cream mixture, cover with a layer of lady fingers, and then add the remaining cream mixture. Chill for at least 4 hours in the refrigerator before serving. SERVES 6.

Pineapple Rice Cream is a good dessert that will use up 1 cup of leftover cooked rice. In a large bowl, combine 1 pound miniature marshmallows and 1 cup canned crushed pineapple; chill thoroughly. Lightly fold in 1 cup cooked rice, then add 1 cup chopped English walnuts or sliced almonds and 1 cup heavy cream, whipped stiff. Spoon into a dessert bowl or individual dessert dishes and chill until ready to serve. Top each serving with a maraschino cherry.

Fig bars are chewy and full of flavor. Try this dessert, using a 1-pound package of these cookies as a base. Cut the fig bars into small cubes and use half of them to cover the bottom of a baking dish. Add the contents of 1 can (1-pound, 14-ounces) drained sliced peaches. Sprinkle the remaining fig bar cubes on top. Add 1 teaspoon grated lemon rind, 1 tablespoon lemon juice, and 1 cup of the peach syrup. Dot with 2 tablespoons butter or margarine. Bake in a moderate oven, 375° F., about 30 minutes. Serve hot or warm, with ice-cold light cream. SERVES 6.

Susan Dathe told me about S'Mores, a dessert that youngsters like very much. All you need are graham crackers, marshmallows, and small chocolate bars. Put a piece of chocolate on top of one graham cracker. Toast a marshmallow and, while it is hot, put it on top of the chocolate; top with another graham cracker.

Cupcakes are easier to serve for a youngster's party than slices of cake. I like Top Hat Cupcakes. Bake or buy cupcakes and slice off the tops where they begin to bulge out. Place a scoop of ice cream on the lower half and add the other half to make the top hat. You can serve them right away or freeze them until you are ready to use them.

Coffee Mousse is a refreshing frozen dessert. In a large bowl, combine ½ pint whipping cream and 1 tablespoon powdered instant coffee. Beat until the cream begins to thicken, then gradually add ½ cup confectioners' sugar and beat until stiff. Turn the mixture into a serving tray or parfait glasses and freeze until firm (about 2 hours at the lowest temperature in your freezer). SERVES 4.

Dream Whip topping makes an easy frozen mousse. Make up 1 package Dream Whip with the ½ cup cold milk as directed on the package. Fold in the contents of 2 cans Gerber's (baby food) puréed apricots. Freeze the mixture in an ice-cube tray and cut it into triangles. It's low in fat and low in calories, but high in flavor.

Coconut Parfait is a simple dessert that can be frozen in parfait glasses, little fruit juice glasses, or cheese glasses. Combine 2⁄3 cup sugar and 1 1⁄2 cups water; bring to a boil and boil rapidly for 5 minutes. Allow to cool. Stir in 2 teaspoons vanilla and 2 cups grated canned or frozen coconut. Mix well. Fold in 1 pint heavy cream, stiffly whipped. Pile in parfait glasses and freeze. Serve frozen with a topping of fresh whipped cream.

Peach Melba is supposed to have been named after Madame Melba, the celebrated singer. Here is a simple method of preparation. Chill canned peach halves. Place each peach half in a sherbet or champagne glass and put a scoop of vanilla ice cream in the center of each half. Top with a commercially prepared Nesselrode topping, an elegant preparation with marrons and pineapple and all good flavors blended together. Pour about 2 teaspoons of Kirschwasser (cherry brandy) over each serving.

To dress up a gelatin dessert, pour the gelatin mixture into parfait or dessert glasses, or even into fruit juice or little cheese glasses, and top with sliced bananas and a whipped topping.

Strawberry Banana Bavarian is a more elaborate but still a "quickie" dessert. Use 1 package strawberry-flavored gelatin, 1⁄2 cup heavy cream, whipped, and 4 ripe bananas. Dissolve the gelatin according to the package directions and let it set until it is the consistency of unbeaten egg whites. Fold in the whipped cream. Fill parfait glasses with the gelatin mixture and sliced bananas. Garnish with more sliced bananas. SERVES 6.

If you want to impress your teatime visitors, serve this pineapple-mincemeat mold. It's delightful with coffee or tea. Just add 1 3-ounce package lemon-flavored gelatin to 1 1⁄2 cups hot canned unsweetened pineapple juice and stir until dissolved. Chill until partially thickened and then stir in 1 cup canned mincemeat. Pour into a mold and chill until firm. Unmold and top with a scoop of whipped cream. SERVES 6.

This quick frozen dessert is like a lovely sherbet. Use 2 No. 303 cans (4 cups) canned applesauce, 1 flat can crushed pineapple, juice and all, and 3 tablespoons slivered candied ginger. Combine all ingredients and freeze. Spoon or scoop out the dessert and serve it with a decoration of two or three fresh mint leaves.

A delightful topping for pineapple sherbet is the commercial pineapple topping mixed with a little green crème de menthe. Serve with a pineapple angel food cake as a base for the sherbet, or serve the sherbet in a glass with slices of cake on the side.

Ice cream is probably the dessert that the new homemaker relies on more than anything else. And why not, with the wonderful assortment of flavors that we have? Make ice cream balls from coffee ice cream and store them in your freezer or the freezer compartment of your refrigerator. Before serving, roll them in chopped roasted almonds. Top with a light chocolate sauce (you can buy it in a can), either hot or cold.

Here is a crisp almond topping that goes well over ice cream, cream puddings, or fruit. Melt 2 tablespoons butter and stir in 3 tablespoons brown sugar. Cook until thick and smooth, stirring often. Add 1 cup cornflakes and 1/4 cup chopped almonds. Blend together and cool.

Maple syrup blended with salted pecans makes a quick ice cream sauce. The little touch of salt gives a nice flavor.

Everyone from six to sixty loves sundaes. To make a banana sundae, use a ripe banana, 1 scoop of ice cream, 2 tablespoons chocolate or fruit syrup, 2 tablespoons crushed fruit or preserves, whipped cream, whole or chopped nuts, and a maraschino cherry.

For a Jamaican sundae, place a scoop of vanilla ice cream in a champagne or sherbet glass, cover it with about 1/4 cup pure maple syrup, spoon about 2 tablespoons of marshmallow cream over the top, and sprinkle with chopped salted cashew nuts.

Ice Cream Mincemeat Flambé is a good dessert for the holiday season. Use 1 quart vanilla ice cream to serve 6 to 8. Warm 1 1/2 cups mincemeat in a saucepan and add 1/3 cup rum or cognac. Just before serving, flame the mincemeat and spoon it over vanilla ice cream in sherbet glasses. SERVES 6 OR 8.

Ice cream pies are an impressive "company touch" and so easy to prepare. Make a crumb crust by combining 1½ cups crushed graham crackers or vanilla wafers, ¼ cup melted butter or margarine, and 2 tablespoons sugar. Press the mixture into a 9-inch pie pan and either set it in the refrigerator to chill or bake it for 5 minutes in a moderate (350° F.) oven and allow to cool. Drain canned peach slices and defrosted red raspberries and swirl the fruit through softened vanilla ice cream. Spoon this mixture into the crumb pie shell and return it to the freezer until the ice cream is firm.

Biscuit Tortoni is a much maligned recipe because we all have our own little frozen desserts that we dignify with this name. Try mine. Beat 1 egg white until it is stiff but not dry; fold in 2 tablespoons sugar. Combine 1 cup whipping cream, 2 tablespoons sugar, and 2 teaspoons vanilla or 1 teaspoon almond extract; beat until stiff. Fold the cream mixture into the egg white. Pour into a freezer tray and freeze until the mixture is solid about ½ inch in from the sides of the tray. Turn it out into a chilled bowl and beat until smooth. Meanwhile, melt 1/3 bar German's Sweet Chocolate and drip the melted chocolate into the chilled mixture. Blend well, pour into little tortoni cups or nut cups, and freeze. Just before serving, sprinkle the tops with slivered almonds.

Any of the instant or cooked pudding mixes may be combined with lady fingers to make a dessert that may loosely be called a "trifle." Split the lady fingers in half and place a layer in the bottom of a serving bowl. Spread red raspberry jam over the lady fingers, and then add pudding, prepared according to package directions. Repeat the layers, ending with lady fingers on top. Chill overnight before serving. This makes a very moist dessert which you spoon out like a pudding. André, the executive chef at the Waldorf Astoria, adds a meringue topping and browns it lightly under broiler heat for just a minute.

Dress up rice pudding with a hot spiced fruit sauce. Bake individual rice puddings in custard cups. Heat canned fruit cocktail with a dash of cinnamon and nutmeg and thicken it slightly with cornstarch. Unmold the rice pudding on a dessert plate and top with the fruit sauce.

Flan, or egg custard, is found in every refrigerator in Mexico City and it's even served as a dessert in all of the hotels in Acapulco. It's good for you and very simple to make. Use 4 eggs, 1/4 cup sugar, 1/4 teaspoon salt, 1 teaspoon vanilla, and 3 cups scalded milk. Beat the eggs slightly, stir in the sugar, salt, and vanilla, then slowly stir in the milk. Strain the mixture into a baking dish, set the dish in a pan of hot water, and bake in a moderate oven, 350° F., for about 1 1/2 hours. Test by a knife in the center of the custard and if it comes out clean, then the custard is done. Immediately remove the baking dish from the pan of hot water. Allow the custard to cool and then chill it in the refrigerator. Serve cold, garnished with fresh sliced strawberries, sliced almonds, or grapenuts.

If you like flan with a burnt-sugar syrup, heat sugar in a heavy skillet, stirring constantly until it liquefies. Don't let it burn. Divide the syrup equally among individual ramekins. It will harden the minute it touches the sides of the ramekin, but as it bakes it will soften. When you turn out the custard you will have a flan exactly like that served at the Hotel Club de Pesca in Acapulco.

Old-fashioned boiled custard topped with an island of meringue makes the dessert called Floating Island Custard. Cooked meringue tastes better than uncooked. Make the meringue with 2 tablespoons sugar to each egg white. Drop each island on top of water in a custard cup. You do this so that the island will retain its shape. Cook until lightly browned in a moderate (375° F.) oven. Lift from the water and float on the custard.

Saboyan is a delightful custardlike dessert, flavored with Madeira wine. To serve 6, use 8 egg yolks, 1 cup confectioners' sugar, a pinch of salt, 1/2 cup Madeira wine, and 8 egg whites beaten until stiff but not dry. Beat the egg yolks, sugar and salt together until very light. (This I do in an electric mixer.) Place in the top of a double boiler, but don't let the boiling water touch the bottom of the top section. Add the Madeira wine gradually and continue to beat with a rotary beater until the mixture doubles in bulk. Remove from the heat, fold in the beaten egg whites, and serve at once in sherbet glasses.

If it's 110° F. in the shade and you feel that you need nourishment and yet something that will revive you, use 1 cup cold milk, 1 mashed ripe banana, a scoop of your favorite ice cream or sherbet and whiz in the blender. I cheat; I use 2 scoops of pineapple sherbet.

For a quick afternoon pick-up, put 1 cup cold fruit juice and 1 mashed ripe banana into your blender and blend until smooth. Or use 1 cup cold milk and 1 mashed ripe banana. For a banana egg-nog, use 1 cup cold milk, 1 mashed ripe banana, 1 egg, and a dash of salt.

Frozen cranberry juice ice cubes add color and tang to tall fruit drinks. Just empty the ice tray and pour in the cranberry juice. Two hours later you'll have cranberry ice cubes.

13

The low-fat, low-cholesterol menu

A PROBLEM THAT IS FACING MANY WOMEN TODAY for the first time is the preparation of low-fat, low-cholesterol meals. Whether one member of the family is on such a diet for medical reasons or whether the whole family is on the diet because they feel that it is healthier for everyone, the problem remains the same. In most instances a consultation with a doctor, nutritionist, or a dietician has been very helpful for finding out the basic do's and don'ts. But this is just the beginning. These do's and don'ts must be translated by the homemaker into interesting menus, three times a day, every day. Somehow the gap between the specifications of the diet and the preparation of the meals must be filled.

It was just two years ago that I began working on a low-fat, low-cholesterol menu for a public eating place. As Food Editor for the *Dallas Morning News,* I had received many questions from men asking what to eat when they were away from home. A civic-minded friend of mine, D. Gordon Rupe, gave me the main incentive I needed to go ahead with the project when he said, "Why isn't there a place in Dallas where businessmen can eat luncheon and know that they are staying on their low-fat, low-cholesterol diets?"

I was offered the Baker Hotel in Dallas as a testing ground. The project was going to take cooperation of an Executive Chef who would give the preparation of the meals meticulous care. Any deviation from the use of unsaturated oils, or the addition of other food elements not permitted in the diet, would make the menu worthless. We certainly had the right man for the job in Chef Edmond Kaspar, the Executive Chef of the Baker Hotel, who last year was a member of the winning American team in Culinary Olympics in Germany.

The project was also going to take a great deal of time, money and research. Complete menus had to be worked out for three meals a day with enough variety so that none of the dishes would be repeated too often. I can never adequately show my gratitude to the Rice Council for making it possible to plan and carry out these special menus, because it was through their generosity that the research and consultation work was done.

Incidentally, this project was not done for publicity. We all agreed that, until the project had a six-month trial period, there would be only enough publicity, through the *Morning News* and my television program, to let people know that such a menu was available.

On September 15, 1960, the Julie Benell Low-Fat, Low-Cholesterol Menu was clipped to the regular menu at the Baker Hotel Coffee Shop and at two private clubs—the Imperial Club and the Petroleum Club. Then we all waited to see whether or not it was the answer to the problem of finding properly prepared low-fat foods when eating away from home. It was.

At the end of the six-month trial period more than 19 per cent of all meals ordered in the Baker Hotel Coffee Shop were being ordered from this special menu and thirty-five per cent of the luncheons served in the Imperial Club and Petroleum Club were selected from this low-fat, low-cholesterol menu.

Visitors to Dallas who stayed at the Baker Hotel spread the news of the new menu, and we have received inquiries from dining rooms and hotels all over the country, asking if this menu is available. At the end of the trial period, the Baker Hotel kept the menu as a permanent part of its regular menu. Through the cooperation of the Rice Council, the Julie Benell Low-Fat, Low-Cholesterol Menu is now ready to be given as a public service to other hotels where Executive Chefs will give it the proper care and attention, as Chef Edmond Kaspar is doing at the Baker Hotel.

On the following pages is a list of the basic do's and don'ts of this diet. This is intended only as a basic guide, since such diets do vary in details according to individuals and their reasons for being on the diet. All amounts given in the list are based on an 1800-calorie-per-day diet.

BASIC DO'S AND DON'TS

Fats

YOU MAY USE unsaturated fats (liquid fats), such as corn, olive, rice, and vegetable oils.

DO NOT USE saturated fats (animal fats and butterfat), such as chicken fat, lard, pork, suet, and butter.

Eggs

YOU MAY USE the whites of eggs.

DO NOT USE the yolks of eggs. Although you may not eat very many eggs, remember that they are often hidden in prepared foods such as noodles, cakes, mayonnaise, and ice cream.

Dairy Products

YOU MAY USE 6 ounces (per serving) of skim milk.

DO NOT USE whole milk, cream, butter, cheese, or ice cream—all of them contain saturated fat.

Meats

YOU MAY USE Canadian bacon; 4 ounces (cooked) roast beef, filet mignon, roast lamb, or roast veal; 5 to 6 ounces (uncooked) lean sirloin tips, lean lamb, or lean veal; 6 ounces (uncooked) chopped round beef.

DO NOT USE ham, pork, or bacon (except Canadian bacon); liver, kidneys, brains, or sweetbreads; red meats with visible fat. (Since red meats contain a certain amount of hidden fat, it is suggested that meals containing red meat be limited to three a week.)

Fish

YOU MAY USE 6 ounces (uncooked) lean fish, such as:

Bluefish	Colorado brook trout
Cod	Flounder

Haddock
Halibut
Ocean perch
Pollock
Pompano
Red fish
Red snapper
Striped bass
Swordfish

DO NOT USE any of the fatty fish.

Seafood

YOU MAY USE clams, crabmeat, shrimp, scallops, and lobster.

DO NOT USE oysters.

Poultry

YOU MAY USE 4 ounces of chicken or turkey with the skin removed; ½ broiled chicken; 1 chicken breast, whole and boned; Texas quail; pheasant; 1-pound Rock Cornish hen.

DO NOT USE livers or giblets.

Potatoes

DO NOT USE potatoes in any form.

Rice

YOU MAY USE ½ cup cooked rice per serving. Rice, incidentally, is an excellent substitute for potatoes.

Vegetables

YOU MAY USE the following vegetables in the amounts indicated:

1 cup per serving

Asparagus
Beet greens
Broccoli
Brussels sprouts
Cabbage
Cauliflower
Celery
Chard
Chicory
Collards
Cucumbers
Dandelion greens
Escarole
Eggplant
Kale
Lettuce
Mushrooms
Mustard greens

1 cup per serving

Okra	String beans
Peppers	Summer squash
Radishes	Tomatoes
Sauerkraut	Turnip greens
Spinach	Water cress

½ cup per serving

Beets	Pumpkin
Carrots	Rutabagas
Onions	Turnips
Peas	Winter squash

¼ cup per serving

Corn	Lima Beans

Gravies and Sauces

YOU MAY USE gravies and sauces *only* if they are made with low-fat chicken or beef stocks and thickened with arrowroot or cornstarch.

Breads

YOU MAY USE 4 thin slices of Melba toast with ½ teaspoon oil.

DO NOT USE other breads or hot breads such as biscuits, pancakes, waffles, etc.

Fruits

YOU MAY USE ½ cup per serving of the following fresh fruits:

Blackberries	Pineapple
Blueberries	Raspberries
Cherries	Strawberries
Peaches	

YOU MAY USE ½ small cantaloupe, ¼ small honeydew melon, or 4 x 8-inch piece of watermelon. And remember that fruit sherbets can replace higher-calorie desserts.

Fruit Juices

YOU MAY USE ¾ cup grapefruit juice, orange juice, tomato juice, or V-8 juice.

Cereals

YOU MAY USE 1 individual box of cold cereal, ⅔ cup of hot oatmeal, or 1 cup of other hot cooked cereals.

Rice is a very important food in a low-fat, low-cholesterol diet. It is delicious, filling, and adaptable not only to main dish variations, but also for desserts and salads. Many men on this kind of diet like hot cooked rice for breakfast.

Rice can be cooked in a saucepan on the top of the range or put into a shallow casserole, covered tightly with a cover or foil, and baked in a moderate (350° F.) oven for 45 minutes.

Each serving of rice should be ½ cup. To make 12 servings using unprocessed rice (long-grain, medium-grain, or brown), use 1 pint rice, 5 cups liquid (water or low-fat chicken or beef broth), and 2 teaspoons salt. Bring the liquid and salt to a boil. Pour the boiling liquid over the rice in a shallow baking pan, approximately 9 x 13 x 2½ inches. Stir to moisten the rice and spread it evenly over the bottom of the pan. Cover tightly with a cover or with aluminum foil. Bake in a preheated moderate (350° F.) oven for 45 minutes.

For processed rice, either white or brown, use 1½ cups rice, 1 quart water, and 2 teaspoons salt. Proceed in the same way, but bake for 55 minutes.

Here are variations for rice served as a vegetable:

Grated Carrots

Use ½ cup grated carrots and ¼ cup diced green pepper. Stir into 6 cups hot cooked rice.

Hawaiian Rice

Use ½ cup crushed pineapple and ¼ cup diced green pepper. Heat the pineapple and pepper and stir into 6 cups hot cooked rice.

Mushroom Rice

Stir into 6 cups hot cooked rice 1 cup sliced, cooked, and drained mushrooms. Very good with brown rice and wild rice.

Peas and Carrot Rice

Use frozen peas and carrots; stir the cooked vegetables into hot cooked rice.

Raisin Rice

Stir 1 cup raisins into 6 cups cooked rice and keep hot until ready to serve. Very good with brown rice.

Rice and Chives

Use 1/4 cup of chopped chives and stir into 6 cups hot cooked rice.

Herbs and spices may be added to the liquid in which rice is cooked, to vary the flavor. You can ad lib your way with the herbs and spices that are favorites at your house. Here are the combinations that we have used, all based on the amount of uncooked rice that will yield 6 cups cooked rice.

Curried Rice

Stir into the liquid before boiling 1 tablespoon curry powder and 1 tablespoon onion flakes. Very good with brown rice.

Herb Rice

Before the rice is cooked, add to the liquid any one of the following:

1/2 teaspoon thyme, sage, basil, rosemary, orégano, or savory.
1 teaspoon celery seeds or dill.
4 small bay leaves.

Parsley Rice

Add 1 tablespoon onion flakes to the water before boiling; add 1 cup chopped parsley to the cooked rice before serving.

Saffron Rice

Stir 1/4 teaspoon saffron into 1 tablespoon water and add to the liquid in which the rice is to be cooked.

Chef Edmond Kaspar has done a wonderful job of developing four sauces that can be used with fish, seafood, chicken, red meats, and fruit salads. With these sauces, the low-fat, low-cholesterol menu becomes really fine eating. Here are the recipes:

Basic Fish Sauce

- 2 tablespoons low-fat chicken soup base
- 1 quart water
- 1 pint clam broth
- 1/4 cup arrowroot
- 1/3 cup lemon *or* lime juice

Blend together the chicken base and 1 quart water and bring to a boil. Blend together and add the clam broth and arrowroot. Stir until the mixture thickens and comes to a boil. Add the lemon or lime juice and serve over fish. Herbs and additional seasoning may be added if desired. Size of serving, 1/2 cup. SERVES 12.

This sauce may be refrigerated and used over a period of one week.

Sauce Supreme

- 1/4 cup low-fat chicken soup base
- 1 quart water
- 1 pint white wine (Chablis or sauterne)
- 1/4 cup arrowroot

Blend together the chicken base and 1 quart water and bring to a boil. Blend together and add the wine and arrowroot. Stir until the mixture thickens and comes to a boil. Strain if desired. If preferred, equal amounts of water may be substituted for all or part of the wine. Herbs and additional seasonings may be added if desired. The same can be refrigerated and used over a period of a week. Size of serving, 1/2 cup. SERVES 12.

Brown Sauce for Meats

- 1/4 cup low-fat chicken soup base
- 1 quart water
- 1 pint red wine
- 1 tablespoon Kitchen Bouquet
- 1/4 cup arrowroot

Blend together the chicken base and 1 quart water and bring to a boil. Blend together and add the wine, Kitchen Bouquet, and arrowroot. Stir until the mixture thickens and comes to a boil. Strain if desired. If preferred, water may be substituted for all or part of the wine. Herbs and additional seasonings may be added if desired. The sauce can be refrigerated for a week. Size of serving, ½ cup. SERVES 12.

Cooked Pineapple Dressing

1½ cups pineapple juice
2 tablespoons arrowroot
½ cup sugar
½ teaspoon dry mustard
½ teaspoon salt
½ cup lemon juice
¼ teaspoon Tabasco sauce

In a saucepan, blend together the pineapple juice and arrowroot. Add the sugar, mustard, and salt. Cook over low heat, stirring until the mixture thickens and comes to a boil. Remove from the heat and stir in the lemon juice and Tabasco. Chill and serve on fruit or in salads. This can be kept in the refrigerator for a week to 10 days. MAKES 1 PINT.

I hope that this chapter will be of help to you in planning low-fat, low-cholesterol meals. I'm sure that by using your own creative ability you can go on to develop your own special recipes for this diet problem.

I would like to emphasize that you should always consult your doctor about a diet of this kind, and follow his advice, because each person on a special diet has a problem that is very personally his own, and only your doctor can advise you about the best diet for your needs.

Here is a list of the brand-name products upon which we have based our calculations of the caloric values and fat and cholesterol content of the recipes in this chapter. There are many other excellent brands available in different parts of the country. If you use a similar product of another brand, be sure to ascertain the caloric value and give close attention to the package directions; these products will serve you well.

Royal custard-flavor dessert mix	Standard Brands, Inc., New York, New York
D-Zerta dietary puddings (except chocolate)	General Foods Corp. White Plains, New York
D-Zerta dietary gelatin dessert	General Foods Corp. White Plains, New York

Good Seasons chicken-flavor base and seasoning	General Foods Corp. Institutional Products Div. White Plains, New York
Good Seasons beef-flavor base and seasoning	General Foods Corp. Institutional Products Div. White Plains, New York
Borden's modified skimmed milk	The Borden Company New York, New York
Le Gout chicken base for soups and seasoning	Fern Foods, Inc., Franklin Park, Ill.
Carnation instant nonfat dry milk	Carnation Company Los Angeles, Calif.
Dream Whip dessert topping mix	General Foods Corp. White Plains, New York
Balanced dietetic-pack fruits	Balanced Foods Inc., New York, New York
Frenchette dressings for salads (French)	The Frenchette Division of Carter Products, Inc. New York, New York
Sucaryl sweetening solution	Abbott Laboratories North Chicago, Ill.
Fruit Fresh (ascorbic acid mixture)	Merck Chemical Division Merck and Co., Inc. Rahway, New Jersey

Seafood Gumbo Soup

2 quarts chicken soup stock
1 pint clam broth
1 pint uncooked shrimp
1 pint diced fresh tomato
1 pint crabmeat, cooked and cleaned
1 pound uncooked fish fillets
1 cup cooked *or* quick-frozen corn
1 pint sliced okra
1 pint diced carrots
½ cup diced onions
Salt to taste
3 cups cooked rice

Bring the soup stock to boiling and add all ingredients except rice. Reduce heat and simmer until the okra is tender, about 15 minutes. Season to taste. Serve in soup bowls with a scoop of hot cooked rice in the center of each. Size of serving: 1½ cups soup, ¼ cup rice. SERVES 12.

Chicken Gumbo Soup

1 gallon fat-free chicken soup stock
3 cups diced fresh tomatoes
1 pint cooked *or* quick-frozen corn
1 pint sliced okra
½ cup diced onion
1 pint diced carrots
1 quart diced chicken
Salt to taste
3 cups cooked long-grain rice

Bring the soup stock to boiling and add all ingredients except rice. Cook until vegetables are tender, about 15 minutes. Season to taste. Serve in soup bowls with a scoop of hot cooked rice in the center of each. Size of serving: 1½ cups soup, ¼cup rice, SERVES 12.

Cucumber Vichyssoise

2 tablespoons low-fat chicken soup base
3 cups coarsely diced cucumber with rind
½ cup uncooked short-grain rice
1 cup scallions, sliced
½ cup chopped celery tops
1 pint instant dry milk crystals
1 teaspoon salt
1 quart water
3 cups modified skimmed milk

Place all ingredients except liquid skimmed milk in a saucepan with 1 quart water. Stir until the milk crystals are dissolved. Cover and simmer until vegetables and rice are tender. Pour into blender jar and blend until contents are smooth. Stir in the skimmed milk. Chill thoroughly or serve hot, garnished with chives. If a thinner consistency is desired, use additional liquid skimmed milk. Size of serving, ⅝ cup. SERVES 12.

Pineapple-Rice Salad

3 cups cooked rice, chilled
¾ cup drained crushed pineapple
2 tablespoons Pineapple Salad Dressing (see index)

Toss crushed drained pineapple and chilled rice together until well mixed. Chill until thoroughly cold. Mix with chilled pineapple salad dressing. Size of serving, ¼ cup. SERVES 12.

Vegetable-Rice Salad

For the ¾ cup uncooked vegetables, use any combination of the following: unpeeled cucumber, radishes, celery, tomato, green pepper, scallions (tops only), carrots.

- ¾ cup diced or sliced uncooked vegetables
- 3 cups cooked rice, chilled
- ¾ cup cooked peas and carrots, chilled
- ½ cup low-calorie salad dressing (Frenchette)

Toss together the vegetables and rice until all are evenly distributed. Add salad dressing and mix well. Size of serving, ¾ cup. SERVES 12.

Chef Edmond Kaspar's Frenchette Dressing

- 1½ quarts chicken stock
- ½ cup arrowroot
- 1 tablespoon dry mustard
- 1 cup tomato catsup
- 1 cup V-8 (vegetable juice)
- 1 cup wine vinegar
- ¾ cup lemon juice
- 1 tablespoon Worcestershire sauce
- 3 tablespoons Sucaryl to flavor
- ½ teaspoon garlic powder
- 1½ teaspoons Fruit Fresh
- 1 teaspoon ground allspice
- 1 tablespoon salt (*or* to taste)
- 2 tablespoons paprika powder

Blend together in a saucepan the chicken stock, arrowroot, and dry mustard. Cook over low heat, stirring constantly, until the mixture thickens. Add the remaining ingredients. Chill in the refrigerator. This dressing can be kept in a jar in the refrigerator indefinitely. MAKES ½ GALLON.

Orange Gelatin Rice Salad Mold

- 5 envelopes low-calorie orange-flavored gelatin dessert
- 3½ cups hot water
- 1 11-ounce can mandarin oranges
- 2 tablespoons lemon juice
- 1 pint cooked rice
- 1 cup coarsely grated carrots

Dissolve gelatin in 3½ cups hot water using the juice from the oranges to replace the remaining water called for in the package directions. Add lemon juice and chill until the gelatin is the consistency of egg white. Add and stir in the rice and carrots. Place three well-drained mandarin oranges in bottom of each mold. Add the gelatin mixture and chill until firm. Use as garnish on Fiesta Fruit Salad plate. Garnish with any remaining orange sections. Size of serving, ½ cup. SERVES 12.

Lime Gelatin and Rice Salad

4 envelopes (7 grams each) low-calorie lime gelatin dessert
3½ cups hot water
2 tablespoons lemon juice
1 pint cooked rice
1 cup grated carrots
1 cup finely chopped cabbage

Dissolve gelatin in 3½ cups hot water. Add the lemon juice and chill until the gelatin is the consistency of egg white. Stir in the rice, carrots, and cabbage. Chill until the gelatin is semisolid. Dip into molds and chill until firm. Turn out on turkey or roast beef cold plates. Size of serving, ½ cup. SERVES 12.

Spanish Rice

5 cups tomato juice
½ cup green pepper
¼ cup onion flakes
2 teaspoons salt
1 pint uncooked rice

Mix together and bring to a boil all ingredients except the rice. Pour the boiling liquid over the rice in shallow 9 x 13 x 2½-inch baking pan. Stir to moisten and spread evenly over bottom of pan. Cover tightly with aluminum foil or cover. Bake in a preheated moderate (350° F.) oven for 45 minutes, until rice is tender. Cut into squares and serve. Size of serving, ½ cup. SERVES 12.

Rice Pilau

1 tablespoon low-fat chicken soup base
1 tablespoon onion flakes
½ cup chopped, cooked mushrooms
5 cups water
1 pint uncooked brown rice

Place all ingredients except rice in a saucepan with 5 cups water. Bring to a boil and pour over rice in a shallow 9 x 13 x 2½-inch pan. Stir to moisten the rice and spread evenly over pan. Cover tightly with cover or aluminum foil. Bake in a preheated moderate

(350° F.) oven for 45 to 50 minutes, or until rice is tender. Size of serving, ½ cup. SERVES 12.

Turkey and Shrimp Supreme

3 pints Sauce Supreme (see index)
3 cups cooked shrimp
1 quart diced cooked turkey *or* chicken
1 tablespoon chopped parsley (optional)
3 pints cooked rice

Heat the sauce, add shrimp and poultry, and heat thoroughly. Stir in the parsley flakes. Serve over hot cooked fluffy rice. Size of serving, 1 cup on ½ cup rice. SERVES 12.

Poached Halibut, Spanish Style

5 ounces halibut
Chopped shallots or green onions
Juice of ¼ lemon
1 cup sauterne wine
½ bell pepper, sliced
3 fresh mushrooms, sliced
1 tomato, peeled and coarsely diced
Salt and white pepper

Combine all ingredients and bring to a boil. Cover the casserole and bake in a hot (400° F.) oven for approximately 10 minutes. Remove the fish from casserole. If the vegetables are not cooked enough, cook them a little longer. Thicken sauce with arrowroot or cornstarch. SERVES 1.

Poached Fresh Fillet of Red Snapper Poulette

6-ounce fillet of red snapper
Fresh chopped shallots *or* sliced green onions
Salt, pepper, Ac'cent
Sauterne wine
Sliced fresh mushrooms
½ cup Basic Fish Sauce (see index)
Chopped chives and parsley garnish

Add to the fish the shallots or onions, salt, pepper, and Ac'cent; cover with sauterne wine. Bring to a boil and add the mushrooms. Cook in a hot (400° F.) oven for 10 minutes. After the fish is cooked, remove it to a hot platter and boil the wine to reduce it to about one-third of the original amount. Add the Basic Fish Sauce and heat through. Add the chopped chives and pour the sauce over the fish. Garnish with parsley. SERVES 1.

Poached Pompano en Papilotte, Sauce Poulette

Pompano
Chopped shallots *or* green onions
Sauterne wine
Chopped chives
Chopped fresh *or* canned mushrooms
Basic Fish Sauce (see index)
Salt and pepper

Season the fish with salt and pepper. Place the fish in an ovenproof saucepan with the shallots or onions, add sauterne wine to cover, and poach. Cover the saucepan and bake in a hot (400° F.) oven until the fish is done. Remove the fish to a heated platter and boil the wine to reduce it to half the original amount or a bit less. Add a couple of spoonfuls of Basic Fish Sauce and chopped chives and mushrooms. Fold the fish, sauce, and mushrooms and chives in a foil envelope. Put into a hot (400° F.) oven until the foil puffs up. Then split the top of the foil and serve the pompano in the foil. The amounts of ingredients used, of course, depend on how many servings are needed.

Back Fin Crabmeat Casserole à la Newburg

Fresh *or* canned crabmeat
Sherry wine
Basic Fish Sauce (see index)
Chopped pimiento (optional)
Chopped green pepper (optional)

Warm the crabmeat in the sherry and add enough Basic Fish Sauce to make the necessary amount of sauce. Stir in pimiento and/or green pepper if desired. Serve on Melba toast or rice.

Casserole of Shrimp Sautéed New Orleans

- 4 tablespoons unsaturated oil
- 4 pounds uncooked shrimp, peeled and deveined
- 1 pint sauterne wine
- 5 onions, sliced
- 12 tomatoes, peeled, diced, without pulp
- ½ gallon fish broth *or* clam juice
- 1 cup bourbon
- 3 tablespoons arrowroot (optional)

Heat the oil, add the shrimp, and cook for 2 minutes. Drain the oil and reserve. (The moisture from the shrimp will add to the oil and make a larger amount of liquid.) Add the bourbon to the shrimp, heat, and flambé. Add the sauterne. Sauté the onion and tomatoes in another skillet. Cover the shrimp with the fish sauce (the oil and juices from the shrimp). Add the onions and tomatoes and cook together for 10 to 15 minutes. If the sauce is not thick enough, sprinkle arrowroot over the top and stir it rapidly into the sauce. Serve over rice. SERVES 12.

Louisiana Shrimp Curry

2 onions, chopped
½ stalk celery, chopped
1 clove garlic, minced
2 apples, peeled and diced
4 tomatoes, peeled and diced
1 cup chutney, chopped
3 tablespoons curry powder
1 pint chicken broth
1 pound peeled and deveined shrimp
Unsaturated oil

Place in a covered saucepan the onions, celery, garlic, apples, tomatoes, chutney, curry powder, and chicken broth; cook very slowly in a 325° F. oven until vegetables and apples are tender. (This is a basic curry sauce and can be kept in the refrigerator and used with a second appearance of lamb, chicken, or seafood.)

Sauté the shrimp in the oil and add curry sauce to taste. Serve over hot rice. SERVES 2.

Jumbo Louisiana Shrimp Casserole, Bombay Style

2 onions, diced
½ stalk celery, sliced thin
1 clove garlic, minced
2 apples, peeled and diced
4 tomatoes, peeled and diced
1 cup chutney, chopped
½ cup curry powder
1 pint chicken broth (no fat)
1 pound shrimp, cleaned and deveined
Shallots *or* green onion, chopped
½ cup sauterne wine

To make the sauce, combine diced onions, celery, garlic, apples, tomatoes, chutney, curry powder, and chicken broth. Cook in a slow oven, 325° F., for about 1 hour. This thick purée can be kept in the refrigerator and used as a sauce for second-day servings of lamb, meat, or chicken.

To make this shrimp casserole, sauté the shrimp very lightly with a few shallots or chopped green onion. Add sauterne and cook 5 minutes, stirring occasionally. Add ½ cup curry sauce, heat through, and serve with rice. SERVES 2 OR 3.

Bahama Lobster Tail Thermidor

6-ounce lobster tail
Lemon juice
Salt and pepper
Small onion, sliced
Half bay leaf
Brandy
Chopped shallots *or* green onions
Sherry wine
Tarragon
Basic Fish Sauce (see index)
½ teaspoon powdered mustard

Boil the lobster tail in water with lemon juice, salt and pepper, onion and bay leaf. (If the lobster tail is defrosted, boil 1 minute after the water has returned to boiling. If it is frozen, boil three minutes longer.) Remove the lobster tail from the water and cut off the membrane on the shell. Remove the lobster meat and cut it into chunks. Put the lobster meat in a skillet with brandy and shallots; flambé. Add a little sherry wine and a touch of tarragon. Add enough Basic Fish Sauce to give the desired consistency and stir in the powdered mustard. Heat all together and refill lobster shell. SERVES 1.

Cape Cod Scallops Florentine

1 pound scallops
Chopped shallots *or* green onions *or* chives
1 cup sauterne
Cornstarch *or* arrowroot for thickening
2 packages frozen chopped spinach, cooked

Put the scallops in a pan with the shallots or onions and braise the scallops. Add the sauterne. Bring to a boil, then cover the pan and place it in a hot (400° F.) oven for about 8 minutes. Remove the scallops from the pan. Boil the liquid until it is reduced to about one half of the original amount. Thicken the sauce with cornstarch or arrowroot. Return the scallops to the sauce and serve over a bed of hot spinach. SERVES 3.

Lemon Wild Rice

6 cups hot cooked wild rice
Juice of ½ lemon
Grated rind of 1 lemon

Blend in lemon juice and rind before serving. This is excellent with poultry.

Arroz con Pollo à la Valencia

- 1 pound uncooked, peeled and deveined shrimp *or* lobster meat
- 6 ready-to-cook chickens (2½ pounds each), quartered
- 3 ounces unsaturated oil
- 3 medium onions, chopped
- 1 pint sauterne wine
- ½ pound lean Canadian bacon, finely diced
- 1 quart chicken stock *or* bouillon
- ½ quart uncooked rice
- Pinch of saffron
- 12 small tomatoes, peeled and chopped coarsely
- 2 cups uncooked peas (frozen or fresh)
- Salt and pepper

Cut the shrimps in half or the lobster meat into chunks. Sauté the chicken in the oil, turning it to brown both sides. Add the onions and simmer until they are golden brown. Add the wine, and bacon; cook slowly for 10 minutes. Add the chicken stock, rice, saffron, tomatoes, peas, and shrimp or lobster. Season to taste with salt and pepper; mix well. Bring to boiling, cover the pan, and place in a moderate (350° F.) oven for 25 minutes to 30 minutes. SERVES 12.

Prawn and Chicken Curry with Rice Pilau

- 1 pound (15 to 20) uncooked shrimp
- 3 pounds chicken breast
- ½ cup unsaturated oil
- 3 bell peppers, cut into eighths
- 3 small tomatoes, peeled and cut into eighths
- 3 small onions, peeled and cut into eighths
- ½ teaspoon salt
- 2 teaspoons sugar
- 2 teaspoons soy sauce
- 2 teaspoons gin
- 2 cups chicken broth *or* water
- 2 tablespoons tomato catsup
- 2 tablespoons cornstarch *or* arrowroot
- 3 tablespoons chutney
- 2½ tablespoons curry powder

Shell and devein the shrimp. Remove the skin from the chicken breast and cut the meat into good-sized chunks. Heat the oil, add the shrimp and chicken pieces, and sauté, turning the pieces over with a wooden spoon until the chicken is lightly browned and the shrimp are pink. Add the bell peppers, tomatoes, onions, salt, sugar, soy sauce, and gin; cook for 3 to 5 minutes, stirring constantly so that the mixture doesn't stick. Add the chicken broth and simmer for 5 minutes longer. Thicken with cornstarch or arrowroot, stirring all the time. Add the chutney and curry powder. Serve over Rice Pilau (recipe in this chapter). SERVES 8 TO 10.

Casserole of Chicken Hawaiian Luau

- 1 pound white meat of chicken
- Salt and Ac'cent
- 2 tablespoons unsaturated oil
- 2 tablespoons sherry wine
- 1 cup diced pineapple
- ¼ cup sliced water chestnuts
- ¼ cup bamboo shoots
- ¼ cup celery, sliced diagonally
- ¼ cup chopped onion
- 3 cups chicken broth
- 2 tablespoons catsup
- ½ green pepper, diced
- 1 tomato, cut into pieces
- 2 tablespoons arrowroot *or* cornstarch

Remove the skin from the chicken and cut the meat into sticks. Season with salt and Ac'cent. Sauté the chicken in the oil until it is golden brown, turning it over and over all the time. Add the sherry, pineapple, water chestnuts, bamboo shoots, celery, onion, chicken broth, catsup, and green pepper. Cook this mixture for about 5 minutes. Add 2 tablespoons arrowroot or cornstarch to thicken. Serve with hot rice. SERVES 2.

Boneless Breast of Chicken Eugenie, Sauce Supreme

- 3 pounds boneless chicken breast
- Salt and pepper
- Cornstarch
- ½ teaspoon unsaturated oil
- ½ cup diced onion
- ¼ cup sliced celery
- Pinch of thyme
- 1 cup sauterne wine
- ½ cup Sauce Supreme (see index)

Remove the skin from the chicken breast. Season with salt and pepper and touch very lightly with cornstarch. In a skillet, sauté the chicken in the oil. Place in a hot (400° F.) oven to brown, uncovered. Add the onion, celery, and thyme. Simmer for about 5 minutes, then add the sauterne and let it cook for 20 minutes longer. Remove the chicken breast from the pan. Add the Sauce Supreme to the pan and let simmer a few minutes longer. Strain the sauce and serve it over the chicken breast. (Breast of pheasant may also be prepared this way.) SERVES 2.

No-Crust Chicken Pot Pie

Clean and remove the skin from one 4-pound hen. Place the chicken in a large covered kettle and add water, not quite enough to cover the hen. Make a bouquet garni by tying parsley, herbs, salt, and Ac'cent in a small piece of cheesecloth; add this to the pot. Cover and bring to boiling; reduce heat and simmer for about 2 hours or until the chicken is tender. Remove the chicken and cut it in large chunks. Skim off all the fat from the broth.

For the vegetables, use boiled small onions, frozen carrots and peas, and sliced mushrooms, and use the chicken broth to make the Sauce Supreme (see index for recipe). Put the chicken chunks and vegetables into the sauce and serve in a pot pie dish. If you like, you can add ½ cup of sauterne wine 30 minutes before the end of the cooking time.

Breast of English Pheasant in Brandy with Mushrooms

3 pounds boneless breast of pheasant
Salt and pepper
Cornstarch
½ teaspoon unsaturated oil
½ cup diced onion
¼ cup diced celery
Pinch of thyme
1 cup brandy
½ pound fresh mushrooms, sliced

Remove the skin from the pheasant breast. Season with salt and pepper and touch very lightly with cornstarch. In a skillet, sauté the pheasant in the oil. Place in a hot (400° F.) oven to brown, uncovered. (This does more than half the cooking of the pheasant breast, so take plenty of time at this point.) Add the celery and thyme. Simmer for about 5 minutes, then add the brandy and let it cook 20 minutes longer. Add the mushrooms, cover, and cook for 10 minutes more. Strain the sauce and serve it over the pheasant breast. SERVES 2.

If you like a slightly thicker sauce, sprinkle it with cornstarch or arrowroot and stir well.

Baked Sliced Turkey Marco Polo on Broccoli

This is an excellent dish for a second appearance of a turkey.

Turkey slices
Sliced canned mushrooms
Hot cooked broccoli
Sauce Supreme (see index)

Put the cooked broccoli in a flameproof casserole. Cover it with slices of white meat turkey and sliced mushrooms. Pour hot Sauce Supreme over all and place the casserole under the broiler until the mixture is heated through and bubbly.

White Meat Chicken à la King with Mushrooms and Sauce Supreme

- 4 cups cooked cubed white meat of chicken
- 1 bell pepper, cubed (optional)
- 2 pimientos, diced
- 1 can (4 ounces) pieces and stems mushrooms, drained
- 4 cups Sauce Supreme (see index)
- ½ cup sherry wine

If you use the bell pepper, parboil the cubes lightly in water for five minutes and drain thoroughly before adding to the other ingredients.

Combine the chicken, pepper, pimientos, mushrooms, and Sauce Supreme. Cook until thoroughly heated. At the last minute add the sherry, stir well, and serve over hot rice.

Scallopini of Veal Sauté Marsala

- 10 ounces veal, cut in thin scallopini cut
- Salt and pepper
- Lemon juice
- Flour
- Sliced shallots *or* green onions *or* chives
- ¼ cup sherry
- ½ cup of Basic Brown Sauce (see index)

Season the veal with salt, pepper, and a dash of lemon juice. Pound a little flour into the meat and brown it in a pan with the shallots, green onions, or chives. After the meat is browned, add the sherry. Cook until the wine has reduced to one half, and then add the Brown Sauce. Heat through and adjust seasonings to taste. SERVES 2.

Slivers of Veal Tenderloin Gourmet

- 1½ pounds veal tenderloin, trimmed of fat and cut in strips
- Salt, pepper, paprika
- Shallots *or* chopped green onions
- 1 cup sauterne
- 1 cup Basic Brown Sauce (see index)
- 5 bottoms of artichokes, cut in eighths
- ½ pound fresh mushrooms, cut in quarters
- 2 tomatoes, peeled and diced

Season the veal with salt, pepper, and paprika. Over very high heat, sauté the meat with the shallots or onions. When the veal is lightly browned, remove it from the pan. Add the sauterne to the pan and boil until the amount of liquid is slightly reduced. Add the Brown Sauce, artichokes, mushrooms, and tomatoes. Cover and let simmer for 5 minutes. Add the meat, mix well, and serve with rice. SERVES 4 TO 6.

Beef Teriyaki

- 3 pounds of sirloin strip
- 1 cup soy sauce
- 1/4 cup red wine
- 2 to 3 tablespoons sugar
- 1/4 teaspoon Ac'cent
- 3 cloves garlic, chopped
- 1-inch piece of ginger root
- 1/4 cup water
- 1 teaspoon unsaturated oil

Cut the meat into 1/4 inch slices. Make a marinade by combining the soy sauce, wine, sugar, Ac'cent, garlic, ginger root, and 1/4 cup water. Put the meat into the marinade and let stand for at least 2 hours. Drain the meat, saving the marinade. Sauté the meat in the oil. When it is browned, add the marinade and cook for 10 to 20 minutes or until the meat is tender. SERVES 6 TO 8.

Old-Fashioned Beef Stew Bourguignonne

- 1 pound beef, bottom round with fat removed
- 1 pint Burgundy wine (or any good domestic red wine)
- 2 onions cut in two
- 2 carrots, halved
- 1/2 stalk celery
- 3 cloves garlic, minced
- 1/2 bay leaf
- Pinch of thyme
- 2 ripe tomatoes, peeled and cut in wedges
- Salt, pepper, and Ac'cent
- 2 tablespoons arrowroot *or* cornstarch
- 1 tablespoon tomato paste
- 1 cup sliced cooked mushrooms
- 1/2 cup small pearl onions
- 1 cup cooked peas

Cut the meat into cubes about 1 inch thick. Add the wine and marinate the beef overnight or at least two or three hours. When ready to cook, lift the meat from the marinade and put it into a Dutch oven. Let it cook, uncovered in a hot (400° F.) oven for 10 to 15 minutes. Add the onions, carrots, celery, garlic, bay leaf, thyme, tomatoes, salt, pepper, and Ac'cent. Continue to cook in the oven, uncovered, for another 10 minutes. Sprinkle the marinade with the arrowroot or cornstarch and add it to the meat and vegetables. Add the tomato paste. If the marinade doesn't cover the meat, add enough water to cover it completely. Cover the Dutch oven and reduce oven heat to moderate, 350° F. Cook for 1 hour. Remove the meat from the sauce. Strain the sauce and, if it doesn't seem quite thick enough, add a little more cornstarch. If it is too thick, add a little more water. Pour the sauce over the meat, add the sliced mushrooms, pearl onions, and cooked peas. Serve with rice. SERVES 3 TO 4.

Beef Tenderloin Teriyaki en Brochette

- 3 pounds beef tenderloin
- 1⅔ cups (1 can) pear nectar
- ½ cup granulated sugar
- 1 cup soy sauce
- 1 cup sweet Sake (Japanese wine)
- ½ teaspoon grated garlic
- 2 teaspoons Ac'cent
- 1 piece ginger root 1″ long
- Fresh pineapple cubes
- Small fresh mushrooms

Cut the meat into 1-inch cubes. Make a marinade by combining the pear nectar, sugar, soy sauce, Sake, garlic, Ac'cent, and ginger root. Add the meat and marinate for 30 minutes. Place the meat, pineapple, and mushrooms on skewers, starting with a mushroom, then a cube of meat, then a pineapple cube and another meat cube; end with a mushroom. Make each skewer a serving of four pieces of meat, four pieces of pineapple, and 2 mushrooms. Broil over charcoal or in your broiler for 8 to 10 minutes for medium, and 15 minutes for well done. Serve with rice. SERVES 6 TO 8.

Slivers of Sirloin Tips in Casserole

- 1 pound sirloin tips, fat removed
- Salt, pepper, Ac'cent
- ½ teaspoon cooking oil
- 1 onion, sliced
- 1 cup sauterne wine
- 2 small green peppers, diced
- 4 fresh tomatoes, peeled and coarsely diced
- 1 clove garlic, minced
- Small spice bag of thyme and bay leaf
- 2 tablespoons cornstarch

Cut the tips into 1-inch strips, season them with salt, pepper, and Ac'cent, and brown them in ½ teaspoon oil. Add the onion and garlic and let simmer for 5 minutes. Add the sauterne, green peppers, tomatoes, and spice bag; blend in the cornstarch. Cover and cook in a moderate (350° F.) oven until tender. Serve with rice. If there is too much liquid, thicken it with more cornstarch; but this dish is best with a thinner gravy. SERVES 3.

Creamy Rice Pudding

5 cups modified skimmed milk	1 tablespoon Sucaryl
1 cup uncooked long-grain rice	2 teaspoons vanilla

Top-of-stove method
Heat the milk over hot water until bubbles form around the edge of the pan. Stir in the rice and Sucaryl. Cover and cook, stirring occasionally, for 1 hour. Stir in vanilla, cover, and allow to cool.
Oven method
Heat the milk and Sucaryl. Pour over the rice in a shallow 9 x 13 x 2½-inch baking pan; add vanilla. Stir to moisten the rice and to spread the mixture evenly over the bottom of the pan. Cover tightly with cover or aluminum foil. Bake in a preheated moderate (350° F.) oven for 1 hour. Remove from the oven and allow to cool, covered. Serve with ¼ cup fresh fruit (blueberries, peaches, raspberries, or strawberries) and 2 level tablespoons whipped topping. Size of serving: ½ cup pudding, ¼ cup fruit, 2 tablespoons whipped topping. SERVES 12.

Fruit Fresh–Sucaryl Mixture

⅓ cup Fruit Fresh	1 cup Sucaryl
1 cup water	

Shake all together in a jar and refrigerate, covered, until needed.

Fruit Fresh is a vitamin C powder which is used to keep the fresh fruit flavor and color of the fruit. Mixed with Sucaryl, it makes a low-caloric sweetener which protects the fruit. Combine 2 tablespoons of the mixture with each pint of fresh fruit before serving.

Seven Jewel Pudding

1 box (24 grams) low-calorie vanilla-flavor pudding mix	4½ cups modified skimmed milk
1 teaspoon powdered ginger	½ cup candied fruit
	¼ cup raisins
	1 quart cooked short-grain rice

Stir the pudding powder and ginger into the milk and heat until the pudding begins to boil. Remove from the heat and stir in the fruits and rice. Cover and chill. Serve with one of the low-fat, low-cholesterol toppings. Size of serving, ½ cup. SERVES 12.

Rice and Raisin Pudding

- 1 box (24 grams) low-calorie vanilla-flavor pudding mix
- 4½ cups modified skimmed milk
- 1 quart cooked short-grain rice
- 1 cup raisins

Stir the pudding powder into the milk and heat until the pudding begins to boil. Remove from the heat and stir in the rice and raisins. Cover and chill. Serve with one of the low-fat, low-cholesterol toppings. Size of serving, ½ cup. SERVES 12.

Old-Fashioned Rice Pudding

- 1 box (24 grams) low-calorie vanilla-flavored pudding mix
- 1 quart modified skimmed milk
- 1 quart cooked short-grain rice, chilled

Stir the pudding powder into the milk. Cook over moderate heat until the mixture comes to a boil. Remove from the heat and stir in the rice. Cover and chill. Serve topped with one of the following fruits:

- 1½ cans apricots, 1-pound can, 2 halves per serving
- 1½ cans cherries, 1-pound can, 5 cherries per serving
- 2 cans Kadota figs, 1-pound can, 2 figs per serving
- 2 cans peach halves, 1-pound can, 1 half per serving

These are dietetic-packed canned fruit. If water-packed fruits are used, sweeten each 1-pound can with:

apricots	1 teaspoon Sucaryl
cherries	½ teaspoon Sucaryl
Kadota figs	½ teaspoon Sucaryl
peaches	½ teaspoon Sucaryl

Size of serving: ½ cup pudding, 2 tablespoons topping fruit. You may add 2 tablespoons low-calorie whipped topping to each serving, if desired. SERVES 12.

Cheese Pudding

1½ cups farmer's cheese
1½ cups cooked short-grain rice, chilled
2 2¼-ounce boxes Royal custard-flavored dessert mix
1 quart skimmed modified milk

Toss together the farmer's cheese and rice until evenly distributed. Divide among twelve individual dessert dishes. Stir the dessert mix into the skimmed milk and heat until the mixture comes to a boil. Pour over the rice and cheese. Allow to cool, then chill until firmly set. Serve with one of the low-fat, low-cholesterol toppings. Size of serving, ½ cup. SERVES 12.

Strawberry and Peach Dessert

2 1-pound cans dietetic-packed canned sliced peaches
1 box (21 grams) low-calorie strawberry gelatin dessert
2¾ cups hot water
3 cups cooked short-grain rice, chilled

Drain the peaches and save the liquid. Dissolve the gelatin powder in 2¾ cups hot water, using peach juice to make up the remaining liquid called for in the package directions. Chill until firm. Beat until the gelatin is light and frothy. Stir in the cooked rice and beat until well blended and frothy. Pour the mixture into individual serving dishes and chill until set. Unmold, if desired. Top with whipped topping and garnish with sliced peaches. If water-packed fruit is used, sweeten each can with 1 teaspoon Sucaryl a few hours before using. Size of serving, ½ cup. SERVES 12.

Orange-Apricot Dessert

2 1-pound cans dietetic-packed canned apricots
1 box (21 grams) low-calorie orange gelatin dessert
2¾ cups hot water
3 cups cooked short-grain rice, chilled

Drain the apricots and save the liquid. Dissolve the gelatin powder in 2¾ cups hot water, using apricot juice to make up the remaining liquid. Chill until firm. Beat until the gelatin is light and frothy. Stir in the cooked rice and beat until well blended and frothy.

Pour into individual serving dishes and chill until set. Unmold and top with whipped topping. Garnish each serving with 2 apricot halves. If water-packed fruit is used, sweeten each can with 1 teaspoon Sucaryl a few hours before using. Size of serving, ½ cup. SERVES 12.

Red Cherry Topping

1 1-pound can dietetic-pack canned cherries
2 tablespoons cornstarch
2 tablespoons lemon juice
2 teaspoons grated lemon rind
1½ teaspoons Sucaryl
Few drops red vegetable coloring

Drain the cherries and save the juice. Combine the cornstarch and cherry juice, adding water to make 1 cup if necessary. Cook over low heat, stirring constantly until the mixture comes to a boil. Cook 3 minutes until liquid becomes clear. Remove from the heat and stir in the lemon juice, rind, cherries, Sucaryl, and coloring. Allow to cool. Serve over puddings. If desired, use port wine to replace all or part of the cherry juice. Size of serving, 1 tablespoon sauce and 3 cherries. SERVES 12.

Whipped Topping

2 24-gram boxes low-calorie vanilla-flavored pudding mix
4 cups modified, skimmed milk
2 2-ounce envelopes dessert topping mix (Dream Whip)
1 teaspoon vanilla

Stir the pudding powder into 3 cups skimmed milk. Cook over moderate heat until the mixture comes to a boil; chill. In a chilled bowl, stir Dream Whip mix into 1 cup skimmed milk and add the vanilla. Beat with an electric mixer until soft peaks are formed. Gently add the chilled pudding to the Dream Whip; beat until well blended. If the mixture thickens after refrigeration, mix well until gloss returns. Skimmed milk may be added if a thinner consistency is desired. Size of serving, 2 level tablespoons. SERVES 24.

Apricot Whip

1 2-ounce envelope dessert topping mix (Dream Whip)
½ cup modified skimmed milk
½ cup Apricot Glacé (see p. 341)

Place the Dream Whip in a chilled bowl and stir in the milk. Beat until soft peaks are formed. Stir in the Apricot Glacé and beat until blended. Chill until ready to use. If the whip thickens after refrigeration, stir it briskly until smoothness and gloss return. Size of serving, 2 tablespoons. SERVES 12.

Apricot Glacé

1 11-ounce box dried apricots
$2\frac{1}{2}$ cups water
1 tablespoon Sucaryl

Place the apricots and $2\frac{1}{2}$ cups water in a saucepan and bring to a boil. Cover, remove from the heat, and let stand for 1 hour. Place the apricots, apricot liquid, and Sucaryl in the blender jar. Blend until smooth, add water if a thinner consistency is desired. This also may be used as a topping. Size of serving, 2 tablespoons. SERVES 24.

Raspberry Melba Topping

1 10-ounce package quick-frozen raspberries
1 12-ounce jar red currant jelly
Few drops red vegetable coloring

Empty the raspberries with their syrup into the blender jar. Add the jelly and cover the jar. Blend at low speed for about 45 seconds, or until well blended. Strain and chill thoroughly. Serve over cheese pudding. Size of serving, 2 tablespoons. MAKES 1 PINT.

The following menus are what I call "go-togethers," showing how a really gourmet meal can be served with these low-fat, low-cholesterol recipes. The choice of appetizer, soup, and dessert has been left to you.

1. Broiled fillet of red snapper with pickled papaya and lemon wild rice, asparagus, julienne of beets salad.
2. Beef tenderloin en brochette on Spanish rice, asparagus, romaine and tomato salad with low-calorie dressing.
3. Baked sliced turkey Marco Polo on broccoli, sliced mushrooms, hot rice, corn O'Brien, hearts of lettuce with low-calorie dressing.

4. Charcoal-broiled chopped steak, tomato, raw onion, dill pickle.
5. Broiled filet mignon, mushroom caps, water cress, brown rice.
6. Broiled lamb chops, Bartlett pear, mint jelly, water cress, Spanish rice, braised celery, asparagus vinaigrette salad.
7. Poached Florida pompano en papilotte, sauce poulette, Spanish rice, julienne of string beans, asparagus vinaigrette salad.
8. Casserole of white meat chicken à la king, wild rice, broccoli with lemon.
9. Broiled lamb shish kebab with orange, oriental rice, braised celery, julienne of string beans.
10. Roast prime ribs of beef au jus (special cut with no fat), Spanish rice, Brussels sprouts with chestnuts, sliced tomato salad.
11. Stuffed fresh mushrooms with crabmeat, broiled tomato, brown rice, plain okra, romaine and tomato salad with special dressing.
12. Broiled Rock Cornish game hen with half peach and cranberries, brown rice, broccoli au citron, hearts of lettuce with plain dressing.
13. Fresh Colorado River brook trout poached in French vermouth with mushrooms, truffles, and chives; wild rice, asparagus, romaine and tomato salad with special dressing.
14. Broiled Puget Sound salmon with grapefruit section, macedoine of fresh vegetables, plain spinach, asparagus salad.
15. Beef roast on Spanish rice with natural gravy, rice pilau with mushrooms, tossed green salad, Frenchette dressing.
16. Back Fin crabmeat casserole à la Newburg, curried rice, fresh string beans, fruit salad with pineapple dressing.
17. Poached fillet of halibut, Spanish style; curried rice, fresh string beans, fruit salad with pineapple dressing.
18. Broiled white meat turkey steak, mustard sauce, pineapple ring, mushrooms, wild rice, fresh green pea pods.
19. Bahama lobster tail thermidor; wild rice, plain succotash, asparagus, tossed green salad.
20. Broiled fresh Colorado River trout with sliced cucumber, wild rice, asparagus, hearts of lettuce salad with special dressing.
21. Sliced roast beef tenderloin with mushrooms, natural gravy, water cress, wild rice, tossed green salad, asparagus.
22. Boneless breast of pheasant Eugenie, Sauce Supreme; wild rice, half nectarine, asparagus, hearts of lettuce with special dressing.
23. Casserole of shrimps sautéed New Orleans, saffron rice, celery roots, fresh broccoli, tossed green salad with Frenchette dressing.

24. Casserole of chicken Hawaiian luau with wild rice, asparagus, fruit salad with pineapple salad dressing.
25. Sliced beef roast au jus on saffron rice, fresh broccoli, tossed green salad with special dressing.
26. Broiled Rock Cornish game hen with a brandied peach, brown rice and green peas, hearts of lettuce with sliced tomato.
27. Broiled boneless fresh trout with grapefruit sections, brown rice, cauliflower, hearts of lettuce and sliced tomato.
28. Scallopini of veal sauté marsala with saffron rice, sliced mushrooms, green peas, hearts of lettuce with Frenchette dressing.
29. Cape Cod scallops Florentine on a bed of fresh spinach, sauce poulette, curried rice, zucchini provençale, fresh fruit salad with pineapple dressing.
30. Slivers of sirloin tips in casserole with rice pilau, string beans sauté, fresh fruit salad, pineapple dressing.
31. Louisiana shrimp curry, wild rice, broccoli lemon, young carrots and peas, Boston lettuce with special dressing.
32. Hawaiian rice, poached fresh fillet of red snapper poulette, chives, mushrooms, young carrots and peas, hearts of lettuce with special dressing.
33. Boneless breast of English pheasant in brandy with mushrooms, rice pilau, Brussels sprouts with chestnuts, hearts of palm salad with Frenchette dressing.
34. Old-fashioned beef stew Bourguignonne with mushrooms, onions, and peas; rice, baby lima beans, orange gelatin rice salad mold.
35. Sliced white meat turkey on rice pilau with mushrooms, Sauce Supreme, fresh turnip greens, baby lima beans, orange gelatin rice salad mold.
36. Scallopini of veal orégano, asparagus spears, mushroom rice, tossed green salad with Frenchette dressing.
37. Hot sliced roast beef in sauce served on a bed of plain spinach, mushroom rice, baked stuffed Italian squash, tossed green salad.
38. White meat chicken à la king with mushrooms, brown raisin rice, yellow squash, asparagus salad with special dressing.
39. Poached halibut, Spanish style; brown rice, fresh green pea pods, asparagus salad with Frenchette dressing.
40. Boneless fresh trout poached in wine and French vermouth,

truffles and mushrooms, Hawaiian rice, peas French style, sliced tomato salad.

41. Chicken casserole delight with water chestnuts, peas, onions, carrots; asparagus, plain spinach, tossed green salad with special dressing.
42. Jumbo Louisiana shrimp casserole, Bombay style with curry; wild rice, asparagus, sliced tomato salad vinaigrette.
43. No-crust chicken pot pie with mushrooms, carrots, peas, Sauce Supreme; plain Italian squash, princesse salad vinaigrette.
44. Fruit fiesta plate with lime rice salad; raspberry sherbet, fruit compote, or creamy rice pudding for dessert.
45. Seafood platter of shrimps and crabmeat on rice vegetable salad with Frenchette dressing; pineapple or lemon sherbet, or half grapefruit.
46. Chicken salad gourmet, rice curry, tomato, artichoke, asparagus, pickle; creamy rice pudding.

For desserts you may have your choice of: melon, any flavor of sherbet, half grapefruit, fruit compote, creamy rice pudding, cheese pudding, rice and raisin pudding, Seven Jewel pudding, cheese pudding with raspberry sauce, old-fashioned rice pudding, strawberry and peach dessert, or orange-apricot dessert. All of these rice dessert recipes will be found in the rice recipes in this chapter.

I hope you are convinced after reading these delightful menus that Chef Edmond Kaspar has served for the past six months that there is no reason for dullness or routine to creep into a low-fat, low-cholesterol menu.

14

Be daring: flaming cookery

DON'T PASS THIS CHAPTER BY if you don't have chafing dishes, brûlot pans, Bourguignonne fondue burners, petite marmites, and all of the other glamorous cooking equipment. I'll venture to say that you have an electric skillet in your pantry and this is a wonderful substitute for almost any of these more specialized pieces of equipment. So let's start right off and talk about some of the flaming dishes that are such fun to make. You can create quite a reputation for yourself with a flaming dessert, but be sure to practice on the family before you venture to do it for your guests.

First of all, remember that when you cook with wines and liqueurs, you are cooking out all of the alcoholic content and leaving only the lovely bouquet that you couldn't find in an extract bottle. A fine wine sauce can make a routine dish into a gourmet's delight.

Jim Beard told me not too long ago that he was a little tired of being called America's No. 1 Gourmet because now anyone who knows how to cook broccoli is a gourmet. A gourmand is something different—a gourmand is a pig. So we'll just say that you are a person who has a flair for the unusual in cooking, which is one of the creative arts, just as is painting a beautiful picture or designing a lovely gown.

The first recipes I am going to give you were from the menu of one of the most fabulous dinners ever to take place in Dallas.

The French Cognac Industry and The Dallas Gun Club gave a dinner which was executed by Executive Chef Willy Rossel of the Sheraton-Dallas Hotel. The menu was set by the one and only James Beard, who is three hundred pounds of the most delightful, jolly human being I know. After the dinner he and I did a flaming cookery demonstration and made these dishes for the guests. I'd like you to have the recipes.

Chicken Liver Pâté Truffle

1½ pounds chicken livers, chopped
3 eggs
¾ cup heavy cream
4 slices bacon, crumbled
⅓ cup cognac
1 teaspoon ginger
2 teaspoons salt
1 teaspoon allspice
½ teaspoon black pepper
4 tablespoons flour
Salt pork, sliced
1 or 2 truffles

Blend ⅓ of the chicken livers with 2 eggs, another ⅓ with the heavy cream, and the remaining ⅓ with the crumbled bacon. Blend the cognac and the remaining egg with the flour. Mix together with the seasonings. Line a loaf tin with the slices of salt pork and pour half of the mixture into the loaf pan. Chop or slice 1 or 2 truffles and add them at this time, following with the remaining mixture. Top with thin slices of salt pork and cover tightly with foil. Bake in a pan of hot water in a slow oven, 325° F., for 1½ to 2 hours. Chill and slice. Serve one thin slice, with Melba toast, for a first course.

Crabmeat Soup Charentais

1 pound crabmeat
½ cup milk
2 tablespoons butter
2 cups Béchamel sauce (recipe on p. 347)
1 cup whipping cream
⅓ cup cognac
Finely chopped parsley

Heat the crabmeat in the milk and butter in the upper part of a double boiler. Prepare a light Béchamel sauce and add the cream to it after it has come to the boiling point. Add to the crabmeat. Season to taste and add more cream if the mixture needs thinning. Just before serving, stir in the cognac. Serve in heated cups with a sprinkling of finely chopped parsley. Depending on the size of your portions, this SERVES 4 TO 8.

Béchamel Sauce

½ cup fish broth
4 tablespoons butter
3 tablespoons flour
1 cup light cream
Salt, pepper, and nutmeg

If you do not have fish broth or stock on hand, use the bones, skin, and fish bits, or buy a pound of frozen fish fillets; boil them in water and strain. To make the sauce, melt the butter, add the flour, and cook until it is slightly colored. Add the fish broth and cream; cook and stir until the sauce is nicely thickened. Cook 5 minutes longer and season to taste with salt, pepper, and nutmeg.

Cognaced Wild Texas Quail

These quail are now being raised in game preserves in our great state of Texas and, although they come a little high in price, they are a wonderful conversation-piece dish.

6 quail, dressed
12 tablespoons foie gras
6 large truffles (optional)
Freshly ground pepper
1 cup cognac
1½ cups chicken broth
Bouquet garni
Salt and pepper
Dash of cognac
6 grape leaves (you can buy these canned)
Rosemary
Larding pork
Melted butter
6 bread slices, crust removed
6 tablespoons butter
1 teaspoon lemon juice
½ pound muscat grapes, seeded

Stuff each quail with 2 tablespoons foie gras and a large truffle. Grind a small amount of fresh pepper over each bird and place the quail in a bowl. Pour 1 cup cognac over them and let stand for 1 hour. Meanwhile, combine the heads, feet, and wing tips with 1½ cups chicken broth and a bouquet garni (parsley and other herbs tied in a piece of cheesecloth). Let simmer over medium heat for 1 hour. Strain well. Season the liquid with salt, pepper, and a dash of cognac, and boil it until the amount is reduced by one third. Wrap each quail in a grape leaf and dab each one with a little rosemary. Cover the breasts with thin slices of larding pork and truss well with fine twine. Roll the quail in melted butter. Roast in a hot oven, 450° F., for just 18 minutes. Fry the bread slices in the 6 tablespoons butter until crisp and arrange them in an ovenproof serving dish. Place each quail on a bread slice. Cover and keep hot. Add to the roasting pan the broth and cognac, lemon juice, and grapes. Bring to boiling and boil until the amount of liquid is reduced by one half. Pour over the quail and serve. SERVES 6.

Fillet of Beef James Beard Flambé

- Fillet of beef, whole, trimmed
- 1 tablespoon freshly ground pepper
- ½ teaspoon ground ginger
- Pinch of nutmeg
- 1 cup olive oil
- ½ cup cognac
- Bay leaf
- Pinch of thyme
- Additional cognac, warmed (optional)

Rub the fillet of beef with freshly ground pepper, ground ginger, and nutmeg; place it in a roasting pan. Pour over this the olive oil and ½ cup cognac. Add a bay leaf and a pinch of thyme. Let the fillet stand for several hours, turning it frequently. To roast, place the meat on a rack in a hot (450° F.) oven and roast for 25 minutes or to an internal temperature of 120° F. for very rare beef. Baste occasionally with the marinade. If desired, the whole fillet may be flamed with warm cognac at the table before carving. (Do be sure to flame it. It's fascinating and it gives a most unusual flavor to the meat.)

Savarin au Cognac

- 1½ packages dry yeast *or* 1 yeast cake
- ⅔ cup warm milk
- 1 teaspoon sugar
- 2 cups all-purpose flour
- 4 eggs, lightly beaten
- 1 tablespoon sugar
- ½ teaspoon salt
- ⅔ cup soft butter

Dissolve the yeast in the warm milk. Add 1 teaspoon sugar. Combine the flour, salt, 1 tablespoon sugar, and the eggs in an electric mixer. Add the yeast mixture and beat until blended. The mixture should have a soft sticky consistency at this point. Beat it for an additional two minutes, then cover the bowl and let the dough rise in a warm place for 45 minutes. Stir the dough down and beat in

⅔ cup soft butter with your hands. Beat for about 4 minutes. Pour the dough into a well-buttered ring mold and let it rise in a warm place (80° F.) until it has doubled in bulk. Bake in a hot (450° F.) oven for 10 minutes. Reduce the heat to moderate, 350° F., and bake until nicely browned and cooked through, about 35 minutes longer. Unmold onto a rack. When the savarin is partially cooled, drench with Cognac Syrup.

Cognac Syrup

- 1 cup sugar
- 1½ cups water
- ½ cup cognac

Boil the sugar and water together for about 15 minutes, then add the cognac. Cool the savarin and fill with fresh or preserved fruits well sugared and flavored with cognac. Top with whipped cream. SERVES 6 TO 8.

Cognaced Carrots

Cook the carrots, then add a mixture of honey, cognac, and chopped parsley.

Wild Rice Angers

To cooked wild rice, add thinly slivered toasted almonds.

Tomatoes Jarnac

Thinly sliced tomatoes, dressed with olive oil, seasoning, and cognac. This is made like French dressing, in the same proportions, except that cognac is used instead of vinegar.

Now, let's do some chafing dish cookery. Remember that the usual chafing dish has a blazer pan with a handle, which is like a skillet, and a hot water bath pan, or the double boiler part of it, which is the pan with no handle that fits over your burner.

Pineapple Jubilee

- 1 9-ounce can pineapple tidbits
- Pineapple juice
- ½ cup white corn syrup
- 2 ounces Jamaica rum
- Hard vanilla ice cream

Drain the tidbits, saving the syrup. Add to the syrup enough pineapple juice to make 2 cups. To this liquid, add the corn syrup.

Place the liquid in the saucepan, or blazer, part of the chafing dish and boil until the volume is reduced by almost one half. Add the pineapple tidbits and heat thoroughly. Pour the rum over the pineapple and ignite. Serve flaming over hard vanilla ice cream. SERVES 4 GENEROUSLY.

This can also be done in an electric skillet.

Strawberries Romanoff

2 quarts choice strawberries, hulled and washed
Sugar
1 cup orange juice
1 cup Grand Marnier (orange liqueur)
3 cups heavy cream

Sprinkle the berries very lightly with sugar. Add the orange juice and Grand Marnier; let stand for 1 hour. Just before serving, whip and fold in the cream. Serve in sherbets. SERVES 8 TO 10.

Cherries Jubilee

2½ cups (No. 2 can) black Bing cherries, pitted
¼ cup cognac
Vanilla ice cream

Heat the cherries in their own juice in a chafing dish blazer pan. Pour half of the cognac in while the cherries are heating, but don't let them boil. When they are steaming hot, dash them with the remaining cognac, put a match to them, and serve flaming over vanilla ice cream. Notice that no thickening is used in this recipe. SERVES 4 TO 6 GENEROUSLY.

Bananas Flambé

4 firm bananas
½ pound butter
2 tablespoons brown sugar
Juice of 2 lemons, strained
Brandy, warmed, to cover

Slice the bananas lengthwise, then cut them into quarters. Place the chafing dish in its hot water jacket over a strong flame. Melt the butter in the chafing dish and add the lemon juice. Arrange the bananas in this sauce and sprinkle with brown sugar. Cover and cook until the bananas are soft but not mushy. Remove the cover. Float the brandy on top, lighting the warmed brandy as you pour it from the small saucepan. It will continue to burn on top of the bananas. When the blue flame dies, serve 4 banana quarters on each of 4 warmed plates. SERVES 4.

Broiled Peaches in Bourbon

Canned or fresh peaches (2 halves to a serving)
Brown sugar
Butter
Cinnamon
Bourbon

Arrange the peach halves in a flat baking dish. Heap the centers with brown sugar, dot lavishly with butter, and sprinkle with cinnamon. Place 4 inches from the broiler and broil 5 minutes or until sugar is melted and peaches are slightly browned. Arrange the peaches on a flameproof serving dish and add 3 tablespoons warmed bourbon for each serving. Flame it as you bring it to the table.

This can be served as a dessert, but I think it is simply elegant with duck, goose, or almost any poultry.

Ice Cream Bermuda

I must confess that I stole this recipe from the Pump Room of the Ambassador East Hotel in Chicago. While attending a Food Editors' Conference, we were entertained at the hotel by one of the food companies. The meal was delicious, with chicken in fresh pineapple shell, with a rim of baked dough to keep the top on the pineapple during the baking period. Everything was perfect. Our Maitre d'Hotel extended himself with this divine dessert and, although there were about one hundred and fifty food editors in attendance, he and his trained staff made this dessert right at the tables. I made mental calculations, then came home and whipped it up. It's been a favorite of Dallas hostesses since that time. So, thanks to the Ambassador East for a lovely dessert. To serve 4, you'll need:

1 quart rich chocolate ice cream
2 bananas
8 teaspoons sugar
1½ ounces Cointreau *or* Triple Sec
4 ounces rum

This dessert is made in a crêpe Suzette skillet (or you can use an electric skillet). Slice the banana into a Suzette pan, add the sugar and carmelize (in other words, turn the sliced bananas over and over in the sugar until the sugar is half melted). Add the Triple Sec or Cointreau (an orange liqueur), stir occasionally, and let come to a bubbling heat. When the mixture becomes a light golden brown, and the bubbling continues, add the rum. Ignite and pour while flaming over the chocolate ice cream which you have served in sherbets. SERVES 4.

Cheese Blintzes

L. J. Lissauer, one of my good friends in Dallas, likes nothing better than to entertain during the summer with swimming parties around his pool at breakfast time. He dotes on cooking, and his cheese blintzes can't be beaten. I am not as good as he is, so forgive me, L.J., but I think that cheese blintzes are a very important recipe for people to know about.

- 4 eggs
- 1 cup water
- 1 cup flour
- 1 tablespoon brandy
- ½ teaspoon salt
- 3 teaspoons sugar
- 2 cups small-curd cottage cheese, drained
- Dash of salt
- 1 teaspoon grated orange rind *or* ¼ teaspoon cinnamon

To make the batter for the thin crêpes, beat 3 eggs, add the water, then add the flour, brandy, salt, and 1 teaspoon sugar. Form into thin pancakes in a buttered 5-inch skillet (the old-fashioned heavy iron skillets are best). Turn these pancakes just once with a spatula and cook them on both sides, then keep them in a warm place. Reserve a little of the batter to seal the blintzes after filling them.

For the filling, beat the remaining egg and add the cottage cheese, 2 teaspoons sugar, dash of salt, and either grated orange rind or cinnamon. Put a spoonful of this mixture on each crêpe, fold like an envelope or roll like an omelet, and seal the edges with the reserved batter. Chill in the refrigerator until serving time, then sauté the blintzes in the blazer pan of your chafing dish or in an electric skillet in ¼ cup butter. Serve with sour cream and preserved cherries.

Café Brûlot

A Café Brûlot pan is a little shallow bowl standing on legs over a burner, either Sterno or alcohol. You must have the proper ladle that has a strainer in one end of the bowl of the ladle in order to flambé this lovely after-dinner drink properly. This brûlot bowl and ladle can be used for cherries jubilee, oranges jubilee, or almost any kind of liquid that you want to flambé and it's a handsome piece of equipment to have on a buffet. Café Brûlot means coffee and blazed brandy.

- 1 slice each lemon and orange peel
- 5 cubes sugar
- 2 cloves
- Piece of cinnamon stick
- 1/4 vanilla bean
- 1 1/2 cups brandy
- 2 cups strong hot coffee

Place in the top of a chafing dish or a brûlot pan the lemon and orange peel, 4 sugar cubes, cloves, cinnamon stick, and vanilla bean. Add the brandy and heat. Warm the ladle and with it dip up a bit of the spiced brandy. Put the additional lump of sugar in the ladle and ignite the sugar and brandy. When the brandy in the ladle is blazing bright, lower the ladle into the pan. Pour the very strong, hot coffee into the chafing dish and blend by dipping some of the liquid and pouring it back again. When the blaze has burned itself out, serve the café in demitasse cups. This is a show-off drink, believe me, and I haven't met anyone yet who enjoys the combination of brandy and coffee who just doesn't love it.

While on the subject of coffee, let me tell you about a delightful coffee liqueur that comes from Jamaica and is made from the coffee grown on the Blue Mountains of this lovely tropical island. It's called Tia Maria and you can use it as an after-dinner drink, just plain or with a little heavy cream floating on top of it. This is called "bottled insomnia" in the Islands, because it is pure Blue Mountain coffee that has been made into a liqueur.

Crêpes Suzette

Crêpes Suzette are a dessert that we use very often at our house because my husband says that he probably cooked his way through the University of Texas making crêpes Suzette at the fraternity house. He is very fancy with his. I am much plainer with mine. Here again is a recipe that you can fancy up or dress down, with as many liqueurs as you want to use; mine is a basic but good recipe. First of all, let me tell you that if you have a friendly husband who loves to show off with his cooking and crêpes are a favorite of his, be prepared. Have your orange butter frozen in the freezer. Have your crêpes frozen, and they have about a thirty-day life in the freezer. When you make crêpes to freeze, cool them down on paper toweling, then stack them in a light weight foil pan, with a layer of foil in between, so they won't stick together. Wrap the whole pan in foil and label it: "Crêpes, such and such a date." Don't let them stay in the freezer too long (although I have kept them for as long as sixty days). The orange butter is more perishable and has about a thirty-day life in the freezer. But here you are, coming out of the theater, and your husband says, "Why don't you come home for crêpes Suzette?" You're dead if you haven't made this pre-preparation. The rest is simple. It's everyone's own preference as to how crêpes Suzette should be put together.

3 eggs, beaten
1 cup water
1 cup flour
1 tablespoon brandy
½ teaspoon salt
1 teaspoon sugar
½ pound sweet butter
Grated rind of 1 lemon
Grated rind and juice of 1 orange
3 tablespoons powdered sugar
2 jiggers Cointreau
2 jiggers Grand Marnier
2 jiggers brandy *or* rum *or* cognac

To make the crêpes batter, combine eggs, water, flour, brandy, salt and 1 teaspoon sugar. For each pancake, use only 1 tablespoon of batter and cook it in a 5-inch buttered skillet, tilting the pan so that the batter covers the bottom. Turn only once. Release the outer edge of the crêpe with the tip of the spatula and it will be easy to turn it. The crêpes can be made ahead of time and kept warm on a warming plate or on a plate over the top of a double boiler.

For the sauce, cream the butter with the grated lemon and orange rind and powdered sugar. Chill until needed. When ready to use, put the butter mixture in the blazer pan of a chafing dish or in a crêpes skillet. When it is bubbling, add the orange juice. Cook until the juice cooks down, then add Cointreau and Grand Marnier. Dip the crêpes, one at a time, into this mixture; swish them around in it and then either fold in quarters or, with the tines of a fork, catch one end of the crêpe and roll it. Put each crêpe to one side in the pan as it is done. When all the crêpes are rolled or folded, sprinkle them with a little sugar and let cook for a minute or two. Then pour on the rum, brandy or cognac, and flame. Spoon this delicious sauce up over the crêpes until the flame dies out, and then serve three of these little crêpes per portion with the sauce divided equally among the servings.

This recipe may be varied, if you wish, by adding 1 teaspoon of guava jelly to each crêpe as you roll it.

Julie's Chili con Carne

This very thought may give you indigestion but very often we will have small bowls of chili with one or two warmed crackers and crêpes Suzette for dessert. I'm sure many of you are saying, "This gal lives dangerously"—but it's fun, believe me.

There are some very good canned chili products on the market and there are two schools of thought about homemade chili. Should the meat be ground or chopped? I am old-fashioned, so I say it should be chopped. I make huge quantities of chili at one time and then freeze it in small portions that I can use for one meal.

- ½ pound suet, coarsely ground
- 2 pounds beef chuck *or* round, cut in small dice
- 1 large onion, cut fine
- 3 pods garlic
- 2 quarts water
- 1 No. 303 can (2 cups) tomatoes
- 4 to 5 hot red pepper pods, cut fine, *or* 1½ tablespoons dried red peppers
- 1 tablespoon (or more) chili powder
- Salt to taste
- 1½ tablespoons ground cumin

Fry the suet and add the meat to it. Add the onions and garlic and brown the meat. Add water, tomatoes, pepper pods, chili powder, and salt. Cook about 2 hours or until the meat is tender. Add the ground cumin about halfway through the cooking time. This chili freezes well. If you like very hot chili, add 1 small can green chilies, chopped fine.

Brack's Chili con Carne Concentrate

At our WFAA Communications Center, we have one of the greatest natural-born cooks in the world in Brack Tennel, who is our authority on game cookery and other specialties of the Southwest. This is his recipe for chili concentrate. In other words, chili that you can make and freeze and then add water when you want to serve it. If there is too much fat from the suet on top of the chili, remove as much as you want before you reheat it.

- 2 pounds coarsely ground chuck
- ½ pound suet, coarsely ground (not with meat)
- 1 large onion, cut fine
- 5 red pepper pods, cut fine *or* 2 tablespoons dried red peppers
- 1 tablespoon (or more) chili powder
- 1½ tablespoons ground cumin
- 6 pods garlic, chopped fine
- 1 tablespoon paprika
- Salt to taste

Brown the chuck with the suet and cook very slowly with the onion, pepper pods, chili powder, cumin, garlic, paprika, and salt to taste. Add no water. Cook slowly until the meat is tender; adjust seasonings to suit your taste. Freeze in quantities that you will use for individual meals. At serving time, add water to make the finished chili con carne the consistency you like.

Beef Tournados with Mushroom Caps

One of our most favorite dinners is beef tournados with a small baked potato and big fat jumbo spears of asparagus. This is a low-fat entrée, because you use beef filets and canned beef bouillon. What little fat you use, you can adapt to any low-fat diet that you might be observing at your house.

- 6 tablespoons butter
- 6 beef filets (without bacon), cut 1 inch thick
- ½ cup shallots *or* chopped chives
- ⅔ cup cognac
- ¾ cup beef bouillon
- Salt, pepper, Ac'cent
- 6 large mushroom caps

Heat the butter in a skillet over high heat until it is almost brown. Brown the beef filets in the butter, turning them only once. Brown on both sides. Add the shallots or chives. Add the cognac, and when it is heated, light it and let it flame. When the flame dies down, add the beef bouillon and seasonings. In the meantime, sauté the large mushroom caps in another skillet until they are partially cooked, not longer than 5 minutes. Add the mushrooms to the tournados and baste with the sauce for 2 to 3 minutes. The meat should be brown on the outside and pink inside. If you prefer your meat well done, have the filets cut thinner. If you would rather have a thicker gravy than the thin sauce, add a little cornstarch mixed with water. Serve one filet and one mushroom cap per serving. SERVES 6.

Rice cooked in bouillon and asparagus with hollandaise sauce round out the meal. This is good company fare, and the tournados can be done in a crêpes Suzette skillet on a Suzette stove.

Lobster Newburg

There isn't any place in the United States where you can't have lobster at the drop of $1.35 or thereabouts per Rock Lobster tail, because the African Rock Lobster industry has done a magnificent job of bringing these delicious, sweet-tasting lobster tails into every market. Bless them, because this is one of my favorite foods.

- 2 cups cooked lobster in chunks
- 3 tablespoons butter
- 1 teaspoon lemon juice
- 1 teaspoon flour
- ½ cup light cream
- 2 egg yolks, slightly beaten
- 2 tablespoons sherry
- Salt and pepper

Cook the lobster for 3 minutes in 2 tablespoons butter. Add the lemon juice and cook for 1 minute more. Melt the remaining 1 tablepsoon butter and stir in the flour. Add the cream gradually and cook until the sauce is thickened. Add the egg yolks, lobster, and sherry. Season to taste with salt and pepper. Reheat. This can be served on fluffy rice, toast points, or toasted English muffins. SERVES 4.

Curried Lobster

- 1 tablespoon butter
- 1 onion, minced
- 1 tart apple, peeled and minced
- Curry powder to taste
- 1 tablespoon cornstarch *or* arrowroot
- ½ pint light cream *or* half and half
- 1 can lobster *or* 1 cup cooked frozen lobster, cut into chunks

Melt the butter in the blazer pan of a chafing dish or in an electric skillet. Add onion and apple and cook thoroughly. Sprinkle with curry powder to taste, from a teaspoon to a tablespoon (be careful, it's powerful). Add the cornstarch or arrowroot mixed with a little of the cream. Add the remaining cream. Stir until the sauce is rich and creamy. Add the lobster and heat through. Serve with plain boiled rice and chutney, or serve in patty shells.

Creamed Potatoes

Here is what I call a "planned-over" dish. I hate the word "left-overs." So, if you have any baked or boiled potatoes left over, enough to make 2½ cups, peel and dice them to use in this lovely vegetable dish that is so good with sliced ham.

2½ cups diced boiled *or* baked potatoes
2 cups medium white sauce (recipe below)
Salt, pepper, and paprika
Parmesan cheese for topping

Combine the potatoes and white sauce in a chafing dish pan over hot water. Season and heat thoroughly. Dash a few grains of paprika on top and sprinkle gently with grated Parmesan cheese. SERVES 4 TO 6. To make white sauce use 2 tablespoons butter or margarine, 2 tablespoons flour, 2 cups of milk and season to taste.

Hashed Brown Potatoes

Here is another recipe for using "planned-over" potatoes.

2 tablespoons butter
2½ cups diced boiled *or* baked potatoes
½ teaspoon salt
½ teaspoon pepper
⅓ cup minced instant onion

Melt the butter in a chafing dish pan over direct heat. Add the onions and sauté them until they are slightly golden in color. Add the potatoes, salt, and pepper. Let cook until browned on one side, about 5 minutes. Using pancake turner, turn the whole mixture over. Brown on the other side, about 5 minutes.

This is wonderful with hamburgers or meat loaf. SERVES 4.

Steak Teriyaki

In Dallas we have the most fabulous restaurant featuring not only the best of Polynesian dishes, but excellent Chicken Bonne Femme, and man-sized Texas charcoal-broiled steaks. Tony Bifano is the owner of the Bali Hai Restaurant, and it is one of the restaurants that you can always recommend and know that the food will be good. There's a secret to this continued excellence in food preparation: Mr. Bifano takes a personal interest in food preparation and has seven international chefs in the kitchen—it's a power-packed, winning combination. This recipe for Steak Teriyaki is one of my favorites and Mr. Bifano was nice enough to share it with me. (There is another recipe in the salad chapter for Bali Hai poppy seed dressing, which is used over their Polynesian salad of diced fresh fruits and romaine lettuce, topped with a cluster of grapes that have been frosted with blue sugar.)

The Oriental cooks measure out and prepare all the ingredients before starting, as this is a quick sautéing over high heat, using a heavy skillet (their skillets are shaped like salad bowls and are called Woks). They also use two implements to toss the ingredients as you do a salad; one is a deep-bowled spoon and the other is like a pancake turner.

Hoisin Sauce is a Chinese vegetable sauce for which there is no American counterpart, but it can be ordered from any Chinese grocery store or supply house.

- 2½ pounds beef tenderloin
- 2 tablespoons Hoisin Sauce
- 1 teaspoon chopped fresh ginger
- ½ clove garlic, finely chopped
- 1 8-ounce can sliced mushrooms, drained
- ½ cup canned pineapple tidbits, drained
- 1 teaspoon sugar *and* 1 teaspoon Ac'cent, mixed
- 2 tablespoons cornstarch
- 2 tablespoons sherry wine
- 3 tablespoons soy sauce

Slice the beef tenderloin in strips 1/16 inch thick, about the thickness of a half dollar. Sauté it in oil until the meat loses its red color. Add the Hoisin Sauce, ginger, garlic, mushrooms, and pineapple tidbits. Mix *gently,* and heat through. Add the sugar and Ac'cent. Mix the cornstarch with a little water to make a smooth paste; add the sherry and soy sauce and add to the mixture. Again handle gently, and combine and heat through. Serve with fried rice, fluffy dry rice, or Chinese noodles. SERVES 6.

A new type of small table cooker in copper, with a regulated alcohol burner under it, is now being imported from Switzerland. It is called a Bourguignonne bowl, but it's nothing in the world but a fondue pan. It is used to prepare Beef Bourguignonne for buffets. This is a do-it-yourself job that your guests will enjoy. You furnish long-handled forks (which, incidentally, come with the bowl), cubes of lean, tender, beef fillet, and a Bourguignonne bowl half full of oil. Heat the oil until smoking hot on your range, then bring it in and set it over the alcohol burner. Arrange around the bowl a complete assortment of sauces—sweet and sour, plum sauce, soy sauce, hot barbecue sauce, and chopped chutney. Your guests cook their own bits of meat—rare, medium, or well done, to their own preference—dunk the meat in one of the sauces, put it on a plate with the other hors d'oeuvres and canapés, and go on their way. This is worlds of fun and truly a conversation piece. This same bowl can be used for a Swiss cheese fondue or Neuchateloise, or for a chili con queso or any hot dip.

Let me tell you about a quick hot cheese dip that is very popular in this part of the country. Use one of the cheese foods, such as Cheez Whiz, add tomato juice to thin it down and a touch of Tabasco (or use the product called Snapee Tom, a highly seasoned tomato juice). Mix thoroughly and keep hot in the blazer pan of your chafing dish over hot water.

Fondue Neuchateloise

- 1 cut clove garlic
- 1 cup light dry white wine
- ½ pound Swiss cheese, shredded or finely cut
- Salt, pepper, and nutmeg to taste
- 1½ tablespoons flour
- 3 tablespoons Kirschwasser *or* applejack *or* cognac *or* light rum
- 1 loaf French bread with hard crust

Rub the blazer pan of the chafing dish thoroughly with the garlic. Pour in the wine and set the pan over very slow fire (to lower the heat, partially close the lid over your alcohol or Sterno burner). When the wine is heated to the point that air bubbles rise to the surface (don't boil it), stir it with a fork and add the shredded Swiss cheese by handfuls, each handful to be completely melted before adding another. Continue stirring until the mixture starts bubbling lightly. Add a little salt, pepper and nutmeg. Finally, add and thoroughly stir in the Kirschwasser, other brandy, or rum. Reduce the heat and keep the fondue hot. Have your guests dip out the fondue with hunks of French bread. Serve the bread in a wicker basket placed beside the chafing dish.

Fruited Flambé

This recipe calls for 2 tablespoons light rum and 1 tablespoon bourbon or dark rum. If you prefer, you may use 3 tablespoons of all one kind of rum.

¼ cup sugar
⅓ cup water
2 tablespoons orange juice
¼ teaspoon grated orange rind
¼ teaspoon grated lemon rind
1 teaspoon butter
4 bananas, whole or cut in half across
2 tablespoons light rum
1 tablespoon bourbon *or* dark rum

Combine the sugar and water in a saucepan and boil until the syrup thickens. Add the orange juice, orange rind, and lemon rind. Return to the heat and bring the syrup to the boiling point. Combine the butter and syrup in a hot chafing dish or heavy skillet. Add the bananas and cook for 3 or 4 minutes, basting frequently with the syrup. Add the rum and bourbon, and serve. Allow one banana per person. If you will heat the bourbon or rum a little before you flame it, it will flame more easily. Never boil it or let it get very hot, just warm it through. SERVES 4.

As a go-together meal, try hamburger Viennese, creamed potatoes, asparagus amandine, and this lovely, light, banana dessert.

Breakfast Corned Beef Balls

1½ cups canned *or* leftover corned beef hash
1 teaspoon chopped chives *or* parsley
1 teaspoon chili sauce
2 eggs, well beaten separately
1 tablespoon water
½ cup fine bread crumbs
2 tablespoons butter

Mix the hash with the chives or parsley and chili sauce. Beat in 1 egg. Mix well and shape into small balls. Dip the balls into the remaining egg mixed with the water, and then dip them into the crumbs. Place the blazer pan of the chafing dish directly over the heat; add the butter and sauté the balls in it until they are lightly browned. Serve with chiffon scrambled eggs, for breakfast or brunch. SERVES 4.

Breakfast Codfish Balls

1 cup cooked shredded salt codfish
1½ cups mashed potatoes
1 teaspoon chopped parsley
2 eggs, slightly beaten separately
½ teaspoon ground ginger
½ teaspoon fresh ground black pepper
½ cup fine bread crumbs
2 tablespoons butter

Mix the codfish, potatoes, parsley, and 1 egg; beat until smooth. Season with ginger and pepper and shape into small balls or croquettes. Dip the balls into the remaining egg and then into the crumbs. These balls may be made early in the day and kept in the refrigerator. When you are ready to cook them, place the blazer pan of the chafing dish over direct heat, heat the butter, and brown the balls until they are golden. Serve with scrambled eggs that have been mixed with diced ripe avocado. SERVES 4.

Eggs and Chicken Livers in Tomato Sauce

- 8 chicken livers, chopped
- 1 tablespoon chopped onion
- 3 tablespoons olive oil
- ½ teaspoon salt
- ¼ teaspoon pepper
- 1 cup tomato sauce
- 4 tablespoons sauterne wine
- 4 eggs
- 4 slices buttered toast *or* toasted English muffin halves

Sauté the livers and onion in oil in the blazer pan over direct heat. Cook for 5 minutes, then season with salt and pepper. Mix the tomato sauce into the livers and cook for 5 minutes longer. Stir in the wine and cook for 3 minutes more. Slip the eggs into the sauce, one at a time, carefully separated from each other. Cover pan, cook 3 minutes or until the eggs are set and soft-cooked (longer if you like hard-cooked eggs). Serve each egg covered with sauce on a slice of buttered toast or on a toasted muffin half. SERVES 4.

Creamed Deviled Ham on Toast

- 2 tablespoons butter
- 2 tablespoons flour
- 2 cups milk
- 1 hard cooked egg, chopped
- 2 2¼-ounce cans deviled ham
- 4 slices buttered toast

Make a medium white sauce by combining the butter, flour and milk. In the chafing dish blazer pan over hot water heat the white sauce until it is thick. When the sauce is steaming, add the egg and deviled ham, stir, and heat through but do not allow to boil. Serve very hot over toast slices. SERVES 4.

Chiffon Scrambled Eggs

- 2 tablespoons butter
- ½ cup cream (half and half)
- 5 eggs, slightly beaten
- ½ teaspoon salt
- Freshly ground black *or* white pepper
- 2 tablespoons minced chives *or* parsley

Melt the butter in the blazer pan over hot water. Add the cream, mix, and pour in the eggs. Cook the eggs slowly, stirring with a whisk until they are set as much as you want them to be. Add salt and pepper and serve at once, garnished with the chives or parsley.

French Toast

3 eggs, slightly beaten
½ teaspoon salt
1 teaspoon sugar
¾ cup milk
4 to 8 slices white bread, ½-inch thick, crusts removed
3 tablespoons butter

Mix the eggs, salt, sugar, and milk in a shallow dish or pie plate. Dip the bread slices into the egg mixture, one at a time. Heat the butter in the blazer pan of the chafing dish set directly over the burner. Brown the bread on one side, then carefully turn it over and brown the other side. Add more butter if necessary to keep the bread from sticking. Serve plain, or as a base for soft scrambled eggs, or with syrup, honey, jam, or powdered sugar.

Canadian Bacon and Eggs

4 to 8 slices lean Canadian bacon
4 eggs
Salt and pepper

Set the chafing dish blazer pan over direct heat. When it is hot, cook the bacon in it, draining off excess fat. When the bacon is crisp, place it on a warm platter while you cook the eggs. Break the eggs one at a time into a saucer and slowly slip each one into the hot fat. Do not cover the pan. Baste the eggs gently with a little of the fat or add 2 tablespoons boiling water to the pan. Cover the pan and cook the eggs until they are set or cooked to desired doneness. Serve at once, garnished with the bacon. SERVES 4. Hot baking powder biscuits and big frosty glasses of orange juice are wonderful with this brunch type of breakfast.

Hominy Grits Cakes

1 quart milk
2 teaspoons salt
¼ cup hominy grits
2 egg yolks, slightly beaten
2 tablespoons butter
Currant *or* apple jelly

Make hominy mush ahead of time and let it set in a shallow pan in the refrigerator so you can cut it into 8 to 10 large slices about

½ inch thick. To make the mush, combine the milk and salt in the upper part of a double boiler; bring to boiling. Slowly stir in the hominy and cook for about 1 hour over boiling water. Stir the mush frequently; it must be very thick. Remove it from the heat and stir in the egg yolks. Pour the mixture into a loaf or shallow square pan, let it cool, and then chill till firm. (This really should chill overnight.) When you are ready to cook it at the table, slice the mush about ½ inch thick, then use a cookie cutter to make rounds. Sauté the rounds in butter in the chafing dish blazer pan over direct heat until brown on both sides, about 8 minutes. Serve hot with jelly or with a sweet syrup and crisp bacon. MAKES ABOUT 8 TO 10 LARGE SLICES.

Creamed Dried Beef

Creamed dried beef is a recipe for a new bride. It is ideal for that first use of your chafing dish and it makes a good quick supper or a pick-up if you come home hungry from a late party. Dried beef is always on your pantry shelf, or should be, because it's a perfect emergency food.

¼ pound sliced dried beef
4 tablespoons butter
3 tablespoons flour
¼ teaspoon pepper
2 cups light cream, half and half
4 slices buttered toast, crusts removed

Pull the beef apart into small pieces. Melt the butter in the blazer pan of the chafing dish over hot water. Add the beef and sauté it until it is lightly browned, about 5 minutes. Sprinkle the flour and pepper over the meat, mix, and add the milk slowly, stirring all the time. Stir and mix while the sauce thickens and boils. Serve at once, on toast. SERVES 4 TO 6.

Red Bean Soup

Down in our part of the country, and through the real Southern states, we use red beans. These are the dried red kidney beans that you can pick up any place in a 1-pound cellophane bag. You have no idea how much goodness is in a package of red beans. Red beans and rice is a great favorite, but my red bean soup is something of which I am very, very proud. I serve it in a petite marmite, another lovely and useful piece of table equipment. It's a brass holder with alcohol or Sterno burner to keep the contents of the large stone crock hot. Use a deep, long-handled dipper to serve the soup.

I like to serve this soup in mugs (regular coffee mugs) in the living room as a first course before a buffet supper. Actually, it's so hearty that you could serve it with toasted or hot French bread, a dessert—and that's a whole meal. It all depends on how well you like the flavor of red beans.

1 pound dry red kidney beans	Crushed red pepper *or* Tabasco sauce
¼ pound salt pork	Sherry wine
1½ cups chopped onion	

Soak the red beans in water overnight. Put the beans in a large covered kettle and add more water to them until the beans are completely covered in water. Cut the salt pork into small chunks and add it to the beans with the chopped onion. Cook until the beans are so tender they squash when you test one of them and the salt pork has cooked all of its tantalizing flavor into the beans. If you like, you can cook the crushed red pepper into the beans with the water; but I prefer to season mine with red pepper or Tabasco, whichever is more convenient, and salt, after they are finished cooking, because you never know how salty salt pork is going to be. Put the bean mixture through a food mill to make a thick purée. Taste again for seasoning and then, as you put it into the petite marmite, add about 2 tablespoons sherry wine. Little chunks of French bread are wonderful with this soup. SERVES 5 OR 6.

Incidentally, if you ever get to New Orleans, don't miss Brennan's red bean soup. It is a specialty of the house and Miss Ella Brennan is so proud of it, she has put it into her new cookbook.

Danish Meat Balls in Sour Cream

This is a wonderful hot hors d'oeuvre and can be served with picks.

2 slices whole wheat bread	½ cup commercial sour cream
1 pound ground beef	¼ teaspoon ground nutmeg
2 large onions, finely minced	4 tablespoons butter
½ teaspoon salt	1 onion, thinly sliced, separated into rings
Pepper	2 tablespoons Worcestershire sauce
1 egg	
Fine dry bread crumbs	

Soak the bread in cold water, then press the slices between your hands to remove as much moisture as possible. Add the bread to the meat. Add the minced onion, salt, pepper, and egg; mix well. Shape into balls about 1 inch in diameter (makes over 2 dozen balls). Roll the balls in fine dry bread crumbs. Mix the sour cream with the nutmeg. Melt the butter in the blazer pan of your chafing dish over direct heat. Add the onion rings and sauté them to a delicate brown. Add the Worcestershire sauce, then fill the pan with meat balls and brown them on all sides. Pile the browned meat balls to one side and keep adding more until all are cooked. Pour the sour cream over the meat balls and serve at once. After the cooking is done, and during serving, put the hot water bath pan under the blazer pan of your chafing dish so that the sour cream doesn't curdle. All you want is just to keep it hot, once it's cooked.

Dirty Rice

Remember the name of this chapter, "Be Daring," when you read this recipe. Dirty Rice is one of the most delicious Southern and Southwestern ways of preparing rice especially to be used with poultry or with wild game.

Thanks to Mrs. Gordon Rupe, this is the original recipe for Dirty Rice. Believe me, it will be a conversation piece at your dinner table, both for its flavor and its name.

- 1 cup uncooked long-grain rice
- 1 uncooked chicken *or* duck liver
- 1 uncooked chicken *or* duck gizzard
- 1 shallot
- 2 stalks celery
- 6 sprigs parsley
- ½ green bell pepper
- Salt to taste
- ⅓ cup bacon fat *or* chicken fat

Bring the rice to a boil with cold water that is ½ inch over the top of the rice. Watch carefully so that the rice doesn't scorch. Keep the saucepan covered during the cooking. After the rice comes to a boil, lower the heat and cook, covered, until the rice is tender and dry. When the rice is done, set it aside in a warm place. Wash the liver, gizzard, and vegetables. Put the vegetables through a food grinder. Then grind the liver and gizzard and mix all together. Add salt to taste. Heat the fat in a skillet and fry the mixture until it is done. Add the cooked rice and mix thoroughly. Serve with fowl or game. This rice may be molded in little ramekins and turned out around the game on a large platter. SERVES 6.

Julie's Dirty Rice

Because I believe in keeping the recipes that make up the American tradition of fine cooking, I like to give the original recipes as well as any short-cut version that I might use. However, because I am so convinced that modern homemakers are going to use the wonderful new convenience foods that we have at our fingertips, I have done my own version of Dirty Rice which uses canned chicken broth, Minute Rice, shredded dehydrated parsley, celery seed, instant minced onion. This takes only minutes to prepare and I believe you'll like it.

- 1 tablespoon instant minced onion
- 1½ cups canned chicken broth
- 1½ cups Minute Rice
- 1 teaspoon shredded dehydrated parsley
- ½ teaspoon whole celery seed
- ½ pound (about 7) chicken livers, very finely chopped
- 3 tablespoons bacon fat *or* unsaturated oil
- 1 teaspoon salt
- ½ teaspoon black pepper
- ½ teaspoon Ac'cent
- 1 teaspoon Worcestershire sauce

Add the onion to the chicken broth and bring to a boil. Add the Minute Rice and allow the mixture to return to a boil. Add the parsley and celery seed, cover the saucepan, remove from the heat and let it stand. Sauté the chicken livers in the bacon fat or oil with the salt, pepper, and Ac'cent, stirring constantly. When the livers are cooked, add them to the rice and broth mixture and let the whole mixture come back to a boil again. Set aside, covered, for 10 minutes. Stir in the Worcestershire sauce. It can be served at once, or you can cook it ahead and then at serving time fry it in 3 tablespoons fat, which gives it a slightly different flavor. SERVES 6.

Fillet of Sole, Sauterne

- 4 fillets of sole
- 1 cup chopped shallots *or* green onions
- 1½ cups sauterne wine
- Salt, pepper, and Ac'cent
- Cornstarch

Sauté the chopped shallots or green onions in a skillet with a very little oil until they are hot, but not wilted. Add the sauterne and heat to the boiling point. Pour the wine sauce over fillets in a casserole that has a cover or that you can cover tightly with foil. Bake for only 20 minutes in a preheated hot (400° F.) oven. Remove the fillets to a hot platter and reduce the wine sauce to one half (in other words, let it boil half away on the top of the range). Thicken with a sprinkling of cornstarch if you want the wine sauce a little thicker. Pour the sauce over the cooked fillets and serve immediately. SERVES 4.

Crème de Menthe Shirred Eggs

Butter
Eggs
White crème de menthe

Butter either pot de crème cups or small individual casseroles. Break 2 eggs into each cup. Pour about 1 tablespoon melted butter over each cup and add 1 tablespoon white crème de menthe. Bake in a preheated moderate (350° F.) oven for about 15 minutes or until the eggs are set as much as you want them. Serve this with little pork sausages and hot baking powder biscuits for a late supper.

Oranges Jubilee Sauce

1 cup orange juice
1 cup water
3/4 cup sugar
1 1/2 tablespoons cornstarch
6 oranges
1/2 cup sliced almonds
2/3 cup brandy, warmed

Combine 3/4 cup orange juice with the water and sugar. Bring to a boil, then reduce the heat and simmer for 5 minutes. Mix the remaining 1/4 cup orange juice with the cornstarch to make a smooth paste. Add the paste slowly to the hot mixture, stirring constantly. Cook stirring occasionally, until the syrup is slightly thickened and glossy, about 10 minutes. Break the oranges into sections and remove the white membrane; place the sections in a chafing dish (or electric skillet). Cover with the thickened syrup, sprinkle with toasted almonds, and cut thin slices of an orange and float them on top. Heat thoroughly. Ignite the warmed brandy in the pan and add to the sauce. Serve flaming over vanilla ice cream. Remember that the ice cream must be very hard; otherwise you will have sherbet glasses of delicious orange jubilee soup. SERVES 12 TO 16.

Café Royale

After-dinner demitasse cups of coffee can be great fun, either a café brûlot or a café royale. Café royale is so simple that it really doesn't require a recipe. Just place a lump of sugar in a teaspoon of cognac, ignite the cognac over a demitasse cup of coffee, and then lower the spoon slowly into the cup. The entire surface of the cup will light up.

Zabaglione Grand Marnier

There are many people who can't stand zabaglione, but I think it's because they have eaten an inferior recipe and feel that it is an insipid dessert. Actually, it is delicious, and Mario's Restaurant in Dallas makes one of the greatest zabagliones I have ever tasted.

6 egg yolks
5 tablespoons sugar
6 drops *or* 1/4 teaspoon vanilla
3 ounces cognac
3 ounces Grand Marnier

Put the egg yolks into the blazer pan of your chafing dish over hot water (or in a double boiler in the kitchen) and whip gently. Add the sugar, stirring constantly and gently with a wire whisk. When it gradually thickens to a very heavy cream consistency, add the vanilla and a little of the cognac and the Grand Marnier. Blend as the custard will absorb this liquid until you have used up all of the cognac and Grand Marnier. Be careful not to add the liqueurs too fast because you will lose that wonderful delicate consistency of the finished dish. Zabaglione may be served hot or cold, in long stemmed champagne glasses; it is eaten with a spoon. I like it served hot. If you prefer it cold, pour it into the champagne glasses, let it cool, then chill it in the refrigerator.

Crêpes Grand Marnier

This recipe is one that I picked up at the Hotel Intercontinental at San Juan, Puerto Rico. This is done with great showmanship, and how wonderful it is to see a master at work at a crêpes Suzette stove and skillet.

6 crêpes (use basic recipe)
3 tablespoons sugar
3 tablespoons butter
3 tablespoons fresh orange juice
1/4 cup Grand Marnier
1 teaspoon grated orange rind
A little more Grand Marnier for the final flaming

In the blazer pan over direct flame, combine the sugar, butter, orange juice, Grand Marnier, and grated orange rind. Heat until well blended, then dip the crêpes into this mixture and swish them around until they are well coated. Fold or roll. Add a little more Grand Marnier, ignite, and serve 3 crêpes to a customer.

Crêpes Luau

We haven't talked too much about using your crêpes Suzette skillet and stove for recipes other than crêpes Suzette. There are many exotic dessert recipes that can be based upon the tiny thin crêpes, and one of them is Crêpes Luau.

- 8 crêpes (use basic crêpes recipe)
- 1½ cups fresh or canned crushed pineapple, drained
- ¾ cup fresh coconut *or* frozen fresh coconut
- 3 tablespoons rum
- Butter
- Sugar
- 2 ounces dark rum

First combine the pineapple with the coconut and 3 tablespoons of rum. Add sugar if you think it's needed. If you use fresh pineapple, you will probably need a little sugar; if you use canned crushed pineapple it will be sweet enough. Put a generous spoonful on each crêpe. Roll the crêpes, brush with melted butter, and sprinkle with granulated sugar. In a hot crêpe pan over direct flame, brown the crêpes in a little more butter. Warm the dark rum, pour it over the crêpes, and ignite. Serve two crêpes to a customer and serve them flaming. Elegant.

Macedoine of Fruit Flambé

- 4 tablespoons butter
- 2 fresh pears, peeled, cored, and sliced
- ½ cup fresh or frozen pineapple cubes
- 1 cup whole fresh strawberries
- 1 banana, peeled and sliced
- 1 cup apricot purée
- ½ cup warm dark rum
- 6 slices pound cake

In the blazer pan of your chafing dish over direct heat, or in a large crêpe skillet, heat the butter and sauté the pears, pineapple, strawberries, and bananas until the fruit is heated. Add the apricot purée and simmer for about 1 minute. Pour the warm rum over the fruit and set aflame. Serve the flaming macedoine of fresh fruit over the slices of pound cake. SERVES 6 TO 8.

This is just the beginning of what you can do with the special pieces of table cooking equipment that you have. Use your griddle for hot canapés for football buffets. Use your hibachi for fun and conversation, for little meat balls with hot barbecue sauce. Use your petite marmite for a wonderful oyster stew for an open house. And use your imagination as to how you can present conversation pieces to make your parties talked about and make you the hostess who always has something different. You can do it!

Index

* Low-fat, low cholesterol

* Low-fat, low cholesterol

* Low-fat, low cholesterol

* Low-fat, low cholesterol

* Low-fat, low cholesterol

* Low-fat, low cholesterol

* Low-fat, low cholesterol

* Low-fat, low cholesterol

* Low-fat, low cholesterol

* Low-fat, low cholesterol